Frommer's®

P9-BYA-906

Alaska Cruises
& Ports of Call

2008

by Jerry Brown & Fran Wenograd Golden

Wiley Publishing, Inc.

Published by:

Wiley Publishing, Inc.
111 River St.
Hoboken, NJ 07030-5774

ISBN: 978-0-470-16907-0

Editor: Jamie Ehrlich
Production Editor: Michael Brumitt
Cartographer: Elizabeth Puhl
Photo Editor: Richard Fox
Anniversary Logo Design: Richard Pacifico
Production by Wiley Indianapolis Composition Services

Front cover photo (main image): Southeast Alaska: Passengers at bow of cruise ship observing glacier
Front cover photo (insert) and back cover photo: Homer, Alaska: Three Bald Eagles in group portrait

For information on our other products and services or to obtain technical support, please contact our Customer Care Department within the U.S. at 800/762-2974, outside the U.S. at 317/572-3993 or fax 317/572-4002.

Wiley also publishes its books in a variety of electronic formats. Some content that appears in print may not be available in electronic formats.

Manufactured in the United States of America

5   4   3   2   1

Contents

List of Maps

An Invitation to the Reader

In researching this book, we discovered many wonderful places—hotels, restaurants, shops, and more. We're sure you'll find others. Please tell us about them, so we can share the information with your fellow travelers in upcoming editions. If you were disappointed with a recommendation, we'd love to know that, too. Please write to:

Frommer's Alaska Cruises & Ports of Call 2008
Wiley Publishing, Inc. • 111 River St. • Hoboken, NJ 07030-5774

An Additional Note

Please be advised that travel information is subject to change at any time—and this is especially true of prices. We therefore suggest that you write or call ahead for confirmation when making your travel plans. The authors, editors, and publisher cannot be held responsible for the experiences of readers while traveling. Your safety is important to us, however, so we encourage you to stay alert and be aware of your surroundings. Keep a close eye on cameras, purses, and wallets, all favorite targets of thieves and pickpockets.

About the Authors

Jerry Brown was born in Edinburgh, Scotland, and worked as a reporter for Scottish newspapers before joining the news department of the *London Daily Mail*. Later, for 31 years, he was the West Coast Bureau Chief of a leading travel trade newspaper. He and Margaret, his wife and best editor, have two grown sons, a granddaughter, Victoria Rose, and two grandsons, Mason Patrick and Maddox Matthew. **Fran Wenograd Golden** is a well-established travel writer and editor whose work appears in numerous newspapers and magazines as well as websites including CruiseCritic.com. She is also author of *TV Vacations: A Fun Guide to the Sites, the Stars, and the Inside Stories Behind Your Favorite TV Shows* as well as other travel books. She lives in Boston and is the proud parent of Erin and Eli.

Other Great Guides for Your Trip:

Frommer's Alaska 2008

Alaska For Dummies

Pauline Frommer's Alaska

Cruise Vacations For Dummies

Frommer's Cruises & Ports of Call 2008

Frommer's Seattle 2008

Frommer's Canada

Frommer's Vancouver with Kids

Frommer's British Columbia & the Canadian Rockies

Vancouver & Victoria For Dummies

The following **abbreviations** are used for credit cards:

AE	American Express	DISC	Discover	V	Visa
DC	Diners Club	MC	MasterCard		

Frommers.com

Now that you have this guidebook to help you plan a great trip, visit our website at **www.frommers.com** for additional travel information on more than 3,600 destinations. We update features regularly to give you instant access to the most current trip-planning information available. At Frommers.com, you'll find scoops on the best airfares, lodging rates, and car rental bargains. You can even book your travel online through our reliable travel booking partners. Other popular features include:

- Online updates of our most popular guidebooks
- Vacation sweepstakes and contest giveaways
- Newsletters highlighting the hottest travel trends
- Online travel message boards with featured travel discussions

What's New in Alaska Cruising in 2008

Just like the glaciers, the world of Alaska travel is always changing. New ships come, and others go—in some years more so than in others. Cruise lines add new shore excursions and land packages, and enhance their onboard offerings. During our travels, we're constantly finding interesting new changes in the tourism industry of the 49th state. In writing this book, we've tried to keep track of the latest and greatest developments.

THE CRUISE INDUSTRY IN GENERAL Cruise lines are notoriously reluctant to publicize their passenger loads. While there were few empty berths in the peak weeks of the summer of 2007 in Alaska, in some shoulder weeks, less than full loads were the order of the day. There were many ships in the market— hey, it's a great market—and because of the additional tonnage, the lines didn't see as much of an increase in passenger traffic as they have in some other recent years. Europe was the big growth cruise market in the summer of 2007, not Alaska. The good news for consumers is the heavy competition in Alaska meant plenty of discounts for the public as the lines pulled out all the stops to try to fill in the gaps in their booking patterns. Discounting is something cruise companies would like to get away from but can't. It's almost a vicious circle: The more big ships they press into service, the more they find themselves forced to offer price breaks to attract passengers. Most of the big lines do not get the full rack rate they'd like to get. We expect the discounting trend to continue in 2008. Some lines' brochures reflect an early booking discount, which they now consider to be the de facto brochure price. We believe your best bet for getting a good deal on a cruise in 2008, as it is every year, is to book early, by mid-February—or earlier, if possible. The kind of discount offers we refer to can be very attractive, especially if you're flexible and prepared to sail in the shoulder season (May or Sept). Chances are, you'll still be able to get a deal even after that date—especially if you're a past passenger of one of the lines. (Cruise lines offer all sorts of deals for repeat passengers. In June last year, for instance, Holland America Line informed its Mariner Society members that a 7-day Gulf cruise was available on the last southbound cruise of the *Statendam* on Sept 16, starting at the astounding price of $399—$57 a day!) You can take your chances and wait for an offer like that one in 2008, but if you do, be prepared to miss out, because these offers don't always exist. It's safer to try to reserve midsummer space long before the season starts in May, the earlier the better. Leave it to April or May and you will almost certainly find that early bookers have snapped up the best cabins on the best ships.

CRUISE LINES & THEIR SHIPS As we mentioned earlier, some years see greater increases in capacity than others.

As we went to press, **Holland America Line** and **Princess** each have (again) scheduled eight ships for Alaska service for 2008. Princess has its two biggest, the *Diamond Princess* and *Sapphire Princess,* in Gulf cruise rotation out of Vancouver. The *Star Princess* is returning to the Alaska fleet after a short hiatus and will run on Inside Passage itineraries. The *Dawn Princess,* which was in Seattle last year, has been switched to San Francisco for a season of 10-day Inside Passage cruises.

New to the Alaska scene this year is the intimate 670-passenger *Tahitian Princess,* which will offer an unusual "Connoisseur Cruise" schedule of 14-day sailings that includes the Gulf ports plus the seldom-visited Kodiak, southwest of Anchorage. Holland America's *Noordam,* built in 2006 and carrying 1,848 passengers, is being deployed elsewhere in 2008, while the *Veendam* is returning. While the two Alaska cruise heavyweights will have the same number of ships in the market, Princess will offer more berths; its ships are generally bigger.

Also plying Alaskan waters for its second year is Norwegian Cruise Line's *Norwegian Pearl.* The ship (93,000 GRT, 2,466 passengers) entered service in 2006 and features the first bowling alley at sea. **Silversea,** one of the truly upscale all-inclusive lines, is back in the Alaska market in 2008 following a 1-year hiatus, with its *Silver Shadow.* This gives the state two luxury ships again—Regent's *Seven Seas Mariner* being the other. There are a total of 28 big ships in Alaska this year, one more than last year. On the small-ship side, Cruise West, the biggest small ship player by far in the Alaska market, is adding an eighth ship, bringing the *Spirit of Nantucket* to Alaska for the first time (the ship has previously cruised in places including the East Coast as the *Nantucket Clipper*). The ship has a new name to go with its new role—the *Spirit of Glacier Bay.*

Clipper Cruise Line left the Alaska market after the 2007 season, and that name is disappearing too (a company called International Shipping Partners bought the two remaining ships, *Clipper Odyssey* and *Clipper Adventurer,* both of which were in Alaska in 2007, and will not be there in 2008). And because we still get asked—Glacier Bay Cruiseline no longer exists at all (it didn't exist for the 2007 book either).

PORTS OF EMBARKATION   Seattle continues to be described as the "hottest port" in the market. For years, cruise lines used Seattle as a port of embarkation for smaller ships, most notably **Cruise West** (whose biggest ship holds fewer than 140 passengers). Then in 2000, **Norwegian Cruise Line** (NCL) pioneered the use of Seattle as a big-ship port, placing its *Norwegian Sky* (now departed for Hawaii) there for the Alaska season. Some competitors predicted that this plan was rash and would never succeed. Then came the September 11, 2001, terrorist attacks, and overnight, every cruise operator started looking for new U.S. ports to use as Americans started looking for ports closer to home. In 2008, NCL will again have the *Norwegian Pearl* and *Norwegian Star* in Seattle for the Alaska seasons and they will join ships from the fleets of Princess, Royal Caribbean, and Holland America. In fact, there will be eight big ships cruising out of Seattle to Alaska in 2008.

Seward and the rather colorless port of Whittier continue to operate as the turnaround ports for Gulf of Alaska cruises. Nondescript as it may be, Whittier is closer to Anchorage, and that translates into time saved in getting people from the ship to Anchorage's hotels and the trains that will carry them on to the Denali Park corridor. **Carnival, Princess,** and **Regent Seven Seas** also use Whittier as their northern terminus. In both Seward and Whittier, rail tracks extend right up to the pier, enabling passengers to board their transportation to Anchorage. It is also, of course, possible to get there by motorcoach, still the most common transfer medium. The town is now getting things like luxury hotels, which it never had before.

The big news in Vancouver unfortunately may be that it's getting increasingly expensive with the Canadian dollar at press time about equal to the U.S. dollar.

The battle for the minds—and pocketbooks—of cruisers is being fought not so much with hardware—new ships, fancier staterooms, more restaurants—but with itineraries, shore excursions, onboard activities, cruisetours, and more welcoming dock facilities.

ONBOARD CHANGES Cruise lines are constantly tweaking their onboard products and services, with the aim of making life easier for passengers and reducing regimentation, especially at mealtimes. All of **Holland America's** Alaska ships have been completely equipped with the Signature of Excellence package—a bundle of onboard amenities such as massage shower heads, fluffier towels and pillows, lighted makeup mirrors, and the like. **Carnival** passengers will also notice comfier beds, thanks to a line-wide upgrade effort (if you really like it, you can even buy the bedding—new, of course). And the line has introduced gourmet low-cal options in its dining rooms for those who don't want their cruise to be a gorge-fest.

Celebrity has also beefed up its concierge program for those who like a little extra attention (who doesn't?). All of the new ships have scads of alternative dining opportunities, some for a price, some gratis. Perhaps the most flexible of all is **Princess,** which offers seven dining options on both the *Diamond* and the *Sapphire,* and **NCL,** with 11 dining areas on the *Pearl,* 11 on *Star,* and 9 on the

Sun. Another change is the cost of top-end offerings: On *Carnival Spirit,* its high-end steakhouse now charges $30 a head; ditto for the fancy restaurants on the three **Celebrity** ships. Most cruise lines have been adding maritime communications networks that now allow passengers to use their cellphones at sea, a cheaper option than shipboard phone lines. You can use the same networks to text-message and check your PDA.

Princess and Holland America have been beefing up their Alaska menus to add more regional specialties and special options such as salmon bakes.

Again this year, guests on Regent's *Seven Seas Mariner* or Silversea's *Silver Shadow* won't have to hassle with bar bills. Silversea has operated a no-charge-for-booze program for some time; Regent introduced it last year.

Getting hitched on a ship is a little bit easier this year, thanks to Princess Cruises. Whereas before the company allowed weddings to take place only on the *Diamond, Sapphire, Island,* and *Coral Princesses,* now such ceremonies are available on every ship in the fleet, including all eight in Alaska in 2008.

CRUISETOURS A lot of the emphasis here is on the Denali Corridor (Anchorage to Fairbanks, through Denali), where rail tours hold sway. **Holland America, Princess,** and **Royal Celebrity Tours** (the tour company for Royal Caribbean and Celebrity) all have new (or at least very late-model) domed-glass railcars in service this year. They are being billed as "the most luxurious," with "the easiest viewing windows," and will serve "gourmet meals." The rhetoric, while perhaps overheated and open to argument, gives a fairly accurate impression of the quality of a truly splendid product. The cars are uniformly spectacular—and, incidentally, a tribute to the power of market forces. Holland America recently upgraded its bus fleet, too, with sparkling new Explorer Coaches.

SHORE EXCURSIONS Cruise lines are increasingly looking at Alaskan ports as just the starting point for exploration. They have to—how else to disperse crowds of thousands? Toward that end, the lines have beefed up their offerings. **Carnival,** for instance, has a brochure that lists over 100 shore excursions, and **Princess** has 19 in Juneau alone. A new name appearing more frequently in listings these days is Icy Strait Point, an area (it can hardly be called a town) between Juneau and Glacier Bay. It is, in essence, nothing more than a single dock, an old cannery unit strategically placed for entry on foot to some of Alaska's most pristine and hitherto inaccessible wilderness areas. **Holland America, Royal Caribbean, Princess,** and **Celebrity** are among lines now making port calls there. New shore excursions from this port include a ZipRide, where you sit in a bucket seat and travel down a mountain on a wire— the one here is the longest in the world. In Sitka, there's now a semi-submersible ride through the harbor, allowing guests a chance to view the ocean floor, seeing the aquatic life and plant forms up close through underwater viewing windows. And yes, for those so inclined there are now Duck Tours (in amphibious vehicles) in Ketchikan.

Increasingly creative excursions in the traditional ports (Ketchikan, Skagway, Juneau, and Sitka) are showing up on the rosters as well. In Juneau, for instance, photographically inclined passengers on Princess's ships can snap away with the help of a professional photographer on a Photo Safari by Land & Sea. In Ketchikan, **Celebrity** added a Coastal Wilderness and Bear Trek, where a narrated boat tour takes you to remote sites in search of bears and other wildlife; you then hop on a floatplane for a 1-hour flight to a prime bear-viewing area. In Ketchikan, several lines offer a relatively new Harley-Davidson Motorcycle Tour and a Rainforest Ropes and Zip Line Challenge and a new stern-wheeler, the 350-passenger *Alaska Queen,* now in service offering 2½-hour narrated harbor tours. In Victoria, B.C., you can see stars; **Princess** offers evening stargazing with a visit to the Dominion Observatory. Prince Rupert is developing new shore excursions, too, including Grizzly Bear Viewing by Boat (at nearby Khutzeymateen Valley). The Thshimshian Tradition Canoe Quest and Rainforest Hike in Prince Rupert includes a trip in a 31-foot Native-design canoe.

EXPLORING Skagway and Ketchikan just keep getting more jewelry stores that cater to cruise passengers. For independent travelers in Ketchikan, **Allen Marine Tours** has added a cruise to the Misty Fjords National Monument on a high-speed catamaran. In Haines, a funky new little museum focuses on the history of hammers. In Vancouver, check out the new audio tours offered by the SkyTrain that use Global Positioning System (GPS) technology. Seattle has a newly expanded Seattle Art Museum and a brand new **Olympic Sculpture Park.** The cruise lines have also added some cool excursions including one that takes you past the home of Bill Gates by boat. **Icy Strait Point** is getting increased visits as Alaska's newest port; it was created by the cruise lines as a jumping-off point for wildlife tours. Check out the new Wild Spice restaurant in Juneau, offering Mongolian grill in Alaska. And in Victoria, have a brew at Spinnaker Gastro Brewpub, recently expanded and Canada's oldest brewpub.

We've made some new additions to this guide based on our recent travels. We discovered a cute little quilt shop in Petersburg, and Haines now has an outdoor coffee and sweets hangout just steps from Fort Seward. We heard so much buzz about Glacier Gardens Rainforest Adventure in Juneau that we had to check it out. It's a gorgeous botanical garden, and an excellent choice for a visit—after Mendenhall Glacier.

We've added back in this book an entire write-up of Valdez, now that cruise ships are visiting there again in 2008 (albeit in small numbers; there's not much to see).

CRUISE ITINERARIES Alaska is somewhat limited in the itinerary variations it can offer. It is essentially either the Inside Passage (through the part of Alaska known as Southeast or the Panhandle) or the popular one-way cruises across the Gulf of Alaska between Vancouver and Anchorage (with embarkation or disembarkation in Seward or Whittier, the ports for Anchorage). Other alternative routes include all-Alaska cruises on small ships beginning and ending in places like Juneau and Ketchikan, cruises to remote Indian villages, and big-ship cruises embarking and disembarking at San Francisco, Seattle, or Vancouver. The *Tahitian Princess*'s visits to Kodiak this year are the latest effort to stretch the Alaska big-ship cruise map.

THE GLACIER BAY ACCESS DEBATE Environmental issues involving passenger-ship entry into Glacier Bay continue to pit environmentalists (who want to limit the number of cruise ships allowed into the bay) against the cruise lines. The subject of how many ships can safely enter the vast wilderness area without upsetting the whales and other forms of aquatic life that inhabit it in the summer has been hotly debated—and disputed— for more than a decade. The environmentalists would like to prohibit all big cruise ships from visiting Glacier Bay in June, July, and August; the cruise lines, naturally, feel that more ships should be granted access during those peak travel

months. As this book is being written, the number of Glacier Bay big-ship visitation permits will be maintained at 2007 levels. (That, though, in the ever-changing world of Alaska, is always subject to revision, up or down, at short notice.)

An environmental-impact study to determine exactly how much damage—if any—ships do to the aquatic population of the bay drags on, its preliminary results open to interpretation. That study ultimately will determine whether to open up the precious bay to more ships.

In 2008, **Holland America** will offer more ships that have access to the park than any other line in the market, and **Princess** will have the most berths visiting the area because the company has larger ships. Many other ships will also have authorizations to enter the park this year.

Don't worry if your cruise doesn't include a visit to Glacier Bay; there are plenty of other equally delightful and— in our opinion, sometimes even more attractive—glacier areas to visit. The cruise lines have found ways to live with the Glacier Bay–entry restrictions by substituting visits to Hubbard Glacier, Icy Bay, Misty Fjords, or Tracy Arm. We would rather visit Hubbard Glacier any day of the week!

ENVIRONMENTAL CONCERNS The state legislature has enacted a series of pollution-mitigating restrictions on cruise lines, including increased environmental-reporting requirements and stricter rules about where cruise ships may legally discard treated waste. And the legislature is likely to continue to turn up the heat to keep the cruise lines honest.

Some cruise execs believe that environmental concerns, serious as they are, are being overplayed and used by some people as an "excuse" to make cruise lines and their passengers pay for the privilege of visiting the state. Whether that's true or not, Alaskans' perception of cruising and their efforts to make cruise passengers pay more are matters that concern ship operators greatly. Cruise lines have done their part to alleviate the locals' fears. They've staggered the timing of their shore excursion vehicle traffic to cut down on crowds in the streets. They've hooked up to city power supplies while in port rather than continuing to operate their own generators, in order to minimize the outflow of pollutants from their smokestacks. They've installed sophisticated garbage-disposal equipment and new procedures to do away with unclean dumping at sea. They've done all kinds of things to respond positively to the concerns of Alaska citizens. It's an uneasy truce—but it's holding. (Nothing illustrates the Alaska environmental conflict more vividly than the debate over the Alaska National Wildlife Reserve, the vast wilderness area in the extreme north that the Bush administration would like to open up to oil drilling. Cruise passengers don't travel that far north [nor do most Alaskans, for that matter], but nevertheless the question "to drill or not to drill" has caused a great deal of discussion, not to say discord, among residents. The slightest suggestion of an incursion into wilderness land and the creatures that inhabit it just seems to raise the hackles of some Alaskans.)

TAXATION Attention, passengers: Prepare to pay more for your cabin in 2008! Many residents of Alaska have become activists in their efforts to increase taxation to cruise companies.

The battle began when voters in Alaska approved a ballot initiative. This initiative comprised the following: imposing a $50 head tax on every passenger, a 33% tax (ouch!) on ships' casino profits (and guess who would end up footing that bill as well), and positioning a pollution practices inspector—to be known as an Ocean Ranger—on every cruise ship sailing in Alaska waters. The initiative called

for the Ocean Rangers' salaries to be paid by the state, but with accommodations taking one cabin out of revenue service on each ship.

Despite a fight financed by the cruise industry—reportedly at a cost of more than $1 million—tax-minded voters approved this initiative by a healthy margin of almost five percentage points. It was the first headache that faced Alaska's new governor, Republican Sarah Palin, when she took office in December 2006.

The $50 per passenger head tax and 33% casino tax were written into law; however, lawmakers backpedaled when they realized the high cost of hiring the estimated 80 new pollution experts to fulfill the Ocean Rangers requirement. They settled on a compromise: Instead of each ship having an onboard Ocean Ranger, pollution experts already on the state's payroll will simply board ships after they dock to ensure the ships' practices are environmentally sound.

Ports will now get their share on a prorated basis out of the $50 passenger head tax collected by the state. Whatever's left over when the ports have been paid will accrue to the general coffers.

Many Alaskans, both incomers and those born in the state, choose to be there because of its tranquility and pristine beauty—the very things that tourism, if improperly managed, has a tendency to erode. Thus, those residents are prone to call for taxes that may discourage cruise passengers from visiting. The cruise lines, of course, deny that their industry is environmentally unfriendly. They also argue that they pay more than enough to Alaska in the form of docking fees, supplies, purchases, and the rest to cover the cost of any demands they may make on the infrastructure and the services of the communities they sail to.

By and large, cruise operators have no objection to paying their fair share—but what they disagree on is what constitutes a fair share. The lines know that Alaska is an essential part of their summer cruise mix. So they will just have to suck it up and, alas, pass the higher costs on to their passengers.

A word to the wise: Don't let all this legislative/taxation wrangling frighten you off. On the whole, you'll find the vast majority of residents of Alaska remain warm to visitors, whether from cruise ships or independent travelers.

1

The Best of Alaska Cruising

Alaska is one of the top cruise destinations in the world, and when you're sailing through the calm waters of the Inside Passage or across the Gulf of Alaska, it's easy to see why: The scenery is simply breathtaking.

Much of the coastline is wilderness, with snowcapped mountain peaks, immense glaciers that create a thunderous noise as chunks break off into the sea (a process known as calving), emerald rainforests, fjords, icebergs, soaring eagles, lumbering bears, and majestic whales, all easily visible from the comfort of your ship.

Visit the towns and you'll find people who retain the spirit of frontier independence that brought them here in the first place. Add Alaska's colorful history and heritage, with its European influences, its spirit of discovery, and its rich Native cultures, and you have a destination that is utterly, endlessly fascinating. Even thinking about it, we get chills of the good kind.

The fact that the number of cruise passengers who come here each year has been steadily increasing—2008 momentously may be the year the number of cruise passengers tops one million for the first time—has had its impact, of course. In the summer, some towns turn into tourist malls populated by seasonal vendors, including jewelry stores geared towards the cruise crowd (15 such stores in Skagway alone at our last count) and shelves filled with imported souvenirs. However, the port towns you'll visit—from Juneau, the most remote state capital in the country, to Sitka, with its proud reminders of Native and Russian cultures—retain much of their rustic charm and historical allure. Sure, you may have to jostle for a seat in Juneau's popular Red Dog Saloon (a must-do beer stop) or ask other visitors to step out of the way as you try to snap a picture of Skagway's historic gold-rush buildings or Ketchikan's picturesque Creek Street, but these are minor hassles for cruise-ship passengers. If you want to get away from the crowds by taking an organized shore excursion or touring on your own, or booking a small-ship cruise that goes to more remote parts, there's opportunity for that, too. In addition, by signing up for the cruise lines' pre- or post-cruise land-tour packages (known as "cruisetours"), you can also visit less-populated inland destinations such as Denali National Park, Fairbanks, the Kenai Peninsula, the Yukon Territory, or the Canadian Rockies.

Even before you cruise, we can predict you'll want to visit again. Jerry first visited in 1973 and claims he's never been the same—the place put such a spell on him that over the years, he's been back upward of 50 times. Fran's first visit to the state wasn't quite that long ago, but she also noticed that her view of the world was forever changed, and she quickly put the state at the top of her list of cruise destinations. Alaska is like that. It grabs you by the scruff of the neck and won't let you go.

Whether you're looking for pampering and resort amenities or a "you and the sea" adventure experience, you'll find it offered by cruise ships in Alaska. Here are some of our favorites, along with our picks of the best ports, shore excursions, and sights.

1 The Best of Alaska's Ships

- **The Best Ships for Luxury:** Luxury in Alaska is defined in 2008 by the midsized ships operated by Regent Seven Seas and Silversea Cruises, the latter returning to Alaska after a 1-year absence. If you want a more casual kind of luxury—a really nice ship with a no-tie-required policy—the *Seven Seas Mariner* offers just that on an all-suite vessel (most cabins have private balconies) with excellent cuisine. Silversea, on the other hand, with its *Silver Shadow,* represents a slick, Italian-influenced luxury experience with all the perks—big suite cabins, fine food, fine linens, and fine companions. Both lines include fine wine and booze and gratuities in their cruise fares. If you're more the small-ship type, for the ultimate Alaska experience in an intimate setting, check out the yachts of American Safari Cruises, where soft adventure comes with luxury accoutrements.

- **The Best of the Mainstream Ships:** Every line's most recent ships are beautiful, but Celebrity's *Infinity* is a stunner as is its sister ship, *Millennium.* These modern vessels, with their extensive art collections, cushy public rooms, and expanded spa areas, give Celebrity a formidable presence in Alaska. And the late-model *Sapphire Princess* and *Diamond Princess* (which both debuted in 2004) have raised the art of building big ships to new heights. Both of these vessels will again be in Inside Passage service this year—departing from Vancouver.

- **The Best of the Small Ships:** Cruise West is the biggest small-ship player now that Clipper and Glacier Bay Cruiseline have vanished from the scene. Our fave of the fleet is the *Spirit of '98,* which has the cool hook of looking and feeling like a Victorian steamship—although it was actually built in 1984. And for real nostalgia, Majestic Cruise Line's *Empress of the North,* a real stern-wheeler, is hard to beat (the ship was out of service for a time in 2007 after it hit some rocks off Juneau, but was expected to be operational in 2008). Sailing on the *Empress,* watching the paddle wheel throw spray, is to take a step back in time to the golden age of steamboat travel.

- **The Best Ships for Families:** All the major lines have well-established kids' programs. Holland America and Norwegian Cruise Line win points in Alaska for their special shore excursions for kids and teens, and Carnival gets a nod for offering shore excursions for teens.

- **The Best Ships for Pampering:** It's a tossup—Celebrity's *Infinity* and *Millennium* offer wonderful AquaSpas complete with thalassotherapy pools and a wealth of soothing and beautifying treatments, and the solariums on Royal Caribbean's *Rhapsody of the Seas, Serenade of the Seas,* and *Radiance of the Seas* offer relaxing indoor pool retreats. Luxury line Regent Seven Seas, of course, pampers all around. Ditto for the very posh Silversea Cruises.

- **The Best Shipboard Cuisine:** Regent Seven Seas is tops in this category, especially in the creative department, although Silversea, with its emphasis on preparation, has plenty to appeal to foodies as well—you want your filet rare, you'll get it rare. Of the mainstream lines, Celebrity has impressed in the past, though they recently dropped their affiliation with renowned French chef Michel Roux. Dinner in the reservations-only specialty restaurants on both the *Infinity* and the *Millennium* ($30 service

Alaska

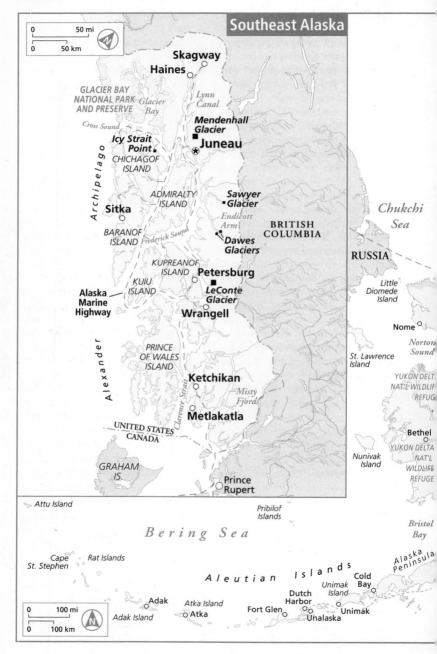

Southeast Alaska

0 — 50 mi
0 — 50 km

Skagway
Haines
GLACIER BAY
NATIONAL PARK
AND PRESERVE
Glacier Bay
Lynn Canal
Cross Sound
Icy Strait Point
CHICHAGOF ISLAND
Mendenhall Glacier
Juneau
Archipelago
ADMIRALTY ISLAND
Sawyer Glacier
Endicott Arm
BRITISH COLUMBIA
Chukchi Sea
Sitka
BARANOF ISLAND
Frederick Sound
Dawes Glaciers
RUSSIA
KUPREANOF ISLAND
Petersburg
KUIU ISLAND
LeConte Glacier
Little Diomede Island
Alaska Marine Highway
Wrangell
Nome
Norton Sound
Alexander
PRINCE OF WALES ISLAND
St. Lawrence Island
YUKON DELTA NAT'L WILDLIFE REFUGE
Ketchikan
Misty Fjords
Clarence Strait
Metlakatla
UNITED STATES
CANADA
Bethel
YUKON DELTA NAT'L WILDLIFE REFUGE
Nunivak Island
GRAHAM IS.
Prince Rupert
Attu Island
Pribilof Islands
Bristol Bay
Bering Sea
Cape St. Stephen
Rat Islands
Aleutian Islands
Cold Bay
Alaska Peninsula
Adak
Adak Island
Atka Island
Atka
Fort Glen
Dutch Harbor
Unimak Island
Unalaska
Unimak
0 — 100 mi
0 — 100 km

Paved Road
State or Provincial Route
Dirt Road

ARCTIC OCEAN

ALASKA

CANADA

USA

0   1000 miles

Barrow

CAPE KRUSENSTERN
NAT'L MON.

BROOKS RANGE

Prudhoe Bay
Deadhorse

Beaufort
Sea

NOATAK NAT'L
PRESERVE

Anaktuvuk
Pass

ARCTIC NAT'L
WILDLIFE
REFUGE

KOBUK VALLEY
NAT'L PARK

GATES OF THE
ARCTIC NAT'L PARK
AND PRESERVE

Dalton Hwy

Kotzebue

Bettles

Fort Yukon

YUKON FLATS
NAT'L WILDLIFE
REFUGE

Dempster Hwy

NORTHWEST

Arctic Circle

TERRITORIES

BERING LAND BRIDGE
NAT'L PRESERVE

Chena
Hot Springs

Circle

YUKON-CHARLEY RIVERS
NAT'L PRESERVE

CANADA

Galena

Manley
Hot Springs

2

6

Fairbanks

Eagle

YUKON

Unalakleet

Nenana

North Pole

5

Yukon River

McGrath

DENALI
NAT'L PARK

Mt. McKinley

3

ALASKA RANGE

8

Delta
Junction

9

Tok

4   1

Dawson City

5

Kuskokwim River

Talkeetna

Glennallen

6

Willow
Wasilla

1

WRANGELL MTS.

4

LAKE CLARK
NAT'L PARK
AND PRESERVE

Anchorage

Palmer

Kenai
Soldotna

Valdez

10

McCarthy

1

2

Whitehorse

4

Dillingham

1

Whittier

Cordova

WRANGELL–ST. ELIAS
NAT'L PARK
AND PRESERVE

1

King
Salmon

Homer

Seward

KATMAI NAT'L
PARK AND PRESERVE

Seldovia

Cook Inlet

Prince
William
Sound

Yakutat

7

BRITISH
COLUMBIA

KENAI FJORDS
NAT'L PARK

Alaska Marine
Highway

Kodiak

GLACIER BAY NAT'L
PARK AND PRESERVE

Juneau

Kodiak Island

Gulf of
Alaska

ANIAKCHAK NAT'L
MONUMENT AND PRESERVE

Southeast Alaska, See Inset

PACIFIC   OCEAN

To Vancouver
& Seattle

Prince Rupert

charge per person) is a very special, pampered dining experience. But somewhat surprisingly, the Nouveau Supper Club on the *Carnival Spirit* (service charge $30 per person) also presents an impressive dining experience that will especially appeal to fans of elegant steakhouses—the beef is properly aged and expertly grilled. Carnival has also upgraded both its main dining room and buffet offerings.

- **The Best Ships for Onboard Activities:** The ships operated by Carnival and Royal Caribbean have rosters teeming with onboard activities that range from the sublime (such as lectures) to the ridiculous (such as contests designed to get passengers to do or say outrageous things). Princess's ScholarShip@Sea program is a real winner, with exciting packaged classes in such diverse subjects as photography, personal computers, cooking, and pottery—they even recently added scrapbooking to the mix.

- **The Best Ships for Entertainment:** Look to the big ships here. Carnival and Royal Caribbean are tops when it comes to an overall package of shows, nightclub acts, lounge performances, and audience-participation entertainment. Princess also offers particularly well-done—if somewhat less lavishly staged—shows.

- **The Best Ships for Whale-Watching:** If the whales come close enough, you can see them from all the ships in Alaska. But smaller ships—such as those operated by Cruise West, Lindblad, and American Safari—might actually change course to follow a whale. Get your cameras ready!

- **The Best Ships for Cruisetours:** With their own fleets of deluxe motorcoaches and railcars, Princess, Holland America, and more recently Royal Caribbean Cruises (which owns Royal Caribbean and Celebrity) are the market leaders in getting you into the Interior of Alaska, either before or after your cruise. Princess and Holland America also own lodges and hotels, and some of the other lines actually buy their land product components from these lines. One of Holland America's strengths is its 3- and 4-night cruises combined with an Alaska/Yukon land package. The company offers exclusive entry into the Yukon's Kluane National Park, and they've added another Yukon gem—Tombstone Territorial Park, near Dawson City, a region of staggering wilderness beauty, Native architecture, stunning vistas, and wildlife. Princess is arguably stronger in 7-night Gulf of Alaska cruises in conjunction with Denali/Fairbanks or Kenai Peninsula cruisetour arrangements.

2 The Best Ports

Juneau and Skagway are our favorites. Juneau is one of the most visually pleasing small cities anywhere and certainly the prettiest capital city in America. It's fronted by the Gastineau Channel and backed by Mount Juneau and Mount Roberts, offers the very accessible Mendenhall Glacier, and is otherwise surrounded by wilderness—and it's a really fun city to visit, too.

As for Skagway, no town in Alaska is more historically significant, and the old buildings are so perfect you might think you stepped into a Disney version of what a gold-rush town should look like. If, that is, you can get over the decidedly turn-of-the-millennium Starbucks at the Mercantile Center and the 15 or so upscale jewelry shops that have followed cruise passengers from the Caribbean (like some of the locals we know, we were thrilled last year to discover that Little Switzerland, one such shop, had actually pulled up stakes and moved on after a not-very-successful run in Skagway). There are people who will tell you that Skagway is hokey, touristy—and it is. But if you can get yourself into the right frame of mind, if you can recall the history of the place, the gold-rush frenzy that literally put the town on the map, it's easier to capture the true spirit of Skagway. The residents have made every effort to retain as much as possible of the architecture and historic significance of their community, and they don't mind sharing it with visitors during the cruise season. For a more low-key Alaska experience, take the ferry from Skagway to Haines, which reminds us of the folksy, frontier Alaska depicted on the TV show *Northern Exposure,* and is a great place to spot eagles and other wildlife. Some ships also stop at Haines as a port of call, usually for a few hours after Skagway, and this is one town we're pleased to report has not been changed by the advent of cruise-ship visitors.

3 The Best Shore Excursions

Flightseeing and helicopter trips in Alaska are unforgettable ways to check out the scenery if you can afford them. But airborne tours tend to be pretty pricey—some of them approaching $600 a head. A helicopter trip to a dog-sled camp at the top of a glacier (usually the priciest of the offerings) affords both incredibly pretty views and a chance to try your hand at the truly Alaskan sport of dog sledding. (Yes, even in summer: The sleds may be fitted with wheels.) It's a great way to earn bragging rights with the folks back home. For a less extravagant excursion, nothing beats a ride on a clear day on the White Pass & Yukon Route Railway out of Skagway to the Canadian border—the route was expanded in 2007 to take passengers to Fraser, at the border, and on to Carcross (also known as Caribou Cross) in the Yukon Territory, some 30 more miles into Canada. The train route is the same one followed by the gold stampeders of 1898. While you're riding the rails, try to imagine what it was like for those gold seekers crossing the same path on foot!

And we also like to get active with kayak and mountain-biking excursions offered by most lines at most ports. In addition to affording a chance to work off those shipboard calories, these excursions typically provide optimum opportunities for spotting eagles, bears, seals, and other wildlife. Ziplining is just plain fun for those who want to try soaring on a wire above the treetops—the adrenaline rush can be addictive.

Another, less hectic shore excursion that goes down well with many passengers is a float ride down one of the more placid stretches of Alaska's myriad rivers, such as the Kenai, the Mendenhall, or the Chilkat. These outings don't involve a lot of paddling—which can be hard work—but instead use the natural flow of the river to propel the four- to six-person rubber raft downstream. And they involve little or no white water. Generally, the group will stop for a picnic lunch en route and return to the staging area by motorcoach or automobile.

2

Choosing Your Ideal Cruise

Just like clothes, cars, and gourmet coffee, Alaska cruises come in all different styles to suit all different tastes; so the first step in ensuring that you have the best possible vacation is to match your expectations to the appropriate itinerary and ship.

In this chapter, we explore the advantages of the two main Alaska itineraries, examine the differences between big-ship cruising and small-ship cruising, pose some questions you should ask yourself to determine which cruise is right for you, and give you the skinny on cruisetours, which combine a cruise with a land tour that gets you into the Alaska Interior.

1 The Alaska Cruise Season

Alaska is a seasonal, as opposed to year-round, cruise destination; the season generally runs from May through September, although some smaller ships start up in April. May and September are considered the shoulder seasons, and lower brochure rates and more aggressive discounts are offered during these months. We particularly like cruising in May, before the crowds arrive, when we've generally found locals to be friendlier than they are later in the season, at which point they're pretty much ready to see the tourists go home for the winter.

Also, at the Inside Passage ports, May is one of the driest months in the season. On a recent late-May cruise, temperatures were in the high 60s (teens Celsius), perfect for hiking and biking. Late September, though, also offers the advantage of fewer fellow cruise passengers clogging the ports. The warmest months are June, July, and August, with temperatures generally around 50°F to 80°F (10°C–27°C) during the day and cooler at night. In the past couple of years the temperature soared even higher. (When temperatures reached 90°F/32°C in Juneau in the summer of 2004, there was much local speculation about global warming.) You may not need a parka, but you will need to bring along some outerwear and rain gear. The trick in coping with Alaska weather is to dress in layers, with maybe a lightweight waterproof jacket on top and a sweater and blouse/shirt underneath. June 21 is the longest day of the year, with the sky lit almost all night. June tends to be drier than July and August (we have experienced trips in July when it rained nearly every day). April and May are drier than September, although in early April you may encounter freezing rain and other vestiges of winter. If you are considering traveling in a shoulder month, keep in mind that some shops don't open until Memorial Day, and the visitor season is generally considered over on Labor Day (although cruise lines operate well into Sept).

2 The Inside Passage or the Gulf of Alaska?

For the purposes of cruising, Alaska can be divided into two separate and distinct areas, known generically as "the Inside Passage" and "the Gulf."

Shore Excursions: The What, When & Why

Shore excursions offered by the cruise lines provide a chance for you to get off the ship and explore the sights up close. You'll take in the history, nature, and culture of the region, from exploring gold-rush-era streets to experiencing Native Alaskan traditions such as totem carving.

Some excursions are of the walking-tour or bus-tour variety, but many others are activity-oriented: Cruise passengers have the opportunity to go sea kayaking, mountain biking, horseback riding, salmon fishing, ziplining, and even rock climbing. You can see the sights by seaplane or helicopter—and maybe even land on a glacier and go for a walk. Occasionally, with some of the smaller cruise lines, you'll find quirky excursions, such as a visit with local artists in their studios. Some lines even offer scuba diving and snorkeling.

With some lines, shore excursions are included in your cruise fare, but with most lines they are an added (though very worthwhile) expense. See chapters 8 and 9 for details on the excursions available at the various ports. For more information, see "Cruisetours: The Best of Land & Sea," later in this chapter, and chapter 10.

THE INSIDE PASSAGE

The Inside Passage runs through the area of Alaska known as Southeast (which the locals also call "the Panhandle"). It's the narrow strip of the state—islands, mainland coastal communities, and mountains—that runs from the Canadian border in the south to the start of the Gulf in the north, just above the Juneau/Haines/Skagway area. The islands on the western side of the area afford cruise ships a welcome degree of protection from the sea and its attendant rough waters (hence the name "Inside Passage"). Because of that shelter, such ports as Ketchikan, Wrangell, Petersburg, and others are reached with less rocking and rolling, and thus less risk of seasickness. Sitka is not on the Inside Passage (it's on the ocean side of Baranof Island) but is included in most Inside Passage cruise itineraries.

Southeast encompasses the capital city, **Juneau,** and townships influenced by the former Russian presence in the state (**Sitka,** for instance), the Tlingit and Haida Native cultures (**Ketchikan),** and the great gold rush of 1898 (**Skagway).** It is a land of rainforests, mountains, inlets, and glaciers (including Margerie, Johns Hopkins, Muir, and the others contained within the boundaries of **Glacier Bay National Park).** The region is rich in wildlife, especially of the marine variety. It is a scenic delight. But then, what part of Alaska isn't?

THE GULF OF ALASKA

The other major cruising area is the **Southcentral** region's Gulf of Alaska, usually referred to by the cruise lines as the "Glacier Discovery Route" or the "Voyage of the Glaciers," or some such catchy title. "Gulf of Alaska," after all, sounds pretty bland.

The coastline of the Gulf is that arc of land from just north of Glacier Bay to the Kenai Peninsula. Southcentral also takes in **Prince William Sound;** the **Cook Inlet,** on the northern side of the peninsula; **Anchorage,** Alaska's biggest city; the year-round

Alyeska Resort at Girdwood, 40 miles from Anchorage; the **Matanuska** and **Susitna** valleys (the "Mat-Su"), a fertile agricultural region renowned for the record size of some of its produce; and part of the Alaska Mountain Range.

The principal Southcentral terminus ports are **Seward** or **Whittier** for Anchorage. No ships in a regular Alaska pattern actually head for Anchorage proper; instead, they carry passengers from Seward or Whittier to Anchorage by bus or train. However, let us stress that going on a Gulf cruise does not mean that you don't visit any of the Inside Passage. The big difference is that, whereas the more popular Inside Passage cruise itineraries run round-trip to and from Vancouver or Seattle, the Gulf routing is one-way—northbound and southbound—between Vancouver and Seward or Vancouver and Whittier. A typical Gulf itinerary also visits such Inside Passage ports as **Ketchikan, Juneau, Sitka,** and/or **Skagway.**

The Gulf's glaciers are quite dazzling and every bit as spectacular as their counterparts to the south. **College Fjord,** for instance, is lined with glaciers—16 of them, each one grander than the last. Recently Fran saw incredible calving at **Harvard Glacier** with chunks of 400- and 500-year-old ice falling off and crashing into the water to thunderous sounds every few minutes (any worries about such a display being caused by global warming aside, the sight was spectacular). Another favorite part of a Gulf cruise, though, is the visit to the gigantic **Hubbard Glacier**—at 6 miles, Alaska's longest—at the head of Yakutat Bay. Nothing beats a sunny day watching the glacier all hyperactive, popping and cracking and shedding tons of ice into the bay. Sometimes ships can get so close to the face that passengers speculate about just how near they might be. Jerry overheard one awestruck golf enthusiast assure all within hearing on one ship, "It's not more than a nine-iron shot away." Now that's close!

We should mention, however, that on a recent visit we couldn't even get into the bay because another ship was blocking our path (and hogging the optimum views). Our fear is that, with so many new ships in Alaska, glacier viewing could become a blood sport.

WHICH ITINERARY IS BETTER?

It's a matter of personal taste. Some people don't like open-jaw flights (flying into one city and out of another)—which can add to the ticket price—and prefer the round-trip Inside Passage route. Others don't mind splitting up the air travel because they want to enjoy the additional glacier visits on the Gulf cruise itineraries. It's entirely up to you. Cruise enthusiasts should not limit themselves to one itinerary; they should try both.

It wasn't so long ago that you wouldn't have had a choice. A few years back, there were practically no Gulf crossings. Then Princess and its tour-operating affiliate decided to accelerate the development of its land components (lodges, railcars, motorcoaches, and so on), particularly in the Kenai Peninsula and Denali National Park areas, for which Anchorage is a logical springboard. To feed these land services with cruisetour passengers, Princess beefed up the number of Gulf sailings it offered. In 2008, five of the eight Alaska ships—four of them built since 2000—will be on that route, with the line also having a formidable Inside Passage capacity. Two of the line's newest and most amenity-filled ships, the *Diamond Princess* and the *Sapphire Princess,* each carrying 2,670 passengers, will do Gulf duty again this year. The other cruisetour giant, Holland America Line, will have five of its eight vessels in the Inside Passage (two out of Vancouver, three out of Seattle), and three vessels cruising across the Gulf (out of Vancouver). HAL tends to go more heavily into the Inside Passage than Princess because it is arguably stronger in Yukon Territory land services, which are more accessible from Juneau or Skagway.

3 Big Ship or Small Ship?

Picking the right ship is the most important factor in ensuring that you get the vacation you're looking for. Cruise ships in Alaska range from **small adventure–type vessels** to really **big resortlike megaships,** with the cruise experience varying widely depending on the type of ship you select. There are casual cruises and luxury cruises; there are educational cruises where you attend lectures, and entertainment-focused cruises where you attend musical revues; there are adventure-oriented cruises where hiking, kayaking, and exploring remote areas are the main activities, and resortlike cruises where aquatherapy and mud baths are the order of the day.

Besides the availability (or nonavailability) of the programs, the spas, the activities, and the like, there is another question you have to answer before deciding on a ship. Do you want, or do you need, to be with people and, if so, in an intimate daily setting or only on an occasional basis? On a small ship, there's no escape. The people you meet on a 12-passenger or even a 130-passenger vessel are the ones you're going to be seeing every day of the cruise. And woe betide you if they turn out to be boring, or bombastic, or slow-witted, or in some other way not to your taste. Some people may think that the megaships are too big, but they do have at least one saving grace. On a 2,600-passenger ship, there's plenty of room to steer clear of people who turn you off. And because all of these big, newer ships have lots of alternative restaurants, it's even easier to avoid those types at mealtimes, something that's not so easy on a smaller ship. Personal chemistry plays a big part in the success or failure of any cruise experience—especially a small-ship cruise experience.

You'll need to decide what overall cruise experience you want. Itinerary and type of cruise are even more important than price. After all, what kind of bargain is a party cruise if what you're looking for is a quiet time? Or an adventure-oriented cruise if you're not physically in the best of shape? Your fantasy vacation may be someone else's nightmare, and vice versa.

Unlike the Caribbean, which generally attracts people looking to relax in the sun, people who want to spend all their time scuba diving and snorkeling, and people who want to party till the cows come home, Alaska attracts visitors with a different goal: They want to experience Alaska's glaciers, forests, wildlife, and other natural wonders. All the cruise lines recognize this, so almost any cruise you choose will give you opportunities to see what you've come for. The main question, then, is how you want to see those sights. Do you want to be down at the waterline, seeing them from the deck of an adventure vessel, or do you want to see them from a warm lounge or from your own private veranda?

In this section, we'll run through the pros and cons of the big ships and the small and alternative ships.

THE BIG SHIPS

Big ships operating in Alaska vary in size, amenities, and activities, and include really, really big and really, really new megaships (the *Diamond Princess* and the *Sapphire Princess* are the biggest; the *Norwegian Pearl* the newest). All the big ships offer a comfortable cruising experience, with virtual armies of service employees overseeing your well-being and ship stabilizers ensuring smooth sailing.

The size of the current crop of ships may keep Alaska's wildlife at a distance (you'll probably need binoculars to see the whales), but they offer plenty of deck space and comfy lounge chairs to sit in as you take in the gorgeous mountain and glacier views, and sip a cup of coffee or cocoa. Due to their deeper drafts (the amount of ship below the waterline), the big ships can't get as close to the sights as the smaller ships, and they can't visit the more pristine fjords, inlets, and narrows. However, the more powerful engines on these ships do allow them to visit more ports during each trip—generally popular ports where your ship may be one of several, and where shopping for souvenirs is a main attraction. Some of the less massive ships in this category may also visit alternative ports, away from the cruise crowds.

It should be noted that the bigger ships being built nowadays are equipped with some pretty powerful stabilizers—something to think about if you have the occasional bout with seasickness.

The big-ship cruise lines put a lot of emphasis on **shore excursions,** which often take you beyond the port city to explore different aspects of Alaska—nature, Native culture, and so on (see the shore excursion listings in chapters 8 and 9 for more information). Dispersing passengers to different locales on these shore trips is a must. When 8,000 passengers from several visiting ships disembark on a small Alaska town, much of the ambience goes out the window. On particularly busy days there are—literally—more cruise passengers in some ports than locals. Take Skagway, for instance: In midsummer, even counting the influx of seasonal tourist services–related employees, its population is far short of 1,000. One large cruise ship will deposit at least twice that many people onto the streets—and on busy days there may be as many as *four* ships in port! The larger ships in the Alaska market fall generally into two categories: midsize and megaships.

Carrying between, say, 1,800 and 2,670 passengers, the **megaships** look and feel like floating resorts. Big on glitz, they offer loads of activities, attract many families and (especially in Alaska) seniors, offer many public rooms (including fancy casinos and fully equipped gyms), and provide a wide variety of meal and entertainment options. And though they may feature one or two formal nights per trip, the ambience is generally casual. The Alaska vessels of the Carnival, Celebrity, Princess, and Royal Caribbean fleets all fit in this category, as do Norwegian Cruise Line's *Sun, Star,* and brand new *Pearl,* and Holland America's *Oosterdam* and *Westerdam.* But a word of caution: Due to the number of people involved, disembarkation from the biggest ships can be a lengthy process.

Midsize ships in Alaska for 2008 fall into two segments: the ultraluxury Regent *Seven Seas Mariner* and Silversea's *Silver Shadow* and the modern midsize *Veendam, Ryndam, Volendam, Amsterdam, Zaandam,* and *Statendam* of the Holland America Line, and the *Tahitian Princess* of Princess Cruises. In general, the size of these ships is less significant than the general onboard atmosphere: Holland America's midsize ships all have a similar calm, adult-oriented feel, while Norwegian's vessels all share the same ultracasual, activities-oriented approach. The *Mariner* offers a casual form of luxury (think country-club set), while the *Silver Shadow* offers luxury with a sleek, Italian flair. Both the midsize ships and the megaships have a great range of **facilities** for passengers. There are swimming pools, health clubs, spas (of various sizes), nightclubs, movie theaters, shops, casinos, bars, and special kids' playrooms. In some cases, especially on the megaships, you'll also find sports decks, virtual golf, computer rooms, and cigar clubs, as well as quiet spaces where you can get away from it all. There are so many public rooms that you more than likely won't feel claustrophobic. **Cabins**

SHIP SIZE COMPARISONS

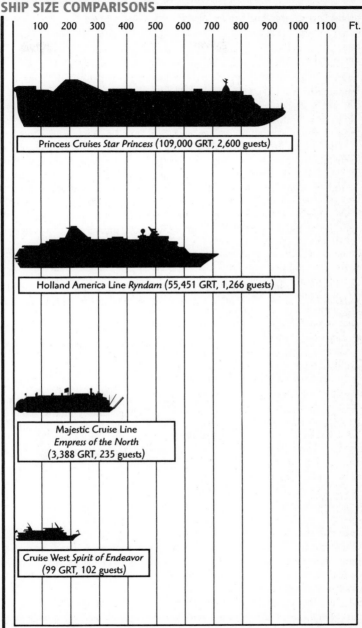

| 100 | 200 | 300 | 400 | 500 | 600 | 700 | 800 | 900 | 1000 | 1100 | Ft. |

Princess Cruises *Star Princess* (109,000 GRT, 2,600 guests)

Holland America Line *Ryndam* (55,451 GRT, 1,266 guests)

Majestic Cruise Line
Empress of the North
(3,388 GRT, 235 guests)

Cruise West *Spirit of Endeavor*
(99 GRT, 102 guests)

Ships in this chart represent the various size vessels sailing in Alaska. See ship reviews in chapters 5 and 6 for comparative sizes of ships not shown here. (*GRT* means gross register tons, which is not literally a measure of weight, but rather a measure of interior space on ships.)

Weighing the Dining Options on Various Cruises

Smaller ships usually serve dinner at a certain time, with open seating, allowing you to sit at any table you want. Large ships may offer only two fairly rigid set-seating times, especially for dinner. This means that your table will be pre-assigned and remain the same for the duration of the cruise. However, increasingly, there are some exceptions to the rule in the large-ship category. The ships of Norwegian Cruise Line, Regent Seven Seas, and Silversea now serve all meals with open seating—dine when you want and sit with whom you want (within the restaurants' open hours and sometimes requiring reservations to be made in the morning for dinner). Princess has its own innovative version of this system, allowing guests to choose before the cruise between traditional early or late seating, or open restaurant-style seating. Most large ships today also offer multiple alternative-dining options, featuring casual buffets and specialty restaurants, some with an additional charge (as a gratuity) of up to $30. See "Choosing Your Dining Options" in chapter 3 for more information on dining choices, and see the individual ship reviews in chapters 5 and 6 for ship-specific dining information.

---

range from cubbyholes to large suites, depending on the ship and the type of accommodations you book. They offer TVs and telephones, and some have minibars, picture windows, and private verandas.

These ships have big dining rooms and buffet areas and serve a tremendous variety of **cuisine** throughout the day, often offering 24-hour-a-day food service. There may also be additional dining venues, such as pizzerias, hamburger grills, ice-cream parlors, alternative restaurants, wine bars, cigar bars, champagne bars, caviar bars, and patisseries.

In most cases, these ships have lots of **onboard activities** to keep you occupied when you're not whale- or glacier-watching, including games, contests, and classes and lectures (sometimes by naturalists, park rangers, or wildlife experts; sometimes on topics such as line dancing and napkin folding). These ships also offer a variety of entertainment options that may even include celebrity headline acts and usually include stage-show productions, some very extravagant (those of Princess and Carnival come to mind). These ships carry a lot of people and, as such, can at times feel crowded—there may be lines at the buffets and in other public areas, and it may take a while to disembark in port.

THE SMALL & ALTERNATIVE SHIPS

While big cruise ships are mostly for people who want every resort amenity, small or alternative ships are best suited for people who prefer a casual, crowd-free cruise experience that gives passengers a chance to get up close and personal with Alaska's **natural surroundings** and **wildlife.**

Thanks to their smaller size, these ships, carrying fewer than 130 passengers (American Safari Cruises's *Safari Spirit* carries only 12), can go places that larger ships can't, such as narrow fjords, uninhabited islands, and smaller ports that cater mostly to small fishing vessels. Due to their shallow draft, they can nose right up to sheer cliff faces, bird rookeries, bobbing icebergs, and cascading waterfalls that you can literally reach out and touch. Also, sea animals are not as intimidated by these ships, so you might find yourself having a rather close encounter with a humpback whale, or watching other sea mammals bobbing in the ship's wake. The decks on these ships are closer to the waterline, too, giving passengers a more intimate view than they would get from the high decks of the large cruise ships. Some of these ships stop at ports on a daily basis, like the larger ships, while some avoid ports almost entirely, exploring natural areas instead. Small ships also have the flexibility to change direction as opportunities arise—say, to go where whales have been sighted and to linger a while once a sighting has been made.

The alternative-ship experience is all about a sense of **adventure** (it's usually adventure of a soft rather than a rugged sort) and offers a generally casual cruise experience: There are no dress-up nights and food may be rather simply prepared. (Although there are notable exceptions: American Safari's fare is excellent and Cruise West has made major strides in recent years in upgrading the quality of its menus.) Because there are so few public areas to choose from—usually only one or two small lounges—camaraderie tends to develop more quickly between passengers on these ships than aboard larger vessels, which can be as anonymous as a big city. **Cabins** on these ships don't usually offer TVs or telephones and tend to be very small and, in some cases (not in the case of American Safari), downright spartan. Meals are generally served in a single open seating (meaning seats are not assigned, but there is a set dinner time), and dress codes are usually nonexistent.

None of these ships offers the kind of significant exercise or spa facilities that you'll find on the big ships—your best exercise bet is usually a brisk walk around the deck after dinner—but many compensate by offering more **active off-ship opportunities,** such as hiking or kayaking. The alternative ships are also more likely to feature in-depth **lectures** on Alaska-specific topics, such as marine biology, history, and Native culture.

There are little or no stabilizers on most of these smaller ships, and the ride can be bumpy in open water—which isn't much of a problem on Inside Passage itineraries, since most of the cruising area is protected from sea waves. These ships are also difficult for travelers with disabilities, as only three (Majestic America Line's *Empress of the North* and Cruise West's *Spirit of '98* and *Spirit of Oceanus*) have elevators. And the alternative-ship lines do not offer specific activities or facilities for children, although you will find a few families on some of these vessels.

4 Cruisetours: The Best of Land & Sea

Most folks who go to the trouble of getting to a place as far off the beaten path as Alaska try to stick around for a while once they're there, rather than jetting home as soon as they hop off the boat. Knowing this, the cruise lines have set themselves up in the land-tour business as well, offering a number of great land-based excursions that can be tacked on to your cruise experience.

We're not just talking about an overnight stay in Anchorage or Juneau before or after your cruise. Almost any cruise line will arrange an extra night's hotel accommodation for you, but, enjoyable as that may be, it doesn't begin to hint at the real opportunities available in Alaska. No, the subject here is **cruisetours,** a total package with a cruise and a structured, prearranged, multiple-day land itinerary already programmed in—for instance, a 7-day cruise with a 5-day land package. There are any number of combinations between 9 and 21 days in length.

In this section, we'll discuss the various cruisetour itineraries that are available through the lines. See chapter 10 for details on the various cruisetour destinations.

CRUISETOUR ITINERARIES

Many parts of inland Alaska can be visited on cruisetour programs, including Denali National Park, Fairbanks, Wrangell–St. Elias, Nome, and Kotzebue. If you're so inclined, you can even go all the way to the oil fields of the North Slope of Prudhoe Bay, hundreds of miles north of the Arctic Circle.

Three principal tour destination areas can be combined with your Inside Passage or Gulf of Alaska cruise—two major ones, which we'll call the **Anchorage/Denali/Fairbanks** corridor and the **Yukon Territory,** and one less-traveled route that we'll call the **Canadian Rockies Route,** which is an option due to Vancouver's position as an Alaska cruise hub.

ANCHORAGE/DENALI/FAIRBANKS CRUISETOUR

A typical Anchorage/Denali/Fairbanks cruisetour package (we'll use Princess as an example, since it is heavily involved in the Denali sector) might include a 7-day Vancouver-Anchorage cruise, followed by 2 nights in Anchorage, and a scenic ride in a private rail car to **Denali National Park** for 2 more nights at Princess's Denali Lodge or Mount McKinley Lodge (or 1 night at each), before heading on to Fairbanks. On a clear day, the McKinley property affords a panoramic view of the Alaska Mountain Range and its centerpiece, **Mount McKinley,** which, at 20,320 feet, is North America's highest peak. A full day in the park allows guests to explore the staggeringly beautiful wilderness expanse and its wildlife before reboarding the train and heading into the Interior of Alaska, to **Fairbanks,** for 2 more nights. Fairbanks itself isn't much to look at, but the activities available in outlying areas are fantastic—the *Riverboat Discovery* paddle-wheel day cruise on the Chena and Tanana rivers and an excursion to a gold mine are two excellent activity options in the area. Passengers on that particular cruisetour fly home from Fairbanks.

A shorter variation of that itinerary might be a cruise combined with an overnight (or 2-night) stay in Anchorage along with the Denali portion, perhaps with rail transportation into the park and a motorcoach back to Anchorage, skipping Fairbanks. Princess also recently introduced cruisetours that include visits to a hitherto largely inaccessible area, **Wrangell–St. Elias National Park,** where they have built the Copper River Princess Wilderness Lodge, the fifth hotel in the company's lodging network.

YUKON TERRITORY CRUISETOUR

Another popular land itinerary offered along with Alaska cruises typically involves a 3- or 4-day cruise between Vancouver and Juneau/Skagway (you either join a 7-day sailing late or get off early), combined with a land program into the **Klondike,** in Canada's Yukon Territory, then through the Interior of Alaska to Anchorage. En route, passengers experience a variety of transportation modes, which may include rail, riverboat, motorcoach, and possibly air. There are a number of variations.

The Yukon, although located in Canada, is nevertheless an integral part of the overall Alaska cruisetour picture, due to its intimate ties to Alaska's gold-rush history. The overnight stops are **Whitehorse,** the territorial capital, and **Dawson City,** a remote, picture-perfect gold-rush town near the site where gold was found in 1896. Holland America offers a drive through Canada's **Kluane National Park,** a Yukon Territory wilderness area designated a UNESCO World Heritage Site, and also through Tombstone

Territorial Park, about 90 minutes' drive from Dawson City, an area of stunning scenery, Native architecture, and abundant wildlife. Kluane Park contains 5 of North America's 10 tallest peaks. And if it's wilderness scenery you want, you'll be hard-pressed to find any that's more awesome than these two exclusive offerings from Holland America.

After heading north through the Yukon, cruisetour passengers cross the Alaska border near Beaver Creek, travel to Fairbanks, and from there go through Denali to Anchorage. Again, the tour can be taken in either direction and on a pre- or post-cruise basis.

CANADIAN ROCKIES CRUISETOUR

A Canadian Rockies tour is easily combined with a Vancouver-originating (or terminating) Inside Passage or Gulf cruise. In 5-, 6-, or 7-day chunks, you can visit such scenic wonders as **Banff, Lake Louise,** and **Jasper National Park** in conjunction with an Alaska sailing.

The Canadian Rockies offer some of the finest **mountain scenery** on earth. It's not just that the glacier-carved mountains are astonishingly dramatic and beautiful; it's also that there are hundreds and hundreds of miles of this wonderful wilderness high country. Between them, Banff National Park and Jasper National Park preserve much of this mountain beauty. Other national and provincial parks make accessible other vast and equally spectacular regions of the Rockies, as well as portions of the nearby Columbia and Selkirk mountain ranges. The beautiful Lake Louise, colored deep green from its mineral content, is located 35 miles north of Banff.

SHOULD YOU TAKE YOUR CRUISETOUR BEFORE OR AFTER YOUR CRUISE?

Though the land portion of both the Denali and the Yukon itineraries can be taken either before or after the cruise, we feel that it's better to take the land portion pre-cruise rather than post-cruise. Why? After several days of traveling around in the wilderness, it's nice to be able to get aboard a ship to relax and be pampered for a while.

Because of the distances that must be covered on some wilderness cruisetour itineraries, passengers often have to be roused out of bed and ready to board the motorcoach by, say, 7:30am. And the day may seem to go on forever, with a stop to view this waterfall, or that river, or mountain. Then, upon arrival at the next stop—in the early evening usually—the request is, "Hurry and get cleaned up for dinner." By the time you've crawled into your new bed often quite late at night, you're beat. It's a nice kind of tired, as the saying goes, but it's tired nevertheless. After a few days of that, it's great to get on a luxurious cruise ship, unpack just once, and rise when you feel like it, comfortable in the knowledge that you haven't missed your transportation and that you'll still make it in time to have a leisurely breakfast.

That, at any rate, is the conventional wisdom, and there's more of a demand for pre-cruise land packages than for post-cruise. Since the lines obviously can't always accommodate everybody on a land itinerary before the cruise (they're hoping to even out the traffic flow by having a like number of requests to go touring after the voyage), it's smart to get your bid in early.

BATTLE OF THE TOP PLAYERS

If we talk in this section more about **Princess** and **Holland America** than we do about other lines, it's because that through investing tens of millions of dollars in land components of Alaska tourism, they have become the 800-pound gorillas duking it out for dominance in Alaska. Other lines offer some of the same cruisetours as these two, but many of them buy at least some of their cruisetour components from Princess and/or Holland America's land operations. It may seem odd to have companies buying from (or selling to) competitors, but with tourism in Alaska, there's practically no other way. As recently as the early 1980s, when Holland America–Westours owned the bulk of the land-tour components, Princess, its number-one rival, was also its number-one customer! Hey, a 4-month season makes for strange bedfellows.

It was partly to carve out a niche for itself and at the same time to lessen its reliance on the services of a competitor that Princess plunged heavily into the lodging and transportation sectors. Princess is arguably stronger in the Denali corridor than any other line, while Holland America could be said to have the upper hand in the Yukon/Klondike market. But each line offers both of these tour areas, among other options.

Princess owns railcars (called the *Midnight Sun Express*) in the Denali corridor. Holland America also owns railcars there (called the *McKinley Explorer*). Both, incidentally, rely on the Alaska Railroad to pull them. Princess owns wilderness lodges; Holland America owns primarily city hotels. Both Princess and Holland America have a fleet of motorcoaches. HAL's fleet is brand new—39 luxurious 45-seat beauties that were phased in last year and will be in service in 2008. For the technically minded, they are MCI LX models, the very latest, offering as much legroom as is offered in most first-class airplane cabins and, according to the operator, 50% more legroom than it offered on its coaches last year. Coaches already in the fleet will either be retired or will be retrofitted to provide the same level of comfort as the newcomers.

But HAL and Princess have not gone unchallenged. With its Royal Caribbean International and Celebrity Cruises brands, Royal Caribbean has become the third well-established player in the game. The company will have three Royal Caribbean ships and three Celebrity ships in the 49th state this summer. A few years ago, it formed Royal Celebrity Tours to operate its own land packages; in 2008 the land affiliate will offer several dozen cruisetour options. Its motorcoaches are luxurious and its railcars are truly state-of-the-art, featuring glass-domed tops so you don't miss any views on the Denali Park run. The railcars have comfortable, airline-style leather seats at least on par with the business-class seating of most major airlines, a fine kitchen on the lower level (meals are extra, with a variety of offerings), and a friendly, knowledgeable staff. Plus, the railcars are more accessible for travelers with disabilities than those run by Princess or Holland America (each of Royal Caribbean's is equipped with a mechanical lift that can carry two wheelchairs at a time to the second level from the station platform).

5 Quiz Time: Questions to Ask when Choosing Your Cruise

After you've decided which itinerary and what kind of ship appeal to you, we suggest you ask yourself some questions about the kind of experience you want, and then read through the cruise-line and -ship reviews in chapters 5 and 6 to see which ones match your vision of the perfect Alaska cruise vessel.

When looking at the attributes of the various ships to make your choice, some determining factors will be no-brainers. For instance, if you're traveling with kids, you'll want a ship with a good kids' program. If you're a foodie, you'll want a ship with gourmet cuisine. If you're used to staying at a Ritz-Carlton hotel when you travel, you'll probably want to cruise on a luxury ship. If you usually stay at B&Bs, you'll probably prefer one of the small ships.

Also ask yourself whether you require resortlike amenities, such as a heated swimming pool, spa, casino, aerobics classes, and state-of-the-art gym. Or do you care more about having an adventure or an educational experience? If you want the former, choose a large cruise ship; if you prefer the latter, a small ship may be more your speed.

Here are some more pertinent questions to help you narrow the field:

How do you get a deal and what's not included? The best way to get a deal on a cruise in Alaska is to book early. Virtually all the lines (with the exception of some of the small-ship lines) offer early booking discounts. The numbers and dates may vary a bit, but the formula has been fairly standard: You get about 25% to 30% off and your best choice of ship, cabin, and itinerary if you book by mid-February and 20% off if you book by mid-April. But with such fierce competition, you can sometimes get big discounts even into May, especially if you're a member of the lines' past-passenger fraternity. As the season gets underway, last-minute fares starting at less than $100 a day are not uncommon (we've even seen them at less than $85 per day). The catch? These are one-shot, very limited deals that are for cruises sailing quickly after the offers are made. Finding a decent airfare at the last minute can be tough, so unless you're driving it really does not pay to be tardy. And one of these years the Alaska cruise lines may find they can sell their berths at the asking price and the last-minute discounts will dry up. We suggest you book your Alaska cruise and particularly your Alaska cruisetour (because these are increasingly popular) as early as possible.

Cruise fares cover onboard accommodations, meals, entertainment, and activities. There are, however, a number of expenses not covered in the typical cruise package, and you should factor these in when planning your vacation budget. Airfare to and from your port of embarkation and debarkation is usually extra (though cruise lines sometimes offer reduced rates). Necessary hotel stays before or after the cruise are also usually not included. Gratuities, taxes, and trip insurance are typically extra as well. Shore excursions are rarely included in the cruise fare, and if you opt for pricey ones like flightseeing, you can easily add $600 to $1,000 to your total. Alcohol is typically extra as is soda and such incidentals as laundry, telephone calls from the ship, beauty and spa services, photos taken by ship photographers, and babysitting.

Because travel agents constantly keep abreast of the latest bargains, we believe they are best equipped to advise you on the best Alaska cruise deals.

See chapter 3 for more information on when to book for the best prices.

How much time is spent in port and how much at sea? Generally, ships on 7-night itineraries spend 3 days in port, and cruise in natural areas like Glacier Bay, College Fjord, or Tracy Arm during the other 3.

Coming into port, ships generally dock right after breakfast, allowing you the morning and afternoon to take a shore excursion or explore on your own. They usually depart in the early evening, giving you an hour or two to rest up before dinner. On rare occasions, a ship might cruise through a glacier area in the morning and dock at the next port in the early afternoon, not leaving until 10 or 11pm.

On days at sea, the emphasis will be on exploring natural areas, viewing glaciers, and scanning for wildlife. Big ships stick to prearranged schedules on these days, but on small-ship, soft adventure–type cruises, days at sea can be very unstructured, with the captain choosing a destination based on reports of whale sightings, for example. Some small-ship itineraries include almost no ports, sticking instead to isolated natural areas that passengers explore by kayak, by Zodiac boat, or on foot.

Is the cruise formal or casual? If you don't care to get dressed up, select a less formal cruise, such as those offered by many of the small ships, by Regent's luxurious but casual *Seven Seas Mariner,* and by the Norwegian Cruise Line ships, which do not have official formal nights (though there's a night when you can dress up if you like). If, on the other hand, having the chance to put on your finery appeals to you, select one of the more formal premium lines such as Princess, Celebrity, or Holland America (and, to a lesser extent, mass-market lines like Royal Caribbean and Carnival), or the posh Silversea. These ships will offer casual, semiformal, and formal nights, meaning women can show off everything from a sundress to an evening gown over the course of a week, and men will go from shirt-sleeves one night, to jacket and tie the next, to full-on tuxedo (or dark suit) the next.

What are the other passengers usually like? Each ship attracts a fairly predictable type of passenger. On small ships, you'll find a more physically active bunch that's highly interested in nature, but you'll find fewer families and single travelers. Larger ships cater to a more diverse group—singles, newlyweds, families, and couples over 55. Alaska sailings from Seattle are attracting a younger, more family-oriented crowd. We've included information on typical passengers in all the cruise-line reviews in chapters 5 and 6.

I'll be traveling alone. Will I have fun? And does it cost more? A nice thing about cruises is that you needn't worry about dining alone because you'll be seated with other guests. (If you don't want to be, seek a ship with alternative-dining options, although a steady diet of "Table for one, please" is likely to raise a few eyebrows among your shipmates.) You also needn't worry much about finding people to talk to because the general atmosphere on nearly all ships is very congenial and allows you to find conversation easily, especially during group activities. Some ships host a party to give singles a chance to get to know one another, and some ships offer social hosts as dance partners.

The downside is that you may have to pay for the privilege of traveling solo. Because their rates are based on two people per cabin, some lines charge a "single supplement" rate (aka an extra charge) that ranges from 110% to an outrageous 200% of the per-person, double-occupancy fare. As a single person, you have two choices: Find a line with a reasonable single supplement rate or ask if the line has a cabin-share program, under which the line will pair you with another single so you can get a lower fare. Some lines also offer a single-guarantee program, which means if they can't find you a roommate, they'll book you in a cabin alone but still honor the shared rate. Singles seeking real savings have the option on some ships of cramming into a shared quad (a room for four). Some older ships and a few small ships have special cabins designed for singles, but these tend to sell out fast and are not necessarily offered at bargain prices.

Is shipboard life heavily scheduled? That depends to a certain extent on you and the ship you choose. Meals are generally served during set hours only, though on larger ships you'll have plenty of alternative options if those hours don't suit you. On smaller ships you may be out of luck if you miss a meal—unless you can charm the cook. On both large and small ships, times for disembarking and reboarding at the ports are strict—if you miss the boat, you miss the boat. (See chapter 4 for tips on what to do in this situation.) Other than these two considerations, the only schedule you'll have to follow on board is your own. It all depends on how busy you want to be.

What are the cabins like? Cabins come in all sizes and configurations. See "Choosing Your Cabin" in chapter 3 for a detailed discussion.

What are meals like? Meals are a big part of the cruise experience. The larger the ship, the more dining options you'll find. When booking your cruise on a larger vessel, you'll be asked ahead of time to decide on your preferred dinner hour since most large ships feature two dining-room seatings each evening, with tables assigned. Norwegian, Princess, Silversea, and Regent ships are the exceptions to this rule, offering open, restaurant-style seating, meaning that you can dine when you want, with whomever you choose. (On Princess ships, you choose in advance of your cruise whether to dine traditional- or restaurant-style; on Norwegian, Silversea, and Regent ships you are encouraged to make reservations each morning for tables at dinner.) On smaller ships, you can sit where you want but dinner will be called for a set time. In the reviews in chapters 5 and 6, we discuss dining options for each line.

If you have any special dietary requirements (vegetarian, kosher, low salt, low fat), be sure the line is informed well in advance—preferably at the time you book your cruise. Almost all ships have vegetarian, vegan, and low-fat options available at every meal, and those that don't can usually meet your needs with some advance warning. With low-carb diets so popular, the lines are getting into these options as well. Carnival, for instance, now features a nightly low-carb menu for those who are so inclined.

What activities and entertainment does the ship offer? On small ships, activities are limited by the available public space and usually up to the passengers to organize—maybe a game of Scrabble or Trivial Pursuit. There may be a showing of a video or two and there will typically also be a lecture series dealing with the flora, fauna, and geography of Alaska, usually conducted by a trained naturalist. These lectures are also becoming more popular on the larger ships.

The big ships offer activities such as fitness, personal finance, photography, and art classes; ping-pong and bingo tournaments; audience-participation games; art auctions; and parties. Glitzy floor shows at night are almost de rigueur. (See the general big-ship and small-ship descriptions earlier in this chapter for more information on activities and entertainment.)

Does the ship have a children's program? More and more parents are taking their kids with them on vacation, and cruises to Alaska are no exception. The lines are responding by adding youth counselors and supervised programs, fancy playrooms, teen centers, and even video-game rooms to keep kids entertained while their parents relax. Some lines offer special shore excursions for children and teens, and most ships offer babysitting (for an extra charge). Some lines have reduced rates for kids, though most discourage parents from bringing infants.

It's important to ask whether a supervised program will be offered on your specific cruise, as sometimes the programs operate only if there are a certain number of children on board. If your kids are TV addicts, you may want to make sure that your cabin will have a TV and VCR. Even if it does, though, channel selection will be very limited (it's not a bad idea to bring along a portable DVD player and your own selection of movies).

I have a disability; will I have any trouble taking a cruise? It's important to let the cruise line know about your special needs when you make your booking. If you use a wheelchair, you'll need to know if wheelchair-accessible cabins are available (and how they're equipped), as well as whether public rooms are accessible and can be reached by elevator, and whether the cruise line has any special policy regarding travelers with disabilities. For instance, some lines require that you be accompanied by a fully mobile companion. We've noted all this information in the cabin sections of the ship reviews in chapters 5 and 6. Note that newer ships tend to have the largest number of wheelchair-accessible cabins, and of the small ships in Alaska, only *Empress of the North, Spirit of '98,* and *Spirit of Oceanus,* are even moderately wheelchair-accessible.

Travelers with disabilities should inquire when they're booking whether the ship docks at ports or uses tenders (small boats) to go ashore. Tenders cannot always accommodate passengers with wheelchairs—in most cases, you can't wheel yourself but, rather, will need crew assistance. One exception is Holland America, which uses a special lift system to get passengers into the tenders without requiring them to leave their wheelchairs. Once on board the ship, travelers with disabilities will want to seek the advice of the tour staff before choosing shore excursions, as not all will be wheelchair friendly.

If you have a chronic health problem, we advise you to check with your doctor before booking the cruise and, if you have any specific needs, to notify the cruise line in advance. This will ensure that the medical team on the ship is properly prepared to offer assistance. There is another, somewhat sensitive, consideration for some would-be small-ship passengers—obesity. We mention this only because we once met, on a small ship, a charming young lady who stood a little over 5 feet tall and weighed about 250 pounds. She told us that she had been advised by the cruise line not to book passage on the ship she first chose because she wouldn't fit in the shower. The company put her instead on one on which her girth would not be such a problem. Understand, please, that the cruise operator is not being judgmental. But if you don't mention such things and end up on an inappropriate ship, you're in for a miserable time. So assess the situation realistically.

What if I want to take a cruise for my honeymoon? One-week Alaska cruises start not only on Saturdays and Sundays, but also on Mondays, Wednesdays, Thursdays, and Fridays, which should help you find an appropriate departure date so that you won't have to run out of your wedding reception to catch a plane. You will want to make sure that the ship you choose offers double, queen-, or king-size beds; and you may want to also request a cabin with a tub or Jacuzzi. Rooms with private verandas are particularly romantic. You can take in the sights in privacy and even enjoy a quiet meal, assuming that the veranda is big enough for a table and chairs (some are not), and that the weather doesn't turn chilly. If you want to dine alone each night, make sure the dining room offers tables for two or that the ship offers room service. Your travel agent can fill you in on these matters. You may also want to inquire as to the likelihood that there will be other honeymooners your age on the ship. Some ships—among them those of Princess, Royal Caribbean, Carnival, Celebrity, and Holland America—offer special honeymoon packages, and there might even be honeymoon suites. Most lines offer special perks such as champagne and chocolates if you let them know in advance that you will be celebrating your honeymoon on the ship.

Can I get married on board? Yes. You can get married at sea in the chapel on any of the Princess ships, with the nuptials conducted by the ship's captain. You can also get married at sea on the *Carnival Spirit,* which has a nice wedding chapel. The captain can perform the ceremony when the ship is in Canadian waters. And by the way, *Carnival Spirit* Capt. Pier Paolo Scala recently informed us he can also now conduct weddings for same-sex couples in Canadian waters. You may be able to get married on other big ships—but only if you're willing to bring your own clergyman along with you at full price. You can also, of course, get married while the ship is in port, but you will have to provide your own clergyman or justice of the peace. Ships without wedding chapels will usually agree to clear a public room for your nuptials and may provide flowers and light refreshments as well.

Will I get seasick? On Inside Passage itineraries, most of your time will be spent in protected waters where there are islands between you and the open sea, making for generally smooth sailing. However, there are certain points, such as around Sitka and at the entrance to Queen Charlotte Strait, where there's nothing between you and Japan but a lot of wind, water, and choppy seas. Ships with sailing itineraries on the Gulf of Alaska and those sailing from San Francisco will of necessity spend more time in rough, open waters. Although ships that ply these routes tend to be very stable, you'll probably notice some rocking and rolling. And keep in mind big ships tend to be more stable than smaller ships.

Unless you're particularly prone to seasickness, you probably don't need to worry much. But if you are, there are medications that can help, including Dramamine, Bonine, and Marezine, which are available over the counter and also stocked by most ships—the purser's office may even give them out free. Another option is the Transderm patch, available by prescription only, which goes behind your ear and time-releases medication. The patch can be worn for up to 3 days but comes with a slew of side-effect warnings. Some people have also had success in curbing seasickness by using ginger capsules, which are available at health-food stores, or acupressure wristbands, which are available at most pharmacies. But we're not doctors. Our best advice is to ask your doctor before your cruise what he or she recommends. If you do get sick shipboard, the ship's doctor may have additional recommendations.

Is there smoking on ships? The short answer is yes, and ardent anti-smokers and those with respiratory issues should be aware cruise ships do not generally offer non-smoking cabins (the cruise lines say it's "too hard to police."). Most lines have banned smoking in dining rooms and relegated smokers to a few select bars. Some go as far as to restrict smoking to certain open deck areas. A problem for both the cruise lines and some passengers, however, is that some smokers consider the private balconies on cabins as smoking rooms. If you're next to one of these cabins, smoke might annoyingly waft into your door. But more importantly, in 2006, a fire on a Princess ship in the Caribbean was believed to have been caused by a lit cigarette chucked off a balcony and blown back onto the ship. Cruise lines have discussed banning smoking on cabin balconies, but at press time none had been enforced.

3

Booking Your Cruise & Getting the Best Price

Okay, you've thought about what type of cruise vacation experience you're looking for. You've decided when and for how long you'd like to travel. You know what sort of itinerary interests you. And after reading through our ship reviews in chapters 5 and 6, and narrowing your focus down to a couple of cruise lines that appeal to you, you'll be ready to get down to brass tacks and make your booking.

1 Booking a Cruise: The Short Explanation

Every cruise line has a brochure, or sometimes many different brochures, full of beautiful glossy photos of beautiful glossy people enjoying fabulous vacations. They're colorful! They're gorgeous! They're enticing! They're confusing!

You'll see low starting rates on the charts, but look further and you'll realize those are for tiny inside cubicles; most of the cabins sell for much more. Sometimes the brochures feature published rates that are nothing more than the pie-in-the-sky wish of cruise lines for what they'd like to sell the cruise (most customers will pay less). We strongly suggest you look at the early-bird savings column and book your cruise early (by mid-Feb for average savings of 25%–30% and sometimes as much as 50%). In reality, you may be able to get the cruise for 40% or 50% off at the last minute. But here's the problem with waiting: Alaska right now is hot, hot, hot. Sure, you may be able to save by taking your chances, but if you don't reserve space early, you may also be left out in the cold (cold in Alaska, get it?). Keep in mind the most expensive and cheapest cabins tend to sell out first. As they say in the cruise business, ships sell out from the top and from the bottom first. Aggressive marketing by the cruise lines to past passengers is adding to the increase in early bookings. Speaking of which, if you've cruised at all before—Caribbean, Europe, Bermuda—check with the cruise line to see if you qualify for a past-passenger deal.

So how do you book your cruise? Traditionally (meaning over the past 30 years or so), people have booked their cruises through **travel agents.** But you may be wondering: Hasn't the traditional travel agent gone the way of typewriters and eight-track tapes and been replaced by the **Internet?** Not exactly. Travel agents are alive and kicking, though the Internet has indeed staked its claim alongside them and knocked some of them out of business. In an effort to keep pace, most traditional travel agencies have created their own websites.

So which is the better way to book a cruise these days? Good question. The answer can be both. If you're computer savvy, have a good handle on all the elements that go into a cruise, and have narrowed down the choices to a few cruise lines that appeal to you, websites are a great way to trawl the seas at your own pace and check out deals, which can be dramatic. On the other hand, you'll barely get a stitch of personalized service searching for and booking a cruise online. If you need help getting a refund or arranging special meals or other matters, or deciding which cabin to choose, you're on your own. In addition, agents usually know about cruise and airfare discounts that the lines won't necessarily publicize on their websites.

However you arrange to buy your cruise, what you basically have in hand at the end is a contract for transportation, lodging, dining, entertainment, housekeeping, and assorted other miscellaneous services that will be provided to you over the course of your vacation. That's a lot of services, involving a lot of people. It's complex, and like any complex thing, it pays (and saves) to study up. That's why it's important that you read the rest of this chapter.

2 Booking through a Travel Agent

The majority of cruise passengers still book through agents. The cruise lines are happy with this system and have only small reservations staffs themselves (unlike airlines). In some cases, if you try to call a cruise line to book your own passage, you may be advised by the line to contact an agent in your area. The cruise line may even offer you a choice of names from its list of preferred agencies, and there are often links to preferred agencies on some of the lines' websites.

A good travel agent can save you both time and money. If you're reluctant to use an agent, consider this: Would you represent yourself in court? Perform surgery on your own abdomen? Tackle complicated IRS forms without seeking help? You may be the rare type that doesn't need a travel agent, but most of us are better off working with one.

Good agents can offer you expert advice, save you time, and (best of all) will usually work for you for free or for a nominal fee—the bulk of their fees are paid by the cruise lines. (Many agents charge a consultation fee—say, $25—which is refunded if you eventually give them the booking.) In addition to advising you about the different ships, an agent can help you make decisions about the type of cabin you will need, your dining room seating choices, any special airfare offerings from the cruise lines, pre- and post-cruise land offerings, and travel insurance. All of these can have a big impact on your cruise experience. We recently saw a complaint by someone who booked a really cheap inside cabin and was very angry it was "a noisy cabin." Had they asked an experienced agent, they might have been advised that the cabin was cheap because it was practically in the engine room—and that had they paid only a few bucks more they would have had a nice quiet cabin.

It's important to realize that not all agents represent all cruise lines. In order to be experts on what they sell, and to maximize the commissions the lines pay them (they're often paid more based on volume of sales), some agents may limit their offerings to, say, one luxury line, one midprice line, one mass-market line, and so on. If you have your sights set on a particular line or have narrowed down your preferences to a couple of lines, you'll have to find an agent who handles your choices. As we mentioned above, you can call the lines themselves to get the name of an agent near you. It's also a good idea to ask if the agent you are working with has actually been to Alaska. The cruise lines have been clamping down on agents who give rebates, and there are fewer of these deals out there than there were a few years ago. The cruise lines themselves post Internet specials on their websites, and the same deals are usually also available through travel agents. The lines don't want to upset their travel agent partners and generally try not to compete against them.

Agents, especially those who specialize in cruises, are frequently in contact with the cruise lines and are continually alerted by the lines about the latest and best deals and special offers. The cruise lines tend to communicate such deals and offers to their top agents first, before they offer them to the general public, and some of these deals will never appear in your local newspaper, on bargain travel websites, or even on the websites of the cruise lines themselves.

Experienced agents know how to play the cruise lines' game and get you the best deals. As an example, the lines run promotions that allow you to book a category of cabin rather than a specific cabin, and guarantees that you'll be placed in that category or better. An informed agent will not only know about these offers, but may be able to direct you to a category on a specific ship in which your chances of an upgrade are better. The cruise lines will also sometimes upgrade passengers as a favor to their top-producing agents or agencies.

To keep their clients alert to specials, agencies may offer newsletters or communicate through other means, such as postcards or e-mail, or post specials on their websites. Depending on the agency you choose, you may run across other incentives for booking through an agent. Some agencies buy big blocks of space on a ship in advance and offer it to their clients at a group price available only through that agency. These are called group rates, although "group" in this case means savings, not that you have to hang out with the other people booking through the agency. In addition, some agencies are willing to negotiate, especially if you've found a better deal somewhere else. It never hurts to ask. Finally, some agencies are willing to give back to the client a portion of their commissions from the cruise line in order to close a sale. This percent may be monetary, or it might take the form of a perk such as a free bottle of champagne or a limo ride to the ship (hardly reasons to book in and of themselves, but nice perks nevertheless).

FINDING A GREAT AGENT

If you don't know a good travel agent already, try to find one through your friends, preferably those who have cruised before. For the most personal service, look for an agent in your area, and for the most knowledgeable service, look for an agent who has cruising experience. It's perfectly okay to ask an agent questions about his or her personal knowledge of the product, such as whether he or she has ever cruised in Alaska or with one of the lines you're considering. The easiest way to be sure that the agent is experienced in booking cruises is to work with an agent at a **cruise-only agency** (that's all they book) or to find an agent who is a cruise specialist within a full-service agency. If you are calling a full-service travel agency, ask for the **cruise desk.** A good and easy rule of thumb to maximize your chances of finding an agent who has cruise experience and who won't rip you off is to book with an agency that's a member of the **Cruise Lines International Association** (CLIA; ✆ 212/921-0066; www.cruising. org). Members are cruise specialists. Membership in the **American Society of Travel Agents** (ASTA; ✆ 800/275-2782; www.astanet.com) ensures that the agency is monitored for ethical practices, although it does not designate cruise experience. You can tap into the Internet sites of these organizations to find reliable agents in your area.

BOOKING WITH DISCOUNTERS

Keep in mind that discounters, who specialize in great-sounding, last-minute offers (usually without airfare) and whose ads you can find in Sunday papers and all over the Internet, don't necessarily offer service that matches their prices. Their staffs are more

Watch Out for Scams

It can be difficult to know whether the travel agency you're dealing with to make your Alaska cruise booking is or isn't reliable, legit, or, for that matter, stable. It pays to be on your guard against fly-by-night operators and agents who may lead you astray.

- **Get a referral.** A recommendation from a trusted friend or colleague is one of the best ways to hook up with a reputable agent.
- **Use the cruise lines' agent lists.** Many cruise-line websites include agency locator lists, naming agencies around the country with whom they do business. These are by no means comprehensive lists of all good or bad agencies, but an agent's presence on these lists is usually another good sign of experience.
- **Beware of snap recommendations.** If an agent suggests a cruise line without first asking you a single question about your tastes, beware. Because agents work on commissions from the lines, some may try to shanghai you into cruising with a company that pays them the highest rates, even though that line may not be right for you.
- **Always use a credit card to pay for your cruise.** A credit card gives you more protection in the event the agency or cruise line fails. (Trust us: It happens occasionally!) When your credit card statement arrives, make sure the payment was made to the cruise line, not the travel agency. If you find that payment was actually made to the agency, it's a big red flag that something's wrong. If you insist on paying by check, you'll be making it out to the agency, so it may be wise to ask if the agency has default protection. Many do.
- **Always follow the cruise line's payment schedule.** Never agree to a different schedule the travel agency comes up with. The lines' terms are always clearly printed in their brochures and usually require an initial deposit, with the balance due no later than 45 to 75 days before departure, depending on the cruise line. If you're booking 2 months or less before departure, the full payment is usually required at the time of booking.
- **Keep on top of your booking.** If you ever fail to receive a document or ticket on the date it's been promised, inquire about it immediately. If you're told that your cruise reservation was canceled because of overbooking and that you must pay extra for a confirmed and rescheduled sailing, demand a full refund and/or contact your credit card company to stop payment.

likely to be order takers than advice givers. Go to these companies to compare prices only when you are certain about what you want.

WATCHING OUT FOR SCAMS

The travel business tends to attract more than its share of scam operators trying to lure consumers with incredible come-ons. If you get a solicitation by phone, fax, mail, or e-mail that just doesn't sound right, or if you are uneasy about an agent you are dealing with, call your state consumer-protection agency or the local office of the Better

Business Bureau. Or you can check with the cruise line to see whether they have heard of the agency in question. Be wary of working with any company, be it on the phone or Internet, that won't give you its street address. You can find more advice on how to avoid scams at the **ASTA** site, www.astanet.com.

BOOKING A SMALL-SHIP CRUISE

The small-ship companies in Alaska—American Safari Cruises, Cruise West, Lindblad Expeditions, and Majestic America Line—all offer real niche-oriented cruise experiences, attracting passengers who have a very good idea of the kind of experience they want (usually educational or adventurous, and always casual and small scale). In many cases, a large percentage of passengers on any given cruise will have sailed with the line before. Because of all this, and because the passenger capacity of these small ships is so low (12–235), in general you don't find the kind of deep discounts that you do with the large ships. For the most part, these lines rely on agents to handle their bookings, taking very few reservations directly. All of the lines have a list of agents with whom they do considerable business, and they can hook you up with one of them if you call or e-mail the cruise line and ask for an agent near you.

3 Cruising on the Internet

For those who know exactly what they want (we don't recommend Internet shopping for first-time cruisers), there are deals to be had on the Internet. Those sites that sell cruises include top online travel agencies (Travelocity.com, Expedia.com, Orbitz.com), agencies that specialize in cruises (I-cruise.com, Uniglobe.com, Cruise.com, Cruise411.com, 7blueseas.com), travel discounters (Bestfares.com, Onetravel.com, Lowestfare.com), and auction sites (Allcruiseauction.com, Priceline.com). For more Internet options, check out the cruise listings at Johnnyjet.com.

There are also some good sites on the Internet that specialize in providing cruise information rather than selling cruises. The best site dedicated to cruising in general (rather than linked with one line) is **Cruisecritic.com** (recently purchased by Expedia). On this website there are reviews by professional writers as well as ratings by cruise passengers, plus useful tips, frequent chat opportunities, and message boards. **AlaskaCruisingReport.com** tracks what's happening specifically in Alaska. In addition, nearly all the cruise lines have their own sites, which are chock-full of information— some even offer virtual tours of specific ships. You will find the website addresses for the various cruise companies in our cruise-line reviews in chapters 5 and 6.

4 Cruise Costs

In chapters 5 and 6, we've included the brochure rates for every ship reviewed, but as noted above, these prices may actually be higher than any passenger will pay. Prices constantly fluctuate based on any special deals the cruise lines are running. The volume of travelers interested in cruising Alaska heavily influences rates. If the sales season (Sept–Jan are the key months) fails to achieve certain predetermined passenger volume goals, the lines are very quick to start slashing rates to goose the market. The prices we've noted are for the following three basic types of accommodations: inside cabins (without windows), outside cabins (with windows), and suites. Remember that cruise ships generally have several different categories of cabins within each of these three basic divisions, all priced differently. That's why we give a range. See "Choosing Your Cabin," below, for more information on cabin types.

The price you pay for your cabin represents the bulk of your cruise vacation cost, but there are other costs to consider. Whether you're working with an agent or booking online, be sure that you really understand what's included in the fare you're being quoted. Are you getting a price that includes the cruise fare, port charges, taxes, fees, and insurance, or are you getting a cruise-only fare? Are airfare and airport transfers included, or do you have to book them separately (either as an add-on to the cruise fare or on your own)? One agent might break down the charges in a price quote, while another might bundle them all together. Make sure you're comparing apples with apples when making price comparisons. Read the fine print!

It's important when figuring out what your cruise will cost to remember what extras are not included in your cruise fare. The items discussed in the section below are not included in most cruise prices and will add to the cost of your trip.

SHORE EXCURSIONS

The priciest additions to your cruise fare, particularly in Alaska, will likely be shore excursions. Rates range from about $30 to $99 for a sightseeing tour by bus (the higher-priced tours will throw in a visit to a museum or other local attraction), to $299 and up (sometimes as high as $600) for a lengthy helicopter or seaplane flightseeing excursion. Although these sightseeing tours are designed to help cruise passengers make the most of their time at the ports the ship visits, they can add a hefty sum to your vacation costs, so be sure to factor these expenses into your budget. Of course, whether you take the excursions is a personal choice, but we suggest you set aside at least $600 per person for trips in port, which might just about cover a short flightseeing trip, a kayak or jeep safari, and a bus tour.

TIPS

You'll want to add tips for the ship's crew to your budget calculations. Crewmembers are usually paid low base wages with the expectation that they'll make up the difference in gratuities. Two exceptions in Alaska this year are Regent Seven Seas and Silversea Cruises, the only lines in the market to include tips in the cruise fare (but you can still leave a few bucks for your favorite crew members if you want to).

Because some people find the whole tipping process confusing, a couple of years ago some lines began automatically adding tips to guests' shipboard accounts. Carnival, Holland America, Norwegian Cruise Line, and Princess, for instance, all add a standard tip of $10 per passenger, per day. In all these cases, you are free to adjust the amount up or down as you see fit, based on the service you received.

Tips are given at the end of the cruise, and passengers should set aside at least $10 per passenger per day for tips for the room steward, waiter, and busperson. In practice, we find that most people tend to give a little more. Additional tips to other personnel, such as the headwaiter or maitre d', are at your discretion. If you have a fancy room with a butler, slip him or her about $3.50 a day. Most lines automatically add 15% to bar bills, so you don't have to tip your bartender. There may be an automatic tip of 15% for spa services. If not, you can add a tip to the bill.

You can tip in cash or, on most lines, add gratuities to your shipboard account. On small ships, tips are typically pooled among the crew: You hand over a lump sum in cash, and they divvy it up. Since tipping etiquette on small ships varies, we include information on tipping specifics for each small-ship line on p. 123 in chapter 6 and general guidelines in "Tips on Tipping," on p. 60 in chapter 4.

BOOZE & SODA

Most ships charge extra for alcoholic beverages (including wine at dinner) and soda. Nonbubbly soft drinks, such as lemonade and iced tea, and hot drinks like coffee and tea are included in your cruise fare. Soda will cost about $2.50, beer $3.50 and up, and mixed drinks $3.95 and up. A bottle of wine with dinner will run anywhere from $15 to upward of $300.

PORT CHARGES, LOCAL TAXES & FEES

Every ship has to pay docking fees at each port. It also has to pay some local taxes per passenger in some places. Juneau, for instance, imposes a $5-a-head tax on arriving cruise passengers. Port charges, taxes, and other fees are sometimes included in your cruise fare but not always, and these charges can add as much as $250 per person onto the price of a 7-day Alaska cruise. Make sure you know whether these fees are included in the cruise fare when comparing rates.

5 Money-Saving Strategies

EARLY-BIRD & LAST-MINUTE DISCOUNTS

As we said earlier, the best way to save on an Alaska cruise is to **book in advance.** In a typical year, lines offer early-bird rates, usually 25% to 30% off the brochure rate, to those who book their Alaska cruise by mid-February of the year of the cruise. If the cabins do not fill up by the cutoff date, the early-bird rate may be extended, but it may be lowered slightly—say, a 15% or 20% savings. In the past couple of years, the lines have been getting even more aggressive with early-booking discounts, hoping to encourage passengers to make their Alaska cruise plans months in advance (cruise-line executives like their ships filled up as early as possible). Princess's lowest early-booking price for Alaska cruises for 2008 is $749; Holland America's is $798; Norwegian Cruise Lines' is $699; and Royal Caribbean's is $665. If the cabins are still not full as the cruise season begins, cruise lines typically start marketing special deals, usually through their top-producing travel agents, and sometimes, but rarely, offering savings of up to 50%. We recently saw an offer from Celebrity through an agent for an early season cruise priced at the last minute from $469. And both Holland America and Princess in 2007 had last-minute specials of under $100 a day. But again, it's our feeling that in 2008, these last-minute discounts will be less common than in some previous years. And keep in mind that last-minute deals are usually for a very limited selection of cabins and rarely offered during the July and August high season. Planning your Alaska cruise vacation well in advance and taking advantage of early booking discounts is still the best way to go.

SHOULDER-SEASON DISCOUNTS

You can also save by booking a cruise in the shoulder months of **May** or **September,** when cruise pricing is lower than during the high-season summer months. Typically, Alaska cruises are divided into budget, low, economy, value, standard, and peak seasons, but since these overlap quite a bit from cruise line to cruise line, we can lump them into three basic periods:

1. **Budget/Low/Economy Season:** May and September
2. **Value/Standard Season:** Early June and late August
3. **Peak Season:** Late June, July, and early to mid-August

THIRD- & FOURTH-PASSENGER DISCOUNTS

Most ships offer highly discounted rates for third and fourth passengers sharing a cabin with two full-fare passengers, even if those two have booked at a discounted rate. You can add the four rates together and then divide by four to get your per-person rate. This is a good option for families (or very good friends) on a budget, but remember that it'll be a tight fit, since most cabins aren't all that big. Some lines also offer **special rates for kids,** usually on a seasonal or select-sailing basis, that may include free or discounted airfare.

GROUP DISCOUNTS

One of the best ways to get a cruise deal is to book as a group, so you may want to gather family together for a reunion or convince your friends or colleagues they need a vacation, too. A "group," as defined by the cruise lines, is generally **at least 16 people** in at least eight cabins. Not only do the savings include a discounted rate, but at least the cruise portion of the 16th ticket will be free. On some upscale ships, you can negotiate a free ticket for groups of eight or more. The gang can split the proceeds from the free ticket or hold a drawing for the ticket, maybe at a cocktail party on the first night. If your group is large enough, you may even be able to get that cocktail party for free, and perhaps some other onboard perks as well.

Some travel agencies buy big blocks of space on a ship in advance and offer it to their clients at a group price available only through that agency. These are called group rates, although, as we mention earlier in the chapter, "group" in this case means savings, not that you have to hang out with (or even know) the other people booking through the agency.

SENIOR CITIZEN DISCOUNTS

Senior citizens might be able to get extra savings on their cruise. Some lines will take 5% off the top for those 55 and up, and the senior rate applies even if the second person in the cabin is younger. Membership in groups such as AARP is not required, but such membership may bring additional savings.

OTHER DEALS

Check each line's website for the latest savings schemes.

If you like your Alaska cruise so much you that decide you want to vacation here again, consider booking your next cruise on the spot. Cruise lines have become smart about the fact that when you're on a ship, you're a captive audience, so they may propose that you make your future vacation plans on board. Before you sign on the dotted line, though, make sure the on-the-spot discount can be combined with other offers you might find later. Keep in mind that if you do choose to book on board, you can still do the reconfirmation and ticketing through your travel agent by giving the cruise line his or her name.

Lines tend to offer cut rates when they are introducing a new ship or moving into a new market. So it pays to keep track of what's happening in the cruise industry—or have your agent do so—when you're looking for a deal.

6 Airfares & Pre-/Post-Cruise Hotel Offerings

Also see the information on cruisetours in chapter 10.

AIR ADD-ONS

Unless you live within driving distance of your port of embarkation, you'll probably be flying to Vancouver, Anchorage, Seattle, or one of the other ports to join your ship.

Your cruise package may include airfare, but if not, you'll have to make other arrangements. You can book air travel separately, but remember that those attractive starting discount fares you see in the newspapers and on the Web may not apply, especially if your cruise departs on the peak travel days of Friday or Saturday. A better option is usually to take advantage of the cruise lines' air add-ons. Why? First of all, as frequent customers of the airlines, cruise lines tend to get decent (if not the best) discounts on airfare, which they pass on to their customers. Second, booking air with the cruise line also allows the line to keep track of you. If your plane is late, for instance, they may hold the boat, though not always. When you book air travel with your cruise line, most lines will include **transfers** from the airport to the ship, saving you the hassle of getting a cab. (If you do book the air travel on your own, you may still be able to get the transfers separately—ask your agent about this.) Be aware that once the air ticket is issued by the cruise line, you usually aren't allowed to make changes.

The only times it may pay to book your own air transportation is if you are using frequent-flier miles and can get your air travel for free, or if you are particular about which carrier you fly or which route you take. You are more or less at the mercy of the cruise line in terms of carrier and route if you take their air offers, and you may even end up on chartered aircraft. Some lines offer special **deviation programs** that allow you to request specific airlines and routing for an extra fee. The deadline for these requests is usually 60 days before the sailing date or, if you book later, on the day your cruise reservations are made. *Tip:* If you're determined to book your own air and your travel schedule is flexible, it's often easier to get the carrier and the flight time you prefer if you choose a cruise that leaves on a Wednesday or Thursday or some such non-peak day of the week.

If airfare is part of the cruise package but you choose not to book your air transportation with the cruise line, you will be refunded the air portion of the fare.

PRE- & POST-CRUISE HOTEL OFFERINGS

Even if you don't take a cruisetour, you may want to consider spending a day or two in your port of embarkation or debarkation either before or after your cruise (see details on exploring the port cities in chapters 8 and 9). An advantage to coming in a day or two early is that you don't have to worry if your flight is running late. Plus, Vancouver, Anchorage, and Seattle, the cities into which most passengers fly, happen to be great cities to explore.

Just as with airfare, you need to decide whether you want to buy your hotel stay from the cruise line or make arrangements on your own. The cruise lines negotiate **special deals with hotels** at port cities, so you will often get a bargain by booking through the cruise line.

When evaluating a cruise line's hotel package, make sure that you review it carefully to see what's included. See whether the line offers a transfer from the airport to the hotel and from the hotel to the cruise ship (or vice versa); make sure that the line offers a hotel that you will be happy with in terms of type of property and location; and inquire if any escorted tours, car-rental deals, or meals are included. You'll also want to compare the price of booking on your own (see chapter 7 for information on hotels in the various ports). Keep in mind that cruise lines usually list rates for hotels on a per-person basis, whereas hotels post their rates on a per-room basis.

7 Choosing Your Cabin

Once you've looked at the ship descriptions in chapters 5 and 6, talked over your options with your travel agent, and selected an itinerary and ship, you're going to have to choose your cabin. The cruise lines have improved things a bit since Charles Dickens declared that his stateroom reminded him of a coffin, but cramped, windowless spaces can still be found. On the other hand, so can penthouse-size suites with expansive verandas, Jacuzzis, and butler service. Most cabins on cruise ships today have twin beds that are convertible to queen-size (you can request which configuration you want), plus a private bathroom with a shower. Some cabins have bunk beds, which are obviously not convertible. Most ships also offer cabins designed for three or four people that will include two twin beds plus one or two bunks that fold down from the wall in some way. In some cases, it is possible to add a fifth bed to the room. Some lines offer special cabins designed for families, with "regular" twin beds that can be pushed together to create a double bed, plus fold-down bunks. Families may also be able to book connecting cabins (although they'll have to pay for two cabins to do so).

Most cabins, but not all, have televisions. Some also have extra amenities, such as safes, minifridges, VCRs, bathrobes, and hair dryers. A bathtub is considered a luxury on ships and will usually be offered only in more expensive rooms.

CABIN TYPES

What kind of cabin is right for you? Price will likely be a big factor here, but so should the vacation style you prefer. The typical ship offers several types of cabins, which are illustrated by floor plans in the cruise line's brochure. The cabins are usually described by **price** (highest to lowest), **category** (suite, deluxe, superior, standard, economy, and other types), and **furniture configuration** ("sitting area with two lower beds," for example—"lower bed" meaning that the bed is a standard floor bed rather than a bunk that pulls out from the wall). The cabins will also be described as being **inside** or **outside.** Simply put, inside cabins do not have windows (or even portholes) and outside cabins do. However, views from some outside cabins may be obstructed—usually by a lifeboat—or look out onto a public area; an experienced travel agent should be able to advise you on which cabin to choose if full views and privacy are important. On the big ships, deluxe outside cabins may also come with **verandas** (also referred to as **balconies**) that give you a private outdoor space to enjoy the sea breezes. This is a great thing to have in Alaska. You can throw on your bathrobe and view the glaciers and wildlife. But remember that the verandas vary in size, so if you're looking to do more than stand on your balcony, make sure the space is big enough to accommodate

Bed Lingo

On cruise ships, "lower beds" refer to standard twin beds, while "bunks" (or, less commonly, "upper beds") refer to beds that passengers pull out from the wall to sleep in.

deck chairs, a table, or whatever else you require. Also keep in mind that these verandas are not completely isolated—your neighbors may be able to see you and vice versa. With few exceptions, veranda cabins will not have obstructed views.

Noise can be a factor that may influence your cabin choice. If you take a cabin on a lower deck, you may hear engine noises; in the front of the ship, anchor noises; and in the back of the ship, thruster noises. A cabin near an elevator may bring door-opening and -closing sounds. And a cabin above or below the disco may pulse until all hours of the night. The loudest areas of a ship vary depending on how well insulated the different areas are, so if noise will be a problem for you, ask what the quietest part of the ship is when you are booking your cabin. We would say that, generally, midships on a higher deck will be the quietest part of the ship (unless, of course, you're near a disco).

If you plan to spend a lot of quiet time in your cabin, you should probably consider booking the biggest room you can afford, and you should also consider taking a cabin with a picture window or, better still, a private veranda. If, conversely, you plan to be off on shore excursions or on deck checking out the glaciers and wildlife, and using your cabin only to change clothes and collapse in at the end of the day, you might be happy with a smaller (and cheaper) cabin. Usually, cabins on the higher decks are more expensive and much nicer, with plusher amenities and superior decor, even if they are the same size as cabins on lower decks. **Luxury suites** are usually on upper decks. The top suites on some ships are actually apartment size, and you'll get lots of space to stretch out. A quirky thing about cabin pricing is that the most stable cabins during rough seas are those in the middle and lower parts of the ship.

On the small ships, cabins can be truly tiny and spartan, though some give the big-ship cabins a run for their money. Generally, the difference lies in the orientation of the cruise line: Those promising a real adventure experience tend to feature somewhat utilitarian cabins.

Aboard both large and small ships, keep in mind that the most expensive and least expensive cabins tend to sell out fast. Also keep in mind that, just as with real estate, it's sometimes better to take a smaller cabin in a nicer ship than a bigger cabin in a less pleasant ship.

CABIN SIZES

The size of a cabin is described in terms of square feet. This number may not mean a lot unless you want to mark it out on your floor at home. But to give you an idea: 120 square feet and under is low end and cramped, 180 square feet is midrange (and the minimum for people with claustrophobia), and 250 square feet and up is suite size.

8 Choosing Your Dining Options

Smaller ships usually serve dinner at a certain time, with unassigned seating, allowing you to sit at any table you want. So if you plan to sail on one of the smaller lines, you don't have to read this section at all. Because most dining rooms on **larger ships** are not large enough to accommodate all passengers at once, large ships typically offer two different seating times, especially for dinner. In this case, your table will be preassigned and remain the same for the duration of the cruise. You will generally make your choice of seating time and table size when you book your cruise. Exceptions to the reserved-seating approaches are noted in the "Open Seating" portion of this section.

MEALTIMES

If you are on a ship with set dinner times, early or main seating is typically at 6pm and late seating is at 8:30pm. There are advantages and disadvantages to both times, and it basically comes down to personal choice. **Early seating** is usually less crowded and the preferred time for families and seniors. The dining experience can be a bit more rushed (the staff needs to make way for the next wave of guests), but food items may be fresher. You can see a show right after dinner and have first dibs on other nighttime venues as well. And you just may be hungry again in time for the midnight buffet.

MODEL CABIN LAYOUTS

Typical Outside Cabins
- Twin beds (can usually be pushed together)
- Some have sofa bed or bunk for third passenger
- Shower (tubs are rare)
- TV and music
- Window or porthole, or veranda

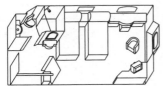

Outside Cabin

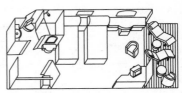

Outside Cabin with Veranda

Typical Suites
- King, queen, or double beds
- Sitting areas (often with sofa beds)
- Large bathrooms, usually with tub, sometimes with Jacuzzi
- Refrigerators, sometimes stocked
- TVs w/VCR and stereo
- Large closets
- Large veranda

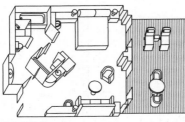

Suite with Veranda

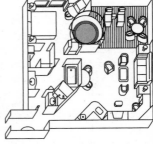

Grand Suite with Veranda

Thanks to Princess Cruises for all photos and diagrams.

READING A SHIP'S DECK PLAN

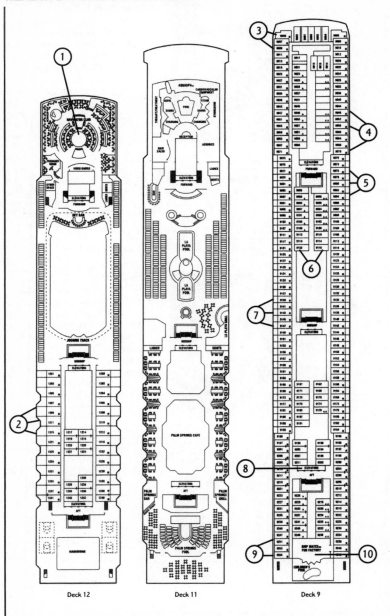

Deck 12

Deck 11

Deck 9

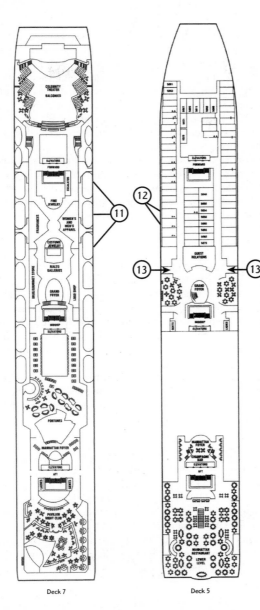

Deck 7

Deck 5

Some cabin choice considerations:

1. Note the location of the ship's disco and other loud public areas, and try not to book a cabin that's too close or underneath.
2. Cabins on upper decks can be affected by the motion of the sea. If you're abnormally susceptible to seasickness, keep this in mind.
3. Ditto for cabins in the bow.
4. Outside cabins without verandas appear as solid blocks of space.
5. Outside cabins with verandas are shown with a line dividing the two spaces.
6. Inside cabins (without windows) can be real money-savers.
7. Cabin midships are the least affected by the motion of the sea, especially if they're on a lower deck.
8. Cabins that adjoin elevator shaftways might be noisy (though proximity makes it easier to get around the ship).
9. Cabins in the stern can be affected by the motion of the sea and tend to be subject to engine vibration.
10. Cabins near children's facilities may not be the quietest places, at least during the day.
11. Check that lifeboats don't block the view from your cabin. The lifeboats in this example adjoin public rooms and so are out of sight.
12. Cabins for travelers with disabilities are ideally located near elevators and close to the ship's entrances (#13).

(Thanks to Celebrity Cruises for use of Mercury's deck plan.)

Late seating, on the other hand, allows you time for a good long nap or late spa appointment before dining. Dinner is not rushed at all. You can sit as long as you want, enjoying after-dinner drinks—unless, that is, you choose to go catch a show, which will usually start at 10:15pm or 10:30pm.

If you also choose to eat **breakfast** and **lunch** in the dining room as opposed to at the more casual venues on the ship, you are theoretically supposed to eat at assigned times as well—typical mealtimes for breakfast are 7 or 8am for the early seating and 8:30 or 9am for the late; for lunch, it's usually noon for the early seating and 1:30pm or so for the late. We've found, though, that most ships aren't hard and fast on this. Crowds in the dining room are typically an issue only at dinner. If you show up outside of your assigned time for breakfast or lunch and your assigned table is full, the staff will probably just seat you elsewhere. Most cruise lines, in fact, operate their dining rooms on a de facto "open seating" basis for both of these meals.

Most large ships today also offer **alternative dining options.** Most have a casual, buffet-style cafe restaurant, usually located on the Lido Deck, with indoor and outdoor poolside seating and an extensive spread of both hot and cold food items at breakfast, lunch, and dinner. Some ships also have **reservations-only restaurants,** seating fewer than 100, where—except on some luxury ships—a small fee is charged, mainly to cover gratuities.

TABLE SIZE

Do you mind sitting with strangers? Are you looking to make new friends? Your dinner companions can make or break your cruise experience. Most ships offer tables configured for two to eight people. For singles or couples who want to socialize, a table of eight seats generally provides enough variety so that you don't get bored and also allows you to steer clear of any individual you don't particularly care for (tables are assigned, not seats). Couples may choose to sit on their own, but singles may find it hard to secure a table for one. A family of four may want to choose a table for four, or request to sit with another family at a table for eight.

You need to state your table size preference in advance, unless you are on a ship with an open-seating policy, but don't worry if you change your mind once you're on board. You'll probably be able to move around. Just tell the dining-room maitre d' and he or she will review the seating charts for an opening.

OPEN SEATING

Put off by all this formality? Want guaranteed casual all the way? Norwegian Cruise Line's ships, Regent's *Seven Seas Mariner,* and Silversea's *Silver Shadow* all serve meals with open seating—dine when you want (within the restaurants' open hours, of course) and sit with whom you want. The catch is, particularly with Norwegian, you are best off deciding in the morning where you want to have dinner and making a reservation or you may find the restaurant of your choice is full up when you decide to eat. Princess has its own version of this system, allowing guests to choose traditional early or late seating, or open restaurant-style seating (you make your choice before the cruise but can change your mind once you're on board).

SPECIAL MENU REQUESTS

The cruise line should be informed at the time you make your reservations about any special dietary requirements you have. Some lines offer kosher menus, and all have vegetarian, vegan, low-fat, low-salt, and sugar-free options available.

SMOKE-FREE DINING

Most ships now feature smoke-free dining rooms, but if smoking is a particular concern to you, check this out with your travel agent. If the room isn't nonsmoking, you can request a nonsmoking table. On the other hand, smokers can request a smoking table.

9 Deposits & Cancellation Policies

You'll be asked by your travel agent to make a **deposit,** either of a fixed amount or of some percentage of your total cruise cost. You'll then receive a receipt in the mail from the cruise line. You'll be asked to pay the remaining fare usually no later than 2 months before your departure date.

Cruise lines have varying policies regarding **cancellations,** and it's important to look at the fine print in the line's brochure to make sure you understand the policy. Most lines allow you to cancel for a full refund on your deposit and payment anytime up to 76 days before the sailing, after which you have to pay a penalty. If you cancel at the last minute, you will typically be refunded only 75% of what you've paid (although post-9/11, some lines have introduced more lenient policies).

10 Travel Insurance

There are three kinds of travel insurance: trip-cancellation, medical, and lost-luggage coverage. Rule number one: Check your existing policies before you buy any additional coverage. **Trip-cancellation insurance** is a good idea if you have paid a large portion of your vacation expenses up front—as is the case with cruises. It offers protection if, for some reason, you're not able to take your cruise or your trip is interrupted. For trip-cancellation insurance information, contact one of the following insurers: **Access America** (© 800/729-6021; www.accessamerica.com), **Travel Guard** (© 800/826-4919; www.travelguard.com), **Travel Insured International** (© 800/243-3174; www.travelinsured.com), or **Travelex Insurance Services** (© 888/457-4602; www.travelex-insurance.com).

Health insurance doesn't make sense for most travelers. Your existing health insurance should cover you if you get sick while on vacation (though if you belong to an HMO, you should check to see whether you are fully covered when away from home). If you require additional medical insurance, try **MEDEX International** (© 800/527-0218 or 410/453-6300; www.medexassist.com) or **Travel Assistance International** (© 800/821-2828; www.travelassistance.com; for general information on services, call the company's Worldwide Assistance Services, Inc., at © 800/777-8710).

Small ships may have someone on staff with nursing skills, though they rarely have a doctor, but such ships in Alaska never get so far from civilization that a plane couldn't be summoned by radio to airlift a sick passenger to a hospital.

Onboard Medical Care

Large ships usually have a fully equipped medical facility and staff (a doctor and a nurse or two) on board to handle any emergency. They work from a medical center that typically offers set office hours but is also open on an emergency basis 24 hours a day. A fee (sometimes a steep one) is charged. They're equipped to do some surgery, but in cases of major medical emergencies, passengers may be airlifted off the ship by helicopter to the nearest hospital.

Lost-luggage insurance doesn't make much sense for most travelers, either. On domestic flights, checked baggage is covered up to $2,500 per ticketed passenger. On international flights (including U.S. portions of international trips), baggage is limited to approximately $9.05 per pound, up to approximately $635 per checked bag. If you plan to check items more valuable than the standard liability, see if your valuables are covered by your homeowner's policy, get baggage insurance as part of your comprehensive travel-insurance package (contact one of the travel insurance providers listed above), or buy Travel Guard's BagTrak product. Don't buy insurance at the airport, as it's usually overpriced. Be sure to take any valuables or irreplaceable items with you in your carry-on luggage, as many valuables (including books, money, and electronics) aren't covered by airline policies.

If your luggage is lost, immediately file a lost-luggage claim at the airport, detailing the luggage contents. For most airlines, you must report delayed, damaged, or lost baggage within 4 hours of arrival. The airlines are required to deliver luggage, once found, directly to your house or destination free of charge.

The cruise line may also offer its own insurance policies, including trip-cancellation insurance, lost-baggage insurance, and death and dismemberment insurance. It may pay to compare these policies with the plans offered by insurance companies (this is another area where your travel agent can be of assistance).

FAST FACTS: Alaska

Area Code All of Alaska is in area code **907**. Well, *almost* all. The tiny community of Hyder, about 90 miles northeast of Ketchikan, lies on the Alaska/British Columbia border, almost a suburb of the larger town of Stewart, B.C. For practical and technical reasons, Hyder uses the same area code as Stewart: **250**. In the Yukon Territory, the area code is **867**. When placing a toll call within the state, you must dial 1, the area code, and the number. See "Telephone," below, for an important tip on phone cards.

Banks & ATMs There are banks and automated teller machines in all but the tiniest town. They may charge a nominal fee for the use of the service.

Business Hours In the larger cities, major **grocery stores** are open 24 hours a day and carry a wide range of products (even fishing gear) in addition to food. At a minimum, stores are open Monday through Friday from 10am to 6pm, are open on Saturday afternoon, and are closed on Sunday, but many are open for much longer hours, especially during summer. **Banks** may close an hour earlier and, if they're open on Saturday, it's only in the morning. Under state law, **bars** don't have to close until 5am, but many communities have an earlier closing time, generally around 2am.

Cellular Phone Coverage Most of the populated portion of the state has cellular coverage. The largest provider is an Alaska company called ACS, which posts maps of its coverage area at **www.acsalaska.com**. AT&T has the second-best network. We've found that usable coverage is often less than what the companies claim, so don't bet your life on being able to make a call. Your cell-phone provider should be able to give you a brochure detailing roaming charges, which can be steep.

Emergencies Generally, you can call ℭ **911** for medical, police, or fire emergencies. On remote highways, there sometimes are gaps in 911 coverage, but dialing 0 will generally get an operator, who can connect you to emergency services. Citizens-band channels 9 and 11 are monitored for emergencies on most highways, as are channels 14 and 19 in some areas.

Holidays Besides the normal national holidays, banks and state and local government offices close on two state holidays: Seward's Day (the last Mon in Mar) and Alaska Day (Oct 18, or the nearest Fri or Mon if it falls on a weekend).

Liquor Laws The minimum drinking age in Alaska is 21. Most restaurants sell beer and wine, and a minority have full bars that serve hard liquor as well. Packaged alcohol, beer, and wine are sold only in licensed stores, not in grocery stores, but these are common and are open long hours every day. More than 100 rural communities have laws prohibiting the importation and possession of alcohol (this is known as being "dry") or only the sale but not possession of alcohol (known as being "damp"). With a few exceptions, these are tiny bush communities off the road network; urban areas are all "wet." Of the communities featured in this book, Kotzebue and Barrow are damp, and the rest are wet. Before flying into a Native village with alcohol, ask about the law—bootlegging is a serious crime (and serious bad manners), or check a list online (go to **www.dps.state.ak.us/abc/Index.asp** and click on "Local Option Restrictions").

Lost or Stolen Credit Cards Be sure to tell all of your credit card companies the minute you discover your wallet has been lost or stolen and file a report at the nearest police precinct. Your credit card company or insurer may require a police report number or record of the loss. Most credit card companies have an emergency toll-free number to call if your card is lost or stolen; they may be able to wire you a cash advance immediately or deliver an emergency credit card in a day or two. **Visa**'s U.S. emergency number is ℭ **800/847-2911** or 410/581-9994. **American Express** cardholders and traveler's check holders should call ℭ **800/221-7282**. **MasterCard** holders should call ℭ **800/307-7309** or 636/722-7111. For other credit cards, call the toll-free number directory at ℭ **800/555-1212**.

If you need emergency cash over the weekend when all banks and American Express offices are closed, you can have money wired to you via **Western Union** (ℭ **800/325-6000**; www.westernunion.com).

Identity theft or fraud are potential complications of losing your wallet, especially if you've lost your driver's license along with your cash and credit cards. Notify the major credit-reporting bureaus immediately; placing a fraud alert on your records may protect you against liability for criminal activity. The three major U.S. credit-reporting agencies are **Equifax** (ℭ **800/766-0008**; www.equifax.com), **Experian** (ℭ **888/397-3742**; www.experian.com), and **TransUnion** (ℭ **800/680-7289**; www.transunion.com). Finally, if you've lost all forms of photo ID, call your airline and explain the situation; they might allow you to board the plane if you have a copy of your passport or birth certificate and a copy of the police report you've filed.

Newspapers The state's dominant newspaper is the ***Anchorage Daily News*** (www.adn.com); it's available everywhere but is not always easy to find in Southeast Alaska. Seattle newspapers and ***USA Today*** are often available, and in Anchorage you can get virtually any newspaper.

Taxes There is no state sales tax, but most local governments have a sales tax and a bed tax on accommodations.

Telephone We have been assured that all major calling cards will work in Alaska, but this certainly hasn't been the case in the past. To make sure, contact your long-distance company, or buy a by-the-minute card.

Time Zone Although the state naturally spans five time zones, in the 1980s Alaska's middle time zone was stretched so almost the entire state would lie all in one zone, known as Alaska Time. It's 1 hour earlier than the U.S. West Coast's Pacific Standard Time and 4 hours earlier than Eastern Standard Time. Crossing over the border from Alaska to Canada adds an hour and puts you at the same time as the West Coast. As with almost everywhere else in the United States, daylight saving time is in effect from 1am on the first Sunday in April (turn your clocks ahead 1 hr.) until 2am on the last Sunday in October (turn clocks back again).

Water Unpurified river or lake water may not be safe to drink. Hand-held filters available from sporting-goods stores for around $75 are the most practical way of dealing with the problem. Iodine kits and boiling also work.

The Cruise Experience

Now that you've made most of the hard decisions—choosing and booking your cruise—the rest of your vacation planning should be relatively easy. From this point on, the cruise lines take over much of the work, particularly if you've booked a package that includes air travel.

You should carefully read the brochure of your chosen cruise line (make sure that your agent gives you one or that you get one directly from the cruise line), because most lines' brochures include sections that address commonly asked questions. In this chapter, we'll add our own two cents' worth on these matters and provide some practical hints that'll help you be prepared for all you'll find in the 49th state, both aboard ship and in the ports of call.

1 Packing for Your Cruise

PREPARING FOR THE WEATHER

The sometimes extreme and always unpredictable Alaska weather will be a big factor in the success of your vacation. During your summertime cruise, you may experience temperature variations from the 40s to the 80s (single digits to 20s Celsius). The days will be long, with the sun all but refusing to set, especially in the more northern ports, and people will be energized by the extra daylight hours. You'll likely encounter some rain, but there could also be weeks of sunny skies with no rain at all. You're less likely to encounter snow, but it is a remote possibility, especially in the spring.

Weather plays a factor in what you need to pack, with the must-haves on an Alaska cruise including a raincoat, an umbrella, and comfortable walking shoes that you don't mind getting wet or muddy. A swimsuit is also a must if your ship has a pool (sometimes covered, sometimes heated) or hot tubs.

Even in the summer, temperatures in Alaska may not go much higher than the 50s or 60s (low or high teens Celsius), although they also may go into the 70s or 80s (low to high 20s Celsius). Having **layers of clothing** that you can peel off if the weather is hot and add if the weather is cold is the most convenient approach.

ESSENTIALS

What you choose to pack obviously involves a lot of personal choice, but here's a checklist of some items that everyone should bring along:

- A lightweight, waterproof coat or jacket
- Two sweaters or fleece pullovers, or substitute a warm vest for one
- A warm hat and gloves
- Two to four pairs of pants or jeans
- Two pairs of walking shoes (preferably waterproof)
- Sunscreen (SPF 15 or higher)
- Bug spray (Alaska has 55 different kinds of mosquitoes)

- Sunglasses
- Binoculars (some small ships stock them for free guest use, but on the bigger ships, it will cost you—if they even have pairs for rent)
- A camera, preferably with a telephoto or zoom lens
- Film (bring more than you think you'll need), or an extra flash card if you use digital
- Formal wear (with accessories) if your ship has formal nights (not all do)
- Semidressy wear for informal nights
- Long underwear if you're on a shoulder-season cruise

ALASKA'S CLIMATE, BY MONTHS & REGIONS

Anchorage: Southcentral Alaska

	May	June	July	Aug	Sept
Average high/low (°F)	54/39	62/47	65/52	63/50	55/42
Average high/low (°C)	12/4	17/8	18/11	17/10	13/6
Hours of light	17:45	19:30	18:15	15:30	12
Sunny days	11	10	9	9	9
Rainy days	7	8	11	13	14
Precipitation	.7	1.1	1.7	2.4	2.7

Juneau: Southeast Alaska

	May	June	July	Aug	Sept
Average high/low (°F)	55/39	61/45	64/48	63/47	56/43
Average high/low (°C)	13/4	16/7	18/9	17/8	13/6
Hours of light	17	18:15	17:30	15:30	12:30
Sunny days	8	8	8	9	6
Rainy days	17	15	17	17	20
Precipitation	3.4	3.1	4.2	5.3	6.7

PACKING FOR FORMAL, INFORMAL & CASUAL EVENTS

Some people agonize over what to pack for a cruise vacation, but there's no reason to fret. Except for the addition of a formal night or two, a cruise vacation is really no different from any resort vacation. And in some cases, it's much more casual.

Don't feel you have to go out and buy "cruise wear." Sweatshirts, jeans, and jogging outfits are the norm during the day. Dinner is dress-up time on most ships, although several have begun to offer more casual alternatives. And the small adventure-type ships are all casual all the time.

Generally, ships describe proper dinner attire as formal, informal or semiformal (the two terms mean the same thing in this case), or casual. There are usually 2 formal nights and 2 informal (or semiformal) nights during a weeklong cruise, with the rest casual; check with your line for specifics. **Formal,** although the term has gotten somewhat more relaxed recently, generally means a tux or dark suit with tie for men, and a nice cocktail dress, long dress, gown, or dressy pantsuit for women. **Informal** (or semiformal) is a jacket, tie, and dress slacks, or a light suit, for men (jeans are frowned upon), and a dress, skirt and blouse, or pants outfit for women (the ubiquitous little black dress is appropriate here). **Casual** at dinner means a sports shirt or open-collar dress shirt with slacks for men (some will also wear a jacket), and a casual dress, pants outfit, or skirt and blouse for women. You may also come across country-club casual; in our experience, this is pretty much the same as informal without the tie. For casual nights, dress as you would to go out to dinner at a midrange restaurant.

Men who don't own a **tuxedo** may be able to rent one in advance through the cruise line's preferred supplier, who will deliver the tux right to the ship. In some cases, the ship will keep a limited supply of tuxes on board. But if you attend a formal evening wearing a dark business suit instead of a tuxedo, you won't be alone.

Cleaned & Pressed

Many ships offer dry-cleaning and laundry services (for a fee, of course), and some offer coin-operated laundry facilities (usually requiring quarters so having some handy is helpful). Check your line's brochures for details. Using these services can save you a lot of packing.

2 Money Matters

There are few forms of travel that are as easy as a cruise, at least as far as money is concerned. That's because you've already paid the lion's share of your all-inclusive vacation by the time you board the ship.

When you check in at the cruise terminal for a large-ship cruise, the cruise-line folks will ask for a major credit card to which you will charge your onboard expenses, unless you've established that you will be paying your onboard expenses by cash or check. On some ships, you must report to the purser's office once on board to establish your onboard credit account. On all cruises, you also have the option of paying your account with cash, traveler's checks, or, in some cases, a personal check. Check the cruise line's brochure for specific rules on this. You may be asked to leave a deposit if you are paying with cash, usually $250 for a 1-week sailing. You should let the cruise line know as early as possible if you wish to pay with cash or checks (some lines like to know at the time you make your cruise reservations).

The staff at the check-in counter will give you a special **ship charge card** (sometimes called a "signature card") that you will use for the length of your cruise. From this point on, on most ships, your time aboard is virtually cashless, except for any gambling you do in the casino. On many ships, you can even put your crew tips on your credit card, though on some you're expected to use cash (more on tipping later in this chapter). The same electronic card, by the way, will also likely serve as your cabin key.

On most small ships, things aren't so formal—since there are so few passengers, and since the only places to spend money aboard are at the bar and the small gift counters, the staff will just mark down your purchases and you'll settle your account at the end of the week.

In all cases, you will need some cash on hand for when you stop at a port, in order to pay for cabs, make small purchases, buy sodas and snacks, tip your tour guides, and so on. Having bills smaller than $20 is useful for these purposes. At all the ports described in this book (even the Canadian ones), U.S. dollars are accepted, as are major credit cards. If you prefer to deal in Canadian currency in Canada, there are exchange counters, banks, and ATMs at most ports you will visit. Ships in Alaska do not usually offer currency-conversion services.

The Cost of Common Cruise Incidentals	US$
Alternative dining (service charge)	12.50–30.00
Babysitting (per hr., for two children)	
Private	10.00
Group	6.00–8.00
Beverages	
Beer (domestic/imported)	3.50–6.00
Latte	3.75–4.25
Mineral water	2.00–3.95
Mixed drink	3.95–6.75 (more for fine liquors)
Soft drink	2.50–2.75
Wine with dinner	15.00–300.00 per bottle
Cruise-line logo souvenirs	3.00–50.00
Laundry	1.25–7.00 per item
E-mail (per min.)	0.40–1.50
Haircuts	
Men's	25.00–32.00
Women's	52.00–77.00
Massage (50 min.)	109.00–139.00
Phone calls (per min.)	4.95–15.00
Photos (5×7)	6.95–9.95

Some ships have their own ATMs aboard, most often located, not surprisingly, in the casino. These give out U.S. dollars. A fee may be involved.

It's recommended that you not leave large amounts of cash in your room. All ships have some sort of safes available, either in-room or at the purser's desk, and passengers are wise to use them. You should also store your plane ticket and passport or ID papers there.

BUDGETING

Before your trip, you may want to make a tentative budget. You should set aside money for shore excursions ($600 per person or more if you plan to do several) and tips (about $10 per passenger per day).

Extras that should also be included in your planning are bar drinks, dry cleaning, phone calls, massage and other spa services, salon services, babysitting, photos taken by the ship's photographer, wine at dinner, souvenirs, and costs for any other special splurges your particular ship might offer (items at the caviar bars or cigar bars, time on the golf simulator, and so on). Above are some rough prices for the more common incidentals.

We suggest that you keep careful track of your onboard expenses to avoid an unpleasant surprise at the end of your cruise.

On big ships, a final bill will be slipped under your door on the last night of your cruise. If everything is okay and you're paying by credit card, you don't have to do anything but keep the copy. If there's a problem on the bill, or if you are paying by cash, traveler's check, or personal check, you will have to go down to the purser's or guest-relations desk and wait in what will likely be a very long line. On small ships, you usually have to settle up directly with the purser on the last full day of the cruise.

3 Your Very Important Papers

About 1 month (and no later than 1 week) before your cruise, you should receive in the mail your **cruise documents,** including your airline tickets (if you purchased them from the cruise line), a boarding document with your cabin and dining choices on it, boarding forms to fill out, luggage tags, and your prearranged bus-transfer vouchers from the airport to the port (if applicable). Also included will likely be a description of shore excursions available for purchase either on board or, in some cases, in advance, as well as additional material detailing things you need to know before you sail. Some lines including Carnival and Norwegian Cruise Line also now allow you to download this information online.

All this information is important. Read it carefully. Make sure that your cabin category and dining preference are as you requested and also check your airline tickets to make sure everything is okay in terms of flights and arrival times. Make sure that there is enough time to arrive at the port no later than half an hour before departure time, and preferably a lot earlier. Be sure to carry these documents in your carry-on rather than in your luggage, since you can't board without them.

PASSPORTS & NECESSARY IDENTIFICATION

With the Western Hemisphere Travel Initiative (WHTI), travel ID requirements were recently changed, though some of the changes were subject to continuing debate. As the rules stood at press time, if you are embarking or disembarking your Alaska cruise in Vancouver in 2008, you will be **required** to have a passport (whereas a photo ID and birth certificate used to suffice). If you are not a U.S. citizen but live in the United States, you will have to carry your alien registration card and passport. Foreign-born travelers who do not reside in the U.S. will be required to show a valid visa to enter the U.S. through Canada. For more information about passports and to find your regional passport office, consult the State Department website (http://travel.state.gov) or call the **National Passport Information Center**'s automated service at © **877/487-2778.**

Even if your cruise does not visit Canada, you will still be required to show a photo ID when boarding the ship; in this case, however, a driver's license is sufficient.

4 Getting to the Ship & Checking In

Before you leave for the airport, attach one of the luggage tags sent by the cruise line to each of your bags. Make sure that you correctly fill in the tags with your departure date, port, cabin number, and so forth. You can find all this information in your cruise documents. Put a luggage tag on your carry-on as well.

AIRPORT ARRIVAL

If you booked your air travel and/or transfers with the cruise line, you should see a **cruise-line representative** holding a card with the name of the line, either when you get off the plane or at the baggage area. (If you're arriving on a flight from the United States to Vancouver, you will need to clear Customs and Immigration. Follow the appropriate signs. The cruise-line rep will be waiting to greet you after you've cleared.) Check in with this person. If you are on a pre-cruise package, the details of what to do at the airport will be described in the cruise line's brochure.

When you arrive at your gateway airport, you will be asked by a cruise-line representative to identify your luggage, which will then go straight to the ship for delivery to your cabin. It won't necessarily go in the same bus as you, and it may not (almost

Where's My Luggage?!

Don't panic if your bags aren't in your cabin when you arrive: Getting all the bags on board is a rather slow process—on big ships, as many as 6,000 bags need to be loaded and distributed. If it gets close to sailing time and you're concerned, call guest relations or the purser's office. They'll probably advise you that it's on the way. If your luggage really is lost rather than just late, the cruise line's customer-relations folks will track it down and arrange for it to be delivered to the ship's first port of call.

certainly will not) be waiting for you when you board, but it'll arrive eventually, have no fear. Make certain that your bags have the cruise line's tags on them, properly filled out, before you leave the airport for the ship.

You will have to turn over the **transportation voucher** you received with your cruise documents to the bus driver, so you'll want to have it handy.

If you're flying independent of the cruise line, claim your luggage at the baggage area and proceed to the pier by cab, by rental car, or by whatever other arrangements you have made. And again, remember to put the luggage tags provided by the cruise line on your bags at this point if you haven't already, because when you get to the pier, your bags will be taken from you by a porter for loading onto the ship. The porter who takes your bags may expect a tip of $1 per bag (some will be more aggressive than others in asking for it).

On the question of identifying your luggage, don't rely simply on appearances; one Samsonite looks just like another, even though yours may have a distinctive yellow ribbon on its handle. Check the ID tags as well! There's nothing worse than getting on a cruise that starts with 2 days at sea with somebody else's luggage and only the clothes on your back.

Also, if you're taking non-cruise-line-operated transportation to the cruise dock, make sure you get to the right ship at the right pier. That may sound silly, but in cities with multiple piers, it can get confusing. And cab drivers don't always know their way around the docks. Know your pier number!

WHAT TO DO IF YOUR FLIGHT IS DELAYED

First of all, tell the airline personnel at the airport that you are a cruise passenger and that you're sailing that day. They may be able to put you on a different flight. Second, have the airline folks call the cruise line to advise them of your delay. There should be an emergency number included in your cruise documents. Keep in mind that you may not be the only person delayed, and the line just may hold the ship until your arrival. (Jerry, however, remembers one embarrassing occasion on which several passengers bound for Vancouver through Los Angeles to join a Holland America ship had had the first leg of their trip from Dallas delayed by an aircraft mechanical problem and were now running late. "Don't worry," Jerry assured them. "You'll only be half an hour late in Vancouver. Holland America will wait for you." Bad advice. The group arrived at Canada Place just in time to see their ship disappear in the distance. Jerry has never offered encouragement in such a situation since!)

WHAT TO DO IF YOU MISS THE BOAT

Don't panic. Go directly to the cruise line's port agent at the pier. You may be able to get to your ship via a chartered boat or tug, assuming that the vessel isn't too far out at sea by that time. (Be aware that if you do follow in a small boat, you'll have to transfer from it to a moving ship at sea—not an exercise to be taken lightly!) Or you may

Safety at Sea in the New World (Dis)Order

Traditionally, safety-at-sea issues have included the occasional hurricane, fire, gastrointestinal bug, petty theft, and rogue iceberg. But in the wake of the September 11, 2001 terrorist attacks, the threat of terrorism immediately assumed a high place on that list, prompting cruise lines, port authorities, and the U.S. Coast Guard to implement a number of new security measures throughout their destination areas—including Alaska.

Logistically, ships are more difficult to protect than planes because of their larger passenger loads; their numerous labyrinthine public and "crew only" areas; their regular presence at public port facilities; the access they offer to the numerous contractors who come aboard on turnaround days to refresh flowers, service machinery, and perform other needed functions; and their multicountry itineraries—Alaska cruises usually include Canadian ports as well. For these reasons, all the major cruise lines have their own dedicated onboard security forces, and events over the years have periodically forced enhancements to security procedures. These have included the hiring of ex–Navy SEALs as top-level security consultants, the drilling of deck officers in how to react to takeover attempts, and a mandate that ships have alternative onboard command sites, making it difficult for a small number of terrorists to take and maintain control of a ship. Following 9/11, all cruise ships went to Security Level III, the highest dictated by the Coast Guard, but because stringent security measures were already in place, onboard changes have been relatively few. The cruise lines already were using metal detectors at the gangways, requiring that anyone boarding be on a preapproved list, and employing computerized systems that could tell instantly who was aboard at any given time. Recent additions to these regulations dictate a no-visitors policy; a 300-foot (or more) security zone around all cruise ships; the use of sniffer dogs, concrete barriers, patrol boats, and other security measures at some ports; and the screening of all luggage, ship's stores, mail, and cargo. Many cruise lines have begun photographing passengers digitally at embarkation and matching face to picture every time travelers get back aboard in port.

Because Level III guidelines apply only to U.S. ports, the cruise lines have been working diligently with foreign port officials to beef up security around the ships and protect passengers on shore excursions. Measures include tightening access to ports and increasing local law-enforcement patrols in the water around the vessels.

be put up in a hotel for the night and flown or provided with other transportation to the next port the next day. If you booked your flight on your own, you will likely be charged for this service.

CHECKING IN

Most ships start embarkation in the early afternoon, and depart between 4 and 6pm. You will not be able to board the ship before the scheduled embarkation time, usually about 2 or 3 hours before sailing, and even then it's likely that you'll have to wait in line unless you're sailing on a small ship carrying very few passengers. If you've booked a suite, you may get priority boarding at a special desk. Special-needs passengers may also be processed separately. Ship personnel will check your boarding tickets and ID and collect any documents you've been sent to fill out in advance. You will then be given a boarding card and your cabin key. (On some lines, your key may be waiting in your cabin.) Be prepared for increased security measures that will include an X-ray of your hand luggage and possibly a search with a metal-detecting wand.

You have up until a half-hour (on some ships, it's 1 hr.) before departure to board, but there are some advantages to boarding earlier, like getting first dibs on spa-treatment times. Plus, if you're early enough, you can eat lunch on the ship.

Protocol for establishing your **dining-room table assignment,** if one is required (some ships have open seating), varies by ship. You may be given your assignment in advance of your sailing (shown on your tickets), you may be advised of your table number as you check in, or a card with your table number may be waiting for you in your cabin. If you do not receive an assignment by the time you get to your cabin, you will be directed to a maitre d's desk, set up in a convenient spot on board. This is also the place to make any changes if your assignment does not meet with your approval.

5 Keeping in Touch with the Outside World

GETTING THE NEWS & KEEPING IN TOUCH

Newshounds don't have to feel out of touch on a cruise ship. Most newer cruise ships offer CNN on in-room TVs, and nearly every ship—even small ships without TVs—will post the latest news from the wire services outside the purser's office. Some lines excerpt information from leading newspapers each day and deliver the news to your room.

Most ships will offer the opportunity to make satellite phone calls, but these can be exorbitantly expensive—usually anywhere from $6.95 to $17 per minute. You may be able to use your cellular phone in some of the more populated areas of Alaska (see "Fast Facts: Alaska," in chapter 3). Check with your cellular provider for details. Ships including those in the Carnival and Silversea fleets have also recently added service that allows you to use your cellphone at sea, although you do have to pay what can be expensive roaming rates—again, check with your provider for details.

Another alternative is e-mail, offered by an increasing number of ships, including most of the large ships reviewed in this book. Rates range from 40¢ to $1.50 per minute. It is generally cheaper if you buy a set plan, for instance paying in advance for 4 hours of usage throughout your cruise (plans vary by line, so check with your ship's Internet cafe to see what plans are available). Some of the small ships also offer e-mail access. The port cities you'll be visiting are also likely to have Internet cafes—usually charging cheaper rates than the ships.

SENDING MAIL

If you want to send mail from the ship, you should be able to find both stamps and a mailbox at the purser's office.

6 Visiting the Ports of Call

Here's where the kind of ship you chose for your cruise, and the itinerary, comes into play. On a big ship, you will likely visit the popular ports of Skagway, Juneau, and

Ketchikan (and possibly Sitka or Victoria, depending on your itinerary) and will have several days at sea to enjoy the glorious glaciers, fjords, and wildlife, as well as participate in shipboard activities and relax. On a smaller ship, you may also visit several smaller ports of call and head into wilderness areas that cannot accommodate larger vessels.

On **days in port,** you will want to have a plan of what you want to see on land—more on that in this section. On **days at sea,** you will probably want to be out on deck much of the time looking for whales and listening to the commentary of glacier and wildlife experts. There will be plenty of activities offered, but these may be reduced at certain times—for instance, when the ship is scheduled to pass one of the famous glaciers.

Nearly every ship in Alaska has naturalists and other Alaska experts on board to share their expertise on glaciers, geography, plant life, and wildlife. Sometimes these experts are on for the entire cruise and offer lectures complete with slides or films. Other times they are Forest Service rangers who come on board

Religion on the High Seas

Religious services depend, of course, on the ship and the clergy on board. Some ships offer Catholic Mass every day. Most ships offer a nondenominational service on Sunday and a Friday-night Jewish Sabbath service, usually run by a passenger. On Jewish and Christian holidays, clergy are typically aboard on large ships to lead services, which are usually held in the library or conference room.

at glacier sites (particularly in Glacier Bay) to offer commentary, usually over the ship's PA system. Depending on the ship, local fishermen, Native Alaskans, teachers, photographers, librarians, historians, or anthropologists may come on board to teach about local history and culture.

Cruise lines carefully arrange their itineraries to visit places that offer a little something for everyone, whether your thing is nature, museum hopping, barhopping, or no hopping at all. You can take in the location's ambience and natural beauty, learn about the local culture and history, eat local foods, and enjoy sports activities. And you'll have the opportunity to shop to your heart's content.

SHORE EXCURSIONS

When the ship gets into port, you'll have the choice of going on a shore excursion organized by the cruise line or going off on your own. The shore excursions are designed to help you make the most of your limited time at each port of call, to get you to the top natural or historical attractions, and to make sure you get back to the ship on time. But shore excursions are also a moneymaking area for the cruise line, and the offerings can add a hefty sum to your vacation costs. Whether you choose to take one of these prearranged sightseeing trips is a matter of both personal preference and budgetary concerns; you should in no way feel that you need to do an excursion in every port. Our picks of some of the best shore-excursion offerings in Alaska's Southeast and Southcentral, as well as in Vancouver and Victoria, are included with all the port listings in chapters 8 and 9, along with advice on exploring on your own.

At most ports, the cruise lines offer **guided tours** to the top sights, usually by bus. The most worthwhile tours take you outside the downtown area or include a meal, a dance or music performance, or a crafts demonstration (or sometimes all of the above). There's a guide on each bus, and the excursion price includes all incidental admission costs. The commentary is sometimes hokey, other times educational.

In most Alaska ports, it's easy to explore the downtown area on your own. There are advantages to independent exploration: Walking around is often the best way to see the sights, and you can plan your itinerary to steer clear of the crowds. In some ports, however, there's not much within walking distance of the docks, and it's difficult to find a cab or other transportation. In these cases, the cruise line's excursion program may be your best and most cost-effective option. For instance, a typical **historical tour** in Sitka will take in the Russian St. Michael's Cathedral in the downtown area plus two great sights a little ways out of downtown: Sitka National Historic Park, with its totem poles and forest trails; and the Alaska Raptor Rehabilitation Center, where injured bald eagles and other birds of prey are nursed back to health. The tour may also include a Russian dance performance by the all-female New Archangel Dancers. Although you could visit the church on your own, it's a long walk to the park, and the bus is the best way to get to see the eagles.

There are plenty of shore excursions in Alaska for those who want to get active, such as **mountain-bike trips, fishing, snorkeling,** and **kayak voyages,** all of which get you close to nature and allow you to experience stunning views. These trips are generally worth taking. They usually involve small groups of passengers, and by booking your activity through the cruise line, you have the advantage of knowing that the vendors having been prescreened: Their prices may be slightly higher than those offered by the outfitters that you'll find once you disembark at the port, but you can be assured that the outfitters the cruise lines work with are reputable.

For those who enjoy trips in small planes or helicopters and are willing to pay for the experience (they are on the pricey side), **flightseeing trips,** offered as shore excursions at many of the ports of call, are a fascinating way to see the Alaska landscape. Again, the ship's offerings may be priced slightly higher than the tours offered at the port, but by booking the ship's package, you should be able to avoid touring with Reckless Mike and His Barely Flying Machine. The extra few bucks you pay will be worth it.

A new trend is private shore excursions—the cruise line arranges a guide just for you and anyone else you want to invite along. Norwegian Cruise Line for instance offers this option in Juneau and Ketchikan. It's the best of both worlds—you get to see what you want to see with an experienced guide—but naturally these tours are pricey.

Regular shore excursions usually range in price from about $45 to $55 for a bus tour, to $299 and up for an elaborate offering such as flightseeing (helicopter sightseeing is typically $400 and up, particularly if landing on a glacier is involved).

You may be in port long enough to book more than one option or to take an excursion and still have several hours to explore the port on your own. You may very well find that you want to do a prearranged shore excursion at one port and go it on your own at the next.

The best way to decide which shore excursions you want to take is to do some research in advance of your trip. In addition to our descriptions in chapters 8 and 9, which detail the most common and popular excursions offered in the various ports, your cruise line will probably send you a booklet listing its shore excursions with your cruise tickets. You can compare and contrast. On board your ship, you'll find a shore-excursion order form in your cabin, available at the purser's desk or shore-excursion desk, or at the shore-excursion lecture that will be offered the first day of your cruise. To make your reservations, check off the appropriate places on the shore-excursion order form, sign the form (make sure to include your cabin number), and drop it off as directed, probably at the ship's shore-excursion desk or at the purser's office. Your account will be automatically charged, and tickets will be sent to your cabin before your first scheduled tour. The tickets will include such information as where and when to meet for the tour. Carefully note the time: If you are not at the right place at the right time, the tour will probably leave without you.

Remember: The most popular excursions (such as flightseeing trips) sell out fast. For that reason, you're best off booking your shore excursions the first or second day of your cruise. Some lines, including Holland America, Princess, Royal Caribbean, and Celebrity, offer the option of booking shore excursions in advance of your trip, which we recommend in order to ensure yourself a spot.

ARRIVING IN PORT
When the ship arrives in port, it will either dock at the pier or anchor slightly offshore. You may think that when the ship docks right at the pier you can walk right off, but you can't. Before the gangway is open to disembarking passengers, lots of papers must be signed, and local authorities must give their clearance, a process that can take as long as 2 hours. Don't bother going down to the gangplank until you hear an announcement saying the ship has been cleared.

If your ship anchors rather than docks (as in Sitka, for instance), you will go ashore in a small boat called a launch or tender, which ties up next to your ship and shuttles passengers back and forth all day. Getting on the tender may require a helping hand from crew members, and the waves may keep the tender swaying, sometimes requiring passengers to literally jump to get aboard. (The tenders, by the way, are part of the ship's ample complement of lifeboats, lowered into the water, usually four at a time, for the day in port.)

Whether the ship is docked or anchored, you are in no way required to get off at every port of call. The ship's restaurants will remain open, and there will be activities offered, though usually on a limited basis.

If you do disembark, before you reboard you may want to use the phones at the docks to call home. This is much cheaper than making calls from the ship. But be prepared to wait for a phone. No matter how many telephones there are on the pier, you will invariably find that off-duty members of the crew, who generally get off the ship earlier than passengers, have beaten you to them. It's an interesting exercise to stand near a dozen public telephones and listen to the Filipino, cockney, French, Norwegian, and other languages and dialects being spoken by the users.

TIPS FOR YOUR PORT VISITS
THE ESSENTIALS: DON'T LEAVE THE SHIP WITHOUT 'EM
You must bring your **ship boarding pass** (or shipboard ID) with you when you disembark or you will have trouble getting back on board (you probably have to show it as you leave the ship anyway, so forgetting it will be hard). You may also be required to show a photo ID or driver's license (the ship will let you know if you have to carry this as well). And also don't forget to bring a little cash—although your ship operates on a cashless system, the ports do not. Many passengers get so used to carrying no cash or credit cards while aboard ship that they forget them when going ashore.

WATCH THE CLOCK
If you're going off on your own, whether on foot or on one of the alternate tours or transportation options that we've listed, remember to be very careful about timing. Cruise lines are very strict about sailing times, which will be posted around the ship. You're generally required to be back at the dock at least a half-hour before the ship's

scheduled departure. Passengers running late on one of the line's shore excursions needn't worry: If an excursion runs late, the ship accepts responsibility and won't leave without the late passengers.

If you're on your own and do miss the boat, immediately contact the cruise-line representative at the port. You'll probably be able to catch your ship at the next port of call, but you'll have to pay your own way to get there.

7 Tipping, Packing for Disembarkation & Other End-of-Cruise Concerns

Here are a few hints that should save you some time and aggravation at the end of your cruise.

TIPS ON TIPPING

Tipping is a subject that some people find confusing. First, let's establish that you are expected on most ships to tip the crew at the end of the cruise—in particular, your cabin steward, server, and busperson—and not to tip is bad form. The cruise line will give suggested tip amounts in the daily bulletin and in the cruise director's disembarkation briefing, but these are just suggestions—you can tip more or less, at your own discretion. Keep in mind, though, that stewards, servers, and buspersons are often extremely underpaid (some lines pay their waiters $1 a day base pay) and that their salaries are largely dependent on tips. Many of these crewmembers support families back home on their earnings.

We think the **minimum tip** you should consider is $4 per passenger per day for your room steward and your waiter, and $2 per passenger per day for your busperson. That totals up to $70 per passenger for a 7-night cruise (you don't have to include disembarkation day). We also recommend leaving about half of these amounts on behalf of child passengers 12 and under. Some lines recommend more, some a little less. Of course, you can always tip more for good service or simply to round out the number. You'll also be encouraged to tip the dining room maitre d', the headwaiter, and other better-salaried employees. Whether to tip these folks is your decision. If you have a cabin with butler service, tip the butler about $3.50 per person, per day. Most lines suggest that you tip in cash, but some also allow you to tip via your shipboard account. And recently, lines including Carnival, Holland America, Princess, and Norwegian Cruise Line have begun automatically adding tips of about $10 per passenger, per day, to your shipboard account. Even if the cruise line automatically adds the tips to your shipboard account, you can visit the purser's office and ask them to increase or decrease the amount, depending on your opinion of the service you received. Bar bills automatically include the tip (usually 15%), but if the dining-room wine steward, for instance, has served you exceptionally well, you can slip him or her a few bucks, too. The captain and his officers should not be tipped—it'd be like tipping your doctor.

Regent Seven Seas Cruises and Silversea Cruises both include tips in the cruise fare, although some people choose to tip key personnel anyway—it's really up to you. Small-ship line Cruise West has a policy that no tipping is required or expected, but the other small-ship lines in Alaska do recommend tips of $8 to $14 per day depending on the line (see details in chapter 6).

If you have spa or beauty treatments, you can tip that person at the time of the service (just add it to your ship account; be aware some ships add 15% automatically) and you can hand a bartender a buck if you like, but otherwise tips are usually given on the last night of your cruise. On some ships (especially small ships), you may be asked to submit your tips in a single sum that the crew will divide among itself after the cruise, but generally you reward people individually, usually in little preprinted envelopes that the ship distributes.

If a staff member is particularly great, a written letter to a superior is always good form and may earn that person an employee-of-the-month honor, and maybe even a bonus.

SETTLING YOUR SHIPBOARD ACCOUNT

On big ships, your shipboard account will close just before the end of your cruise, but before that time you will receive a preliminary bill in your cabin. If you are using a credit card, just make sure the charges are correct. If there is a problem, you will have to go to the purser's office, where you will likely encounter long lines. If you're paying by cash or traveler's check, you'll be asked to settle your account during either the day or night before you leave the ship. This will also require you to go to the purser's office. A final invoice will be delivered to your room before departure.

On small ships, the procedure will be simpler. Often you can just mosey over to the purser's desk on the last evening, check to see that the bill they give you looks right, and sign your name.

LUGGAGE PROCEDURES

With thousands of suitcases to deal with, big ships have established the routine of requiring guests to pack the night before they disembark. You will be asked to leave your bags (except for your carry-ons) in the hallway before you retire for the night—usually, you will be required to leave them in the hallway by midnight. The bags will be picked up overnight and placed in the cruise terminal before passengers are allowed to disembark. It's important to make sure that your bags are tagged with the luggage tags given to you by the cruise line toward the end of your cruise. These are not the same tags you arrived with; rather, they're color-coded to indicate deck number and disembarkation order—the order in which they'll likely be arranged on the dock. If you need more tags, alert your cabin steward or the purser's staff. You may also have the option of carrying your own bags off if they are not too heavy for you to do so.

If you booked your air travel through the cruise line, you may be able to check in your luggage for your flight at the cruise terminal. Make sure you receive your luggage claim checks. You may even be able to get your flight boarding passes at the cruise terminal, saving you waiting in line at the airport. You will then proceed to a bus that will take you to the airport.

If you're signed up for a **post-cruise tour,** special instructions will be given by the cruise line.

DISEMBARKATION

You won't be able to get off the ship until it is cleared by Customs and other authorities, a process that usually takes 90 minutes or more. In most cases, you'll be asked to vacate your cabin by 8am and wait in one of the ship's lounges. If you have a flight home on the same day, you will disembark based on your flight departure time. Passengers with mobility problems, those who booked suites, and travelers who will be staying on in the port will often be disembarked early. If you have booked a land package through the cruise line, they will have transportation waiting to take you from the ship to your hotel.

CUSTOMS & IMMIGRATION

If your cruise begins or ends in Canada, you'll have to clear Canadian Customs and Immigration, which usually means that your name goes on a list that is reviewed by authorities. You must fill out a Customs declaration form, and you may be required to show your passport.

When disembarking in U.S. ports after starting out from Vancouver, non-U.S. citizens (including green-card holders) will be required to meet with U.S. Immigration authorities, usually in a lounge or theater, when the ship arrives at the port. You will have to bring your passport receipt with you, and all family members must attend.

The U.S. Customs & Border Protection Service has a preclearance program in Vancouver that allows cruise passengers to go through Customs there before boarding their flights home. The procedure in Vancouver—purely because of the lower number of travelers to be processed—is generally a lot faster than it is at LAX, JFK, or other U.S. airport facilities, where half a dozen flights arrive close together.

5

The Cruise Lines, Part 1: The Big Ships

Here's where the rudder hits the road: It's time to choose the ship that will be your home away from home for the duration of your Alaska cruise.

As we said earlier, your biggest decision is whether you want to sail on a big ship or a small ship. So that you can more easily compare like with like, in this chapter we'll deal with the big and midsize ships; in chapter 6, we'll discuss the small ships.

For some years, the ships in Alaska have been getting bigger and bigger, and in terms of total tonnage offered, Princess ships still lead. The company's *Diamond Princess* and *Sapphire Princess,* both in their fifth Alaska season, will again be plying the waters of the 49th State, as will the *Golden Princess* and the *Star Princess,* two of the company's three 109,000-ton Grand Class vessels. The *Star Princess* is returning to Alaska after an absence of 5 years. The *Diamond Princess* and *Sapphire Princess,* each weighing in at 113,000 tons and capable of carrying 2,670 passengers, will sail from Vancouver; the *Golden* and *Star Princesses* from Seattle.

There are other megaships that don't sport the Princess colors: Celebrity Cruises' returning *Summit* and *Infinity* each weigh 91,000 tons and carry 1,950 passengers. Royal Caribbean's 90,000-ton, 2,100-berth *Radiance of the Seas* will be spending its sixth summer in Alaska, joined by similarly dimensioned sister *Serenade of the Seas.* Carnival Cruise Lines' returning *Carnival Spirit* weighs 88,500 tons and carries 2,124 passengers. Holland America Line again has eight ships in Alaska this year, though none of them is technically a "megaship." The largest of the lot—the *Noordam, Oosterdam, Zuiderdam,* and *Westerdam*—are "only" a little in excess of 80,000 tons and carry fewer than 2,000 passengers apiece. (By today's standards, that's positively mid-size!) The Regent's *Seven Seas Mariner* and Silversea's returning *Silver Shadow*—the only true luxury ships in this market—are tiny compared to the vessels we mention here. However, they're a good bit bigger than the ships in the next chapter, and they offer a full range of big-ship amenities, so we've kept them in with the big guys. The beauty of some of the latter-day megaships is that they are designed so that it doesn't seem as though you're sharing your vacation with thousands of others. There are lots of nooks and crannies in which to relax and hide far from the maddening crowd, so to speak.

The evolution of cruise ships is almost worth a chapter all by itself, but we'll address it here in shorter order. Two decades ago, major cruise lines operated ships that ranged from about 20,000 to 40,000 gross registered tons. These were considered "big" ships. Their cabins had portholes or, at best, picture windows that didn't open. The ships had one dining room, with two seatings for lunch and dinner, and a snack bar/buffet as pretty much the only alternative. Many of them had large numbers of inside cabins, and all of their cabins, inside and outside, tended to be rather basic (in some cases, downright spartan). Only the very best half-dozen or so suites on some of them had private verandas. The *Royal Princess* of Princess Cruises, which debuted in 1984, set industry standards for number of verandas. Of its 600 staterooms, no fewer than 150 of them were balcony equipped. The elegant ship also had no inside rooms. At 45,000 tons, it was getting up there in size and was proving to the industry that extra luxury could be provided at the prevailing rate. Its builder, the Wartsila Yard in Helsinki, Finland, trumpeted the message that *Royal Princess* was the "most advanced cruise ship ever built."

Whether that claim was strictly accurate or not, other cruise lines took notice. Suddenly, verandas were included on their new builds. In some cases, inside rooms were greatly reduced in number, or eliminated entirely. As the demand for cruises grew—stoked by the popular TV show *The Love Boat*—the lines began to look for bigger and better ways to make life at sea enjoyable for their passengers. Advances in shipbuilding technology allowed them to move up from 45,000 GRT, as in the case of the *Royal Princess,* to 65,000 GRT, to 90,000 GRT, and now to 145,000 GRT. The additional space made possible more technologically advanced showrooms, million-dollar collections of original art, better trained and higher-paid entertainment directors, flashy and extensive children's and teens' centers—and alternative dining facilities. Lots and lots of alternative dining facilities! Nowadays, the roster of available food choices on cruise ships would do credit to the Manhattan telephone directory. Depending on your ship, you can have Italian, Tex-Mex, Cajun, Asian fusion, French, even good old British fish and chips. And more and more cruise ships are going to an open seating policy (come when you like, eat with whom you like). On some ships, it is possible nowadays to eat dinner in a different restaurant every night of your cruise.

Now, the *Royal Princess* didn't make all *that* happen; in fact, the ship has virtually no alternative dining sites. But there can be no question that it raised the standards for cruising, so Princess's rivals had to get a little more creative. Improvements in marine architecture and building techniques did the rest. (The *Royal Princess,* by the way, left the fleet 2 years ago and is now sailing for P&O Cruises in London.)

The ships featured in this chapter vary in size, age, and offerings, but share the common thread of having scads of activities and entertainment offerings. You will not be roughing it. On these ships you'll find swimming pools, health clubs, spas, nightclubs, movie theaters, shops, casinos, multiple restaurants and bars, special kids' playrooms, and, in some cases, sports decks, virtual golf, computer rooms, martini bars, and cigar clubs, as well as the aforementioned quiet spaces where you can get away from it all. Onboard activities generally include games, contests, classes, and lectures, plus a variety of entertainment options and show productions, some very sophisticated. An array of shore excursions is offered, for which you will have to pay extra. Cabins vary in size and amenities but are usually roomy enough for the time you'll be spending aboard. And with all the public rooms, you won't be spending much time in your cabin anyway.

1 Some Components of Our Cruise-Line Reviews

Each cruise line's review begins with a quick word about the line in general and a short summation of the kind of cruise experience you can expect to have aboard that line. The text that follows fleshes out the review, providing all the details you need to get a feel for what kind of vacation the cruise line will give you.

The individual ship reviews that follow the general cruise-line description get into the nitty-gritty, giving you all the details on the ships' accommodations, facilities, amenities, comfort levels, and upkeep.

New Cruisers

There is a saying in the industry that nobody should cruise just once. On any voyage, a ship could encounter bad weather. On any given day at sea, the only seat left in the show lounge might be behind an unforgiving pillar. Or a technical problem might affect the enjoyment of the onboard experience. Jerry remembers vividly one occasion on which the air-conditioning on a ship on which he was traveling—which shall remain nameless—went out for half a day. It was an uncomfortable time and could have turned a neophyte off cruising forever. That would have been a mistake. In travel, there is liable to be an occasional snafu. Your hotel room is not available, even though you have a valid confirmation number. Your flight is canceled. The luxury car you thought you rented is not on the lot, and all that's available is a minisubcompact. But you don't stop flying, you don't refuse to stay in a hotel ever again, and you don't stop renting cars. Nor should one unforeseen problem on a cruise ship cause you to swear off the product forever. Give it another go. On a different cruise line, if you prefer. If you still haven't had the enjoyable experience that millions of others have discovered, then, and only then, maybe it's time to abandon hope of becoming a cruise aficionado.

People feel very strongly about ships. For centuries, mariners have imbued their vessels with human personalities, usually referring to an individual ship as "her." In fact, an old (really old) seafaring superstition holds that women should never be allowed aboard a ship because the ship, being a woman herself, will get jealous. It's a fact that people bond with the ships aboard which they sail. They find themselves in the gift shop loading up on T-shirts with the ship's name emblazoned on the front. They get to port and the first question they ask other cruisers they meet is "Which ship are you sailing on?" They engage in a (usually) friendly comparison, and both parties walk away knowing in their hearts that their ship is the best. We know people who have sailed the same ship a dozen times or more and feel as warmly about it as though it were their own summer cottage. That's why, when looking at the reviews, you want to look for a ship that says "you."

We've listed some of the ships' vital statistics—ship size, years built and most recently refurbished, number of cabins, number of crew—to help you compare. Size is listed in tons. Note that these are not actual measures of weight, but gross register tons (GRTs), which is a measure of the interior space used to produce revenue on a ship. One GRT equals 100 cubic feet of enclosed, revenue-generating space. Among the crew/officers statistics, an important one is the **passenger/crew ratio,** which tells you, in theory, how many passengers each crew member is expected to serve and, thus, how much personal service you can expect.

Note that when several vessels are members of a class—built on the same design, with usually only minor variations in decor and attractions—we've grouped the ships together into one class review.

STARS
THE RATINGS

To make things easier on everyone, we've developed a simple ratings system that covers those things that vary from vessel to vessel—quality and size of the cabins and public spaces, comfort, cleanliness and maintenance, decor, number and quality of dining options, gyms/spas (and for the small-adventure lines that don't have gyms and spas, a slightly different system, see p. 124), and children's facilities—plus a rating for the overall enjoyment of the onboard experience. We've given each ship an overall **star rating** (for example, ★★★) based on the combined total of our poor-to-outstanding ratings, translated into a 1-to-5 scale:

1	=	**Poor**	4	=	**Excellent**
2	=	**Fair**	5	=	**Outstanding**
3	=	**Good**			

In instances when the category doesn't apply to a particular ship (for example, none of the adventure ships has children's facilities), we've simply noted "not applicable" (N/A) and absented the category from the total combined score, as these unavailable amenities will be considered a deficiency only if you plan to travel with kids.

Now for a bit of philosophy: The cruise biz today offers a profusion of experiences so different that comparing all ships by the same set of criteria would be like comparing a Park Avenue apartment to an A-frame in Aspen. That's why, to rate the ships, we've used a sliding scale, rating ships on a curve that compares them only with others in their category—big vs. small (more mainstream vs. adventure). Once you've determined what kind of experience is right for you, you can look for the best ships in that category based on your particular needs.

ITINERARIES

Each cruise-line review includes a chart showing itineraries for each ship the line has assigned to Alaska for 2008. Often a ship sails on alternating itineraries—for instance, sailing southbound from Seward (or, in the case of Princess and Carnival, Whittier) to Vancouver 1 week and doing the same route in reverse the next. When this is the case, we've listed both and noted that they alternate. These cruises represent the Gulf of Alaska routing, as opposed to the Inside Passage itinerary, which is generally round-trip from Seattle or Vancouver. (Some longer round-trip cruises depart San Francisco.) All itineraries are subject to change. Consult your travel agent for exact sailing dates.

The variety of cruise itineraries and of ports of embarkation (and disembarkation, for that matter) also demonstrates the maturing of the cruise industry and the growth in demand for the product. Not so long ago, just about the only thing you could do in Alaska cruising was a Vancouver–Vancouver Inside Passage loop. Very few lines had Gulf itineraries. It was simply easier for the ship operators to stick with the tried and true. People wanted it. Ships' crews got into a rhythm—arrive in Vancouver at 8am, discharge passengers, take on new ones, and start all over again. But demand began to outstrip the available berths. San Francisco became an attractive alternative, then Seattle. People who had done the Inside Passage round-trip began to demand a new experience—a cruise across the Gulf. Princess and Holland America, sister companies in the Carnival Corp. family who had invested heavily on a physical presence in Alaska (hotels/lodges, motorcoaches, railcars for land tour add-ons in the Denali Park corridor between Anchorage and Fairbanks), began to see that route as the way to go. Princess and another affiliate company, Carnival Cruises, have further tweaked the itinerary by using Whittier rather than Seward as the northern terminal of the Gulf cruises because it's closer to Anchorage. (Not much, but when you're on vacation, every minute counts!) Royal Caribbean Cruises has also invested heavily in Denali railcars and motorcoaches for its Royal Caribbean International and Celebrity brands. Those lines that do not have a strong investment in Alaska land components still tend to stick with the Vancouver (or Seattle) originating round-trip.

Weddings at Sea

Lovers have long known that there is nothing as romantic as cruising. Luxury cruise ships have been vastly popular honeymoon vehicles for decades. And recently, with the growing popularity of cruises, they have assumed new significance in the marriage business. Ship operators now make it easier to tie the knot either in a port of call during the voyage or on board the vessel. Most lines will help you set it all up—if you give them enough advance notice. They will provide the music, the photographer, the bouquets, the champagne, hors d'oeuvres, the cake, and other frills and fripperies. All you have to do is bring somebody to share your "I do" moment. The wedding package might cost you $1,000 or so over the price of your cabin.

In Alaska this year, Carnival, Celebrity, NCL, Royal Caribbean, and Holland America Line allow you to hold your marriage ceremony in a specially decorated lounge on board while in port, officiated by a local clergyman or justice of the peace. Princess goes one better: Whereas before you could be married only on the *Diamond, Sapphire, Island,* and *Coral Princesses,* all of them equipped with wedding chapels in which the captain himself can conduct the ceremony, now you can be wed on any ship in the Princess fleet, including those in Alaska in 2008. It's all perfectly legal. The ships have been reflagged to Bermuda registry, the authority under which your nuptials will be certified. The captain of the *Carnival Spirit* can also marry couples at sea (including homosexual couples) in the waters off British Columbia.

If you want guests to attend your special onboard moment while in port, the ship line must be notified well in advance, and your guests will be required to produce valid ID and to go through the same kind of screening process that passengers go through. Princess makes it easy for friends and family on shore to share the event by filming the entire process and then posting it on a special webcam found on its website (**www.princess.com**). Click on "Ships" and then "Bridge Cams." And, no, it's not really live. The images are there for all to see long after the rites are concluded.

No matter where you wed, you have to have a valid U.S. marriage license (or a Canadian license, if you want to bid farewell to the single life in one of the British Columbia ports). The cruise line's wedding planner will help you set that up. Just remember to plan in advance—these things take time.

For your convenience, we've listed the **cruisetours and add-ons** you can book with your cruise, and we've provided brochure prices for these as well—where possible! Though some lines make their plans (and set their prices) early, others do not. Therefore, at press time, some of the numbers were not readily available.

PRICES

We've listed the prices for cabins and suites. We stress that all of the prices listed reflect the line's **brochure rates,** so depending on how early you book and on any special deals the lines are offering, you may get a rate substantially below what we've listed.

(Discounts can run as high as 60% or thereabouts.) Rates are per night for a 7-night cruise, per person, and are based on double occupancy. If the ship does not sail 7-night itineraries, we've noted that and offer per diem rates for whatever itineraries it does sail. (The *Dawn Princess,* for instance, operates a 10-night round-trip Inside Passage pattern out of San Francisco.)

Our rates are based on the basic types of accommodations:

- Inside cabin (one without windows)
- Outside cabin (one with windows)
- Suite

Remember that cruise ships generally have several different categories of cabins within each of these three basic divisions, all priced differently, which is why on some ships you'll see a rather broad range in each category.

Please keep something else in mind. As they say in the business, "Buy as much cruise as you can afford." If you go in with the attitude that you refuse to buy anything but the least expensive inside cabin, you may be doing yourself a disservice. The idea that "Oh, I'm not going to spend any time in my cabin anyway, so what does it matter if it's inside or outside, big or small?" isn't really valid. You *will* spend time in your cabin, and sometimes having no exposure to the outside world can be awfully claustrophobic. You may find that for a few hundred dollars more, you can upgrade to an outside room. Or, if you're planning to invest in an outside cabin, you may find that you could reserve a room with a balcony if you dug just a little deeper into the purse. This is not to say you have to go deeply into debt to buy the best—just that you should investigate the possibility of buying something a little better.

2 Carnival Cruise Lines

Carnival Place, 3655 NW 87th Ave., Miami, FL 33178-2428. ℭ 800/CARNIVAL. Fax 305/471-4740. www.carnival.com.

THE LINE IN A NUTSHELL   Almost the definition of mass market, Carnival is the Big Kahuna of the industry, boasting a modern fleet of big ships that are the boldest, most innovative, and most successful on the seas. And nonstop fun (if you have the energy after a hearty day of Alaska cruising) is the name of the game on board.

THE EXPERIENCE   The decor on Carnival's ships is eclectic and definitely glitzy, offering something of a theme-park ambience. Translating the line's warm-weather, fun-in-the-sun experience to Alaska has meant combining the "24-hour orgy of good times" philosophy with opportunities to experience the natural wonders of the state, so you may find yourself bellying up to the rail with a multicolored party drink to gawk at a glacier. Drinking and R-rated comedians are part of the scene, and the casino is nearly always hopping, although the party scene is not as hearty in Alaska as on the line's Caribbean sailings. This, of course, is either a plus or a minus, depending on your taste. Carnival does not pretend to be a luxury experience. It doesn't claim to have the best food (although its recently upgraded food offerings are pretty darn good) and it doesn't promise 'round-the-clock pampering. The motto is "fun," and with a big focus on entertainment, friendly service, and creative cruise directors (they can be corny sometimes, but at least they're lively), that's what Carnival delivers.

Pros

- **Entertainment.** Carnival's entertainment is among the industry's best, with each ship boasting dozens of dancers, a 10-piece orchestra, comedians, jugglers, and numerous live bands, including a resident jazz trio, as well as a big casino.

- **Children's program.** Carnival attracts a slew of families, and its children's program does an expert job of keeping them occupied, with some Alaska-specific activities thrown into the mix of other amusements. The line offers a special series of shore excursions designed for teens.

Cons

- **Service.** The international crew doesn't provide terribly refined service, but that's not the point here, is it?
- **Crowds.** This is a big ship with lots of people on board, and you are occasionally aware of that fact, like when you want to get off at a port and have to wait in line.

THE FLEET   The 2,124-passenger megaship *Carnival Spirit* returns to Alaska in 2008. It offers plenty of activities, great pool and hot-tub spaces (some covered for use in chillier weather), a big ocean-view gym and spa, and more dining options than your doctor would say is advisable.

PASSENGER PROFILE   Overall, Carnival has some of the youngest demographics in the industry; the crowd on Alaska cruises is a tad older than on the line's Caribbean sailings, however. There will be more people over 50 than under. You'll find couples, a few singles, and a good share of families. In fact, the line carries some 575,000 kids a year. This is the same crowd that can be found in Las Vegas and at Florida's megaresorts. Even though passengers on the Alaska sailings may be older, they tend to be young at heart. This is not your average sedentary, bird-watching crowd. Passengers want to see whales, but they will also dance the Macarena.

DINING   Food is bountiful, and the cuisine is traditional American: Red meat is popular on these ships. Carnival has Georges Blanc, one of France's master chefs (three Michelin stars for the past 25 years), creating one-of-a-kind dishes that appear on dining room menus. You'll spot them as the Georges Blanc Signature Selections. In addition, they do delicious preparations of more "nouveau" dishes such as broiled Chilean sea bass with truffle butter, and smoked turkey tenderloin with asparagus tips. The line features fresh salmon on Alaska sailings. In 2007, the line introduced the new gourmet Spa Carnival fare on menus, for those seeking healthier options. Pasta and vegetarian choices are also offered nightly. Meals are served at assigned tables, with two seatings per meal. The casual lunch buffets include international (Japanese, Indian, et al, with a different cuisine featured daily), deli, rotisserie, and pizza stations; and the breakfast buffet, in the same location—La Playa Grill, on Lido Deck—offers everything from made-to-order egg dishes to cold cereals and pastries. Many passengers prefer to eat these meals in La Playa rather than in the main dining room. The *Spirit* also adds the special treat of a truly superb reservations-only supper club, where for a fee of $30 per person, you can dine on a great steak, dancing between courses to music provided by a singer and keyboardist.

ACTIVITIES   If Atlantic City and Las Vegas appeal to you, Carnival will, too. What you'll get is fun—lots of it, professionally and insistently delivered and spangled with glitter. Cocktails inevitably begin to flow before lunch. You can learn to country-line dance or ballroom dance, take cooking lessons, learn to play bridge, watch first-run movies, and practice your golf swing by smashing balls into a net. Among the newer offerings is a photo safari in Juneau led by a professional photographer. Plus, there are always the onboard staple activities of eating, drinking, and shopping, and the Alaska-specific naturalist lectures that are delivered daily. Once in port, Carnival lives up to its "more is more" ethos by offering more than 100 shore excursions in Alaska. These are divided into categories of easy, moderate, and adventure. Internet cafes offer Internet

Carnival Fleet Itineraries

Ship	Itineraries
Carnival Spirit	**7-night northbound Gulf of Alaska:** From Vancouver to Whittier, visiting Ketchikan, Juneau, Skagway, and Sitka, and cruising Prince William Sound (to view College Fjord). May–Aug. **7-night southbound Gulf of Alaska:** From Whittier to Vancouver, visiting Sitka, Juneau, Skagway, and Ketchikan, and cruising Prince William Sound (to view College Fjord). May–Sept. **7-night Glacier Bay:** Sails round-trip from Vancouver, visiting Juneau, Skagway, Ketchikan, the Inside Passage, and Glacier Bay. May–Sept.

access for 75¢ a minute, with a 10-minute minimum, and more discounted bulk use packages. The ships in the fleet have also all been outfitted with Wi-Fi for those who bring their own laptops (for the same fee as above).

Ships also offer wine tastings, motivated by former Carnival president and oenophile Bob Dickinson, and Carnival's Presidential Wine Club program, where membership buys you monthly wine shipments, among other wine benefits. The ships also now offer technology that allows you to use your own cellphone at sea, rather than having to pay steep shipboard phone rates.

CHILDREN'S PROGRAM   Camp Carnival is an expertly run program for children and teens that's loaded with kid-pleasing activities, giving Mom and Dad some downtime. In Alaska, these activities include everything from Native American arts-and-crafts sessions to lectures conducted by wildlife experts, and there are special shore excursions for teens. On the *Spirit,* parents of little kids can even request beepers so that they can keep in touch.

ENTERTAINMENT   Carnival consistently offers the most lavish entertainment extravaganzas afloat, spending millions on stage sets, choreography, and acoustical equipment that leave many other floating theaters in their wake. Each Carnival mega-ship carries flamboyantly costumed dancers and singers (on the *Spirit,* there's a cast of about 20) and a 10-piece orchestra, plus comedians, jugglers, acrobats, rock 'n' roll bands, country-western bands, classical string trios, jazz trios, pianists, and big bands.

SERVICE   As we said before, Carnival service ain't exactly what you'd call "refined," but it is professional. A Carnival ship is a well-oiled machine, and you'll certainly get what you need—but not much more. When you board the ship, for instance, you're welcomed by polite staff at the gangway, given a diagram of the ship's layout, and then pointed in the right direction to find your cabin on your own, carry-on luggage in tow. It is possible on the *Spirit* to have your gratuities (about $10 per passenger per day) automatically charged to your shipboard account.

There is a laundry service on board (for washing and pressing only) that charges by the piece, as well as a handful of self-service laundry rooms with irons and coin-operated washing machines and dryers. Dry cleaning is not available.

CRUISETOURS & ADD-ON PROGRAMS   Three- and 4-night land packages are available in the Denali corridor in conjunction with the services of one of Carnival's affiliate companies, Holland America Line. These range in price from $1,188 to $1,439 per person, double occupancy, in addition to the cruise price. Pre- and post-cruise nights are available in a number of hotels in Seattle, Vancouver, and Anchorage, starting at $178 per night double.

Carnival Spirit

The Verdict

The *Spirit* is glitzy Vegas, with more bars and lounges than you'll be able to visit. The dining room is multistory, and there are cool extras like a reservations-only dinner club and a wedding chapel.

Carnival Spirit *(photo: Gero Mylius, Indav Ltd.)*

Specifications

Size (in Tons)	88,500	Crew	920
Passengers (Double Occ.)	2,124	Passenger/Crew Ratio	2.3 to 1
Passenger/Space Ratio	41.7	Year Launched	2001
Total Cabins/Veranda Cabins	1,062/682	Last Major Refurbishment	N/A

Frommer's Ratings (Scale of 1–5)   ★★★★ ½

Cabin Comfort & Amenities	5	Dining Options	4
Ship Cleanliness & Maintenance	4	Gym, Spa & Sports Facilities	5
Public Comfort/Space	4	Children's Facilities	5
Decor	4	Enjoyment Factor	4

THE SHIP IN GENERAL   The *Spirit* is big and impressive, even if some may find the interior a bit over the top (but after a few days on board, it may grow on you). Rooms reflect a purposeful mismatch of styles, including Art Nouveau, Art Deco, Empire, Gothic, and Egyptian, with the decor featuring expensive materials, such as burled wood, marble, leather, copper, and even gold gild. In other words, legendary Carnival designer Joe Farcus showed little restraint. Love it or not, you'll certainly be wowed.

CABINS   Some 80% of the cabins on this ship boast ocean views, and of those, 80% have private balconies, a big plus in a market like Alaska where views are the main draw. Cabins are larger than those you'll find on other lines in the same price category, and they are mostly furnished with twin beds that can be converted to king size. (A few have upper and lower berths that cannot be converted.) All cabins come with a TV, wall safe, and telephone; oceanview cabins also come with bathrobes and coral-colored leather couches with nifty storage drawers underneath. There are connecting cabins available for families or groups traveling together. Suites are offered at several different levels, each with separate sleeping, sitting, and dressing areas, plus double sinks, a bathtub, and a large balcony. Sixteen cabins are wheelchair accessible. In 2006, Carnival introduced the Carnival Comfort Bed sleep system featuring plush mattresses, fluffy duvets (no more scratchy wool blankets for this line), and a choice of pillow for its suite guests. And not to miss a marketing opportunity, if you fall in love with the new linens and more, you can buy them online at www.carnival comfortbed.com.

Cabins & Rates

Cabins	Per Diem Rates	Sq. Ft.	Fridge	Hair Dryer	Sitting Area	TV
Inside Passage						
Inside	$118–$125	185	yes	yes	no	yes
Outside	$161–$189	220–260*	yes	yes	yes	yes
Suites	$261	340–430*	yes	yes	yes	yes
Gulf of Alaska						
Inside	$121–$128	185	yes	yes	no	yes
Outside	$164–$192	220–260*	yes	yes	yes	yes
Suites	$264	340–430*	yes	yes	yes	yes

Includes veranda

PUBLIC AREAS The ship's soaring atrium spans 11 decks. There are dozens of bars and lounges, including a piano bar, a sports bar, and a jazz club. A lobby bar offers live music and a chance to take in the vast dimensions of the ship. A particularly fun room is the two-level Jackson Pollock–inspired disco, with paint-splattered walls, which, depending on your particular Alaska sailing, may be hopping till dawn or may just host a dozen or so heavy drinkers. A better hangout spot, we think, is the nearby Deco bar, where a jazz trio plays nightly and cigar smoking is allowed (we've even seen the captain hanging out here).

The ship, which debuted as a new class for Carnival, consciously offers the best features of the line's earlier ships, including an expansive outdoor area with three swimming pools (there is a retractable dome over the main pool so that you can take a dip no matter what the weather), four whirlpools, and a water slide; a high-tech children's play center with computers and wall of video monitors; a multilevel oceanview fitness facility; numerous clubs and lounges; and a variety of eating and entertainment options. Among the interesting features is what was the line's first wedding chapel (you can get married at sea on this ship when it sails in Canadian waters, same-sex marriages included), as well as a mostly outdoor promenade (if you are doing a full tour around the ship, you have to take a few steps inside). The ship also has ultra-modern engines and waste treatment and disposal systems to make it more environmentally friendly. And the *Spirit* offers more space per passenger than most ships in the Alaska market.

The hundreds of onboard activities for which Carnival is famous, including Vegas-style shows and casino action (the ship's Louis XIV casino is one of the largest at sea), keep passengers on the *Spirit* on the fast track to that famous and oft-mentioned fun. It's up to you to find time to stop and catch the scenery, which you can do both from the generous open-deck spaces and from some (but not many) indoor spaces. For kids, there's a children's playroom, children's pool, and video arcade. The *Spirit*'s library doubles as an Internet cafe, and the clicking of the computers may be annoying to those who want to read a book there. Shoppers will find plenty of enticements at the ship's shopping arcade, including Fendi and Tommy Hilfiger products.

Carnival passengers also have the capability of using their personal cellphones anywhere at sea.

DINING OPTIONS The ship's handsome atrium is topped with a red stained-glass dome that is part of the Nouveau Supper Club, a reservations-only ($30 per person supplement) steakhouse-style restaurant featuring live entertainment. Some people might consider the spot a little steep, but this is not your run-of-the mill restaurant, operating on getting tables filled by two or three changes of customers in the evening. Rather, it's an intimate room in which passengers are encouraged to linger, to savor, to dance between courses, and to enjoy the music—a truly elegant and enjoyable experience. The two-level main dining room is done up in Napoleonic splendor, and a 24-hour pizzeria and 24-hour room service will keep you from getting hungry.

POOL, FITNESS, SPA & SPORTS FACILITIES   The ship has three pools, including one with a retractable dome, as well as a children's splash pool. There is a freestanding water slide on the top deck. The gym offers an interesting tiered design and more than 50 exercise machines, as well as a spacious aerobics studio. There are windows, so you won't miss the scenery. The spa has a dozen treatment rooms and an indoor sunning area with a whirlpool. The ship also offers three additional whirlpools and a jogging/walking track (15 laps = 1 mile).

3 Celebrity Cruises

1050 Caribbean Way, Miami, FL 33132. © **800/437-3111** or 305/262-8322. Fax 800/437-5111. www.celebrity cruises.com.

THE LINE IN A NUTSHELL   With a premium fleet that's among the best designed in the cruise industry, Celebrity Cruises offers a great experience: classy, tasteful, and luxurious. You'll be pampered (as their commercials say)—at a moderate price.

THE EXPERIENCE   Each of the Celebrity ships is spacious and comfortable, mixing modern and Art Deco styles and throwing in an astoundingly cutting-edge art collection. The line's genteel service is exceptional: Staff members in our experience are polite and professional, and contribute greatly to the cruise experience. Dining-wise, Celebrity shines, offering innovative cuisine that's a cut above the fare offered by some the other mainstream lines.

Celebrity gets the "best of" nod in a lot of categories: The AquaSpas on the line's megaships are tops for mainstream lines, the art collections fleetwide are the most compelling, and the onboard activities are among the most varied. Like all the big-ship lines, Celebrity offers lots for its passengers to do, but it focuses on mellower pursuits and innovative programming.

It's interesting to note that Celebrity (and its affiliate company, Royal Caribbean International) has created the new port of Icy Strait Point. The port is growing—it was created from a cannery dock—and lies between Juneau and Glacier Bay, offering a prime vantage point for whale- and wildlife-watching and easier access to the Alaskan wilderness.

Pros

- **Spectacular spas and gyms.** Beautiful to look at and well stocked, the spas and gyms on the *Infinity, Mercury,* and *Millennium* (and Celebrity's other non-Alaska megaships) are among the best at sea today.
- **Fabulous food.** Celebrity cuisine is rated highly among mainstream cruise lines.
- **Innovative everything.** Celebrity's entertainment, art, service, spas, and cuisine are some of the most groundbreaking in the industry. Its ships were among the first in the industry to display major art collections onboard, and its menus have long recognized the need for vegetarian, low-sodium, heart-conscious, and other dishes.

Cons

- **Occasional crowding.** Pack a couple thousand people onto a ship (pretty much any ship), and you'll get crowds at times, such as during buffets and when disembarking.

THE FLEET Celebrity's current Alaska fleet comprises *Infinity* and *Millennium* (both 91,000 tons, 1,950 passengers), and the slightly older *Mercury* (77,713 tons, 1870 passengers). All three ships offer a high degree of decorative panache and offer just the right combination of elegance, artfulness, excitement, and fun.

PASSENGER PROFILE The typical Celebrity guest is one who prefers to pursue his or her R & R at a relatively relaxed pace, with a minimum of aggressively promoted group activities. The overall atmosphere leans more toward sophistication and less to the kind of orgiastic Technicolor whoopee that you'll find aboard, say, a Carnival ship. Celebrity passengers are the type who prefer wine with dinner and maybe a tad more decorum than on some other ships, but they can kick up their heels with the beer-and-skittles crowd just fine if the occasion warrants. Most give the impression of being prosperous but not obscenely rich, congenial but not obsessively proper, animated and fun but not the types to wear a lampshade for a hat. You'll find everyone from kids to retirees, with a good number of couples in their 40s.

DINING Celebrity's cuisine, plentiful and served with style, is extra special, and leans toward American/European. This means that dishes are generally not low fat, although the line has eliminated trans-fats, and more healthy alternatives are always available. The company recently realigned its dining program by hiring Jacques Van Staden as head of our fleet's F&B program; Staden was nominated for a "rising star" by the prestigious James Beard Foundation.

Alaska cruises offer an array of Pacific Northwest regional specialties, and vegetarian dishes are featured at both lunch and dinner. If three meals a day in both informal and formal settings are not enough for you, Celebrity offers one of the most extensive 24-hour room-service menus in the industry, plus themed lunch buffets and late-night "Gourmet Bites" offered by waiters who roam all the public areas with trays of goodies. Meals in the alternative dining rooms on the *Millennium* and *Infinity,* offered on a reservations-only basis, are worth the $30 charge of admission; they may be the best romantic alternative restaurants at sea.

You can dine formally in the dining room or informally at buffets for breakfast and lunch, with a sushi bar and made-to-order pastas and pizzas offered nightly in the Casual Dining Boulevard. Dinner is served at two seatings in the main dining room. The Spa Cafe in a corner of the thalassotherapy pool area serves low-cal treats, including raw veggie platters, poached salmon with asparagus tips, vegetarian sushi, and pretty salads with tuna or chicken.

ACTIVITIES The line offers a variety of different activities, although many passengers prefer to go it on their own, enjoying the passing landscape and the company of friends. A typical day might offer bridge, darts, a culinary demonstration, a trapshooting competition, a fitness fashion show, a wine tasting, an art auction, and a volleyball tournament. Lectures on the various ports of call, the Alaska environment, glaciers, and Alaska culture are given by resident experts, who also provide commentary from the bridge as the ships arrive in port and, at other times, are available for one-on-one discussions with passengers. Cybercafes offer e-mail access for 95¢ a

Celebrity Fleet Itineraries

Ship	Itineraries
Infinity	**7-night Hubbard Glacier:** Round-trip cruises from Seattle visiting Ketchikan, Juneau, and Victoria, B.C., in addition to cruising the Inside Passage and beside Hubbard Glacier, May–Sept.
Mercury	**7-night Hubbard Glacier:** Round-trip cruises from Vancouver visiting Ketchikan, Hubbard Glacier, Sitka, Juneau, and Inside Passage, May–Sept.
Millennium	**7-night Northbound Gulf of Alaska:** Sails from Vancouver to Seward and reverse, visiting Juneau, Skagway, Icy Strait Point, Ketchikan, and Hubbard Glacier, May–Sept.

minute. The line also offers an Acupuncture at Sea program with medical specialists in Oriental medicine on board.

CHILDREN'S PROGRAM   For children, Celebrity ships employ a group of counselors who direct and supervise a camp-style children's program with activities geared toward different age groups. There's an impressive kids' play area and a separate lounge area for teens. Private and group babysitting are both available.

ENTERTAINMENT   Although entertainment is not generally cited as a reason to sail with Celebrity, the line's stage shows are none too shabby. You won't find any big-name entertainers, but you also won't find any obvious has-beens either—there's just a whole lot of singin' and dancin'. If you tire of the glitter, you can always find a cozy lounge or piano bar to curl up in, and if you tire of that, the disco and casino stay open late.

SERVICE   In the cabins, service is efficient and so unobtrusive you might never see your steward except at the beginning and end of your cruise. In the dining rooms, service is polite, professional, and cheerful. Five-star service can be had at the onboard beauty salon or barbershop, and massages can be scheduled at any hour of the day in the AquaSpa. Laundry, dry cleaning, and valet services are also available. If you stay in a suite, you really will be treated like royalty with a tuxedo-clad butler at your beck and call. The butler will serve you afternoon tea (or free cappuccino or espresso) and bring pre-dinner hors d'oeuvres. And yes, the butler will gladly shine your shoes too, at your request. Also available for those who can't quite afford a suite are Concierge Class rooms that come with perks like fresh flowers and fruit, a choice of pillow type, and oversized towels.

CRUISETOURS & ADD-ON PROGRAMS   Celebrity offers a couple of dozen cruisetours in conjunction with its three Alaska ships this year, ranging in length from 9 to 13 nights and priced from $1,700 per person double to $3,190 per person double, depending on the season and the staterooms chosen. Sixteen of the tours include a ride in Royal Celebrity Tours' luxurious domed railcars on the Denali Corridor and 2- or 3-night stays in the park area. These land portions complement the Gulf of Alaska cruises of the Summit. Other packages feature the Kenai Peninsula and the 650,000-acre Kenai Fjords National Park. Pre- and post-cruise hotel packages are also offered: from $249 per person per night, double occupancy, in Anchorage; from $149 per person per night, double occupancy, in Vancouver.

Celebrity Infinity • Celebrity Millennium

The Verdict

These ships are true winners, combining the kind of luxury you'd expect at a grande dame hotel with all the leisure, sports, and entertainment options of megaships. If these ships were high school seniors, they'd be heading to Harvard. They are the best in their class.

Infinity *(photo: Celebrity Cruises)*

Specifications

Size (in tons)	91,000	Crew	999
Passengers (Double Occ.)	1,950	Passenger/Crew Ratio	2 to 1
Passenger/Space Ratio	46	Year launched	2001
Total Cabins/Veranda Cabins	975/590	Last major refurbishment	N/A

Frommer's Rating (Scale 1–5)   ★★★★★

Cabin Comfort & Amenities	5	Dining Options	5
Ship Cleanliness & Maintenance	5	Gym, Spa & Sports Facilities	5
Public Comfort/Space	5	Children's Facilities	4
Decor	5	Enjoyment Factor	5

THE SHIPS IN GENERAL   When the *Millennium* debuted in 2000, it was hailed as one of the most beautiful ships afloat; guests were equally struck by the debut of its sister ship *Infinity* in 2001. Their design includes lots of glass through which to view the spectacular Alaska vistas.

CABINS   The smallest inside cabins are 170 square feet and boast a minibar, a sitting area with a sofa, and an entertainment unit with a TV. Premium oceanview cabins measure 191 square feet, and large oceanview cabins with verandas are indeed large—271 square feet, with floor-to-ceiling sliding-glass doors leading outside. Suites come in several sizes and offer such accoutrements as whirlpool tubs, DVD players, and walk-in closets. The fanciest suites also have whirlpools on the veranda. The two apartment-size Penthouse Suites (1,432 sq. ft. each), designed to evoke Park Avenue apartments, offer all of the above plus separate living and dining rooms, a foyer, a grand piano, a butler's pantry, a bedroom, exercise equipment, outbound fax, and— sure to be a favorite accessory—motorized drapes. Twenty-six cabins are wheelchair accessible.

Cabins & Rates

Cabins	Per Diems	Sq. Ft.	Fridge	Hair Dryer	Sitting Area	TV
Millennium						
Inside	$150–$291	170	yes	yes	yes	yes
Outside	$178–$414	170–191	yes	yes	yes	yes
Suites	$1,028–$1,456	251–1,432	yes	yes	yes	yes
Infinity						
Inside	$150–$320	170	yes	yes	no	yes
Outside	$178–$414	170–191	yes	yes	yes	yes
Suites	$800–$1,257	251–1,432	yes	yes	yes	yes

PUBLIC AREAS   Highlights on *Infinity* and *Millennium* include the flower-filled botanical conservatories located on top of each ship. Pull up a rattan chair, sit under a ceiling fan, and enjoy a drink. You won't miss the Alaska views from this oasis thanks to two-story-high windows. The conservatories offer classes in flower arranging. Want more? How about Acupuncture at Sea, a shopping center, pizzeria, casino, champagne bar, martini bar, cinema, theater, beauty salon, medical center, library, cybercafe, children's center, teen room, and arcade?

DINING OPTIONS   Both ships have two-tier dining rooms that feature live music by a pianist or a quartet. And they also offer gourmet dining experiences in intimate and romantic alternative restaurants: the SS United States on *Infinity* and the Olympic Restaurant on *Millennium* (a fee of $30 is charged to dine in these and reservations are required). Breakfast, lunch, and dinner also are offered in both formal and informal venues. Dinner is served in the main dining room, a two-story affair, in two seatings, as well as in the Casual Dining Boulevard and the Spa Café. After dinner, Michael's Club (on both ships), decorated like the parlor of a London men's club and devoted to the pleasures of live jazz and piano entertainment and fine cognac, comes into its own. Each ship also offers a coffee bar, Cova Café, which becomes a wine bar with light, live music by night, and if you're looking to spend the evening socializing with friends, there are various other bars tucked into nooks and crannies throughout the ship.

POOL, FITNESS, SPA & SPORTS FACILITIES   Spa aficionados, listen up: The *Infinity* and *Millennium* will not disappoint. The 25,000-square-foot AquaSpa complexes on both ships feature a range of esoteric hydrotherapy treatments; site-specific attractions such as the Persian Garden, a suite of beautiful New Age steam rooms and saunas; and a huge free-of-charge thalassotherapy whirlpool. In addition, there is the usual array of massage and beauty procedures, plus some unusual offerings, such as an Egyptian ginger-and-milk treatment. Next door to the spa, there's a very large, well-equipped cardio room and a large aerobics floor. On the top decks are facilities for basketball, volleyball, quoits (a game akin to horseshoes), and paddle tennis; a jogging track; a golf simulator; two pools; four whirlpools; and a multi-tiered sunning area. The swimming pool features a waterfall.

Celebrity Mercury

The Verdict

One of the most all-around attractive ships out there; a real winner.

Mercury *(photo: Matt Hannafin)*

Specifications

Size (in tons)	77,713	Crew	900
Passengers (Double Occ.)	1,896	Passenger/Crew Ratio	2 to 1
Passenger/Space Ratio	41	Year launched	1997
Total Cabins/Veranda Cabins	639/220	Last major refurbishment	N/A

Frommer's Rating (Scale 1-5)   ★★★★½

Cabin Comfort & Amenities	5	Dining Options	4
Ship Cleanliness & Maintenance	4	Gym, Spa & Sports Facilities	5
Public Comfort/Space	5	Children's Facilities	4
Decor	5	Enjoyment Factor	5

THE SHIP IN GENERAL   It's hard to say what's most striking about *Mercury*. The elegant spa and its 15,000-gallon thalassotherapy pool? The twin three- and four-story atria with serpentine staircases that seem to float without supports, and domed ceilings of painted glass? The two-story, old-world dining room set back in the stern, with grand floor-to-ceiling windows, allowing diners to spot the glow of the wake under moonlight? An intriguing modern-art collection? Take your pick: Any one points to a winner. We really like this ship!

CABINS   Inside cabins are about par for the industry standard, but outside cabins are larger than usual, and suites, which come in five different categories, are particularly spacious. Some, such as the Penthouse Suites, offer more living space than you find in many private homes, and the Sky Suites offer verandas that, at 179 square feet, are among the biggest aboard any ship.

Cabins are accented with wood trim and outfitted with built-in vanities. Closets and drawer space are roomy, and all standard cabins have twin beds that, when pushed together, convert into one full-size bed. Bathrooms are sizable and stylish. Celebrity is fond of high-tech gizmos, and you can actually order food, gamble, or check your bill from the comfort of your cabin via your interactive TV.

Butler service is offered to suite passengers. Eight cabins are wheelchair accessible.

Cabins & Rates

Cabins	Per Diem Rates	Sq. Ft.	Fridge	Hair Dryer	Sitting Area	TV
Inside	$128–$277	175	yes	yes	no	yes
Outside	$150–$343	210	yes	yes	yes	yes
Suites	$757–$1,757	1,433	yes	yes	yes	yes

PUBLIC AREAS   The interior of this ship is the product of a collaboration between a dozen design firms, who have created a diverse yet harmonious whole that provides just the right atmosphere without resorting to glitz. Our favorite is the champagne bar with champagne bubbles etched into the wall.

Throughout the ship, works from a multimillion-dollar art collection sometimes greet you at unexpected moments. Read the tags and you'll be impressed to find names such as Sol LeWitt, who designed a mural specifically for the vessel. There is a coffee bar for those craving caffeine, and various other bars pepper the ship and are great venues to spend time with friends.

There's a two-deck theater with an unobstructed view from every seat if you want to take in a stage show, and there's a cinema if you're in the mood for film. If you're looking for more active pleasures, there's always the disco and casino. For kids, there's a children's playroom, a children's pool, a teen center, and a video arcade.

DINING OPTIONS   As a somewhat older ship—built in the days when alternative dining was not considered a cruise-ship essential—the *Mercury* has a main dining room for breakfast, lunch, and dinner and the Lido Buffet for breakfast, lunch, and a more casual dinner, with menu and buffet service, as well as the options of a sushi bar and made-to-order pasta and pizza bar

POOL, FITNESS, SPA & SPORTS FACILITIES   *Mercury*'s Aqua Spa features a Moorish theme, with ornate tile work and latticed wood. There is a large hydrotherapy pool, plus steam rooms and saunas. The spa also features sometimes-pricey Elemis of London health and beauty services, including hairdressing, pedicures, manicures, massages, and various herbal treatments. We highly recommend the Rasul mud treatment for two. It's both relaxing and giggle-inducing—in the right company! The attached fitness area offers exceptionally large cardiovascular floors and a full complement of exercise machines. An 18-member fitness staff is on hand in the spa and gym area to assist you. Prearranged spa packages that you book before your cruise are available and are a wise idea, as some services (including Rasul) sell out fast.

The Resort Deck features a pair of good-size swimming areas rimmed with teak benches for sunning and relaxation. Even when the ship is full, these areas don't seem particularly crowded. A retractable dome covers one of the swimming pools during inclement weather. A basketball court, jogging/walking track, fitness center, golf simulator, and volleyball court fill out the offerings.

4 Holland America Line

300 Elliott Ave. W., Seattle, WA 98119. © 800/426-0327 or 206/281-3535. Fax 206/286-7110. www.hollandamerica.com.

THE LINE IN A NUTSHELL   More than any other line in Alaska, Holland America has managed to hang on to some of its seafaring history and tradition, offering a moderately priced, classic, casual yet refined ocean liner–like cruise experience.

THE EXPERIENCE   In Alaska terms, everybody else is an upstart when it comes to the cruise and cruisetour business. The line calls itself Alaska's most experienced travel operator, and the key to that claim is HAL's 1971 acquisition of the tour company Westours, founded in 1947 by the late Charles B. "Chuck" West, often called "Mr. Alaska" and widely recognized as the absolute pioneer of tourism to and within the state. (West later founded the small-ship line known as Cruise West.)

Cruising with HAL is less hectic than cruising on most other ships. The line strives for a quieter, sometimes almost sedate, presentation, although it has brightened up its entertainment package and its menus in recent years. Overall, the ships tend to be more evocative of the days of grand liners, with lots of dark wood and displays of nautical artifacts.

Late in 2003, the company embarked on a $225-million Signature of Excellence product- and service-enhancements program aimed at bringing all of the ships in the fleet up to the standards of the *Westerdam,* which debuted in 2004. One problem that always faces cruise lines is ensuring that their new builds—which are invariably fitted with all of the latest bells and whistles—don't overshadow their existing, older fleet mates. HAL's now completed $225-million investment was one way to minimize the disparity between the old and the new.

Since the inception of what it called the Signature of Excellence initiative, HAL has spent much of the upgrade dollars on such items as new amenities in all staterooms— massage showerheads, lighted magnifying makeup mirrors, hair dryers, extra-fluffy towels, terry-cloth robes, upgraded mattresses, and Egyptian-cotton bed linens. Guests in all rooms are now welcomed with a complimentary fruit basket. Suites will have plush duvets on every bed, VCR/DVD player, access to a well-stocked library of tapes and discs, and a fully stocked minibar. The entire fleet, including, of course, the ships in Alaska this year have now been completely equipped with the package.

The Pinnacle Grill, once a popular alternative restaurant on only some of the ships in the fleet, is now a fixture on them all. Table service and a wider range of hot meals have been added for evening dining in the Lido, formerly a buffet-style bistro.

The company allows passengers to board as early as 11:30am—a couple of hours earlier than the norm. And it makes the sometimes tedious and lengthy process of disembarking less onerous by letting passengers stay longer in their staterooms until they are called to leave.

Pros

- **Expertise that comes with experience.** The company's ships are young, but Holland America's experience is apparent. The company was formed in 1873 as the Netherlands-America Steamship Company. In 130-plus years, it figures that you'd get to know a little about operating oceangoing vessels.
- **Warm interiors.** Holland America ships, especially the more recent builds, tend to be understated, inviting, and easy on the eye; nothing garish here.
- **Signature of Excellence.** That mega-upgrade has really made HAL's accommodations much more attractive.

Cons

- **Sleepy nightlife.** If you're big on late-night dancing and barhopping, you may find yourself partying mostly with the entertainment staff, although the company is making an effort to offer more for night owls on its newer ships. You'll find more piano lounges, a bigger casino, and the like on the line's new ships.
- **Homogenous passenger profile.** To a certain degree, passengers tend to be a pretty homogenous group of low-key, 55+ North American couples who aren't overly adventurous. However, this profile is changing as younger passengers and families come aboard.

THE FLEET   Over the years, Holland America Line has picked up a lot of "stuff"— Holland America Tours (formed by the merger of Westours and Gray Line of Alaska), Gray Line of Seattle, Westmark Hotels, the Yukon Queen II river-/day boat that operates between Eagle, on the Alaska/Canada border, and Dawson City on the Yukon River, the *MV Ptarmigan* day boat that visits Portage Glacier outside Anchorage, a fleet of railcars (some built in the Old West style but with better viewing opportunities, and some built in more contemporary style more recently), an almost completely new fleet of motorcoaches, and a lot more.

HAL's control of so many of the components of tour packages once gave the cruise company a position of preeminence in the Alaska market, though that's been well and truly challenged in the past decade by Princess, which now has a heavy presence in the accommodations and ground-transportation business as well. (Actually, the similarities don't end there: Both lines have large fleets of primarily late-model ships, both strive for and achieve consistency in the cruise product, and both are pursuing and acquiring younger passengers and families.) HAL's philosophy is to stick with ships of fewer than 2,000 passengers—many of them significantly smaller—eschewing the 2,200- and 2,600-passenger megaships being built by some other lines, including Princess.

The company's 1,266-passenger Statendam-class ships—the *Statendam* (1993), *Maasdam* (1993), *Ryndam* (1994), and *Veendam* (1996)—are virtual carbon copies of the same attractive, well-crafted design, with a dash of glitz here and there. The 1,440-passenger *Volendam* officially debuted in 1999, and the 1,440-passenger *Zaandam* debuted in 2000. Brighter and bolder than the earlier ships, the *Volendam* and *Zaandam* share many features of the Statendam-class ships, though they are slightly larger in size (63,000 tons, as opposed to 59,652) and carry more passengers (1,440, against the Statendam class's 1,266). The 1,380-passenger *Amsterdam* is 61,000 tons and is one of two flagships in the fleet. (The other is the Amsterdam's sister ship, the *Rotterdam*.) The *Oosterdam* (85,000 tons and carrying 1,848 passengers) is one of four of HAL's Vista-class ships, the others being the *Zuiderdam*, which entered service in the winter of 2002; the *Westerdam*, which joined the fleet in 2003; and another similarly dimensioned vessel, the *Noordam*, checked in early in 2006. The company's smallest ship is the luxurious *Prinsendam*, just 38,000 tons and with a passenger capacity of under 800.

The company has never shown any inclination to plunge into the 100,000-plus-ton megaship market. Keeping the size down allows HAL to maintain its high service standards and a degree of intimacy while enabling the line's ships to offer all of the amenities of its larger brethren.

In 2008, the line will have 168 cruises on eight vessels on either Inside Passage of Gulf of Alaska patterns.

PASSENGER PROFILE   Holland America's passenger profile used to reflect a somewhat older crowd than on other ships. Now the average age is dropping, thanks to both an increased emphasis on the line's Club HAL program for children and some updating of the onboard entertainment offerings. HAL's passenger records in Alaska show a high volume of middle-aged-and-up vacationers (the same demographic as aboard many of its competitors' ships), but on any given cruise, records are also likely to list a few dozen passengers between the ages of, say, 5 and 16. This trend gathered its initial momentum a few years ago in Europe, a destination that, parents seem to think, has more kid appeal. It's spilled over into Alaska more recently, mainly thanks to the cruise line's added emphasis on generational travel and family reunion travel, a growing segment of the market, and also due to the industry's post–9/11 concentration on domestic destinations.

The more mature among Holland America's passengers are likely to be repeat HAL passengers, often retirees. They are usually not Fortune-500 rich—they are looking for solid value for their money, and they get it from this line.

DINING Years ago, HAL's meals were as traditional as its architecture and its itin- eraries. In the last few years, though, it's become a lot more adventurous in all three areas. The variety of dishes on the menu is as good as on any other premium line, and the quality of the food is generally high throughout the fleet. Don't look for lots of pastas; do look for excellent soups. Vegetarian options are available at every meal, and the line has excellent veggie burgers at the on-deck grill.

The kids' menu usually includes spaghetti, pizza, hamburgers, fries, and hot dogs. In addition, a few variations on what's being offered to the adults at the table are often served.

Buffets are offered at the Lido Restaurant as an alternative to breakfast and lunch in the main dining room. HAL also recently expanded its dinner options to include a casual table-service dinner on the Lido Deck (offered on all but the final night of the cruise), in addition to its formal dining-room dinner service. There are also intimate, reservations-required alternative Italian restaurants on the *Volendam, Oosterdam,* and *Zaandam* in Alaska. Dinner there will cost you $30 a head (lunch $15 a head.) It's money well spent.

ACTIVITIES Young swingers need not apply. Holland America's ships are heavy on more mature, less frenetic activities and light on boogie-till-the-cows-come-home, party-hearty pursuits. You'll find good bridge programs and music to dance to or lis- ten to in the bars and lounges, plus health spas and all of the other standard activities found on most large ships—bingo, golf-putting contests (on the carpet in the lobby), dance lessons, art auctions, and the like. All ships offer Internet access for 75¢ a minute.

In 2008, the line will continue its **Artists in Residence Program,** arranged through the Alaska Native Heritage Center in Anchorage, with Alaska Native artists accompa- nying all 7-night cruises and demonstrating traditional art forms such as ivory and soapstone carving, basket weaving, and mask making. The line will also be continu- ing its Huna Interpretive Program, with a member of the Huna tribe joining National Park Service employees in providing commentary as the ships visit Glacier Bay. The Huna tribe has called Glacier Bay home for centuries.

CHILDREN'S PROGRAM Club HAL is more than just one of those half-hearted give-'em-a-video-arcade-and-hot-dogs-at-dinner efforts. This children's program offers expert supervisors, a fitness center, and dedicated kids' common rooms (adults, keep out!) on the Alaska ships *Zaandam, Volendam, Oosterdam,* and *Ryndam.* On the other ships, some of the meeting rooms and lounges—the Half Moon Lounge on the *Statendam,* for instance—are set aside for the younger set during the day and revert to their general-population purposes at night.

Kids' activities are arranged in three divisions, by age—5 to 8, 9 to 12, and teens. The youngest group might have, say, singalongs, while the older kids will try their hand at karaoke. The middle group will compete in golf putting and the teens in fake Monte Carlo nights. (Don't worry, Mom, there's no real gambling involved!) The line also has a portfolio of **kids-only shore excursions** (floatplane rides, treasure hunts, hikes, and the like), on which parents can send their teens and preteens before setting off for their own adventure.

ENTERTAINMENT The line has improved its nightly show-lounge entertain- ment, which was once, frankly, not so hot. The change, to a large extent, reflects the tastes of the younger passengers who are starting to book in greater numbers with HAL. The quality of the professional entertainers on HAL ships has perceptibly improved over the last 5 or 6 years. And then there are the amateurs! Each week

Holland America Fleet Itineraries

Ship	Itineraries
Oosterdam/ Amsterdam/ Noordam	**7-night Inside Passage:** Round-trip from Seattle, visiting Victoria, Ketchikan, Juneau, Sitka, and either Glacier Bay or Hubbard Glacier. May–Sept.
Zaandam/ Zuiderdam	**7-night Inside Passage:** Round-trip from Vancouver, visiting Juneau, Skagway, Ketchikan, and either Glacier Bay or Sawyer Glacier. May–Sept.
Ryndam*/ Statendam	**7-night Gulf of Alaska:** North- and southbound between Vancouver and Whittier/ Anchorage, visiting Juneau, Ketchikan, Haines or Skagway, and either College Fjord or Glacier Bay. May–Sept.
Volendam*	**7-night Gulf of Alaska:** North- and southbound between Vancouver and Whittier/ Anchorage, visiting Ketchikan, Icy Strait Point, Juneau, Sitka, and Hubbard Glacier. May–Sept.

*The Volendam *and* Ryndam *also make one 7-night Inside Passage cruise from Vancouver; the* Ryndam *cruise sails in May and September at the beginning and end of the season, and the* Volendam *sails the itinerary twice in September.*

includes a crew talent show in which the international staff members perform their countries' songs and dances. Even if that sounds a bit corny, try it—many of the staff members are fabulous!

SERVICE   The line employs primarily Filipino and Indonesian staff members who are generally gracious and friendly without being cloying.

Jerry once sailed on the old *Rotterdam V* alongside one of those passengers who must make service people cringe. Three times in 6 nights in the dining room, he sent a dish back with a complaint—"Needs more paprika" was one of his more exotic gripes. Nobody else at the table had any problem with the food—just this obnoxious character. He never once wanted a meal as is. Whatever the menu said, it was always, "I'd like this on the side," or, "That instead of such and such." In short, the guy was an absolute pain. But the waiters never once reacted negatively to this aggravating man. No matter what he demanded, the staff (the table captain and the maitre d', as well as the waiters) treated him exactly as they did the others at the table—with courtesy and warmth. He always got an apology when he sent his food back, no matter how spurious his complaint. The manner in which the dining-room staffers dealt with this difficult customer (even though they must have been seething inside) said a great deal about their commitment to service.

On another occasion, Jerry somehow managed to get his baggage on board a Holland America ship in Vancouver in preparation for sailing—while the keys to the bags were lying on the bedside table at home 1,000 miles away. (You may well feel that you haven't heard many dumber moves than that!) The cabin steward refused to let him break the locks and ruin the rather expensive (and brand-new) luggage. Instead, he called an engineer and together they toiled patiently with a variety of tools—and a huge ring of keys—until, about half an hour after boarding, they managed to free the offending locks. Luggage saved—and score one for the HAL service spirit!

Onboard services on every ship in the fleet include laundry and dry cleaning. Each ship also maintains several self-service laundry rooms with irons.

CRUISETOURS & ADD-ON PROGRAMS   As might be expected of a company that owns its own tour company (Royal Caribbean and Princess also own tour companies in the Alaska market), HAL offers a variety of land arrangements in combination with its cruises. The offerings are extensive. Cruisetours are available ranging from 10 to 20 days in length and vary widely in price. It depends entirely on what category of cabin, and in some cases, hotel accommodations you choose. As an example of what's available, there's HAL's 14-day package (Anchorage-Vancouver), which includes a rail ride through the Denali Corridor with 2 nights in the park, an overnight in Tok, a cruise on the Yukon River from Eagle, overnights in Dawson and Whitehorse, in the Yukon Territory, and ending with a 4-day cruise from Skagway. The per diems for this comprehensive tour range from $191 to $444, the former for an inside cabin on the ship, the latter for the best suite. All land transportation is, of course, included. Overnight hotel stays are also available in Fairbanks, Vancouver, Seattle, and Anchorage—again, with a wide price range. (Staying at an airport hotel in Anchorage, for example, will cost you less than bunking in at the Pan Pacific, next to the Canada Place Passenger Pier—a lot less.) This year again, the cruisetour brochure includes tours featuring Tombstone Territorial Park, 90 minutes' drive from Dawson City in the heart of Canada's Yukon Territory, and to the Yukon Territory's Kluane National Park (a HAL exclusive), which has been designated by UNESCO as a World Heritage Site. The opening up of these two vast, hitherto untouched wilderness areas a couple of years ago reflects HAL's preeminent position in the Yukon tourism market. Whereas other lines (in particular, Princess and Celebrity/Royal Caribbean) have tended to concentrate their investment focus in the Denali Corridor, the Interior, and the Kenai Peninsula, HAL has built instead in the Yukon Territory. Its entry into Kluane and Tombstone allows it to offer, in conjunction with Parks Canada, fixed-wing flightseeing over Kathleen Lake, a Tatshenshini River white-water rafting outing, a hike though the King's Throne region (all in Kluane), and a motorcoach tour from Dawson City to Tombstone for wildlife viewing and hiking.

Ryndam • Statendam

The Verdict

If there is such a thing, these two are "typical" HAL ships, comfortably sized, quite spacious, and with enough room for passengers to spread out—or to hide out, if that's their thing.

Ryndam *(photo: Holland America Line)*

Specifications

Size (in Tons)	55,451	Crew	588
Passengers (Double Occ.)	1,266	Passenger/Crew Ratio	2.2 to 1
Passenger/Space Ratio	43	Year Launched	1991/1994
Total Cabins/Veranda Cabins	633/150	Last Major Refurbishment	N/A

Frommer's Ratings (Scale of 1–5) ★★★★

Cabin Comfort & Amenities	4	Dining Options	3.5
Ship Cleanliness & Maintenance	4	Gym, Spa & Sports Facilities	4
Public Comfort/Space	4	Children's Facilities	3.5
Decor	4	Enjoyment Factor	4

THE SHIPS IN GENERAL   These two nearly identical vessels were built within a 3-year span and fall somewhere between midsize and megaships. They demonstrate an extremely good use of space that pays attention to passenger traffic flows. The interiors feature leather, glass, cabinets, textiles, and furniture from around the world. Touches of marble, teakwood, polished brass, and around $2 million worth of artwork on each vessel evoke the era of the classic ocean liners. The decor often illustrates the seafaring traditions of the Netherlands and the role of Holland America in opening commerce and trade between that country and the rest of the world.

CABINS   All the cabins have a sitting area that can be closed off from the sleeping area with curtains, plus lots of closet and drawer space. The outside doubles have either picture windows or verandas. The least expensive inside cabins run almost 190 square feet (quite large by industry standards) and have many of the amenities of their higher-deck counterparts—sofas, chairs, desks-cum-dressers, stools, hair dryers, safes, and coffee tables. The Signature of Excellence upgrades that we mention earlier in this section have made the rooms much more welcoming—and functional. All cabins have TVs and telephones, and some have bathtubs (including some whirlpool tubs), VCRs, and minibars. Penthouses (one only on each ship) are huge—almost 1,200 square feet. Six cabins on each ship are wheelchair accessible.

Cabins & Rates

Cabin	Per Diem Rates	Sq. Ft.	Fridge	Hair Dryer	Sitting Area	TV
Ryndam						
Inside	$136–$174	182	no	yes	some	yes
Outside	$179–$214	197	no	yes	yes	yes
Suites	$409–$625	292–1,159	yes	yes	yes	yes
Statendam						
Inside	$158–$195	182	no	yes	some	yes
Outside	$200–$243	197	no	yes	yes	yes
Suites	$423–$712	292–1,159	yes	yes	yes	yes

PUBLIC AREAS   The striking dining rooms and the two-tiered showrooms are among these ships' best features; the latter are comfortable and have great views of the stage area from all seats. It helps, of course, that Holland America has made huge strides in upgrading its entertainment package.

The lobby area on each ship is not just the place to board the ship, but a place to hang out in as well. The *Statendam's* lobby houses a magnificent three-story fountain, while the *Ryndam* has a smaller version of the same fountain.

Other public rooms include a coffee bar, a card room, a casino, a children's playroom, a cinema, conference facilities, and a library. We especially like the Crow's Nest forward bar and lounge up on the Sports Deck, an inviting place to while away an hour or three.

DINING OPTIONS   The only alternative to the lovely main dining rooms on these ships are the reservations-only Pinnacle Grill ($30-a-head charge for dinner) and the casual Lido Deck Buffet, which is open in the evenings as well as for breakfast and lunch. That doesn't give guests the five or six alternatives that are available on some other ships, but on a vessel this size, it's perfectly adequate for a 1-week cruise.

POOL, FITNESS, SPA & SPORTS FACILITIES   Both ships have a sprawling expanse of teak-covered aft deck surrounding a swimming pool. One deck above that is a second swimming pool plus a wading pool, with a spacious deck area, bar, and two hot tubs that can be sheltered from inclement weather with a sliding-glass roof. Both areas are well planned and wide open. There's a practice tennis court and, on the *Statendam,* an unobstructed track on the Lower Promenade Deck for walking or jogging. The ships' roomy, windowed gyms have a couple dozen exercise machines, a large separate aerobics area, steam rooms, and saunas. The spas lack pizzazz but offer the typical menu of treatments.

Volendam • Veendam • Zaandam

The Verdict

Although a little older than some of their Alaska fleetmates this year, these three markedly similar vessels raised the bar a little for the cruise line, being somewhat bigger than the company's other Alaska ships at the time they entered service. They signaled the start of a HAL fleet expansion that brought the larger, more luxurious *Oosterdam, Westerdam, Noordam,* and *Zuiderdam.*

Volendam *(photo: Holland America Line)*

Specifications

Size (in Tons)	63,000	Crew	647
Passengers (Double Occ.)	1,440	Passenger/Crew Ratio	2.2 to 1
Passenger/Space Ratio	43	Year Launched	1999/2000/2000
Total Cabins/Veranda Cabins	720/197	Last Major Refurbishment	N/A

Frommer's Ratings (Scale of 1–5)   ★★★★

Cabin Comfort & Amenities	4	Dining Options	3.5
Ship Cleanliness & Maintenance	4.5	Gym, Spa & Sports Facilities	4
Public Comfort/Space	4	Children's Facilities	3.5
Decor	4	Enjoyment Factor	4

THE SHIPS IN GENERAL   Holland America pulled out all the stops on these ships. The centerpiece of the striking triple-decked oval atrium on the *Volendam,* for instance, is a glass sculpture by Luciano Vistosi, one of Italy's leading practitioners of the art—and that's just part of the ship's $2-million art collection, which reflects a flower theme. On the *Zaandam,* the focal point of the atrium is a 22-foot-tall pipe organ that is representative of the ship's music theme, which is filled out by a collection of guitars signed by rock musicians, including the Rolling Stones, Iggy Pop,

David Bowie, and Queen (an attempt to attract a younger, baby-boomer clientele?). Apart from the artwork and overall decorating motifs, there aren't many differences among these magnificent vessels; they really are virtually indistinguishable from one another. The *Zaandam* may look just the teeniest bit brighter than the *Volendam* and the *Amsterdam,* but hardly enough to make a real difference.

CABINS   The 197 suites and deluxe staterooms on each ship have private verandas, and the smallest of the remaining 523 cabins is a comfortable 190 square feet. All cabins come complete with sofa seating areas, hair dryers, telephones, and TVs. The suites and deluxe rooms also have VCRs, whirlpool baths, and minibars. The ships have more balcony cabins than other HAL vessels. Twenty-three of the cabins on each are equipped to accommodate wheelchairs.

Cabins & Rates

Cabins	Per Diem Rates	Sq. Ft.	Fridge	Hair Dryer	Sitting Area	TV
Veendam						
Inside	$122–$159	182	no	yes	yes	yes
Outside	$161–$260	197	no	yes	yes	yes
Suites	$385–$985	292–1,159	yes	yes	yes	yes
Volendam **and** *Zaandam*						
Inside	$137–$153	182	no	yes	yes	yes
Outside	$158–195	197	no	yes	yes	yes
Suites	$392–$711	292–1,159	yes	yes	yes	yes

PUBLIC AREAS   Each ship has five entertainment lounges, including the main two-tiered showroom. The Crow's Nest, a combination nightclub and observation lounge, is a good place to watch the passing Alaska scenery during the day. Each ship also has a casino, a children's playroom, a cinema, a library, an arcade, and an Internet center where you can surf for 75¢ a minute, with a 5-minute minimum.

DINING OPTIONS   All three ships have an alternative restaurant, the Pinnacle Grill (a staple on all HAL ships), which features Pacific Northwest cuisine, available on a reservations-only basis ($30 per-person supplement; $10 per person on the first night of the cruise). Designed to inspire an arty bistro vibe, these restaurants also feature drawings and etchings on the walls.

POOL, FITNESS, SPA & SPORTS FACILITIES   The gym is downright palatial on these ships, with dozens of state-of-the-art machines surrounded by floor-to-ceiling windows. There is an adjacent aerobics room. The spa and hair salon are not quite as striking. Three pools are on the Lido Deck, with a main pool and a wading pool under a retractable glass roof that also encloses the cafe-like Dolphin Bar. A smaller and quieter aft pool is located on the other side of the Lido buffet restaurant. On the Sports Deck is a pair of paddle-tennis courts as well as a shuffleboard court. Joggers can use the uninterrupted Lower Promenade Deck for a good workout.

Oosterdam • Westerdam

The Verdict

The biggest of the HAL ships in Alaska, these two are nevertheless intimate, and certainly well equipped to support HAL's position as a force in the Alaska market.

Oosterdam *(photo: Holland America Line)*

Specifications

Size (in Tons)	82,000	Crew	825
Passengers (Double Occ.)	1,848	Passenger/Crew Ratio	2.2 to 1
Passenger/Space Ratio	44	Year Launched	2003/2003
Total Cabins/Veranda Cabins	924/621	Last Major Refurbishment	N/A

Frommer's Ratings (Scale of 1–5)   ✦✦✦✦

Cabin Comfort & Amenities	4	Dining Options	3.5
Ship Cleanliness & Maintenance	5	Gym, Spa & Sports Facilities	4
Public Comfort/Space	4	Children's Facilities	4
Decor	4	Enjoyment Factor	4

THE SHIPS IN GENERAL   This will be the *Oosterdam*'s third summer in the 49th State, and the first for the *Westerdam*. The ships' thoughtful layout prevents bottlenecks at key points—outside the dining room, for instance, and at the buffet and pool area. Art worth about $2 million, according to HAL, is well displayed throughout each of the vessels, and the decor reflects Holland's (and Holland America's) contribution to the development of cruising and, indeed, of ships as a trade and transportation medium. The nautical pieces on display are plentiful but never overwhelming.

CABINS   Nearly 85% of the ships' cabins have ocean views, 67% of them with verandas. The smallest of the inside cabins is just 136 square feet—tiny enough to induce claustrophobia in some people. But the standard outside rooms start at 185 square feet, a considerable improvement. Suites here go up to 1,380 square feet, making them the biggest in the HAL fleet. All rooms have Internet/e-mail dataports. All of the rooms—even the smallest—have ample drawer and closet space, are tastefully decorated in quiet colors, and have quality bathroom fittings. All have VCRs and minibars. On each ship, 28 cabins, in several categories, are wheelchair accessible.

Cabins & Rates

Cabin	Per Diem Rates	Sq. Ft.	Fridge	Hair Dryer	Sitting Area	TV
Inside	$142–$177	154–185	no	no	no	yes
Outside	$194–$207	171–249	yes	yes	yes	yes
Suites	$464–$578	389–1,318	yes	yes	yes	yes

PUBLIC AREAS   The ships include a disco, a two-level main dining room; a library; a 24-hour cafe; an alternative, reservations-requested restaurant; and seven lounges/bars, including HAL's signature splendid Crow's Nest observation lounge/nightclub. And each has not one, but two showrooms—a spectacular three-level main showroom and a smaller "cabaret-style" venue for smaller-scale performances.

The Club HAL children's facilities are extensive and have both indoor and outdoor components. The ships have two interior Promenade decks, affording walkers protection against the elements—these decks can prove very useful in Alaska!

Wheelchair users are well catered to on this vessel. Besides the 28 cabins specially designed for them, they have wheelchair elevators dedicated for use in boarding the tenders in port, two tenders equipped with special wheelchair-accessible platforms, and accessible areas at virtually all public desks, bars, and lounges.

The ships have well-equipped casinos, offering passengers the chance to try their luck at stud poker, slots, craps, and roulette. Dozens of original art works, whose combined value ranks in the millions, dot the public areas.

DINING OPTIONS   Both of these ships have HAL's signature Pinnacle Grill (at $30 per person for dinner, $15 for lunch) and a more casual, 24-hour cafe. There is also 24-hour room service for those who prefer in-cabin dining.

POOL, FITNESS, SPA & SPORTS FACILITIES   The main pool on the Lido Deck has a retractable dome—a feature that has proven popular on other ships in Alaskan waters and on this one as well. A couple of hot tubs and a smaller pool complement the main pool. A huge spa, complete with the usual array of treatments and services (reserve in advance), occupies part of the topmost deck.

5 Norwegian Cruise Line

7665 Corporate Center Dr., Miami, FL 33126. (℃ **800/327-7030** or 305/436-4000. Fax 305/436-4120. www.ncl.com.

THE LINE IN A NUTSHELL   The very contemporary Norwegian Cruise Line offers an informal and upbeat atmosphere on medium- to megasize ships; its new addition, the 93,000-ton *Norwegian Pearl,* entered the fleet late in 2006 with a passenger capacity of 2,466. This year, both the *Pearl* and the *Norwegian Star* will be in Seattle for the summer's Inside Passage schedule, while the *Norwegian Sun* returns to Vancouver for its Inside Passage round-trips. All three ships are in 7-night rotation.

THE EXPERIENCE   NCL excels in activities, lack of regimentation, and alternative dining. Recreational and fitness programs are among the best in the industry and include programs where attendance at fitness events earns you points that you can cash in for prizes. The line's children's program is also top-notch. The company, which was bought by Star Cruises of Malaysia in 2000, has gradually changed its program to what it calls "Freestyle Cruising," which makes life a whole lot easier for passengers. The line was, in fact, the pioneers of the concept in the North American cruise market. One of the main components of Freestyle Cruising is freedom in when, where, and with whom passengers dine. Guests can eat in their choice of a variety of restaurants pretty much any time between 5:30pm and midnight (you must be seated by 10pm), with no prearranged table assignment or dining time. Other features of Freestyle Cruising are that tips are automatically charged to room accounts, dress codes are more relaxed (resort casual) at all times, and at the end of the voyage, passengers can remain in their cabins until their time comes to disembark, rather than huddling in lounges or squatting on luggage in stairwells until their lucky color comes up. Freestyle Cruising has since been copied, to whatever extent possible, by other lines operating in the U.S., although it was standard for Star Cruises in Asia for years before the company bought NCL. Naturally, with each new ship in a line's fleet, there usually comes innovation. In this case, one special addition has been a four-lane bowling alley tied in with an ultra-chic South Beach–like lounge.

Pros

- **Flexible dining.** NCL's dining policy lets you sit where and with whom you want, dress as you want, and dine when you want (dinner is served 5:30–10pm) at a wide variety of restaurants including one open 24 hours, along with room service.
- **Sports orientation.** Sports fans will be happy to find that ESPN Domestic or International is broadcast (depending on the location of the ship) into passengers' cabins and at the sports bars.
- **Smoke-free zones.** Norwegian promotes a smoke-free environment for those who want it, and all dining rooms are smoke-free. Smoke-free tables in the casino can be requested.

Cons

- **Not all Freestyle.** Shows and activities have specific start and end times; it's not up to the passenger.
- **Few quiet spots.** Other than the library, there's not a quiet room to be found. And the adults-only pool area is usually surrounded by kids.
- **Crowded dining areas.** The most popular of the alternative restaurants can get booked up early; best to make reservations as quickly as one can.

THE FLEET   The 1,900-passenger *Norwegian Sun* and the slightly larger *Norwegian Star* joined the fleet in 2001, within 3 months of each another. Both have now been overtaken in size by the *Norwegian Pearl*. All three ships have lots of windows for great viewing. Though these ships are relatively large and have a lot of public areas, some of the cabins are on the small side and some have insufficient closet space.

PASSENGER PROFILE   In Alaska, the overall demographic tends more toward older, affluent retirees than on the line's warmer-climate sailings, but you'll find an increasing number of younger couples and families as well, attracted by the line's flexible dining policy and relaxed dress code. Generally, passengers are not seeking high-voltage activities or 'round-the-clock action. The disco is seldom the most-used room on an NCL ship, the exception being the Bliss Lounge on Norwegian Pearl. There is a good mix of first-timers and veteran cruisers (many of whom have cruised with this line before).

DINING   The cruise line handles the business of dining in an innovative way, with its extensive number of alternative restaurants as well as smallish main dining rooms. And you can dress pretty much however you like, too—guests are allowed to wear blue jeans, shorts, and T-shirts in the evenings at the buffets, outdoor barbeques, and 24-hour venues. There is one optional formal night for those who want to dress up. On this night, some of the dining outlets are dressier while others remain casual. As on all ships, breakfast and lunch are available either in the dining room, on an open-seating basis, or in the buffet up top, where passengers can help themselves, dress pretty much as they please (many of them have come straight from the pool), and enjoy a more relaxed meal. In addition to the main dining rooms, the ships all have a variety of other food options. Both the *Star* and the *Pearl* have 10 dining venues, and the *Sun*

NCL Fleet Itineraries

Ship	Itineraries
Norwegian Sun	**7-night Inside Passage/Sawyer Glacier:** Round-trip from Vancouver, visiting Ketchikan, Juneau, and Skagway. May–Aug.
Norwegian Star	**7-night Inside Passage/Sawyer Glacier:** Round-trip from Seattle, visiting Ketchikan, Juneau, Skagway, and Prince Rupert, B.C. May–Sept.
Norwegian Pearl	**7-night Inside Passage/Glacier Bay:** Round-trip from Seattle, visiting Juneau, Skagway, Ketchikan, and Victoria, B.C. May–Sept.

runs a close second with 9 options. Included in the mix, depending on the ship, are French, sushi, sashimi, and teppanyaki; Italian eateries; and an a la carte Californian/Hawaiian/Asian outlet for which reservations are strongly recommended. A chocolate buffet, offered once during each cruise, has become an NCL standard on all its ships; NCL's was an industry first and it's quite possible still the best.

ACTIVITIES   In Alaska, the line offers a destination lecturer or two on the history, landscape, and culture of the state; wine-tasting demonstrations; art auctions and dance classes; a fitness program; daily quizzes; crafts; board games; and bingo, among other activities. Passengers also tend to spend time at sports activities, which include basketball and mini-soccer. The ships all have Internet cafes that cost 75¢ a minute a la carte with package rates available. In addition, Alaska sailings feature over 130 options for exciting shore excursions, including the Great Canadian Rafting Adventure, Whale Watching and Wildlife Quest, and the Historic Gold Mine & Pan For Gold. NCL Alaskan voyages also feature one-of-a-kind Freestyle Private Tours on all cruises calling in Juneau and Ketchikan. Freestyle Private Touring is a completely personalized experience comprised of carefully chosen tours created exclusively for NCL guests, encouraging them to customize their time ashore and discover Alaska at their own pace. Tours include a personal guide, giving guests an exclusive insider's perspective.

CHILDREN'S PROGRAM   NCL ships tend to be very family friendly: There's at least one full-time youth coordinator per age group, a kids' activity room, video games, an ice-cream stand, and group baby-sitting for ages 2 and up, plus a Polar Bear Pajama Party and a visit from a park ranger for the ships that sail to Glacier Bay National Park. The line is constantly upgrading its kids' program. More family features aboard ships include a splash pool on the Star, bowling alley and jungle gym with ball pit and tunnels on Pearl, and arcades on all NCL ships.

ENTERTAINMENT   Entertainment is an NCL hallmark, with Vegas-style productions that are surprisingly lavish and artistically ambitious; the gymnasts are superb. On some nights, the showrooms also feature magic, comedians, and juggling acts. The three ships boast the NCL fleet's big splashy casinos, and all have intimate lounges that present pianists and cabaret acts. Music for dancing—usually by a smallish band and invariably the kind of dancing that mature passengers can engage in (that is, not a lot of rock n' roll)—is popular aboard and takes place before or after shows. Each ship also has a late-night disco for those who prefer a more frenetic beat.

SERVICE   In the past, service has been inconsistent, ranging from just okay to great, but the line has worked very hard to upgrade and standardize the focus on personalized service. Generally, room service and bar service fleetwide is speedy and efficient, and the waitstaff is attentive and accommodating. In the alternative dining rooms, service can be slow if it's a large group at one table. With the introduction of the line's flexible dining program, additional crewmembers, mostly waiters and kitchen staff, have been added to each ship. To eliminate tipping confusion, the line automatically adds a charge of $10 per passenger per day to shipboard accounts (you are free to adjust the amount up or down as you see fit based on the service you received). Full-service laundry and dry cleaning are available.

CRUISETOURS & ADD-ON PROGRAMS   Hotel and Land Packages: With the Norwegian *Sun* calling Vancouver home, the line offers 3 night pre- and post-cruise packages to Vancouver, Vancouver Island, Butchart Gardens, and Victoria. Three night hotel packages with tours cost from $579 per person, double occupancy. 1, 2, and 3 night hotel packages are available from $125 per person, double occupancy. Two Seattle-based ships (*Pearl* and *Star*) offer a two-night Classic Seattle package with tours from $489 per person, double occupancy; 1-, 2-, and 3-night hotel packages are available from $95 per person, double occupancy.

Norwegian Pearl

The Verdict

NCL's newest baby, *Norwegian Pearl*, is an excellent evolutionary step beyond *Norwegian Jewel*, the line's previous newest ship.

Norwegian Pearl *(photo: NCL)*

Specifications

Size (in Tons)	93,530	Crew	1,010
Passengers (Double Occ.)	2,394	Passenger/Crew Ratio	2.4 to 1
Passenger/Space Ratio	37	Year Launched	2006
Total Cabins/Veranda Cabins	1,197/568	Last Major Refurbishment	N/A

Frommer's Ratings (Scale of 1–5)   ★★★★

Cabin Comfort & Amenities	4	Dining Options	5
Ship Cleanliness & Maintenance	5	Gym, Spa & Sports Facilities	4.5
Public Comfort/Space	4	Children's Facilities	3.5
Decor	4	Enjoyment Factor	4.5

THE SHIP IN GENERAL   Launched in December 2006, *Norwegian Pearl* is NCL's newest ship.

CABINS   *Norwegian Pearl* has 1197 cabins, 542 of which have balconies. The smallest of the rooms is about 142 square feet, about average for this new breed of ship—not big, but not cramped, either. The ship's biggest accommodations—the spectacular three-bedroom Garden Villa—runs to a staggering 4,390 square feet. One oft-voiced complaint in some of the lower-end cabins is an age-old NCL bugbear—not enough closet and drawer space. (That doesn't apply, of course, to the suites—and most assuredly not to the Garden Villa.) This should not be an issue for a one-week Alaska cruise when there are two to a cabin. All of the rooms are tastefully furnished—no glitz, no glare.

Cabins & Rates

Cabins	Per Diem Rates	Sq. Ft.	Fridge	Hair Dryer	Sitting Area	TV
Inside	$114–$164	143	no	yes	no	yes
Oceanview	$136–$271	161	no	yes	yes	yes
Suites	$271–$2,857	285–4,390	some	yes	yes	yes

PUBLIC AREAS   Public areas are bright and airy, if just a tad too colorful and varied; the casino's red and yellow pillars, for instance, and the nightclub's lilac and blue chairs and carpeting are definitely a bit overheated. The Library, on the other hand, is a tastefully decorated, relaxing room and the only quiet room on the ship. As part of the "Freestyle" concept, *Pearl* has a vast array of eating and drinking spots. Other spaces include has a huge casino, offering blackjack, roulette, craps (with wonderfully fair odds), and Caribbean Stud Poker—plus more than 200 slot machines—and a Texas Hold 'em table. The main showroom, the two-story Stardust Theater, holds about 1,100 in comfy seating, with good sightlines from either floor (and an air-conditioning flow from the back of each chair, helping to keep the room nice and cool). With its massive stage and loads of technological bells and whistles, the Stardust pulls off some pretty ambitious Broadway-style revues. The Internet cafe isn't a cafe at all (no coffee or pastries here), but it can keep you in e-touch with the outside world for 75¢ a minute. Packages lowering the per-minute cost are available. The Aqua Kids Club and Metro Center, for ages 2 through 17, has trained supervisors and is fully equipped with cinema, nursery and sleep/rest area, computer area, arts and crafts area, and dance floor.

DINING OPTIONS   In addition to its two main dining rooms (Indigo and the Summer Palace), the ship houses several other eateries in keeping with NCL's promise of providing maximum dining flexibility. Guests choose from two main dining rooms, a French bistro, Italian trattoria, steakhouse, teppanyaki, sushi, tapas/Tex-Mex, and more, including Blue Lagoon, open 24 hours a day. Supplemental fees ($10–$20 per person) are added for some of the restaurants. Colorful electronic signage around the ship lets passengers know which restaurants are full and which ones have space.

POOL, FITNESS, SPA & SPORTS FACILITIES   The *Pearl* has an adult pool, six hot tubs, a kiddie pool, a spa with exceptional thermal offerings highlighted by the large thalassotherapy pool, and a salon. Active types should check out the Body Waves fitness center, the jogging/walking track, the rock-climbing wall, bowling alley and the court used for basketball, volleyball, mini-soccer, and tennis. Also nice in this day and age is the deck seven promenade, which goes around the entire ship (2⅔ laps to a mile).

Norwegian Star

The Verdict

As the first ship introduced after Star Cruises bought NCL, this ship firmly established Norwegian Cruise Line as a revitalized player in the cruise game. It's big and handsome—inside and out—and offers a great choice of optional dining rooms.

Norwegian Star *(photo: NCL)*

Specifications

Size (in Tons)	91,000	Crew	1,100
Passengers (Double Occ.)	2,240	Passenger/Crew Ratio	2 to 1
Passenger/Space Ratio	40	Year Launched	2001
Total Cabins/Veranda Cabins	1,120/515	Last Major Refurbishment	N/A

Frommer's Ratings (Scale of 1–5)   ★★★★

Cabin Comfort & Amenities	4	Dining Options	4.5
Ship Cleanliness & Maintenance	4	Gym, Spa & Sports Facilities	4
Public Comfort/Space	4	Children's Facilities	3.5
Decor	4	Enjoyment Factor	4.5

THE SHIP IN GENERAL   The *Norwegian Star* came to Alaska in 2004 straight from the other non-contiguous state, Hawaii. In Hawaii, it operated an imaginative interisland itinerary with a trip to and from Fanning Island, a day's sail west of Hawaii, thrown in. The *Star* looks a lot like its new fleetmate, the *Norwegian Pearl,* particularly from behind, with that blunt rear end so favored by ship designers these days. Its real strength is the quality of the interior. The decor is modern, but not jarringly so, with muted but not washed-out colors. There are lots of pastel shades of green and blue, some gold (on drapes and bed-top covers, for instance), and a lot of blond wood. The overall effect is a pleasing meld of functionality and aesthetics.

CABINS   Almost 800 of the *Star*'s accommodations are outside, and about two-thirds of those have verandas. The inside cabins are smallish, ranging from 142 to 150 square feet. Suites have floor-to-ceiling windows, refrigerators, and private balconies. All cabins are equipped with TVs, telephones, small dressing tables, soundproof doors, individual climate control, and sitting areas that are actually big enough to stretch out in. Closet and drawer space is quite limited, so pack lightly. Twenty cabins are suitable for wheelchair access.

Cabins & Rates

Cabins	Per Diem Rates	Sq. Ft.	Fridge	Hair Dryer	Sitting Area	TV
Inside	$100–$143	142–150	yes	yes	no	yes
Outside	$89–$257	160–204	yes	yes	some	yes
Suites	$200–$2,857	284–5,750	yes	yes	yes	yes

PUBLIC AREAS   The *Star* has 10 eateries, for snacks on up to full meals. Its two main dining rooms (Versailles and Aqua) offer traditional (that is to say, multiple-course meals) and a range of lighter fare. It's not in the traditional assigned-seating style ("If it's 8pm, it must be dinnertime"), but on a no-reservations, come-as-you-please basis in a wide variety of restaurants. A card room, theater, casino, cigar bar, conference facilities, disco, library, karaoke bar, wine-tasting cellar, English pub, ice-cream counter, and three-level show lounge round out the public room offerings. For kids, there's a children's playroom (Planet Kids) and a video arcade.

DINING OPTIONS   You won't go hungry on the *Star:* Choose from Le Bistro, a French/Mediterranean restaurant ($15 supplement charge); Ginza, serving Japanese/Chinese cuisine; the SoHo Room, specializing in Pacific Rim/Hawaiian/Californian fusion dishes; the Hawaiian-themed Endless Summer; and much, much more. As if that weren't enough, the Blue Lagoon serves hamburgers, hot dogs, soups, salads, and pizza 24 hours a day.

POOL, FITNESS, SPA & SPORTS FACILITIES   The *Star* is well equipped for the sports-minded and active vacationer. In addition to the fitness center, there are heated pools (a main pool and a children's pool), a jogging/walking track (3½ laps = 1 mile), and an array of sports facilities, including ping-pong tables and two golf-driving ranges.

The Fitness Center, on Deck 12, and the Barong Spa and Beauty Salon, on Deck 11, are well stocked with Jacuzzis, hydrotherapy baths, and saunas. The spa has facilities for couples to take their treatments together.

Norwegian Sun

The Verdict

One of the first of NCL's new breed of ships, built after the line's acquisitions by Star Cruises, *Norwegian Sun* is NCL's first purpose-built entry for "Freestyle Cruising." It offers plenty of amenities, but—in common with other NCL ships—its smaller cabins could use more closet space.

Norwegian Sun *(photo: NCL)*

Specifications

Size (in Tons)	78,309	Crew	968
Passengers (Double Occ.)	1,936	Passenger/Crew Ratio	2.1 to 1
Passenger/Space Ratio	40	Year Launched	2001
Total Cabins/Veranda Cabins	1,025/432	Last Major Refurbishment	N/A

Frommer's Ratings (Scale of 1–5)   ★★★★

Cabin Comfort & Amenities	4	Dining Options	5
Ship Cleanliness & Maintenance	4	Gym, Spa & Sports Facilities	4
Public Comfort/Space	4.5	Children's Facilities	3.5
Decor	4	Enjoyment Factor	4

THE SHIP IN GENERAL   The *Norwegian Sun* was a groundbreaker for NCL when it debuted late in 2001, because it was the first ship specifically built by the company with the Freestyle Cruising concept in mind. Its nine restaurants were vital to the company's vision of dining flexibility, making it possible to eat in a different place every night of the week without stepping foot in either of the two main dining rooms. It's a peaceful ship, with plenty of room to get away from it all, if that's what you have in mind. The *Sun's* eight-story midship atrium is not as ornate as those on some other ships, but it is nevertheless a striking area, giving a great feeling of airiness. That same airiness pervades much of the *Sun's* interiors, including its sleeping accommodations.

CABINS   More than two-thirds of the ship's guest rooms have ocean views, a total of about 650 cabins in all. Of these, 432 have balconies. The smallest cabins are 172 square feet and, having noted earlier passenger comments, NCL has built in additional closet and drawer space. Thirty mini-suites each measure 267 square feet. All rooms have TV, radio, telephone, refrigerators, and safes, as well as individually controlled air-conditioning units. The ship has 20 wheelchair-accessible cabins.

Cabins & Rates

Cabins	Per Diems	Sq. Ft.	Fridge	Hair Dryer	Sitting Area	TV
Inside	$107–$143	147	yes	yes	yes	yes
Outside	$136–$257	147–222	yes	yes	yes	yes
Suites	$214–$2,857	300–829	yes	yes	yes	yes

PUBLIC AREAS   Located midship, the glass-domed, eight-story atrium of the *Sun* is a striking feature, built to offer at least the illusion of space. Bright and airy, it's home to the reception desk, the shore-excursion office, and various passenger services. Four glass elevators whisk passengers to the higher decks. A grand spiral staircase, also midship, links the Atlantic Deck with the International Deck, two flights up. Internet facilities (24 terminals) are available for 75¢ a minute (packages lowering the per-minute cost are available). The two-story show lounge doubles as a disco that jumps into the wee hours. Also entertaining is the *Sun's* large casino and a choice of 11 bar/lounges, including one that welcomes cigar smokers.

DINING OPTIONS   Besides Le Bistro, a standard on all NCL's ships, the Sun offers Il Adagio, a rather formal Italian dining room; Ginza, for Japanese food; East Meets West, presenting a fusion of California, Asian, and Hawaiian cuisine, with a live lobster tank in the middle of the room as a focal point; a Spanish tapas bar called Las Ramblas; the Garden Buffet/Great Outdoor Café, serving lunch and dinner; a healthy-living restaurant called Pacific Heights; and two main dining rooms (some of the alternative restaurants have a modest surcharge). Have a sweet tooth? Look for Sprinkles Ice Cream Parlor near the pools. There is also a 24-hour room-service menu.

POOL, FITNESS, SPA & SPORTS FACILITIES   The ship has two pools and four hot tubs on Pool Deck 11, and a children's splash pool one deck up on the Sports Deck. The Sports Deck features a net for driving golf balls, a basketball/volleyball court, a batting cage, shuffleboard courts, and sunbathing areas. Mandara, one of the premier spa operators in the world, manages this spa, as well as the spas on all NCL ships. Simultaneous spa treatments for couples, in-cabin spa service, hydrotherapy baths incorporating milk and honey or mineral salts, exotic Asian treatments, de-stress treatments, and all of Mandara's signature "Best of East and West" techniques are available here.

6 Princess Cruises

24305 Town Center Dr., Santa Clarita, CA 91355. ℂ **800/LOVE-BOAT** or 661/753-0000. Fax 661/753-1535. www.princess.com.

THE LINE IN A NUTSHELL   The company strives, successfully, to please a wide variety of passengers. It offers more choices in terms of accommodations, dining, and entertainment than nearly any other line.

THE EXPERIENCE   If you were to put Carnival, Royal Caribbean, Celebrity, and Holland America in a big bowl and mix them all together, you'd come up with Princess Cruises' megas. The *Coral, Island, Diamond,* and *Sapphire Princesses*—its latest creations—are less glitzy and frenzied than the ships of, say, Carnival and Royal Caribbean; not quite as cutting-edge as Celebrity's *Infinity* and *Summit;* and more exciting, youthful, and entertaining than Holland America's near-megas. The Princess fleet appeals to a wider cross section of cruisers by offering loads of choices and activities, plus touches of big-ship glamour, along with plenty of the private balconies, quiet nooks, and calm spaces that characterize smaller, more intimate-size vessels. Aboard Princess, you get a lot of bang for your buck, attractively packaged and well executed. The *Dawn Princess* is one of the company's older vessels; it entered service a decade ago. As a function of its age, the *Dawn* lacks some of the pizzazz of its newer fleetmates; it doesn't have as many dining options, for instance. It is nevertheless a worthy representative of the Southern California–based line and has a loyal band of supporters.

Although its ships serve every corner of the globe, nowhere is the Princess presence more visible than in Alaska. Through its affiliate, Princess Tours, the company owns wilderness lodges, motorcoaches, and railcars in the 49th state, making it one of the major players in the Alaska cruise market, alongside Holland America and, increasingly, Royal Caribbean Cruises' two brands, Celebrity and Royal Caribbean International. Princess also operates spectacular wilderness lodges, the newest—opened in 2002—the Copper River Lodge at Cooper Landing near Wrangell–St. Elias National Park.

In 2004, Princess became the first line to use the rather nondescript Whittier as the northern terminus for its Gulf cruises instead of the more commonly used Seward and has done so ever since. Carnival, Princess's affiliate line, relocated its northern turnaround there as well not long afterward. Whittier's primary advantage over Seward is that it's about 60 miles closer to Anchorage. Passengers bound for rail tours of Denali National Park are able to board their trains right on the pier instead of taking a bus to Anchorage and then embarking on their rail carriages. The inauguration of the service was yet another effort by a cruise line to gain a competitive edge over its Alaska rivals. The battle for the minds and wallets of the public is being fought as much on land as at sea these days. With so many ship lines striving to attract new passengers or persuade old ones to come back, every little bit helps. The competition goes on, to the benefit of the traveling public. Princess Cruises is now a member of the same group that owns Holland America and Carnival, both of them highly visible in the Alaska cruise market. That gives the parent, Miami-based Carnival Corp., control of no fewer than 18 ships in Alaska in 2008.

Pros

- **Good service.** The warm-hearted Italian, British, and Filipino service crew do a great job. On a Princess cruise a few years ago, one barman with a glorious cockney accent (which we noted he could mute or emphasize at will) was a huge hit with our group, dispensing one-liners, simple magic tricks, and drinks with equal facility. We've met others on Princess ships with the same gift for making passengers feel welcome without being overly familiar.
- **Private verandas.** Virtually all of the line's Alaska ships have scads and scads of verandas, some of them in as many as 75% of the cabins.

Cons

- **Average food.** The ships' cuisine is perfectly fine if you're not a gourmet, but if you are, you'll find that it's pretty banquet hall–esque.

THE FLEET   Princess's diverse fleet in Alaska essentially comprises eight ships, five of which entered service since the millennium. The fleet includes the *Diamond* and *Sapphire*, which were completed in 2004; the *Star, Coral,* and *Island,* of 2002/2003 vintage, and the *Golden* (2001), not to mention the *Tahitian Princess,* which was built in 1999 and extensively refurbished in 2002 when it was purchased from Renaissance Cruises. The *Dawn* (1997) completes Princess's Alaska fleet this year. The ships generally are pretty but not stunning, bright but not gaudy, spacious but not overwhelmingly so, and decorated in a comfortable, restrained style that's a combination of classic and modern. They're a great choice when you want a step up from Carnival, Royal Caribbean, and NCL but aren't interested in (or can't afford) the slightly more chic ambience of Celebrity or the luxury of Seven Seas or Silversea.

PASSENGER PROFILE   Typical Princess passengers are likely to be between about 50 to 65 and are often experienced cruisers who know what they want and are prepared to pay for it. The line's recent additional emphasis on its youth and children's facilities has begun to attract a bigger share of the family market, resulting in the passenger list becoming more diverse overall.

DINING   In general, Princess offers meals that are good, if hardly gourmet. But you've got to give them points for at least trying to be flexible: A few years ago, Princess implemented a new fleetwide dining option known as Personal Choice. Basically, this plan allows passengers to sign up for the traditional first or second seating for dinner, or for a come-as-you-please restaurant-style dining option. The latter allows you to eat dinner any time between 5:30pm and midnight, though you must be seated by 10pm. Passengers who choose the restaurant-style option may request a cozy table for two or bring along a half-dozen shipmates, depending on their mood that evening. A $10-a-day gratuity will be automatically added to your bill for both the restaurant service and tips for your room steward. If you want to raise or lower that amount, you should do so when you make your cruise reservation (it will be harder to do it once you're on board). It's also possible to eat all your meals in the 24-hour Lido Deck cafe on all Princess ships in Alaska. If you don't go to the main dining room, though, you may miss one of Princess's best features: its pastas. The newest ships also offer a variety of alternative-dining restaurants—Italian, Mexican, Creole, and the like—and it's our experience that meals at these restaurants are well worth the price of admission, ranging from $15 to $25 per person.

ACTIVITIES   Princess passengers can expect enough onboard activity to keep them going from morning to night if they've a mind to, and enough hideaways to let them

Princess Fleet Itineraries

Ship	Itineraries
Diamond *Sapphire/Island/Coral*	**7-night Gulf of Alaska:** North- and southbound between Vancouver Whittier/Anchorage, visiting Ketchikan, Juneau, and Skagway, and cruising Glacier Bay and College Fjord. May–Sept.
Golden/Star	**7-night Inside Passage:** Round-trip from Seattle, visiting Ketchikan, Juneau, Skagway, and Tracy Arm. May–Sept.
Dawn	**10-night Inside Passage:** Round-trip from San Francisco, visiting Victoria, Juneau, Ketchikan, Sitka and Glacier Bay. May–Sept.
Tahitian	**14-night Inside Passage/Kodiak:** Round-trip from Vancouver, visiting Ketchikan, Glacier Bay, Skagway, Valdez, Seward, Kodiak Island, Juneau, Sitka, and Victoria. May–Sept.

do absolutely nothing, if that's their thing. The line doesn't go out of its way to make passengers feel that they're spoilsports if they don't participate in the amateur-night tomfoolery, or putt for dough, or learn to fold napkins. These activities are usually there, along with the inevitable bingo, shuffleboard, and the rest, but they're low-key. Internet access is offered on all the ships for 75¢ per minute. Various packages that bring the cost down are also available for those who use the net more—$55 for 100 minutes, for instance, 150 for $175, and 250 minutes for $100. The line's ScholarShip@Sea program, which allows passengers to take classes in subjects as diverse as photography, computers, cooking, and even pottery, has been hugely popular since it was pioneered by Princess in 2004.

Specifically in Alaska, the line has naturalists and park rangers on board to offer commentary.

CHILDREN'S PROGRAM   Supervised activities are offered year-round for ages 2 to 17, clustered in two groups: Princess Pelicans for ages 2 to 12, and teens age 13 to 17. Princess is seeking to broaden its appeal and distance itself from its old image as a staid, adults-only line, and all of the ships are now well equipped for children and clearly intended to cater to families. Each ship has a spacious children's playroom and a sizable area of fenced-in outside deck for kids only, with a shallow pool and tricycles. Teen centers have computers, video games, and a sound system. Wisely, these areas are placed as far away as possible from the adult passengers.

ENTERTAINMENT   From glittering Vegas-style shows, to New York cabaret-singer performances, to a rocking disco, this line offers a terrific blend of musical delights, and you'll always find a cozy spot where some soft piano or jazz music is being performed. You'll also find entertainers such as hypnotists, puppeteers, and comedians, plus karaoke for you audience-participation types. In the afternoons, there are always a couple of sessions of that ubiquitous cruise favorite, the Newlywed and Not-So-Newlywed Game. Each of the ships also has a wine bar selling caviar by the ounce and vintage wine, champagne, and iced vodka by the glass. The Princess casinos are sprawling and exciting places, too, and are bound to excite gamblers with their lights and action. Good-quality piano-bar music and strolling musicians, along with dance music in the lounge, are part of the pre- and post-dinner entertainment.

For years, Princess has had a connection to Hollywood—this is the *Love Boat* line, after all. It's the only line we know of where you can watch yesterday's and today's television shows on your in-room TV. Also shown are A&E, Biography, E! Entertainment

TV, Nickelodeon, Discovery Channel, BBC, and National Geographic productions, as well as recently released movies.

SERVICE Throughout the fleet, the service in all areas—dining room, lounge, cabin maintenance, and so on—tends to be of consistently high quality. An area in which Princess particularly shines is the efficiency of its shore-excursion staffs. Getting 2,600-plus people off a ship and onto motorcoaches, trains, and helicopters—all staples of any Alaska cruise program—isn't as easy as this company makes it look. And a real benefit of the Princess shore-excursions program is that passengers are sent the options about 60 days before the sailing and can book their choices on an advanced-reservations basis before the trip (tickets are issued on board), either by mail or on the Internet at www.princess.com. The program improves your chances of getting your first choice of tours before they sell out. All of the Princess vessels in Alaska offer laundry and dry-cleaning services and have their own self-service laundromats.

CRUISETOURS & ADD-ON PROGRAMS Princess offers an array of land packages this year that can be used in more than 100 different cruisetour itineraries in Alaska in conjunction with its Gulf of Alaska and Inside Passage voyages (not to mention another dozen or so options in the Canadian Rockies). Virtually every part of the state is covered—from the Kenai Peninsula to the Interior to the Far North. The land portions come in 4- to 9-night segments, all combinable with a 7-night cruise. No fewer than 98 different land itineraries are offered in conjunction with Princess's five wilderness lodges.

Coral Princess • Island Princess

The Verdict

These two are plenty big, but such is the sophistication of marine architecture nowadays that passengers don't have the feeling of living with a couple of thousand others: There are lots of places to get away from it all.

Coral Princess *(photo: Matt Hannafin)*

Specifications

Size (in Tons)	88,000	Crew	900
Passengers (Double Occ.)	1,974	Passenger/Crew Ratio	2.2 to 1
Passenger/Space Ratio	44	Year Launched	2003/2003
Total Cabins/Veranda Cabins	987/727	Last Major Refurbishment	N/A

Frommer's Ratings (Scale of 1–5)   ★★★★

Cabin Comfort & Amenities	4	Dining Options	4.5
Ship Cleanliness & Maintenance	4	Gym, Spa & Sports Facilities	5
Public Comfort/Space	4	Children's Facilities	4.5
Decor	4	Enjoyment Factor	4

THE SHIPS IN GENERAL   These two ships are essentially twins, offering the same amenities and services, with nothing but relatively minor cosmetic differences between them. Roominess is the key here. Weighing 11,000 tons more than, say, the *Dawn,* each nevertheless carries only about 24 additional passengers.

The ships reflect the marine design inventiveness that is becoming more obvious with the arrival of every new ship. Each has a 9-hole putting green, a world-class art collection, a spacious kids' and teen center, a wedding chapel, a cigar lounge, a martini bar (the last two features have become almost standard on new ships), and much more. Decor is tasteful and rich, with a lot of teak decking, stainless-steel and marble fittings, and prominent use of light shades of gray, blue, and brown in the soft furnishings.

CABINS   The two ships have a remarkable number of outside rooms (almost 90%) and a huge number of private balconies—727, or more than 7 out of 10 of the outside units. The smallest accommodations on either of the ships are about 160 square feet, and the largest, the 16 top suites, stretch to 470 square feet, including the veranda. In between, the *Coral* and *Island* offer rooms with square footage ranging from 217 to 248. Don't assume when making a reservation that a minisuite will necessarily come with a veranda; each of the ships has eight minisuites without that amenity, so if you want one be sure to specify that when you make your reservation. Twenty of the cabins (16 outside, 4 inside) are configured for wheelchair use. They are very spacious—between 217 square feet and 248 square feet.

Cabins & Rates

Cabins	Per Diem Rates	Sq. Ft.	Fridge	Hair Dryer	Sitting Area	TV
Inside	$114–$120	156–166	yes	yes	no	yes
Outside	$128–$171	217–248	yes	yes	no	yes
Suites	$180–$428	280–470	yes	yes	yes	yes

PUBLIC AREAS   In keeping with the trend these days, the *Coral* and *Island* each offer a comfy cigar bar and a martini lounge—the Churchill Lounge and the Rat Pack Bar, respectively. Their nautical-themed Wheelhouse Bars are warm, inviting places to spend time after-hours. Also appealing but more frenetic is the Explorers Lounge, which functions as the disco after dinner. The huge casino on the *Coral* and *Island* is a London-themed room, with frescos and knickknacks reflective of the ships' British heritage. An AOL Internet cafe, a wedding chapel, children's and teens' centers, a golf putting green, and a golf simulator are located on the top deck.

DINING OPTIONS   The ships have two main dining rooms and four smaller alternative dining areas—Sabatini's Trattoria, a fast favorite on most recent vintage Princess ships for which there is a $25-per-head charge (well worth the price); a Creole restaurant called The Bayou Café ($15 per head); the poolside hamburger grill; and the poolside pizza bar. In combination, they allow passengers to eat pretty much when they want, and to be as formal or as relaxed as they wish.

POOL, FITNESS, SPA & SPORTS FACILITIES   There are three pools and five whirlpool tubs. The fitness center is a large, well-stocked, airy room with absolutely the last word in equipment. The Lotus Spa offers one of the widest arrays of massage and beauty treatments afloat, including oxygenating facials, an "aromaflex" package that combines the ancient healing therapies of massage and reflexology, and a treatment that involves the placing of heated, oiled volcanic stones on key energy points of the body to release muscular tension and promote relaxation.

Dawn Princess

The Verdict

It's not so long since this ship was one of the huge ships in the fleet. Not anymore. Now some of their fleetmates outweigh it by almost 40,000 tons—about the weight of a good midsize ship!

Dawn Princess *(photo: Princess Cruises)*

Specifications

Size (in Tons)	77,000	Crew	900
Passengers (Double Occ.)	1,950	Passenger/Crew Ratio	2.2 to 1
Passenger/Space Ratio	39	Year Launched	1995/1997
Total Cabins/Veranda Cabins	975/410	Last Major Refurbishment	N/A

Frommer's Ratings (Scale of 1–5)   ★★★★

Cabin Comfort & Amenities	4	Dining Options	3.5
Ship Cleanliness & Maintenance	4.5	Gym, Spa & Sports Facilities	4
Public Comfort/Space	4	Children's Facilities	3.5
Decor	3.5	Enjoyment Factor	4

THE SHIP IN GENERAL   On paper, passengers on the *Dawn* might be expected to be a little cramped for space. Not so. Despite its size and passenger complement, you'll probably never feel crowded: There always seems to be lots of space on deck, in the buffet dining areas, and in the lounges.

CABINS   More than 400 of the ship's 975 cabins and suites have private balconies, including many in the midprice range, such as those on Baja Deck. All cabins, including the 408 inside units, come equipped with minibars, TVs, and twin beds that easily convert to a queen. Closet space is adequate, although it's a little tight in the lower-end cabins. The smallest cabins are 135 square feet, and the six suites measure up at 695 square feet, offering a large living room, separate bedroom/dining area, stall shower and bathtub with whirlpool, two TVs, refrigerator, and safe. The 32 minisuites are somewhat less lavish, though they're still highly desirable. The ship has 19 wheelchair-accessible cabins located on several decks and in several different categories.

Cabins & Rates

Cabins	Per Diems	Sq. Ft.	Fridge	Hair Dryer	Sitting Area	TV
Dawn Princess						
Inside	$99–$131	135–148	yes	yes	no	yes
Outside	$149–$199	155–179	yes	yes	no	yes
Suites	$359–$458	370–695	yes	yes	yes	yes

PUBLIC AREAS   This ship shines when it comes to communal areas. It has a decidedly unglitzy decor that relies on lavish amounts of wood, glass, and marble. Collections of original paintings and lithographs worth $2.5 million are featured onboard. The one-story showroom offers unobstructed viewing from every seat, and several seats in the back are reserved for passengers with mobility problems. The smaller Vista Lounge also offers shows with good sightlines and comfortable cabaret-style seating. The twin dining rooms are broken up by dividers topped with frosted glass. The elegant Wheelhouse Bar is the perfect spot for pre- or post-dinner drinks; done in warm, dark-wood tones, it features live entertainment (a pianist or a duo mostly). More spaces include a dark and sensuous disco; a bright, spacious casino; card room; cinema; and show lounge. Other lounges, scattered throughout the ship, provide opportunities for an intimate rendezvous (check out the Entre Nous) or a bigger bash (try the popular Atrium Lounge, the setting for the captain's opening cocktail party). Another striking feature on this ship is the library, with leather easy chairs equipped with built-in headphone sound systems. They absolutely cry out, "Sit here!"

The ship has an extensive children's playroom with ball drop, castles, computer games, puppet theater, and more.

DINING OPTIONS   If you'd like a break from the main dining rooms and buffet, check out the bistro-style restaurant, where you can get a full dinner until 4am, or Lago's Pizzeria, a sit-down restaurant open afternoons and nights (no takeout or delivery). Pizza is also available by the slice in the Horizon Court between 4 and 7pm daily.

POOL, FITNESS, SPA & SPORTS FACILITIES   The *Dawn* has four pools (one of which is the kids' wading pool) plus hot tubs scattered around the Riviera Deck. The ship boasts some of the best-designed, most appealing health clubs of any of Princess's vessels, though the gyms are on the small side for ships of this size. The spa offers all of the requisite massages and spa treatments. A teakwood deck encircles the ship for joggers, walkers, and shuffleboard players, and a computerized golf center called Princess Links simulates the trickiest aspects of some of the world's most legendary golf courses.

Fitness classes are available throughout the day in a very roomy aerobics room, where stretching and meditation classes are also offered.

Diamond Princess •
Sapphire Princess

The Verdict

If the aim in the ship-designing business nowadays is "keeping up with the Joneses," these two succeed completely. Classy interiors, for sure. But let's face it—there's no way to hide from 2,669 other passengers.

Diamond Princess *(photo: Princess Cruises)*

Specifications

Size (in Tons)	116,000	Crew	1,100
Passengers (Double Occ.)	2,670	Passenger/Crew Ratio	2.4 to 1
Passenger/Space Ratio	43	Year Launched	2004
Total Cabins/Veranda Cabins	1,337/746	Last Major Refurbishment	N/A

Frommer's Ratings (Scale of 1–5)

★★★★ ½

Cabin Comfort & Amenities	4	Dining Options	4.5
Ship Cleanliness & Maintenance	5	Gym, Spa & Sports Facilities	4
Public Comfort/Space	4.5	Children's Facilities	4
Decor	4.5	Enjoyment Factor	4

THE SHIPS IN GENERAL For all practical purposes, these two giants are also virtual twins, offering only the inevitable cosmetic (no structural) differences. Built in Nagasaki, Japan, they are the youngest ships in Princess' Alaska fleet.

CABINS Almost 60% of these ships' accommodations come with private balconies (78% of all the outside rooms)—a lot, though not as high a percentage as on some other ships in the market, including some of their own fleetmates. These are very much mass-market vessels. That requires ample space for people who want less pricey inside and standard outside (nonbalcony) cabins. The rooms range from 168 square feet in the low-end inside units to between 354 and 1,329 square feet (including the veranda) in the suite category. Twenty-seven cabins (16 outside, 11 inside) are wheelchair accessible.

Cabins & Rates

Cabins	Per Diem Rates	Sq. Ft.	Fridge	Hair Dryer	Sitting Area	TV
Inside	$100–$119	168	yes	yes	no	yes
Outside	$135–$192	197–277	yes	yes	yes	yes
Suites	$224–$442	354–1,329	yes	yes	yes	yes

PUBLIC AREAS As in the case of other ships in the fleet, these two vessels cater to a range of tastes. There is, for example, the high-tech Club Fusion, a lounge with flashing lights and modernistic furnishings. At the other end of the spectrum, for those with a more traditional bent, there is the classic Wheelhouse Bar, with dark wood and a cozy feeling.

You wanna dance? Take your pick. For those whose taste runs to the more frenzied, there's Skywalkers, a lounge/disco in the sky with a balcony where you can cool off, and the Explorers Lounge, another disco lower on the ship. For those who prefer more sedate venues, numerous lounges and bars throughout the ships offer more traditional, less hectic dance opportunities. There's also a cozy well-stocked library, a large casino, an Internet cafe, children's and teens' centers, a wedding chapel, and an art gallery. Up top, there's a Sports Deck with a jogging track, basketball/paddle tennis courts, a golf putting course, and a golf simulator.

DINING OPTIONS The *Sapphire* and *Diamond* each feature multiple dining venues. The main dining room is a handsome, somewhat traditional large room with two seatings for dinner; four small dining venues (on decks 5 and 6; no cover charge) offer a variety of "theme" menus. For a great Italian meal, worth every cent of its $25 cover, try the upscale Sabatini's, perhaps the finest—and surely the most filling—Italian restaurant at sea.

During strategic times of the day, hamburgers, hot dogs, and sandwiches are available at the Trident Grill, located poolside, and Häagen-Dazs ice cream is served at Sundae's, also on the Pool Deck. And, of course, 24-hour room service is also available. Sad news for pizza-eaters, though: The pizzerias on these two ships had to be yanked to make room for Sabatini's.

POOL, FITNESS, SPA & SPORTS FACILITIES   There are three major outdoor pool areas and a generously supplied spa and fitness center on each ship, each offering the expected (and demanded) full range of treatments, facials, herbal wraps, and massage. Trainers are present to conduct stretching, meditation, and aerobics classes.

Golden Princess •
Star Princess

The Verdict

These ships, two of three 109,000-ton Grand Class vessels in the Princess fleet (the other is the *Grand*) are real winners. Despite their size and megacapacity (2,600 passengers!), you won't usually feel the crush of all those other guests, thanks to plenty of opportunities to "get away from it all."

Golden Princess *(photo: Princess Cruises)*

Specifications

Size (in Tons)	109,000	Crew	1,200
Passengers (Double Occ.)	2,600	Passenger/Crew Ratio	2.1 to 1
Passenger/Space Ratio	42	Year Launched	2001
Total Cabins/Veranda Cabins	1,301/710	Last Major Refurbishment	N/A

Frommer's Ratings (Scale of 1–5)   ★★★★½

Cabin Comfort & Amenities	4	Dining Options	5
Ship Cleanliness & Maintenance	4	Gym, Spa & Sports Facilities	4
Public Comfort/Space	5	Children's Facilities	4
Decor	5	Enjoyment Factor	4.5

THE SHIP IN GENERAL   With 15 towering decks, the *Golden* and *Star Princesses* are taller than the Statue of Liberty (from pedestal to torch). In fact, they're so big that the *Pacific Princess* (take your pick: either the now-departed ship that inspired the original *Love Boat* series or the one of the same name that the company introduced into service recently) could easily fit inside the hulls of these two and still have lots of room to spare.

Inside and out, they are a marvel of size and design. Their massive white, boxy body, with its spoiler-like aft poking up into the air, cuts a slightly bizarre, space-age profile. But the ships' well-laid-out interior design makes them easy to navigate. Amazingly, they seldom feel crowded—a characteristic, we've found, of the bigger, newer ships of Princess and many other lines—a tribute to the growing sophistication and creativity of the marine architecture community.

The ships offer an amazing variety of entertainment, dining options, and recreational activities. They have five restaurants (plus a pizzeria and outdoor grill), four swimming pools, and three show lounges, as well as expansive deck space.

Even the ships' medical center is grand, boasting high-tech "telemedicine" programs that, via a live video hookup, link the ship's doctors to the emergency room at Cedars Sinai Medical Center in Los Angeles.

CABINS Even the smallest of their inside cabins is quite adequate, at about 160 square feet; standard outside units, sans balcony, go from 165 to 210 square feet; and larger oceanview rooms run between 215 and 255 square feet, including balcony. All of the rooms have twin beds that easily convert to queens, along with refrigerators, televisions, spacious closets, robes, safes, and plenty of drawer space. The larger of the outside rooms comes with a small writing desk. Minisuites give you 325 square feet (including balcony), and the suites range from 515 to about 800 square feet—again, including the balcony—and feature a tub and shower. (Nonbalcony staterooms have only shower stalls.) The rooms are tastefully decorated with subdued, hidden lighting; soft furnishings in quiet colors; and eye-catching, though not gallery-quality art. The ships have 28 wheelchair-accessible cabins. (The Skywalkers disco has a wheelchair lift up to the elevated dance floor, too.)

Nearly two-thirds of each ship's 992 staterooms have balconies. But be forewarned: The verandas are tiered, as they are on so many new ships these days, so passengers in levels above may be able to look down on you. While they might be said to be private, they're really rather exposed. Don't do anything out there you wouldn't want the neighbors to see! TV stations available (geography permitting) include CNN, ESPN, Nickelodeon, BBC programming, and TNT (as well as the inevitable *Love Boat* reruns).

Cabins & Rates

Cabins	Per Diem Rates	Sq. Ft.	Fridge	Hair Dryer	Sitting Area	TV
Inside	$121–$135	160	yes	yes	no	yes
Outside	$142–$214	170–274	yes	yes	no	yes
Suites	$228–$422	323–740	yes	yes	yes	yes

PUBLIC AREAS Hey, where'd everyone go? Thanks to the smart layout of these vessels, with lots of small rooms rather than a few large rooms, passengers are dispersed rather than concentrated into one or two main areas; you'll have no problem finding a quiet retreat.

The public areas have a contemporary and upscale appeal, thanks to pleasing color schemes and the well-designed use of wood, marble, and brass. Two full-time florists create and care for impressive flower arrangements and a large variety of live plants.

Besides the three—count 'em, three—main dining rooms, there are two principal alternative eateries: Sabatini's, a fine Italian staple found on every new Princess ship, and a Southwestern-themed eatery. Other options include the casual 24-hour Horizon Court and two spaces—the Trident Grill (poolside) and a pizza counter—both with limited hours and serving snacks and light meals. Each of the ships' restaurants is on the small side, designed that way so you don't feel like you're dining with a crowd and in order to maintain good acoustics (although you may also feel like the ceiling is closing in on you a bit).

Gamblers will love the sprawling and dazzling 13,500-square-foot casino, among the largest at sea. Near the casino, two lounge areas are ideal for whiling away a few moments before attacking the gaming tables.

The ships' most striking design feature (part of the Grand Class design) is its disco, which juts out over the stern and is suspended—scarily, in our opinion—some 155 feet above the water. From this space, you can literally look forward as if you were following in a helicopter. It's really quite spectacular. If you're scared of heights, of course, don't even think of looking backward; you're so far above the water that it's (literally!) breathtaking. Smoke machines and other high-tech gizmos add to the spooky effect at night. During the day, its banquettes make a particularly cozy spot to snuggle up with a good book.

The *Golden* and *Star Princesses* also have a library, small writing room, card room, and business center with computers and e-mail access (see introduction above for prices).

DINING OPTIONS   The principal alternative eating area is Sabatini's Trattoria. The $25 cover charge gets you the finest Italian food there is—and gobs of it. That's the only additional charge required anywhere on the ships—a function of Princess's Personal Choice dining program.

POOL, FITNESS & SPA FACILITIES   These ships each have something like 1.7 acres of open deck space, so it's not hard to find a quiet place to soak in the sun. They have four great swimming pools, including one with a retractable glass roof so it can double as a sort of solarium (of special importance in Alaska), another touted as a swim-against-the-current pool (although, truth be told, there really isn't enough room to do laps if others are in the water with you), and a third, aft under the disco, that feels miles from the rest of the ship (and is usually the least crowded). There are also nine whirlpool tubs up front.

On the forward Sun Deck, surrounding the lap pool and its tiered, amphitheater-style wooden benches, is the large Plantation Spa, which almost appears to be separate from the rest of the ship. Personally, we find the layout to be a bit weird: For instance, there are no showers in the dressing area. The complex includes a very large oceanview salon and an oceanview gym, which is surprisingly small and cramped for a ship of this size (although there is an unusually large aerobics floor). Unfortunately, the sports deck is located just above the spa, so if you're trying to get a relaxing massage when someone is playing basketball, you'll hear it.

Other active diversions include a jogging track, basketball, paddle tennis, a nine-hole putting green, and computerized simulated golf.

Tahitian Princess

The Verdict

Arguably the most luxurious of Princess's Alaska fleet in 2008. If it were an all-inclusive vessel, we might be inclined to put it in the luxury class, alongside Silversea's *Silver Shadow* and Regent's *Seven Seas Mariner.*

Tahitian Princess *(photo: Princess Cruises)*

Specifications

Size (in Tons)	30,227	Crew	373
Passengers (Double Occ.)	688	Passenger/Crew Ratio	1.8 to 1
Passenger/Space Ratio	44	Year Launched	1999*
Total Cabins/Veranda Cabins	344/232	Last Major Refurbishment	2002

Ship entered service for Renaissance Cruises.

Frommer's Ratings (Scale of 1–5)

Cabin Comforts & Amenities	5	Dining Options	4
Ship Cleanliness & Maintenance	4.5	Gym, Spa & Sports Facilities	3.5
Public Comfort/Space	4	Children's Facilities	N/A
Decor	4	Enjoyment Factor	4.5

THE SHIP IN GENERAL   This delightful little ship—carrying fewer than 700 passengers—is something of a departure for Princess, which has gotten into the habit of building massive vessels. The *Tahitian* (and the other Renaissance-built ship, now renamed the *Pacific Princess*) gave the company a greater degree of intimacy and luxury than it ever had before but leaves few of the big-ship amenities out—namely, a children's center and some alternative dining options.

CABINS   The ship has very few inside rooms—just 27 out of a total of 344—and about 75% of those outside rooms have balconies. The rooms are beautifully done in pastel shades and blond wood, outfitted with spacious closets, TVs, VCRs, sofas, and desks. The smallest inside accommodations are about 160 square feet; outside rooms range from 206 square feet to the largest suites that go from 786 square feet to 962 square feet. Oceanview rooms all have tub/showers; the inside rooms have only a shower stall. Three rooms are handicap-accessible.

Cabins & Rates

Cabins	Per Diem Rates	Sq. Ft.	Fridge	Hair Dryer	Sitting Area	TV
Inside	$164–$179	160–174	yes	yes	yes	yes
Outside	$199–$249	206–216	yes	yes	yes	yes
Suites	$285–$403	322–962	yes	yes	yes	yes

PUBLIC AREAS   The ship's show lounge is an intimate, one-level facility, big enough to put on some interesting presentations, but not big enough to offer those huge glitzy Broadway-style reviews possible on the bigger ships in Alaska. There is a small casino and eight bars, though not all are open all the time. The Observation Lounge is an inviting place to watch the passing scenery; by night, it becomes an equally inviting bar.

DINING OPTIONS   There are two primary alternatives to the main dining room—Sabatini's ($25 cover) and a sushi bar/Japanese restaurant (no fee). You can enjoy a somewhat less structured buffet/bistro on the top deck 24 hours a day or have hamburgers and pizza poolside for lunch.

POOL, FITNESS, SPA & SPORTS FACILITIES   The *Tahitian Princess* comes with a swimming pool and two whirlpool tubs. The Lotus Spa is small but well equipped. Joggers will find the track on the topmost deck.

7 Regent Seven Seas Cruises

1000 Corporate Dr., Suite 500, Fort Lauderdale, FL 33334. © 800/285-1835. www.theregentexperience.com.

THE LINE IN A NUTSHELL   Regent's guests travel in style and extreme comfort. Its brand of luxury is casually elegant and subtle, its cuisine among the best in the industry. The line operates four upscale small to midsize ships and one expedition ship, geared toward affluent and worldly travelers. This year marks the line's eighth full season in Alaska and the return for the sixth year of the all-suite, all-balcony *Seven Seas Mariner.*

THE EXPERIENCE   The Regent Seven Seas experience offers outstanding food, service, and accommodations in an environment that's a little more casual than Crystal's traditional luxury, as evidenced by the country-club-casual attire that passengers wear throughout the cruise. The *Mariner* is one of the most comfortable ships at sea, offering its guests large suites and spacious public areas.

Pros

- **Overall excellence.** The line has a no-tipping policy, excellent food, open seating for meals, generally fine service, great accommodations, and creative shore excursions.
- **Great room service.** It's about the best we've found on a ship, with the food served promptly, fresh, and course by course (rather than all at once).
- **Liquor included in the price.** As of January 1, 2007, guests haven't had to worry about signing bar tabs and settling up at the end of the cruise; that's when Regent switched to a fleetwide liquor-inclusive policy on all departures.

Cons

- **Sedate nightlife** (although the line has recently upgraded its evening entertainment). Many guests, exhausted after a full day in port, retire early, perhaps to watch a movie on their in-suite DVD player, leaving only a few night owls in the disco and other lounges.

THE FLEET   *Seven Seas Mariner* is a regular in the Alaska market; it's the largest ship in the Regent fleet, and it offers an elegant yet comfortable modern design and a graceful yet casual onboard atmosphere.

PASSENGER PROFILE   Regent tends to attract travelers from their 40s to their 60s, with a high household income but who don't like to flaunt their wealth. The typical guest is well educated, well traveled, and inquisitive. They may also be a mixed bunch. Jerry remembers one *Mariner* cruise on which his shipmates included a former NBA basketball coach, a retired High Court judge, a window blinds manufacturer, and a midranking London policeman. (Guess they pay their cops well in England!)

DINING   Regent's cuisine would gain high marks even if it were on land. Service by professional waiters adds to the experience, as do little touches such as fine china and fresh flowers on the tables. Company policy has always been to serve complimentary wine at dinner—that is, unless you want a very expensive bottle of champagne, for example. But because the line serves excellent wines, there's very little reason to want to trade up. The pretty, windowed main dining room has open seating, so you can eat when and with whom you wish. Lavish buffets are offered for breakfast and lunch in the Veranda Restaurant. Other dinner options include Signatures (where the menus and cooking are Le Cordon Bleu School creations) and the Asian and Vietnamese-inspired Latitudes (reservations only, no additional fee).

ACTIVITIES   The line assumes that, for the most part, guests want to entertain themselves on board, but that doesn't mean there isn't a full roster of scheduled activities. These include lectures by local experts and well-known authors, and instruction

Regent Seven Seas Fleet Itineraries

Ship	Itineraries
Seven Seas Mariner	**7-night Gulf of Alaska:** North and southbound between Vancouver and Seward/Anchorage, visiting Ketchikan, Tracy Arm, Juneau, Skagway, Sitka, and Hubbard Glacier. May–Sept.

in the fine arts of pom-pom making and juggling. There are card and board games, blackjack and ping-pong tournaments, bingo, and big-screen movies with popcorn. Bridge instructors are on board on select sailings, and the ships offer facilities for e-mail interaction. Le Cordon Bleu–trained chefs offer cooking classes.

CHILDREN'S PROGRAM   The line is adult-oriented, but a children's program, Club Mariner, is offered on Alaska cruises, where you might find a dozen or so youngsters on any given sailing. Activities, held in borrowed spaces such as the nightclub or card room (there is no dedicated children's facility), include games, tournaments, Alaska-oriented crafts projects, storytelling, and the use of Sony PlayStations. There are also a limited number of special kids' shore excursions. Starting in 2007, Regent began offering special Circles of Interest programs for young guests. Called "Ambassadors of the Environment," these programs were created and are operated by counselors from Jean-Michel Cousteau's Ocean Futures Society, with whom Regent has an exclusive partnership and fleet-wide programming. The program, which has an additional cost, features special lectures and educational and fun activities on board, as well as dedicated shoreside activities and excursions.

ENTERTAINMENT   Entertainment includes medium and small-scale production shows (much improved in recent years), cabaret acts, and headliners including comedians and magicians, and sometimes members of philharmonic orchestras and other musical groups. The library stocks books and movies, which guests can play on their in-suite DVD player.

SERVICE   The senior dining room staff generally has had experience at fine hotels as well as on ships; they provide service so good that you don't really notice it. The same applies for the excellent room stewards. Bar service is outstanding. The *Mariner* also offers dry cleaning and full-service and self-service laundry.

CRUISETOURS & ADD-ON PROGRAMS   Land packages along the Denali Corridor between Anchorage and Fairbanks, to the Arctic Circle, and in the Canadian Rockies are among the cruise/tour options available in conjunction with the Gulf schedule of the *Mariner.* As an example of the prices, a 2-night sky-trekking tour of the Interior with a private pilot/guide starts at $2,690 per person double, while a 5-night Fairbanks/Arctic Circle package starts at $4,620 per person double. A 3-night package at British Columbia's venerable Chateau Whistler is priced at $1,195 per person double.

Pre- or post-cruise hotel nights are available in Anchorage (from $310 per person double) and in Vancouver (from $265 per person double).

Seven Seas Mariner

The Verdict

The true luxury leader among the big ships in Alaska. With very spacious public and deck areas and every suite outside with its own veranda, the viewing is easy and supremely comfortable.

Seven Seas Mariner *(photo: Regent Seven Seas)*

Specifications

Size (in Tons)	50,000	Crew	445
Passengers (Double Occ.)	700	Passenger/Crew Ratio	1.6 to 1
Passenger/Space Ratio	71.4	Year Launched	2001
Total Cabins/Veranda Cabins	350/350	Last Major Refurbishment	2007

Frommer's Ratings (Scale 1–5)

★★★★½

Cabin Comfort & Amenities	5	Dining Options	4
Ship Cleanliness & Maintenance	5	Gym, Spa & Sports Facilities	4.5
Public Comfort/Space	5	Children's Facilities	N/A
Decor	4.5	Enjoyment Factor	4.5

THE SHIP IN GENERAL The *Seven Seas Mariner* is a luxurious vessel that carries 700 guests in extreme comfort. The amount of public space per person is enormous for a ship this size, and its all-outside, all-suite design gives everyone lots of private space as well. There are plenty of mealtime options, especially for dinner. And while the daytime activities offered are not extensive, that seems to suit the clientele nicely. The company has made enormous strides in service and entertainment in recent years, putting the ship in the upper echelon of luxury cruises. The ship underwent a $7 million refurbishment in 2007.

CABINS The cabins are all oceanview suites, and all have private verandas. The Standard Suite is a very large 301 square feet (including veranda); the largest two suites are a whopping 1,580 square feet, with two bedrooms and two balconies. Some of the suites interconnect if you want to book two for a family or just have additional space. All suites offer separate living-room areas, and top levels of suites have dining areas as well. All suites come with queen-size beds that convert to twins, walk-in closets, marble-appointed bathrooms with full-size tubs, TVs and DVD player, refrigerators stocked with complimentary bottled water and soft drinks, safes, phones, and 24-hour room service. You can even order full meals from the dining room menu served in-suite. Fifteen of the cabins are wheelchair accessible.

Cabins & Rates

Cabins	Per Diem Rates	Sq. Ft.	Fridge	Hair Dryer	Sitting Area	TV
Suites	$528–$2,079	301–1,580*	yes	yes	yes	yes

Includes veranda.

PUBLIC AREAS Italian-designed and -built, the *Mariner* features an eclectic modern design that's elegant yet comfortable. An impressive atrium starts on Deck 4 and rises to Deck 12. The two-tiered Constellation Theater is modeled after a 1930s nightclub. There are two additional lounges and a Connoisseur Club, a cushy venue for pre-dinner drinks and after-dinner fine brandy and cigars. The casino offers blackjack, roulette, Caribbean stud poker, and slots. Shoppers can indulge in two small boutiques offering clothes, jewelry, and your usual array of cruise-line logo items. The library offers books and DVDs, as well as a few computer terminals. Additional computer terminals fill the adjacent room, where you can send and receive e-mail for about a buck per message (guests only pay for transmission time, a very nice feature).

DINING OPTIONS   Meals are served in the pretty, windowed Compass Rose main dining room on an open-seating basis. Buffets are also offered at breakfast and lunch at the indoor/outdoor La Veranda. At night, part of La Veranda is closed off and serves Mediterranean cuisine in a casual, intimate space. Other dinner options, on a reservations-only basis, include the Vietnamese-Asian fusion Latitudes and Signatures (where the menus and cooking are Le Cordon Bleu School creations). With these four options (plus room service) available for dinner, *Mariner* offers a range of excellent dining experiences, with no additional cover charges.

POOL, FITNESS, SPA & SPORTS FACILITIES   The ship's Carita of Paris spa offers treatments using a variety of herbal and water-based therapies, as well as a variety of beauty services (the spa areas themselves are a bit spartan). The seawater pool is flanked by three heated whirlpools and surrounded by lots of open deck space. Recreational facilities include a fitness center, golf-driving cages, paddle tennis, a jogging track, ping-pong, and shuffleboard.

8 Royal Caribbean International

1050 Caribbean Way, Miami, FL 33132. ✆ **800/327-6700** or 305/379-2601. www.royalcaribbean.com

THE LINE IN A NUTSHELL   A bold, brash industry-innovating company that ranks up there in size with Carnival and Princess, Royal Caribbean introduced the concept of the megaship with its *Sovereign of the Seas* in 1988, and the industry hasn't been the same since. The mass-market style of cruising that Royal Caribbean sells aboard its megaships is reasonably priced and offers nearly every diversion imaginable.

THE EXPERIENCE   The ships are more informal than formal and are well run, with a large team of friendly service employees paying close attention to day-to-day details. Dress is generally casual during the day and informal most evenings, with just one formal night on each 7-night cruise. The contemporary decor on Royal Caribbean vessels doesn't bang you over the head with glitz like, say, Carnival. It's more subdued, classy, and witty, with lots of glass, greenery, and art. All the Royal Caribbean vessels feature the line's trademark Viking Crown Lounge, an observation area located in a circular glass structure on the upper deck (in some cases, encircling the smokestack), which looks like a Martian spacecraft atop the vessels. Another popular trademark feature are the ships' nautically themed Schooner bars.

Pros

- **Great spas and recreation facilities.** Royal Caribbean's Alaska ships for 2008 all have elaborate health-club and spa facilities, a covered swimming pool, and large, open sun-deck areas.
- **Great observation areas.** The Viking Crown Lounge and other glassed-in areas make excellent observation rooms for gazing at the Alaska sights.

- **Quality entertainment.** Royal Caribbean spends big bucks on entertainment, which includes high-tech show productions. Headliners are often featured.

Cons

- **Crowds.** As with some other big ships, you almost need a map to get around, and you'll likely experience the inevitable lines for buffets, debarkation, and boarding of buses during shore excursions.

THE FLEET   Royal Caribbean owns the largest ship in the world, the new *Freedom of the Seas,* at 160,000 tons, and four 142,000-ton Voyager-class vessels. Although these 3,000-plus-passenger ships—which introduced such cruise-ship design features as ice-skating rinks, rock-climbing walls, and cabins overlooking interior atrium areas—are not in Alaska this year, Royal Caribbean does offer the very up-to-date 2,112-passenger *Radiance of the Seas,* which in 2001 introduced a new category of ship for the line, offering many innovations, including a billiards room with self-leveling pool tables. The ship is joined in Alaska for by its sister ship, the similarly dimensioned *Serenade of the Seas.* The *Radiance* is in Gulf of Alaska service between Vancouver, B.C., and Seward; the *Serenade* is in Inside Passage service out of Vancouver. Also sailing in Alaska in 2008 is the 1,998-guest *Vision of the Seas.*

PASSENGER PROFILE   The crowd on Royal Caribbean ships, like the decor, tends to be a notch down on the whoopee scale from what you'll find on Carnival and perhaps a notch up from those on the somewhat more formal ships of, say, Princess or the Holland America Line. Guests represent an age mix from 30 to 60, and a good number of families are attracted by the line's well-established and fine-tuned kids' programs.

In Alaska, Royal Caribbean focuses more on international sales than the entrenched market leaders, Princess and Holland America, which often results in sailings populated by a good many overseas guests.

DINING   Food on Royal Caribbean has been upgraded and improved in recent years, and occasionally a dish will knock your socks off. The dining rooms feature two seatings with assigned tables at dinner, and open seating at breakfast and lunch. Every menu contains selections designed for low-fat, low-cholesterol, and low-salt dining, as well as vegetarian and children's dishes. On the *Radiance* and the *Serenade,* you also have the option of dining on a reservations-only basis at Chops Grille, a classy steakhouse, or Portofino, an upscale Italian eatery. A fee of $20 a head is charged at these venues, but in our experience, the food soars above what's offered in the dining room. Casual table-service dining is offered in Cascades for all three meals, as an alternative for those who don't want to sit in the dining room (no extra charge). Buffet-style breakfasts and lunches are available in the Windjammer Café, on Deck 10. In addition to the midnight buffet, sandwiches are served throughout the night in the public lounges. A basic menu is available from room service 24 hours a day, and during normal dinner hours, a cabin steward can bring you anything being served in the dining room that night. Royal Caribbean bans smoking in the dining rooms on all its vessels.

ACTIVITIES   On the activity front, Royal Caribbean offers plenty of the standard cruise-line fare (craft classes, horse racing, bingo, shuffleboard, deck games, line-dancing lessons, wine-and-cheese tastings, cooking demonstrations, and art auctions). But if you want to take it easy and watch the world go by or scan for wildlife, nobody will bother you or cajole you into joining an activity. Port lectures are offered on topics

Royal Caribbean Fleet Itineraries

Ship	Itineraries
Serenade of the Seas	**7-night Inside Passage:** Round-trip from Vancouver, visiting Hubbard Glacier, Skagway, Juneau, and Icy Strait Point. May–Sept.
Rhapsody of the Seas	**7-night Inside Passage:** Round-trip from Seattle, visiting Juneau, Tracy Arm, Skagway, and Prince Rupert, B.C. May–Sept.
Radiance of the Sea	**7-night Gulf of Alaska:** Northbound and southbound between Vancouver, B.C., and Seward, visiting Juneau, Skagway, Icy Strait Point, and Hubbard Glacier. May–Sept.

such as Alaska wildlife, history, and culture. The ships also offer an extensive fitness program called ShipShape.

CHILDREN'S PROGRAM   Children's activities are some of the most extensive afloat and include a teen disco, children's play areas, and the Adventure Ocean program, which offers a full schedule of scavenger hunts, arts-and-crafts sessions, and science presentations—so many activities, in fact, that kids get their own daily activities program delivered to their cabin.

ENTERTAINMENT   Royal Caribbean's entertainment package, which incorporates sprawling, high-tech cabaret stages into each of its ship's showrooms, some with a wall of video monitors to augment live performances, is as good as anybody's. It begins before dinner and continues late, late into the night. There are musical acts, comedy acts, sock hops, toga parties, talent shows, and that great cruise favorite, karaoke. The Vegas-style shows are filled with all the razzle-dazzle guests have come to expect, and these large-cast revues are among the best you'll find on any ship. Royal Caribbean uses 10-piece bands in its main showroom. Show bands and other lounge acts keep the music playing all over the ship. All of the entertainment options are first rate.

SERVICE   Overall, service in the restaurants and cabins is friendly, accommodating, and efficient. You're likely to be greeted with a smile by someone polishing the brass in a stairwell. That said, big, bustling ships like Royal Caribbean's are no strangers to crowds and lines, and harried servers may not be able to get to you exactly when you'd like them to. Considering the vast armies of personnel required to maintain a line as large as Royal Caribbean, it's a miracle that staffers appear as motivated and enthusiastic as they do. Laundry and dry-cleaning services are available on all the ships, but none has a self-service laundromat.

CRUISETOURS & ADD-ON PROGRAMS   Royal Caribbean International offers 10- to 13-night Alaska cruisetours combining a 7-night cruise with a 3- to 6-night land package in the Denali Corridor, in conjunction with the Northbound/Southbound Inside Passage sailings onboard *Radiance of the Seas.* In addition, Royal Caribbean features 3 and 5 night cruisetours to the Canadian Rockies and Whistler, in combination with the 7-night Alaska Inside Passage sailings onboard *Serenade of the Seas,* sailing round-trip from Vancouver. Ten-night Alaska cruisetours prices start at $1,269 per person with package prices varying depending on the stateroom category, land package, and departure date. Additionally, Royal Caribbean offers pre- and post-cruise hotel stays in Anchorage (from $263 per person, double, including transfers) and Vancouver (from $132 per person, double, including transfers).

Rhapsody of the Seas

The Verdict

This ship has it all—a great spa, good shopping, and lots of glass for premium viewing of the passing Alaska scenery.

Rhapsody of the Seas *(photo: Royal Caribbean International)*

Specifications

Size (in Tons)	78,491	Crew	765
Passengers (Double Occ.)	1,998	Passenger/Crew Ratio	2.6 to 1
Passenger/Space Ratio	39	Year Launched	1998
Total Cabins/Veranda Cabins	999/229	Last Major Refurbishment	2000

Frommer's Ratings (Scale of 1–5)   ★★★½

Cabin Comfort & Amenities	3.5	Dining Options	3.5
Ship Cleanliness & Maintenance	4	Gym, Spa & Sports Facilities	4
Public Comfort/Space	3.5	Children's Facilities	3.5
Decor	3.5	Enjoyment Factor	3.5

THE SHIP IN GENERAL The *Rhapsody* is a true floating city, offering elegant trappings from multimillion-dollar art collections to a wide range of onboard facilities. Plenty of nice touches—a sumptuous, big-windowed health club/spa with lots of health and beauty treatments, and loads of fine shopping, dining, and entertainment options—give the *Rhapsody* the feel of a top-flight shore resort.

CABINS Staterooms are not large—inside rooms measure 138 square feet and outsides 153 square feet—but do have small sitting areas. All staterooms have TVs, phones, twin beds that convert to queens, ample storage space, and well-lit, moderately sized bathrooms. TVs feature movies, news, and information channels, and excursion and debarkation talks are rebroadcast in-room just in case you missed any information. Nearly a quarter of the staterooms have private verandas, and about a third of the rooms are designed to accommodate third and fourth guests. For bigger digs, check out the Royal Suite—it measures a mammoth 1,150 square feet and even has a grand piano. Fourteen rooms on the ship are wheelchair accessible.

Cabins & Rates

Cabins	Per Diem Rates	Sq. Ft.	Fridge	Hair Dryer	Sitting Area	TV
Inside	$100	138	no	no	yes	yes
Outside	$128–$199*	153	some	no	yes	yes
Suites	$221 and up	1,150	yes	no	yes	yes

*with balcony

PUBLIC AREAS The *Rhapsody* soars 10 stories above the waterline and features a seven-story glass-walled atrium with glass elevators (a la Hyatt Regency) and a winding brass-trimmed staircase. At the top of the staircase, the Viking Crown Lounge affords a 360-degree view of the passing scenery. You'll also appreciate the view through the glass walls of the bi-level dining room. Actually, other than in the windowless casino and show lounge, there are great views to be found virtually everywhere on this ship—perfect for scoping glaciers.

A playroom, teen center, and video arcade provide plenty to keep kids happily occupied while parents relax, gamble, attend one of the many activities (there are dozens to select from each week, including informative nature lectures), take in a show, or dance the night away in the disco or one of numerous lounges and bars, which include a champagne/caviar bar and piano bar. Other rooms include a card room, a library, several shops, and a conference room.

DINING OPTIONS Meals are served both in the windowed, two-story dining room and in the casual, open-seating Windjammer Café (an indoor/outdoor facility open for breakfast and lunch), so there's freedom as to when you dine and, since the menus in each venue are different, choices as to what you'll eat. Pizza is served in the Solarium.

POOL, FITNESS, SPA & SPORTS FACILITIES The spa on the ship is one of the most attractive around—truly a soothing respite from the hubbub of ship life. It offers a wide selection of treatments, as well as the standard steam rooms and saunas. Adjacent to the spa, the spacious solarium has a pool, lounge chairs, floor-to-ceiling windows, and a retractable glass ceiling. This is a peaceful place to repose before or after a spa treatment, or any time at all. Surprisingly, the gym is small for the ship's size—and in comparison to those on Carnival's, Holland America's, and Celebrity's megaliners—but it's well equipped.

The main pool area has four whirlpools, and there are two more in the Solarium. The observatory on deck (complete with stargazing equipment) is protected from wind by glass windbreaks. The *Rhapsody* also offers a cushioned jogging track and a half basketball court.

Radiance of the Seas • Serenade of the Seas

The Verdict

So what if you need a map to find your way around these large vessels? It's worth it if the map leads you to the superb spa, the self-leveling billiards tables, or the revolving bar in the disco.

Radiance of the Seas *(photo: Royal Caribbean International)*

Specifications

Size (in Tons)	90,090	Crew	857
Passengers (Double Occ.)	2,112	Passengers/Crew Ratio	2.5 to 1
Passenger/Space Ratio	43	Year Launched	2001/2003
Total Cabins/Veranda Cabins	1,056/577	Last Major Refurbishment	N/A

Frommer's Ratings (Scale of 1–5)   ★★★★

Cabin Comfort & Amenities	3.5	Dining Options	4.5
Ship Cleanliness & Maintenance	5	Gym, Spa & Sports Facilities	4.5
Public Comfort/Space	4	Children's Facilities	4
Decor	4	Enjoyment Factor	4

THE SHIPS IN GENERAL   These were Royal Caribbean's first ships of the 21st century, as well as being the first vessels in a new class, and they continue the line's tradition of being an innovator in the industry. Highlights include a billiards room with custom-made, self-leveling tables (in case there are big waves) and a revolving bar in the disco. The ships are designed to remind guests that they are at sea. With that goal in mind, they feature huge expanses of glass in some rooms through which to view the passing Alaska scenery. You won't even miss the views when you are in the 12-story lobby elevators because they, too, are made of glass and face the ocean. Even the Internet cafe has an ocean view! These ships are slightly more upscale than the line's other vessels—Royal Caribbean seems to have borrowed a page from sister company Celebrity. They feature wood, marble, and lots of nice fabrics and artwork, adding up to a pretty, low-key decor that lets the views provide most of the visual drama.

CABINS   Staterooms on these vessels are larger than on the *Rhapsody*—the smallest is 170 square feet—and more come with verandas than on the earlier vessels. All rooms are equipped with an interactive TV (which allows guests to check their bills, contact the purser's office, and, on some ships, make shore excursion reservations), telephone, computer jack, vanity table, refrigerator/minibar, and hair dryer. Suites also come with a veranda, sitting area with a sofa bed, dry bar, stereo and VCR, and bathtub and double sinks. The Royal Suite on each ship has a separate bedroom (with a king-size bed) and living room, a whirlpool bathtub, and a baby grand piano. Family staterooms and suites can accommodate five. Fourteen rooms are wheelchair accessible.

Cabins & Rates

Cabins	Per Diem Rates	Sq. Ft.	Fridge	Hair Dryer	Sitting Area	TV
Serenade of the Seas						
Inside	$121	170	yes	no	no	yes
Outside	$142–$207*	185	yes	yes	yes	yes
Suites	$250 and up	293–1,001	yes	yes	yes	yes
Radiance of the Seas						
Inside	$107	170	yes	no	no	yes
Outside	$128–$186*	185	yes	yes	yes	yes
Suites	$257 and up	293–1,001	yes	yes	yes	yes

*with balcony

PUBLIC AREAS   These ships are full of little surprises. There's that billiards room we mentioned and a card club where five tables are dedicated to poker. You can, of course, also find more gaming options in the ships' massive French Art Nouveau–inspired Casino Royale. Bookworms will want to check out the combo bookstore and coffee shop (a first at sea).

The numerous cushy bars and lounges include a champagne bar and piano bar. If you tire of the ocean views, you can gaze into the atrium, eight decks below, from a porthole-like window in the floor of the Crown and Anchor Lounge. The ships' Viking Crown Lounge holds the disco and its revolving bar, as well as an intimate cabaret area. The three-level theater on each ship recalls the glacial landscapes of not only Alaska, but the North Pole as well.

Other public rooms include a show lounge, conference center, library, shopping mall, and business center. For kids, there's a children's center equipped with computer and crafts stations. Teens get their own hangout space. There's also a video arcade.

DINING OPTIONS   The elegant two-level main dining room features a grand staircase but is a rather noisy space. On both ships, casual buffet breakfasts and lunches are offered in the Windjammer Café, and casual dinners, with waiter service, are offered in the Windjammer Café and the Seaview Café. The ships also feature two reservations-only restaurants: Chops Grill, featuring steaks and chops, and Portofino, featuring Italian cuisine. Pizza is served in the Solarium.

POOL, FITNESS, SPA & SPORTS FACILITIES   For the active sort, there's a rock-climbing wall and a nine-hole mini-golf course on the *Radiance* (the latter designed as a baroque garden, of all things). On both vessels, there is a nice spa (including a sauna and steam rooms), an oceanview fitness center with dozens of machines (including 18 Stairmaster treadmills), a jogging track, a sports court (including basketball), golf simulators (for those who like to play virtual golf), and three swimming pools—one outside, one enclosed (the indoor pool features an African theme complete with 17-ft.-high stone elephants and cascading waterfalls), and the third a teen/kiddie pool with slide. Whirlpools can be found in the Solarium and near the outdoor pool.

9 Silversea

110 E. Broward Blvd., Fort Lauderdale, FL 33301. ℂ 800/774-9966. www.silversea.com.

THE LINE IN A NUTSHELL   There can be no argument. Silversea is a very worthy member of the band of operators of truly luxury small ships. Its only rival to its *Silver Shadow* in that category in Alaska this year is Regent's *Seven Seas Mariner*. The company isn't in Alaska every year. It likes to offer past passengers as much variety as possible and it withdrew from the 49th State in 2007 to deploy the vessel in more exotic trades—Southeast Asia, South America, and the like.

THE EXPERIENCE   All of the Silversea vessels represent the last word in elegance and service. Spacious accommodations, all suites, no tipping expected, free beverages (alcoholic and otherwise), swift and caring baggage handling—these are the hallmarks of the Silversea product.

Pros

- **All around excellence.** A no-tipping policy is always a hit and the cuisine, open seating for meals, exemplary service, and great accommodations make Silversea well worth the money.
- **Surprisingly little formality.** Considering the economic status of most of the passengers, there's very little stuffiness.
- **A huge number of private verandas.** More than 80% of the suites on the Silver Shadow offer this desirable feature.

Silversea Fleet Itineraries

Ship	Itineraries
Silver Shadow	**9-night Inside Passage:** North and southbound between San Francisco and Vancouver visiting Ketchikan, Sitka, Haines, Sawyer Glacier, Juneau, and Prince Rupert, B.C. May–Sept.

Cons

- **Not a great deal of nightlife.** Although the ship has a show lounge, it's not really big enough for anything overly lavish. But most passengers—more mature perhaps than on some other ships—don't have any need for high-tech discos or high-energy Broadway reviews.

THE FLEET The *Silver Shadow*, which joined the fleet in 2000, is one of four Silversea ships. Its twin, the *Silver Whisper*, entered service the following year. The others are the smaller and virtually identical *Silver Cloud* (1994) and *Silver Wind* (1995).

PASSENGER PROFILE Guests tend to be in their 60s and up. They are generally well educated with definite ideas on just what luxury means in accommodations, cuisine, and service. And they have the means to pay for it!

DINING Food is one of Silversea's strengths—both in preparation and in presentation—not only in the main dining room (known simply as The Restaurant) but also in the breakfast/lunch buffets in the Terrace Café as well. That room doubles as a low-capacity bistro-type eatery in the evening.

Silversea offers very acceptable complimentary wine with dinner (and at other meals) but if you must upgrade to something really, really expensive (Opus One and Dom Perignon are a couple of tipples that come to mind) you should expect to pay the going rate.

ACTIVITIES There's not a lot and what there is tends toward the sedentary. Bridge, Trivial Pursuit, a quiz given by the cruise director in the lounge at tea time—that's about what you can expect. It's enough for most Silversea devotees.

CHILDREN'S PROGRAM In a nutshell—there isn't one. It's not a company that caters to the younger set.

ENTERTAINMENT It's better on the two bigger ships, but it's still pretty muted. It's just not possible to stage extravagant song-and-dance presentations on a ship—and a stage—as small as this one. But the talent is there and the shows are about as good as they can be given the size constraints facing the performers. Outside the main show room there's usually a small combo for dancing to (no disco, puleeze!). The library has an ample supply of books.

SERVICE Uniformly of the highest order. These people could take their places in the finest restaurants and hotels ashore—from where, in fact, many of them came. The finest compliment that anybody can pay the Silversea staff is that they provide the kind of service that you just don't notice. There is a self-service laundry and remarkably speedy valet service, including laundry and dry cleaning.

Silver Shadow

The Verdict

If Silversea had a movie equivalent, it would have to be Jack Nicholson's *As Good as It Gets*.

Silver Shadow *(photo: Silversea Cruises)*

Specifications

Size (in Tons)	24,258	Crew	295
Passengers (Double Occ.)	382	Passenger/Crew Ratio	1.3 to 1
Passenger/Space Ratio	63	Year Launched	2001
Total Cabins/Veranda Cabins	194/168	Last Major Refurbishment	N/A

Frommer's Ratings (Scale of 1–5)   ★★★★ ½

Cabin Comfort & Amenities	5	Dining Options	4.5
Ship Cleanliness & Maintenance	5	Gym, Spa & Sports Facilities	4
Public Comfort/Space	4	Children's Facilities	N/A
Decor	4.5	Enjoyment Factor	5

THE SHIP IN GENERAL   This ship has one of the highest passenger/space rations in the industry—technically determined as 63. That's a rather esoteric measurement that's arrived at by dividing the ship's gross tonnage (the volume of its interior space) by the lower berth capacity. It's complicated, but take our word for it—this ship is plenty spacious. The *Silver Shadow* takes Silversea's concept of luxury cruising to new heights. Walk-in closets, dressing table with hair dryer close at hand, real marble, double-vanity basin, bathtubs and separate showers, VCR units in every stateroom—no detail has been overlooked.

CABINS   All outside, all suites. All but a few of them have private verandas. The smallest of the units—there are only a handful—have none. But they're a roomy 278 square feet, with picture windows. From there, the sizes go up and up, ranging from 354 square feet all the way up to 1,450 square feet. Every suite comes with convertible twin-to-queen beds, minibar (stocked), and safes.

Ten of the suites are handicap-accessible.

Cabins & Rates

Cabins	Per Diem Rates	Sq. Ft.	Fridge	Hair Dryer	Sitting Area	TV
Suites	$660–$2,200	278–1,450	yes	yes	yes	yes

PUBLIC AREAS   The Silver Shadow's two-level showroom is not the biggest we've ever seen, but it has good sightlines and it's a good place to while away an hour after dinner. There is a small champagne bar and a smaller cigar bar, known as The Humidor. The casino offers the usual array of money-speculating ventures—roulette, blackjack, and a few slots. You can have a drink in the casino or in a bigger room called The Bar. (Who thinks up these names?)

DINING OPTIONS   There are only two places to eat on the ship—The Restaurant and the Terrace Café. Because it is small, the Terrace Café requires reservations for dinner—but there is no charge for eating there.

POOL, FITNESS, SPA & SPORTS FACILITIES   The spa is, like most of the other public rooms, small when measured alongside its megaship competition. But it offers the same range of hydrotherapy, massage and beauty treatments, men's and women's saunas, and more. For fitness buffs, there are aerobics classes and a small jogging track. The beauty shop provides pedicures, manicures, and facials as well as hair styling. The one pool is quite adequate for a ship this size.

6

The Cruise Lines, Part 2: The Small Ships

Big ships show you Alaska while immersed in a vibrant, resort-like atmosphere—but small ships let you see it from the waterline, with no distraction from anything un-Alaskan—no glitzy interiors, no big shows or loud music, no casinos, no spas, no crowds. The largest of these ships (the stern-wheeler *Empress of the North*—more on that later) carries only 223 passengers. On the small ships, you're immersed in the 49th state from the minute you wake up to the minute you fall asleep, and for the most part, you're left alone to form your own opinions, although there invariably will be a naturalist, a historian, or some such expert along to provide a running commentary en route.

These vessels allow you to visit more isolated parts of the coast. Thanks to their smaller size and shallow draft (the amount of hull below the waterline), they can go places larger ships can't, and they have the flexibility to change their itineraries as opportunities arise—say, to go where whales have been sighted. (But bear in mind that ships are prohibited from "stalking" wildlife for too long: They must keep their distance and break off after a relatively short while.) Depending on the itinerary, small-ship ports of call might include popular stops such as Juneau, Sitka, or Ketchikan; lesser-visited areas such as Elfin Cove or Warm Springs Harbor; or a Tlingit Native village such as Kake. The one thing you can be confident of is that all itineraries will include **glacier viewing** and **whale-watching.** Most of the itineraries also have time built in for passengers to explore the wilder parts of Alaska, ferrying passengers ashore for hikes in wilderness areas and, in some cases, carrying sea **kayaks** and **Zodiacs** for passenger use. Rather than glitzy entertainment, you'll likely get informal and informative **lectures** and sometimes video presentations on Alaskan wildlife, history, and Native culture. In most cases, at least some shore excursions are included in your cruise fare. Meals are served in open seatings, so you can sit where and with whom you like; and time spent huddled on the outside decks scanning for whales fosters great camaraderie among passengers. It must be noted, though, that the size of the ships precludes any kind of spacious dining rooms. Generally, they're quite small—some would say cramped. And on most of the smaller ships, room service is not an option—unless you are sick, of course.

Cabins on these ships don't always offer TVs or telephones, and they tend to be tiny and sometimes spartan. (See the individual reviews below for exceptions.) Most do not have e-mail access. There are no stabilizers on most of these smaller ships, so the ride can be bumpy in rough seas. Since the vessels tend to spend most of their time in the somewhat protected waters of the Inside Passage, this is not usually a major concern. But it can be a problem when the vessels ply open seas.

Of the small ships, only Cruise West's *Spirit of '98* and *Spirit of Oceanus* and Majestic Cruise Line's *Empress of the North* are even moderately wheelchair friendly. Small ships may not be the best choice for families with children, unless those kids are avid nature buffs and are able to keep themselves entertained without a lot of outside stimuli.

READING THE REVIEWS

In this chapter, you'll also see the following terms used to describe the various small-ship experiences:

- **Soft adventure:** These ships don't provide onboard grandeur, organized activities, or entertainment, but instead give you a really close-up Alaska experience. These ships often avoid large ports.
- **Active adventure:** These ships function less like cruise ships than like base camps. Passengers use them only to sleep and eat, getting off the ship for hiking and kayaking excursions every day.
- **Port-to-port:** These ships are for people who want to visit the popular Alaska ports (and some lesser-known ones), but also want the flexible schedules and maneuverability of a small ship and a more homey experience than you would find aboard a glitzy big ship.

RATES

Cruise rates in these reviews are brochure rates. Some discounts may apply, including early booking and last-minute offers (see more in chapter 3), although small-ship lines do not traditionally discount their fares as much as bigger ship lines. As we do in chapter 5, all rates have been calculated by nights spent on ship, based on 7-night sailings unless otherwise indicated.

TIPPING

Tipping on small ships is not exactly standardized, as it tends to be on the big ships. It varies quite wildly from company to company. Gratuities on the following lines are pooled among the crew. Below is a rundown of suggested tips per passenger, for a 1-week cruise:

- **American Safari Cruises:** 5% to 10% of the cost of the cruise.
- **Majestic America Line:** $84 to $98 ($12–$14 per day).
- **Cruise West:** No tipping is required or expected.
- **Lindblad Expeditions:** $56 to $70 ($8–$10 per day).

DRESS CODE

The word is *casual.* You're fine with polo shirts, jeans, khakis, shorts, and a fleece pullover and Gore-Tex shell. Having a pair of rubber sandals or old sneakers is handy as going ashore in rubber landing crafts might require you to step out into the surf. Hiking boots are also recommended.

1 American Safari Cruises

19101 36th Ave. W., Suite 201, Lynnwood, WA 98036. ☏ **888/862-8881**. Fax 425/776-8889. www.amsafari.com.

THE LINE IN A NUTSHELL   Directed toward the slightly jaded high-end traveler, American Safari Cruises sails luxury soft-adventure cruises aboard three full-fledged luxury yachts.

A Note on Ship Ratings

Because the small-ship experience is so completely different from the mega-ship experience, we've had to adjust our ratings. For instance, because all but a tiny fraction of these ships have just one dining room for all meals, we can't judge them by the same standard we use for ships with 5 or 10 different restaurants. So we've set the default **Dining Options** rating for these ships at 3, or "good," with points deducted if a restaurant is particularly uncomfortable and points added for any options above and beyond. Similarly, we've changed the "Gym, Spa & Sports Facilities" rating to **Adventure & Fitness Options** to reflect the fact that on small ships the focus is what's outside, not inside. Options covered in this category include kayaks, trips by inflatable Zodiac, and frequent hiking trips.

When reading the reviews in this chapter, bear in mind, too, that small-ship lines often measure their ships' gross register tonnage, or GRT (a measure of internal space, not actual weight), differently than the large lines. There's not even a definite standard within the small-ship market, so to compare ship sizes, it's best to just look at the number of passengers aboard. Also note that where GRT measures are nonstandard, passenger/space measurements are impossible or meaningless.

THE EXPERIENCE   American Safari Cruises promises an intimate, all-inclusive yacht cruise to some of the more out-of-the-way stretches of the Inside Passage—and it succeeds admirably. The price is considerable—but so is the pampering. The vessels carry between 12 and 21 guests, guaranteeing unparalleled flexibility, intimacy, and privacy. Once passenger interests become apparent, the expedition leader shapes the cruise around them. Black-bear aficionados can chug off in a Zodiac boat for a better look, active adventurers can explore the shoreline in one of the yacht's four kayaks, and slacker travelers can relax aboard ship. A crew-to-passenger ratio of about one to two ensures that a cold drink, a good meal, or a sharp eagle-spotting eye is always nearby on the line's comfortable 120-foot ships.

Pros

- **Near-private experience.** With only a handful of fellow passengers, it's like having a yacht to yourself. (In fact, if you have the money and the inclination, you can literally have the yacht to yourself: Whole charters are available, for a stiff price. A 7-night charter of, say, the *Safari Quest* [the 21-seater] could set you back a cool $149,995 in midseason in 2008.)
- **Built-in shore excursions.** All off-ship excursions, including a flightseeing trip, are included in the cruise fare, as are drinks.
- **Night anchorages.** A great boon to light sleepers is that the route taken allows time for the vessels to overnight at anchor, making for quieter sleeping than aboard most ships, which travel through the night.
- **More time to explore.** This year again, the *Safari Quest* will spend the better part of 3 days and 2 nights in Glacier Bay, giving passengers the opportunity to get to know the territory in greater depth, in the lap of luxury.

American Safari Cruises Fleet

Ship	Itineraries
Safari Escape	**8-night Inside Passage:** Between Juneau and Prince Rupert, B.C., visiting Tracy Arm, Ketchikan, Misty Fjords, Canoe Cove, and Petersburg, May–Aug.*
Safari Quest	**7-night Inside Passage:** North- and southbound between Juneau and Sitka, visiting Glacier Bay (2 nights) and Elfin Cove, on Chichagof Island. May–Sept.*
Safari Spirit	**7-night Inside Passage:** North- and southbound between Juneau and Petersburg, visiting Tenakee Springs and Misty Fjords. May–Aug.*

In addition to the itineraries above, all three yachts offer 14-night repositioning cruises between Seattle and Juneau, the Spirit *and* Escape *one each (northbound in May, southbound in Sept), the* Quest *one southbound in Sept.*

Cons

- **The price.** Shore excursions and drinks are included, but even when you remove these costs, the price is still high (the least expensive accommodations start at about $650 a head per day). At a recommended 5% to 10% of the tariff, gratuities can add mightily to the outlay. You pay for all the luxury you get.

THE FLEET   The 21-passenger *Safari Quest* (1992) and the 12-passenger *Safari Escape* (1993) and *Safari Spirit* (1991) are the closest things you'll find to private yachts in the Alaska cruise business. They're sleek, they're stylish, and they're as far as you can get from the megaship experience without owning your own boat.

PASSENGER PROFILE   Passengers—almost always couples—tend to be more than comfortably wealthy and range from about 45 to 65 years of age. Most hope to get close to nature without sacrificing luxury. (You know the old saying: "Some people will go to the ends of the air-conditioned earth in search of adventure.") They've paid handsomely for food, drink, and service, all of which American Safari delivers—and then some. Dress is always casual, in a Saks Fifth Avenue sort of way, with comfort being the prime goal.

DINING   A shipboard chef assails guests with multiple-course meals and clever snacks (wild-mushroom cups, rack of lamb, thyme-infused king salmon, amaretto cheesecake, fresh-baked bread), barters with nearby fishing boats for the catch of the day, and raids local markets for the freshest fruits and vegetables—say, strawberries the size of a cub's paw and potent strains of basil and cilantro. Between meals, snacks such as Gorgonzola and brie with pears, walnuts, and table crackers are set out. Guests may always serve themselves from the ludicrously well-stocked bar, which during our visit had two kinds of sherry and four brands of gin alone, all of them premium.

ACTIVITIES   When passengers aren't eating or drinking, an expedition leader is helping them into Zodiac boats or kayaks to investigate black bears at shoreline or prancing river otters, or to navigate fjords packed with ice floes and lolling seals. Expeditions include trips to boardwalked cannery towns and Tlingit villages, where local people receive the yachts more personally and gracefully than they might a larger ship. Activities throughout the day are well spaced, with many opportunities to see wildlife.

From time to time, local bush pilots may swoop down for a landing beside the ships and take two or three passengers for a whirl over a glacier or a nearby fjord. Because these are private operations, they're not included in the cruise fare.

CHILDREN'S PROGRAM   There is none of any consequence. American Safari really isn't that kind of cruise line, but your kids are welcome, provided neither you nor your children come expecting game rooms or supervised activities.

ENTERTAINMENT   A big-screen TV in the main lounge forms a natural center for listening to impromptu lectures during the day and watching a movie at night. Guests may choose from a library of 100-plus videotapes (guests in the Owner's and Captain's staterooms have TV/VCRs in their cabins) or opt for a casual game of cards or Scrabble in the public rooms upstairs.

Given that these vessels spend a huge percentage of their time at sea—far more than other ships—land visits are kept to a minimum. Wherever possible—at the beginning or end of a trip for instance—the crew and passengers may gather for an all-you-can-eat salmon bake and local saloon crawl.

SERVICE   Crew members cosset passengers cheerfully and discreetly, fussing over such details as the level of cilantro in lunchtime dishes or making elaborate cocktails from the fully stocked open bar. They've even been known to call ahead to upcoming anchorages to arrange for a passenger's favorite brand of beer to be brought aboard. Laundry service is not available on board except in "emergency situations." (The company recommends, by the way, a crew gratuity of 5%–10% at the end of each voyage; a hefty sum when you're paying, say, $4,500 for a cruise.)

CRUISETOURS & ADD-ON PROGRAMS   There are no organized land tours in 2008. But the line will seek to satisfy passengers' wishes—if they ask for help in arranging 1- to 6-day land packages in Alaska and British Columbia in conjunction with their cruises. Inquire about the possibilities when you call, and ASC will try to tailor a land-tour program geared toward your specific interests. Also see the line's website for information on these opportunities.

Safari Quest • Safari Escape • Safari Spirit

The Verdict

Aah—the good life!

Safari Quest *(photo: American Safari Cruises)*

Specifications

Size (in Tons)	N/A	Crew	6/9
Passengers (Double Occ.)	12/21	Passenger/Crew Ratio	2 to 1 (approx.)
Passenger/Space Ratio	N/A*	Year Launched	1993/1992/1991
Total Cabins/Veranda Cabins			
Safari Escape	6/0		
Safari Quest	11/0		
Safari Spirit	6/0		
Last Major Refurbishment	2005 *(Safari Spirit)*		

These ships' sizes were measured using a different scale than the others in this book, so comparison is not possible.

Frommer's Ratings (Scale of 1–5)

★★★★ ½

Cabin Comfort & Amenities	5	Dining Options	3
Ship Cleanliness & Maintenance	4	Adventure & Fitness Options	4
Public Comfort/Space	5	Children's Facilities	N/A
Décor	4.5	Enjoyment Factor	5

THE SHIPS IN GENERAL   More private yacht than cruise ship, these three vessels are an oddity in the cruise community, and as far from the Alaska cruising norm as it's possible to get. Some ships in Alaska are so big, you sort of feel they should have their own zip code, maybe a couple of time zones. The biggest of these three, the *Safari Quest,* is just 120 feet long. The ASC ships have sleek, contoured, Ferrari-looking exteriors. Inside, virtually no area is out of bounds, including the captain's work space: He'll welcome your visit, provided he's not involved in some critical nautical maneuver at the time. It all leads to the feeling that you're vacationing on an impossibly rich friend's space-age yacht.

CABINS   Sleeping quarters are comfortable and clean, with large, firm beds, adequate light, and art (of varying quality if hardly museum-standard) on the walls. Bathrooms are roomy, even in the standard cabins; cabins on the *Safari Escape* have showers only. The showers shoot a steady but not spectacular stream of reliably hot water. The Admiral's Cabins have a large picture window and a small sitting area. Down below, deluxe rooms are tidy, filled with a surprising amount of natural light, and fairly spacious. A few of the top staterooms have televisions with VCRs. There are no special facilities for travelers with disabilities and no cabins designed specifically for single occupancy.

Cabins & Rates

Cabins	Per Diem Rates	Sq. Ft.	Fridge	Hair Dryer	Sitting Area	TV
Safari Escape						
Outside	$574–$824* $564–$713***	112–164	no	yes	some	yes
Safari Quest						
Outside	$699–$1,013** $563–$721***	112–164	no	yes	some	yes
Safari Spirit	$770–$1,070** $571–$714***	115–165	no	yes	some	yes

Rates are per day based on 8-night cruises.
**Rates are per day based on 7-night cruises.*
***Rates are per day based on 14-night cruises.*

PUBLIC AREAS   Sitting rooms are intimate and luxurious, almost as if they had been transported intact from a spacious suburban home. Four or five prime vantage points for spotting wildlife (one is a hot tub!) ensure as little or as much privacy as you desire. All public rooms have generous panoramic windows to gaze out of when you can't be on deck because of cold or inclement weather. All three meals are served family-style at a single table in a casual room, usually when the ship is anchored in some quiet cove or off of some incredibly beautiful shoreline or mountain range. Expect paper napkins at lunch, cloth serviettes at dinner—and gourmet cuisine. There are 24-hour coffee/tea facilities, a fully stocked open bar, and a small library/video library.

POOL, FITNESS, SPA & SPORTS FACILITIES There are stair-steppers on *Safari Quest* and *Safari Spirit*, and sea kayaks for passenger use: eight on *Safari Quest* and two each on *Safari Escape* and *Safari Spirit*. All three ships have hot tubs on the top deck.

2 Cruise West

2301 5th Ave., Suite 401, Seattle, WA 98121. ℂ 800/426-7702 or 206/441-8687. Fax 206/441-4757. www.cruisewest.com.

THE LINE IN A NUTSHELL Like all small ships, Cruise West's ships can navigate in tight areas such as Misty Fjords and Desolation Sound, visit tiny ports such as Petersburg and Haines, and scoot up close to shore for wildlife-watching. But these are not adventure cruises. These vacations are for people who want to visit Alaska's coastal communities and see its wilderness areas up close and in a relaxed, comfortable, small-scale environment without big-ship distractions. They're not for people who want to spend their days hiking and kayaking—unless they really want to on their own, that is.

THE EXPERIENCE The operative words here are *casual, relaxed,* and *friendly.* At sea, the lack of organized activities on the line's port-to-port itineraries leaves you free to scan for wildlife, peruse the natural sights, or read a book. In port—whether one of the large popular ports or a less visited one—the line arranges some novel, intimate shore excursions, such as a visit with local artists at their homes outside Haines or an educational walking tour led by a Native guide in Ketchikan. There is one shore excursion included in the cruise fare in each port, most of the walking tour variety, such as a walk with a local guide around Fort Seward in Haines.

Pros

- **The staff.** The line's friendly, enthusiastic staff is a big plus, making guests feel right at home.
- **Great shore excursions.** Cruise West's list includes some real gems, at an additional charge.
- **Good food.** You might not necessarily expect it on small ships like these, but the dishes served are quite good. Portions are small, but you can order as much as you like.
- **Itineraries.** Because the line has eight ships in Alaska service, it's able to offer more of the varied itineraries that aficionados have come to expect from small ships.

Cons

- **Wacky bathrooms on some ships.** Some of the line's ships have the kind of awkward, head-style, no-shelves bathrooms that are common to many small vessels.
- **Poor lighting** in some of the cabins on some of the ships. Woe betide the lady who's particular about applying her makeup just so!
- **Little to do at night.** If you want nighttime entertainment, you have to make it up yourself. There may be few people hanging in the lounge, but other than a nightly lecture that's about it for the offerings.

THE FLEET The 96-passenger *Spirit of '98* is one of the most distinctive small ships in Alaska, a replica 19th-century coastal steamer. The charming *'98* was even featured in the Kevin Costner film *Wyatt Earp*. The Cruise West fleet also includes

Cruise West Fleet Itineraries

Ship	Itineraries
Spirit of '98	**8-night Inside Passage*:** One-way between Ketchikan and Juneau, visiting Misty Fjords, Metlakatla, Haines, Skagway, Petersburg, Tracy Arm, Sitka, and Glacier Bay. May–Sept. **10-night Gold Rush Inside Passage:** One-way between Seattle and Juneau or reverse, visiting the San Juan Islands, Ketchikan, Frederick Sound, Tracy Arm, Petersburg, Sitka, and Glacier Bay. May and Sept.
Spirit of Alaska	**8-night Inside Passage:** Round-trip from Juneau, visiting Sitka, Icy Strait, Elfin Cove, a small Alaska town (one of four based on itinerary) and Glacier Bay. June-Aug.
Spirit of Discovery	**8-night Inside Passage*:** Same as *Spirit of '98.* May–Aug. 10-night Inside Passage, May and Sept, same as *Spirit of '98.*
Spirit of Endeavour	**8-night Inside Passage*:** Same as *Spirit of '98.* May–Sept. 10-night Inside Passage, May and Sept, same as *Spirit of '98.*
Spirit of Columbia	**3- and 4-night Glacier Bay,** Round-trip from Whittier, visiting Icy Strait and Cordova, and College Fjord. May–Aug. **10-night Inside Passage:** May and Sept, same as *Spirit of '98.*
Spirit of Glacier Bay	**3- and 4-night Glacier Bay:** Round-trip from Juneau, cruising Icy Strait and with 1 full day in Glacier Bay; the 4-night also does port calls in Skagway and Haines. May–Aug. **10-night Inside Passage:** May and Sept, same as *Spirit of '98.*
Spirit of Oceanus	**12-night Coastla Odyssey:** between Vancouver and Whittier, visiting Metlakatla, Misty Fjords, Petersburg, Skagway, and Glacier Bay. May-Sep. **13-night Bering Seas*:** From Whittier to Nome, visiting Kodiak Island, Katmai National Park, Shumagin Islands, the Pribilof Islands, the Yukon Delta Wildlife Refuge, and Russia's Chukotka Peninsula. July.
Spirit of Yorktown	**8-night Inside Passage:** Same as *Spirit of '98.* May–Sept. **10-night Gold Rush Inside Passage:** One-way between Juneau and Seattle. Same as *Spirit of '98.* May and Sept.

*Includes one pre- or post-cruise hotel overnight.

three former Clipper Cruise ships: the 102-passenger *Spirit of Endeavour* (the former *Newport Clipper*), the 138-passenger *Spirit of Yorktown* (formerly *Yorktown Clipper*), and the *Spirit of Glacier Bay* (previously the *Nantucket Clipper*). The *Endeavour, Glacier Bay,* and *Yorktown,* which share a similar design and the same kind of low-key comfort, will all be plying Alaskan waters in 2008. The 78-passenger *Spirit of Alaska* and *Spirit of Columbia,* and the 84-passenger *Spirit of Discovery* are all very similar ships, with less fancy decor than the *Endeavour* and *'98.* The 114-passenger *Spirit of Oceanus* (1984), the former *Renaissance V* of Renaissance Cruises, is its most luxurious ship.

PASSENGER PROFILE   Passengers with Cruise West tend to be older (typically around 60–75), financially stable, well educated, and consider themselves adventuresome. There are likely to be a good number of current or retired physicians and teachers aboard, a smattering of farmers and ranchers, several high-tech types, and a few youngish adults traveling with their single parents. We've also encountered families with kids, including grandparents traveling with grandkids, although the line does not have an organized children's program. Passengers such as these want to visit Alaska in a relaxed, dress-down atmosphere—and on this count, Cruise West delivers.

DINING   Breakfast, lunch, and dinner are served at set times at one unassigned seating. You sit with whoever you want, assuming you get to the dining room on time (otherwise, you sit where seats are available). An early riser's buffet is set out in the lounge before the set breakfast time, but if you're a late riser, you'll miss breakfast entirely, as no room service is available (though if you ask, a crew member will probably fetch you something in the lounge). A hearty cocktail-hour snack (baked brie, meatballs, shrimp, buffalo wings, and the like) is provided every day to tide passengers over until dinner, and the chef will often whip up a batch of cookies. At mealtimes on Cruise West ships, the fare used to be primarily home-style American—not overly fancy, but tasty and varied. In recent years, though, the line has made a concentrated effort to upgrade the quality of its menus and presentation—with considerable success, adding variety and consistency to the table. Each chef makes a point of stocking up as often as possible on such fresh items as salmon and crabs while in port. The galley can accommodate special diets (kosher, low salt, low fat), but you should make special arrangements for this when booking your cruise. There is a vegetarian entrée offered nightly. Service can sometimes be slow, as each waitperson must cover several tables, though it's universally friendly.

ACTIVITIES   As with other small ships, Cruise West vessels don't offer much in the way of diversions. What onboard activities there are might include post-dinner discussions of the port or region to be visited the next day, talks by the cruise host or hostess while at sea, and perhaps a tour of the engine room or galley. Onboard fitness options are an exercise bike or Stairmaster on some of the ships, while the others have nothing—but several times around the deck gives you a decent walk. One shore excursion in each port is included in the cruise fare, and there are additional options for an extra charge.

A cheerful and knowledgeable cruise coordinator accompanies each trip to answer passengers' questions about Alaska's flora, fauna, geology, and history (enthusiastically, though not always at an advanced level); and Forest Service rangers, local fishers, and Native Alaskans sometimes come aboard to teach about the culture and industry of the state. Alaska DVDs may be shown on a screen in the lounge. Binoculars are provided for onboard use in each cabin. If you have your heart set on a port activity that the line doesn't offer, the cruise coordinator will do his or her best to set something up for you.

CHILDREN'S PROGRAM   None. But if kids are onboard the crew may show a children's movie in the lounge, accompanied by a dinner of burgers and dogs, on an ad hoc basis.

ENTERTAINMENT   Videos are available on some of the ships for in-cabin use. Organized entertainment, such as it is, is provided by the crew or by your fellow passengers, often in a humbly (and perhaps appropriately) titled "No-Talent Night" or in a game of Truth or Dare or The Liar's Club. However, on some sailings there is no nighttime entertainment at all.

SERVICE   The line strives for a family feeling and, toward this end, employs a young, energetic crew (many of them college students) who radiate enthusiasm and perform all shipboard tasks, waiting tables at breakfast, making beds and cleaning cabins, polishing the handrails, and unloading baggage at journey's end. They may not be consummate pros, but passengers tend to find them adorable. Just be sure you don't come aboard expecting luxury and white-gloved service. Crew members once told us of being sent into crisis mode when the occupants of the ship's most deluxe suite went into spasms because they couldn't order room service. If you see yourself in that scenario, cruise elsewhere. Tips are included in the cruise fare.

CRUISETOUR & ADD-ON PROGRAMS   Cruise West offers land extensions in various parts of Alaska, including Denali Park, the Aleutians, Prince William Sound, and the major interior city of Fairbanks in conjunction with its cruises. The prices vary greatly, dictated by the length of the tour, of course, but also by the category of cabin chosen for the cruise portion. This year, for example, the land portion of a 12-night package combining cruise and Denali National Park and Fairbanks starts at $2,050 per person, double occupancy, plus the cruise price. The company also offers hotel night add-ons in Seattle (from $175), Anchorage ($175), Juneau ($125), and Ketchikan ($150).

Spirit of '98

The Verdict

The ship was built a little over 2 decades ago, but it has the flavor of a turn-of-the-century (20th century, that is) yacht. Maybe that's why it's so appreciated by authors and filmmakers.

Spirit of '98 *(photo: Cruise West)*

Specifications

Size (in GRTs)	96	Crew	23
Passengers (Double Occ.)	96	Passenger/Crew Ratio	4.2 to 1
Passenger/Space Ratio	N/A*	Year Launched	1984
Total Cabins/Veranda Cabins	49/0	Last Major Refurbishment	1995

These ships' sizes were measured using a different scale from the others in this book, so comparison is not possible.

Frommer's Ratings (Scale of 1–5)   ★★★★

Cabin Comfort & Amenities	3.5	Dining Options	4
Ship Cleanliness & Maintenance	5	Adventure & Fitness Options	2.5
Public Comfort/Space	4	Children's Facilities	N/A
Decor	4.5	Enjoyment Factor	4

THE SHIP IN GENERAL   The *Spirit of '98* is a time machine. Built in 1984 as a replica of a late-19th-century steamship and extensively refurbished in 1995, it carries its Victorian flavor so well that fully two-thirds of the people we've met on board think the ship was a private yacht at the turn of the century.

If you use a wheelchair or otherwise have mobility problems, note that the *'98* is one of only four small ships in Alaska that has an elevator. (Cruise West's *Spirit of Oceanus*, Clipper's *Clipper Odyssey*, and Majestic Cruises Line's *Empress of the North* are the others.)

If you want to get a look at this ship, rent Kevin Costner's *Wyatt Earp* at your video store—one of the final scenes was filmed on board. Also, Sue Henry's 1997 mystery novel *Death Takes Passage* is set entirely aboard the *'98* and provides detailed descriptions of the ship.

CABINS   Cabins are comfortable and of decent size, and continue the Victorian motif. Each features TV/VCR combos and either twin, convertible twin, or double beds with firm, comfortable mattresses. Deluxe cabins have a refrigerator, a seating area, and a trundle bed to accommodate a third passenger. One Owner's Suite provides a spacious living room with a meeting area, a large bathroom with whirlpool tub, a king-size bed, a stocked bar with refrigerator, a TV/VCR, a stereo, and enough windows to take in all of Alaska at one sitting. Bathrooms are larger than aboard most other small ships, though they lack any hint of Victorian frills. One glaring weakness is the lack of shelf space.

Cabin 309, located on the upper deck right next to the elevator, is fully wheelchair accessible. Two cabins (321 and 322, in the stern) are singles.

Cabins & Rates

Cabins	Per Diem Rates	Sq. Ft.	Fridge	Hair Dryer	Sitting Area	TV
Outside	$629–$759*	100–264	some	no	some	yes
Suites	$919	550	yes	no	yes	yes
Outside	$494–$689**					
Suites	$912					

Rates are for 10-night cruises.
Rates are for 8-night cruises.

PUBLIC AREAS   The Grand Salon Lounge holds the ship's main bar, a 24-hour tea/coffee station, and a small video library. The Klondike Dining Room is beautifully decorated and large enough to seat all guests in booths and around center tables. The booths seem to suffer less ambient noise than the round tables in the middle, so try to snag one of those if you can. Both rooms carry the 19th-century theme with pressed-tin ceilings (aluminum actually, but why be picky?), balloon-back chairs, ruffled draperies, and plenty of polished woodwork and brass throughout. A small bar called Soapy's Parlour sits just off of the dining room. There's a bartender at Soapy's at mealtime, but it otherwise gets little use—so if you want to sneak off and read, this is a good spot.

Out in the air, passengers congregate in the large bow area, on the open-top deck, or at the railing in front of the bridge, which is open to visitors except when the ship is passing through rough water.

DINING OPTIONS   Your only choice is the family-style main dining room.

POOL, FITNESS, SPA & SPORTS FACILITIES   None to speak of.

Spirit of Endeavour and Spirit of Glacier Bay

Spirit of Endeavour *(photo: Matt Hannafin)*

The Verdict

These very similar ships carry more than 100 passengers and were the first in the Cruise West fleet to do so. They also helped raise the service bar for the company's other vessels.

Specifications

Size (in GRTS)	95	Crew	28/29
Passengers (Double Occ.)	102	Passenger/Crew Ratio	4 to 1
Passenger/Space Ratio	N/A*	Year Launched	1983/1984
Total Cabins/Veranda Cabins	51/0	Last Major Refurbishment	1999/2006

These ships' sizes were measured using a different scale than the others in this book, so comparison is not possible.

Frommer's Ratings (Scale of 1–5) ✯★★★

Cabin Comfort & Amenities	4	Dining Options	3
Ship Cleanliness & Maintenance	5	Adventure/Fitness Options	2.5
Public Comfort/Space	4.5	Children's Facilities	N/A
Decor	4	Enjoyment Factor	4

THE SHIP IN GENERAL   The Endeavour was previously the *Newport Clipper,* and the Glacier Bay formerly the *Nantucket Clipper,* both for Clipper Cruise Line. They are similar to the *Spirit of Yorktown* in style and layout. The ships offer a higher level of comfort than most other small ships in the Alaska market. (By the way, in case you're wondering about the spelling of the name of the Endeavour, it's correct: The British spelling pays tribute to Captain Cook's first major Pacific exploration ship, the *Endeavour.*)

CABINS   Well appointed, with a writing desk and two large windows in all but the lowest price category (which has portholes), all cabins have firm, comfortable twin beds (convertible to queen-size only in Deluxe cabins); TVs/VCRs, on the *Endeavour* only; adequate closet space; and decent-size bathrooms. Deluxe cabins feature a refrigerator on the *Endeavour* only, and several in the top two categories have a Pullman berth to accommodate a third passenger. Six pairs of cabins on the *Endeavour* and four on the *Glacier Bay* have the option of being adjoined. There are no special facilities aboard for travelers with disabilities and no cabins designed specifically for single occupancy.

Cabins & Rates

Cabins	Per Diem Rates	Sq. Ft.	Fridge	Hair Dryer	Sitting Area	TV
Spirit of Endeavour						
Outside	$494–$700*	152	some	no	some	yes
Spirit of Glacier Bay						
Outside	$450/$625*/$469–$660**	108–155	no	yes	no	no

*For 3-night cruises.
**For 4-night cruises.

PUBLIC AREAS   As with almost all small ships, the *Endeavour* and *Glacier Bay* both have only two indoor public areas: the dining room—the largest room on the ship, lined with wide picture windows—and the plush lounge/bar, decorated with considerable style including light woods as accents. Up top, the large Sun Deck and Stern Deck (both of beautiful teakwood) and a bow viewing area just below the bridge allow plenty of space for wildlife and nature observation. Occasionally, weather permitting, luncheon barbecues are possible in this space as an alternative to the dining room. There is a 24-hour tea/coffee station and a video library both located in the lounge.

DINING OPTIONS   Not much apart from those indicated above.

POOL, FITNESS, SPA & SPORTS FACILITIES   None on either ship.

Spirit of Oceanus

Spirit of Oceanus *(photo: Cruise West)*

The Verdict

The biggest and arguably the most comfortable of Cruise West's fleet.

Specifications

Size (in Tons)	4,200	Crew	54
Passengers (Double Occ.)	120	Passenger/Crew Ratio	2 to 1
Passenger/Space Ratio	39.5	Year Launched	1991
Total Cabins/Veranda Cabins	57/12	Last Major Refurbishment	2001

Frommer's Ratings (Scale of 1–5)   ★★★★

Cabin Comfort & Amenities	4	Dining Options	4
Ship Cleanliness & Maintenance	4.5	Adventure & Fitness Options	5
Public Comfort/Space	4.5	Children's Facilities	N/A
Decor	4	Enjoyment Factor	4

THE SHIP IN GENERAL　Cruise West took ownership of the former *Renaissance V* in June 2002. The addition of the oceangoing vessel has allowed Cruise West to pursue itineraries outside its traditional Alaska coastal cruising waters, such as the Russian Far East, Southeast Asia, and the South Pacific.

CABINS　Launched in 1990, the renamed *Spirit of Oceanus* has 57 outside suites ranging in size from 215 to 353 square feet, each containing a walk-in closet or wardrobe, a marble-topped vanity, a lounge area separated from the bedroom by a curtain, an in-room safe, minibar, and satellite telephone access. Twelve cabins have private balconies. None of the cabins is wheelchair accessible.

Cabins & Rates

Cabins	Per Diem Rates	Sq. Ft.	Fridge	Hair Dryer	Sitting Area	TV
Suites	$692–$1,223* $654–$1,177**	215–353	no	no	yes	yes

Rates are based on 13-night cruises.
**Rates are based on 11-night cruises.*

PUBLIC AREAS　Public rooms include two lounges, a library, a beauty salon, laundry, an outdoor dining terrace, a piano bar, and a small swimming pool. The vessel is one of the few small ships in Alaska with an elevator, making it a better choice for passengers with mobility problems.

DINING OPTIONS　Only the main dining room and an outdoor snack bar.

POOL, FITNESS, SPA & SPORTS FACILITIES　One small swimming pool and one exercise machine.

Spirit of Alaska • Spirit of Columbia • Spirit of Discovery

The Verdict

Not by any means the youngest ships in the Cruise West fleet, but each has a steady and loyal following. And there's a reason for that: They're small enough to get into places that bigger vessels can't in search of wildlife, in effect almost customizing the cruise as they go.

Spirit of Alaska *(photo: Cruise West)*

Specifications

Size (in GRTs)	97/98/94	Last Major Refurbishment	1995/1995/1992
Passengers (Double Occ.)	78/78/84	Crew	21/21/21
Passenger/Space Ratio	N/A*	Passenger/Crew Ratio	3.7 to 1
Total Cabins/Veranda Cabins		Year Launched	1980/1979/1976
Spirit of Alaska	39/0		
Spirit of Columbia	39/0		
Spirit of Discovery	43/0		

These ships' sizes were measured using a different scale than the others in this book, so comparison is not possible.

Frommer's Ratings (Scale of 1–5)   ★★★½

Cabin Comfort & Amenities	3.5	Dining Options	3
Ship Cleanliness & Maintenance	4.5	Adventure & Fitness Options	2.5
Public Comfort/Space	4	Children's Facilities	N/A
Decor	4	Enjoyment Factor	3.5

THE SHIPS IN GENERAL   Though of slightly different sizes and passenger capacities, the *Spirits of Alaska, Columbia,* and *Discovery* are easily lumped together because they are similarly designed ships, all offering the friendly Cruise West experience, though in somewhat less fancy surroundings than the *Spirits of Endeavour, Oceanus,* and *'98.* Though they're older ships, all have been extensively refurbished.

These three ships, however, share a problem common to all others built originally for the American Canadian Caribbean Line (ACCL): They're not good choices for very tall people, as ceilings throughout are set at about 6 feet, 4 inches; many beds are also too short for those 6 feet, 2 inches or taller. On a positive note, though, the *Alaska* and *Columbia* have ACCL's patented bow ramp, which, in combination with their shallow draft, allows the ships to basically beach themselves, disembarking passengers right onto shore in wild areas without ports. Some people claim that they're better able to give passengers an experience of the "real" Alaska, because of their ability to disembark them in such off-the-beaten-path places.

CABINS   Cabins aboard all three ships are very snug (smaller than those on the *Spirit of '98* and *Endeavour*) but comfortable, with light, airy decor and lower twin or double beds. Aboard the *Discovery,* one category has upper and lower bunks, and deluxe cabins have queen-size beds. Storage space is ample, and outside cabins feature picture windows. Bathrooms aboard the *Discovery* and *Columbia* are slightly better than those aboard the *Alaska,* which has tight, head-style arrangements. There are no special facilities aboard for travelers with disabilities. There are two single-occupancy cabins on *Discovery* and three (small) suites on *Spirit of Columbia.*

Cabins & Rates

Cabins	Per Diem Rates	Sq. Ft.	Fridge	Hair Dryer	Sitting Area	TV
Spirit of Alaska						
Inside	$387–$399*	90	no	no	no	no
Outside	$587–$737	95–118	some	no	some	some
Spirit of Columbia*						
Inside	$366–$383**	75	no	no	some	some
Outside	$599–$766	95–110	some	no	some	some
Inside	$562–$718***					
Suites	$912					
Spirit of Discovery						
Inside	$562–$718***	105	no	no	no	no
Suites	$912	110–125	no	no	no	some

Rates are based on 4-night cruises.
**Rates are based on 3-night cruises.*
*** Rates are based on 8-night cruises.*

PUBLIC AREAS   All three ships have a main dining room and a comfortable, if rather small, lounge with a bar that is generally crowded before dinner, at the end of a day that probably included a busy shore excursion. An all-day self-service tea/coffee station is against one wall in the lounge, and predinner nibbles are within easy reach of the bar.

DINING OPTIONS   None.

POOL, FITNESS, SPA & SPORTS FACILITIES   Nothing elaborate—a stationery bicycle and weight machine on the open deck. No pool, either.

Spirit of Yorktown

The Verdict

The ship got an upgrade after the 2007 season, including the addition of four deluxe cabins on the top deck, outfitted with queen-sized beds and offering private balconies.

Spirit of Yorktown *(photo: Cruise West)*

Specifications

Size (in GRTs)	97	Crew	42
Passengers (Double Occ.)	138	Passenger/Crew Ratio	3.5 to 1
Passenger/Space Ratio	N/A*	Year Launched	1988
Total Cabins/Veranda Cabins	68/4	Last Major Refurbishment	2007

This ship's size was measured using a different scale than the others in this book, so comparison is not possible.

Frommer's Ratings (Scale of 1–5)   ★★★½

Cabin Comfort & Amenities	4	Dining Options	N/A
Ship Cleanliness & Maintenance	4	Adventure & Fitness Options	3
Public Comfort/Space	4	Children's Facilities	N/A
Decor	3.5	Enjoyment Factor	3.5

THE SHIP IN GENERAL   The impression we kept coming back to when sitting in the spacious lounge of this ship, or in our cozy cabin, was that someone had taken one of the Holland America or Princess ships and shrunk it to a fraction of its normal size. Though not boasting the multitude of public rooms of those large ships, the four-deck *Spirit of Yorktown* offers similar clean styling and easy-to-live-with decor, while also offering the small-ship advantage of taking passengers into shallow-water ports and other out-of-the-way locations away from the megaship crowds.

CABINS   Although smallish (average cabin size is 123–140 sq. ft.), cabins are very pleasantly styled, with blond-wood writing desks, chairs, and bed frames, and a good amount of closet space, plus additional storage under the beds. There are no phones or TVs, but each cabin does have a music channel. There are no actual safes in the cabin, but two drawers in the closet can be locked.

Cabins come in six categories, differentiated mostly by their location rather than by their size. Most have two lower-level beds, permanently fixed in either an L-shape corner configuration or as two units set parallel to one another (taller passengers—over 6 feet, 2 inches—would be better off with the L-shape arrangement). Some cabins contain upper berths that unfold from the wall to accommodate a third person.

Brand new are four deluxe cabins on the Sun Deck with queen-size beds, private balconies (a rarity on small ships), and minifridges.

All cabins on the Promenade Deck and a handful at the stern on the Lounge Deck open onto the outdoors walkway (rather than onto an interior corridor). While we normally prefer this layout because it makes us feel closer to nature, here it doesn't seem to matter because the doors open out—meaning you can't really leave the door open to breezes without blocking the deck. It's worth noting that passengers in the Promenade Deck cabins should be careful when opening their doors from the inside, lest you end up braining one of your poor fellow passengers walking on the Promenade.

Cabin bathrooms are compact, though not nearly so tiny as aboard many of Cruise West's ships. Toilets are wedged between the shower (no tub) and sink area and may prove tight for heavier people.

There are no special facilities on board for travelers with disabilities and no cabins designed specifically for single occupancy.

Cabins & Rates

Cabins	Per Diem Rates	Sq. Ft.	Fridge	Hair Dryer	Sitting Area	TV
Inside	$449–$474*	108	no	yes	no	no
Outside	$509–$742	126	some	yes	some	no
Inside	$462–$505**					
Outside	$522–$722					

Rates are based on 10-night cruises.
Rates are based on 8-night cruises.

PUBLIC AREAS   As on board most small ships, there are only two public areas: the dining room and the Observation Lounge. The pleasant lounge has big windows, a bar, a small but informative library, and enough space to comfortably seat everyone on board for lectures and meetings. It's the main hub of onboard activity. The dining room is spacious and comfortable. Other than that, there are no cozy hideaways on board other than your cabin. There is, however, plenty of outdoor deck space for wildlife- and glacier-watching.

DINING OPTIONS   None.

POOL, FITNESS, SPA & SPORTS FACILITIES   There are no set exercise facilities, but you could jog or walk around the deck (18 laps = 1 mile).

3 Lindblad Expeditions

96 Morton St., 9th Floor, New York, NY 10014. 𝒞 **800/397-3348** or 212/765-7740. Fax 212/265-3770. www.expeditions.com.

THE LINE IN A NUTSHELL   In 1984, Sven-Olof Lindblad, son of adventure-travel pioneer Lars-Eric Lindblad, followed in his father's footsteps by forming Lindblad Expeditions, which specializes in providing environmentally sensitive soft-adventure/educational cruises to remote places in the world, with visits to a few large ports. A few years ago, the company entered into a joint program with the National Geographic Society, with that organization taking over the onboard lecturers and marketing. The venture lifted Lindblad's educational offerings out of the commonplace. As part of the program, the line awards a cruise to two exceptional K–12 teachers each year, in perpetuity.

THE EXPERIENCE   Lindblad's expedition cruises are explorative and informal, designed to appeal to the intellectually curious traveler seeking a vacation that's educational as well as relaxing. Passengers' time is spent learning about the outdoors (from National Geographic experts and high-caliber expedition leaders trained in botany, anthropology, biology, and geology) and observing the world either from the ship or on shore excursions, which are included in the cruise package. Lindblad Expeditions' crew and staff emphasize respect for the local ecosystem, and flexibility and spontaneity are keys to the experience, as the route may be altered at any time to follow a pod of whales or school of dolphins. Depending on weather and sea conditions, there are usually two or three excursions offered every day.

Pros

- **Great expedition feeling.** Lindblad's programs offer innovative, flexible itineraries; outstanding lecturers/guides; and a friendly, accommodating staff.
- **Built-in shore excursions.** Rather than relying on outside concessionaires for their shore excursions (which is the case with most other lines, big and small), Lindblad Expeditions runs its shore excursions as an integral part of its cruises and includes all excursion costs in the cruise fare.

Cons

- **Cost.** Cruise fares tend to be a little higher than the line's small-ship competition.

Lindblad Expeditions Fleet Itineraries

Ship	Itineraries
Sea Bird/ *Sea Lion*	**11-night Alaska, British Columbia, San Juan Islands:** North- and southbound between Juneau and Seattle, visiting Point Adolphus, Chichagof Island, Glacier Bay, Sitka, Frederick Sound, Misty Fjords, Alert Bay and Johnstone Strait, B.C., and the San Juan Islands, Washington. Apr–Aug. **7-night Coastal Wilderness:** North- and southbound between Juneau and Sitka, visiting Tracy Arm, Petersburg, Frederick Sound, Chatham Strait, Glacier Bay, and Point Adolphus. May and Sept.

THE FLEET   The 62-passenger *Sea Lion* and *Sea Bird* (built in 1981 and 1982, respectively) are nearly identical in every respect. Both are basic vessels built to get you to beautiful spots and have a minimum of public rooms and conveniences: one dining room, one bar/lounge, and lots of deck space for wildlife and glacier viewing.

PASSENGER PROFILE   Lindblad Expeditions tends to attract well-traveled and well-educated, professional, 55+ couples who have "been there, done that" and are looking for something completely different in a cruise experience. The passenger mix may also include some singles and a smattering of younger couples. Although not necessarily frequent cruisers, many passengers are likely to have been on other Lindblad Expeditions programs, and share a common interest in history and wildlife.

DINING   Hearty buffet breakfasts and lunches and sit-down dinners include a good variety of both hot and cold dishes with plenty of fresh fruits and vegetables. Many of the fresh ingredients are obtained from ports along the way, and meals may reflect regional tastes. Although far from haute cuisine, dinners are well prepared and presented, and are served at single open seatings that allow passengers to get to know each other by moving around to different tables. Lecturers and other staff members dine with passengers.

ACTIVITIES   During the day, most activity takes place off the ship, aboard Zodiac boats or kayaks and/or on land excursions. While on board, passengers entertain themselves with the usual small-ship activities: wildlife-watching, gazing off into the wilderness, reading, and chatting. Shore excursions are included in the cruise fare.

CHILDREN'S PROGRAM   Family cruising to Alaska is big business and Lindblad has stepped up to the plate and now offers special family activities on all sailings. Activities have a nature slant, such as exploring an Alaskan rainforest. Don't look for a video arcade or playroom for the kiddies, however.

ENTERTAINMENT   Lectures and slide presentations are scheduled throughout the cruise, and documentaries or movies may be screened in the evening in the main lounge. Alaska-centric books are available in each ship's small library.

SERVICE   Dining-room staff and room stewards are affable and efficient, and seem to enjoy their work. As with other small ships, there's no room service unless you're ill and unable to make it to the dining room.

CRUISETOURS & ADD-ON PROGRAMS   The company offers no land packages in 2008.

Sea Lion • Sea Bird

The Verdict

Get up close and personal in Alaska on these comfortable small ships, and expect excellent commentary from naturalists along the way.

Sea Lion *(photo: Lindblad Expeditions)*

Specifications

Size (in Tons)	100	Crew	22
Passengers (Double Occ.)	70	Passenger/Crew Ratio	3.2 to 1
Passenger/Space Ratio	N/A*	Year Launched	1981/1982
Total Cabins/Veranda Cabins	37/0	Last Major Refurbishment	N/A

*These ships' sizes were measured using a different scale than the others in this book, so comparison is not possible.

Frommer's Ratings (Scale of 1–5)   ★★★½

Cabin Comfort & Amenities	3	Dining Options	3
Ship Cleanliness & Maintenance	4	Adventure & Fitness Options	5
Public Comfort/Space	3	Children's Facilities	N/A
Decor	3.5	Enjoyment Factor	4

THE SHIPS IN GENERAL   The shallow-draft *Sea Lion* and *Sea Bird* are identical twins, right down to their decor schemes and furniture. Not fancy at all, they have just two public rooms and utilitarian cabins.

CABINS   Postage-stamp cabins are tight and functional rather than fancy. No cabins are large enough to accommodate more than two, and each features twin or double beds, a closet (there are also drawers under the bed for extra storage), and a sink and mirror in the main room. Behind a folding door lies a Lilliputian bathroom with a head-style shower (toilet opposite the shower nozzle). All cabins are located outside and have picture windows that open to fresh breezes (except the lowest-price cabins, which have a small "portlight" that allows light in but provides no view). The vessels have no wheelchair-accessible cabins.

Cabins & Rates

Cabins	Per Diem Rates	Sq. Ft.	Fridge	Hair Dryer	Sitting Area	TV
Outside	$712–$941* $635–$817**	118–152	no	no	no	no

*Rates are based on 7-night cruises.
**Rates are per day based on an 11-night cruise; includes shore excursions.

PUBLIC AREAS   Public space is limited to the open sun deck and bow areas, the dining room, and an observation lounge that serves as the nerve center for activities. In the lounge, you'll find a bar; a library of atlases and books on Alaska's culture, geology, history, plants, and wildlife; a gift shop tucked into a closet; and audiovisual aids for the many naturalists' presentations. A couple of years ago, a *bowcam*—an underwater camera attached to the ship's bow—was wired to a monitor in the lounge allowing cruisers every more opportunities for wildlife sightings; a joystick for changing camera angles adds to the fun.

DINING OPTIONS   None.

POOL, FITNESS, SPA & SPORTS FACILITIES   As is the case with the majority of small ships, there is no gym aboard either ship, nor are there any other onboard exercise facilities. However, Lindblad's style of soft-adventure travel means you'll be taking frequent walks/hikes in wilderness areas, usually accessed via Zodiac landing craft.

4 Majestic America Line

2101 4th Ave., Suite 1150, Seattle, WA 98121. ℂ **800/434-1232** or 206/292-9606. Fax 206/340-0975. www. majesticamericaline.com.

THE LINE IN A NUTSHELL   In 2006, American West Steamboat Company was purchased by California-based Ambassadors International, and it has undergone some ups and downs since. First, it bought the Delta Queen Steamboat Company, operator of the *American Queen, Mississippi Queen,* and *Delta Queen* paddle-wheelers on the Mississippi, Ohio, and other rivers in the Midwest and southern U.S. The companies were merged under the corporate name of Majestic America Line. Shortly thereafter the company added the Executive Explorer, of the defunct Glacier Bay Cruiseline, and renamed the 48-passenger ship the *Contessa.* Last summer, however, Majestic laid up the venerable *Delta Queen* after its safety facilities failed to pass muster with the U.S. Coast Guard Service. Then it also took the *Contessa* out of service for the 2008 season, and all indications are that it is unlikely ever to sail again as a Majestic vessel. As far as Alaska is concerned, that leaves the company with one ship, which also had its problems last year when it hit a submerged reef near Juneau and lost several weeks of revenue sailing while repairs were made. But don't let that deter you from trying it out.

Although it clearly belongs in the small-ship category, the *Empress of the North* is quite a bit bigger than the others in its field. Carrying 223 passengers, it has almost twice the capacity of the second largest of the small ships. In a very real sense, this ship belongs in a separate category—stern-wheelers. But it would be a category of one in Alaska. There had not been a paddle-wheel-driven ship in the Inside Passage for a century or more until the *Empress of the North* debuted there in 2003. When not in Alaska, the *Empress* operates with its companion ship, *Queen of the West,* on the Columbia and Snake rivers in Oregon and Idaho along the Lewis and Clark Trail. This year in Alaska, the *Empress of the North* is offering a program of 7-night round-trip cruises out of Juneau, with a 12-nighter at the beginning and end of the season—from Seattle to Juneau in May and from Juneau to Seattle in September.

THE EXPERIENCE   Pure Americana—that's what the *Empress of the North* (and others of the Majestic fleet) represents. Steamboats—side-wheelers and stern-wheelers— were a major mode of transportation at the turn of the 20th century; they brought the gold-rush pioneers to Alaska to join the hunt for Yukon riches more than a century ago. Who could travel on such a vessel in Alaska and not think of the Stampede of

Majestic America Line Fleet Itineraries

Ship	Itineraries
Empress of the North	**7-night Inside Passage:** Round-trip from Juneau, visiting Skagway, Glacier Bay, Sitka, Petersburg, Wrangell, and Dawes Glacier. May–Sept. **12-night Inside Passage:** One-way between Seattle and Juneau, visiting Anacortes and the San Juan Islands, WA., Ketchikan, Wrangell, Petersburg, Sitka, and Glacier Bay. May and Sept.*

*Northbound positioning cruise in May, southbound in Sept.

'98, of the glory days of riverboats on the mighty Mississippi, of calliopes, of Mark Twain? We may not have been around when these colorful vessels held sway over America's rivers and waterways. But we've read about them.

The *Empress of the North* experience is laid-back: no hassle, no heavy entertainment schedule, no formality. The boats move slowly—top speed is about 14 knots on the open seas—which leaves plenty of time to contemplate the passing scenery. The unstuffy atmosphere makes it easy to meet and mingle with complete strangers who quickly become friends; a newly expanded dance floor makes it even easier—to the music of bands not much bigger than, say, a trio. It will never be confused with the disco-style action on the bigger ships, but it's totally in keeping with the *Empress* experience.

Pros

- **Nostalgia.** The ship is a breed apart from most others in the market—a totally different experience.
- **Lots of private verandas.** All outside cabins—90% of which have verandas.
- **Shore excursions included.** Most explorations ashore are covered in the price.

Cons

- **Shallow draft.** Despite the presence of state-of-the-art stabilizers, ships with drafts as shallow as that of the *Empress* are liable to feel heavy seas more than some other ships. But the waters of the Inside Passage *are* fairly well protected, when all is said and done.

THE FLEET   The *Empress of the North,* built in 2003, is a somewhat larger fleet mate of the 163-passenger *Queen of the West* (1995), another stern-wheeler. (Hmm . . . wonder if an empress outranks a queen?) The latter is in service on the Columbia and Snake rivers year-round, joined by the *Empress* in the fall.

PASSENGER PROFILE   Not necessarily filthy rich, but probably comfortably off. And they are experienced cruisers, as not many people would choose a stern-wheeler in open water for their first experience at sea. Many of them have already tried the *Empress of the North* or the *Queen of the West* on the Columbia or Snake rivers. They're not looking for wild adventure ashore or frenzied activity on board.

DINING   Casually elegant on both ships, with an emphasis on local produce. Look for three or four thoughtfully prepared choices on the menu. With the number of passengers on these ships, it's difficult to get too extensive. But nobody leaves the table hungry. Half an hour before lunchtime, sandwiches, hamburgers, and hot dogs are available on the deck aft for those who can't wait for lunch to be served or who want to eat outdoors by the stern wheel, which can be most enjoyable when the Alaska weather cooperates.

ACTIVITIES   Not a lot of organized fun and games. *Empress* passengers don't require it and don't want it. A lecturer accompanies each cruise, offering insights into the passing scenery and cultures. But don't look for kayaks off the back of the vessel, or scuba diving, or anything of that nature.

CHILDREN'S PROGRAM   None.

ENTERTAINMENT   Live entertainment—music for dancing—begins in the early evening in both showrooms on the *Empress* and continues after dinner in the Paddlewheel Lounge. Local performers will board in port to present Native song and dance shows.

SERVICE   All American, which isn't unusual in the small-ship category these days. The seeming lack of sophistication shown by some members of the crew is refreshing—part of the appeal, really—and adds to the experience.

CRUISETOUR & ADD-ON PROGRAMS   The company does not offer any cruisetour or add-on programs.

Empress of the North

The Verdict

If it's a different kind of experience you're looking for, the *Empress* might just be for you. It's one of the most original cruising vessels to hit Alaska in a long time, being the only one using stern-wheeler propulsion.

Empress of the North *(photo: Majestic American Line)*

Specifications

Size (in Tons)	3,200	Crew	84
Passengers (Double Occ.)	223	Passenger/Crew Ratio	2.6 to 1
Passenger/Space Ratio	N/A*	Year Launched	2003
Total Cabins/Veranda Cabins	112/105	Last Major Refurbishment	N/A

These ships' sizes were measured using a different scale than the others in this book, so comparison is not possible.

Frommer's Ratings (Scale of 1–5)   ★★★★

Cabin Comfort & Amenities	4.5	Dining Options	3
Ship Cleanliness & Maintenance	5	Pool, Fitness, Spa & Sports Facilities	2
Public Comfort/Space	4.5	Children's Facilities	N/A
Decor	5	Enjoyment Factor	4.5

THE SHIP IN GENERAL   This ship has gotten a lot of attention in Alaska because of its distinctive profile and the historical musings it evokes. It has four decks, two lounges, and two elevators. Although it is a stern-wheeler, it must be noted that the 360-foot ship does have other propulsion capability—for the technically minded, it has two Z drives that rotate 360 degrees and provide additional power in any direction.

CABINS   Cabins are large by small-ship standards. The least expensive is a roomy 178 square feet, and the accommodations range up to two-bedroom suites measuring

476 square feet. All of the cabins have views of the ocean and 105 (out of 112) also have verandas. Two of the cabins are wheelchair accessible.

Cabins & Rates

Cabins	Per Diem Rates	Sq. Ft.	Fridge	Hair Dryer	Sitting Area	TV
Outside	$457–$629*	178–298	yes	no	yes	yes
Suites	$657–$893	392–476	yes	yes	yes	yes
Outside	$450–$609**					
Suites	$650–$842					

Rates are for 7-night cruises.
**Rates are for 12-night cruises.*

PUBLIC AREAS   Elegance and opulence are the bywords in the *Empress*'s public rooms. Plush burgundy and dark green–hued carpeting, drapes, and upholstery; windows everywhere; two elevators; comfy lounge seating—it's all here. And we must say that one of the most interesting rooms afloat is the Paddlewheel Lounge aft, from which tipplers and dancers both become mesmerized by the thrum, thrum of the paddle wheel seen through the floor-to-ceiling window.

DINING   There's not much variety of location here. You can either dine on the (usually excellent) food in the main dining room or help yourself to the sandwiches, hot dogs, and hamburgers made available on the top deck an hour before lunch. Many people find that kind of help-yourself al fresco (in good weather) dining a welcome change from the necessarily more structured service down below.

POOL, FITNESS, SPA & SPORTS FACILITIES   Nope, not here.

5 Alaska Marine Highway System

7559 N. Tongass Hwy., Ketchikan, AK 99901. © 800/642-0066 or 907/228-7255. Fax 907/277-4829. www.dot.state. ak.us/amhs.

In Alaska, which has fewer paved roads than virtually any other state, getting around can be a problem. There are local airlines, of course, and small private planes—lots and lots of small private planes, some with wheels, some with skis, some with floats for landing on water. (In fact, there are more private planes per capita in Alaska than in any other state in the union.) But given the weather conditions in many northland areas for large parts of the year, airplanes are not always the most reliable way of getting from Point A to Point B.

That's why the Alaska Marine Highway System (aka the Alaska Ferry, or AMHS) is so important. Sometimes in inclement weather even the state capital, Juneau, cannot be reached by road and relies heavily on the ferryboats of the AMHS to bring in visitors, vehicles, supplies, and even, now and then, the legislators who run the state. (Although the AMHS relocated its administrative headquarters to Ketchikan in 2005, its reservations center remains in Juneau, the state capital.)

Although the ferry system was originally created with the aim of providing Alaska's far-flung, often-inaccessible smaller communities with essential transportation links with the rest of the state and with the Lower 48, the boats have developed a following in the tourism business as well. Each year, thousands of visitors eschew luxury cruise ships in favor of the more basic services of the 10 vessels of the AMHS. The service is of particular value to independent travelers, enabling visitors to come and go as they please among Alaska's outposts. Some of the ferries carry both passengers and vehicles, some only passengers.

In 2005, AMHS was officially designated an "All American Road" by the U.S. Department of Transportation. To qualify for such recognition, according to federal rules, a road must have qualities that are nationally significant and contain features that do not exist elsewhere—it must be "a destination unto itself." AMHS definitely fits the bill.

The AMHS's southernmost port is Bellingham, WA. Its network stretches throughout southeast and southcentral Alaska and out to the islands to the west of Anchorage.

THE EXPERIENCE   It must be stressed that ferry-riding vacations are different than cruise vacations, to say the least. Don't even think about one if you're looking for a lot of creature comforts—fancy accommodations, gourmet food, spa treatments, Broadway-style shows, and the rest. You won't find any of the above on the sturdy vessels of the AMHS. In fact, not all ferry passengers get sleeping berths—5 of the 11 ferries in the fleet have no bedroom accommodations.

It's in the lounges or on deck that riders may encounter the only entertainment on board, all created by passengers on a strictly impromptu basis. It might be a backpacker strumming a guitar and singing folk songs. It might be a bearded, burly local reciting the poetry of Robert Service ("A bunch of the boys were whooping it up in the Malamute Saloon . . ."). Or it could be a father keeping his children occupied by performing magic tricks. Occasionally, spirited discussion groups will form in which all are welcome to participate. The subject might be the environment (always a hot, hot topic in Alaska, especially now with talk of opening up the Alaska Wildlife Preserve for oil exploration), politics (Alaskan or federal), the northern lights, the effect of tourism on wildlife (as much a hot-button issue as the environment), or any of a thousand other topics. Occasionally, sports will be discussed—but don't look for the locals to want to talk about anything as much as dog-sledding. It's almost a religion in the 49th State.

Pros

- **Unique way to travel.** The ferry system offers the chance for adventuresome travel that is not too taxing.
- **Lots of flexibility.** Passengers can combine the varied journeys that the ferry system has scheduled to customize their vacation package.

Cons

- **No doctor on board.** None of the vessels carries a doctor, so this may not be a good way to travel if you have health concerns.
- **Space books up quickly.** The only way you will be able to find a space on most of the ferries is by booking promptly. Don't call in May and expect to get what you want in June. It ain't gonna happen! If you're serious about experiencing Alaska by ferry, book now. Call the company at **800/642-0066** or book electronically through the website at www.dot.state.ak.us/amhs.
- **Spartan cabins.** Sleeping accommodations, when available, are basic, to say the least—no fridge, no telephone, and so on. (One traveler was once overheard to say, "I've known Trappist monks with more luxurious quarters!")

THE FLEET   All of the AMHS boats are designated M/V, as in motor vessel. Below is a thumbnail sketch of each one.

- One of the newest and fastest in the fleet is the *Fairweather,* which operates between Juneau and Sitka, and between Juneau and Haines and Juneau and Skagway through the Lynn Canal. It is a 235-foot, 250-passenger catamaran that cuts travel times in half. Interestingly, and somewhat surprisingly, while it links Juneau with Skagway and Haines, it does not link those two latter neighboring communities. The vessel has no sleeping quarters; it is designed purely to provide fast access to and from the capital. Its value to locals is immense; they can now be in the grocery and clothing stores of Juneau, or in the offices of the Legislature, twice as fast as they once were. Its value to tourists is that it enables them to spend less time in transit.
- A sister high-speed vessel, the *Chenega* (pronounced Che-*nee*-ga), is entering its third year of service. It also has no sleeping accommodations.
- The *Lituya,* the smallest and slowest of the ferry company's boats, joined the fleet in 2004. Carrying just 149 passengers, the *Lituya* was built to operate between Ketchikan and the Indian village of Metlakatla. Although built with a specific local market in mind, it also allows tourists to visit a Native community 17 miles from Ketchikan.
- The *Kennicott* (in service since 1998) was built in Gulfport, Mississippi. It is 382 feet long (about one-third as long as the biggest of today's cruise ships), has a service speed of just under 17 knots, and carries 748 passengers. Five of its 109 cabins are wheelchair accessible. The Kennicott has a dining room for sit-down fine dining and a cafeteria.
- The *Taku* was built in 1981 in Seattle. It is 352 feet long and carries 450 passengers at 16.5 knots. Two of its 44 cabins are wheelchair accessible. The boat has a cocktail lounge and cafeteria.
- The Wisconsin-built *Aurora,* which is used only for runs of a few hours, has room for 250 riders. Although it offers no sleeping berths, it has a cafeteria.
- The *Columbia* is the largest (though it doesn't have the biggest capacity) of the AMHS vessels. The ferry, built in Seattle in 1974, is 418 feet long and holds 625 passengers and 134 vehicles. Of its 104 sleeping rooms, 3 are suitable for wheelchair users. The vessel has a cafeteria, dining room for fine dining, and cocktail lounge.
- The 250-passenger *Le Conte,* built in Wisconsin in 1973, is a no-sleeper short-run ferry that offers cafeteria food service.
- The *Matanuska* entered service in 1968 after leaving the builder's yard in Seattle. In 1972, the boat was lengthened and renovated in Portland, bringing it to its current capacity of 500. It has 107 cabins, one of which can accommodate a wheelchair user. The vessel has a cafeteria and a cocktail lounge.
- Another Wisconsin product, the *Tustumena,* began in Alaska waters in 1964 and was extensively renovated in San Francisco 5 years later. Its has 26 sleeping rooms, with one adapted for wheelchair use. It carries 210 passengers. The *Tustumena* has a cafeteria and a cocktail lounge.
- The 500-passenger *Malaspina,* another Seattle build, has 73 cabins. One is suitable for a wheelchair user. The *Malaspina* has a cafeteria and a cocktail lounge.

PASSENGER PROFILE   The travelers who use the ferries are looking for a laid-back, totally casual Alaska experience. Jeans and climbing boots (sometimes not removed for days), anoraks and backpacks—these are the basic accessories of ferry travelers in the 49th state. Ferry passengers who are on vacation (the AMHS is also heavily used as basic transportation by Alaska locals) are mostly young and don't often bring their families. They are definitely not looking for luxury.

PORTS OF CALL   Those seeking a change from the more popular and frequently congested larger Inside Passage and Gulf ports find that the ferries are an ideal way to get around the less-visited Alaska, where paved roads are in short supply and reliable air connections—especially when the weather turns ugly—are nonexistent. A trip on one of the ferries can deposit you in, say, Pelican, on Chichagof Island, where you can enjoy fishing and scenery and join in the banter of the local fisherfolk in Rosie's Bar, the center of activity in town. A trip on another ferry will transport you to Tenakee Springs, a popular spa as far back as the gold-rush days, where you can "take the waters" and take advantage of saltwater fishing opportunities. The ferry will get you to Port Lions, which is located on the northeast coast of Kodiak Island at the eastern end of the Aleutian Chain; to other areas of the Aleutians—False Pass and King Cove for instance; to Chenega Bay, in Prince William Sound; to the Indian settlements at Kake, on Kupreanof Island; and to Metlakatla on Annette Island, among many other destinations. These are not, and never will be, ports with mass appeal. No luxury liner will ever disgorge 2,600 cruise passengers in any of them. But those people who seek a taste of down-home spirit, Alaska style, find these ports to be attractive destinations. In short, the Alaska Marine Highway System can get you to places that cruise ships just don't go. Of course, the ferry system can also get you to big-ship cruise ports such as Ketchikan, Juneau, Whittier, and the rest, but much of the system's appeal, to many visitors, is its ability to transport travelers to lesser-known outposts.

DINING   Only 2 of the 10 AMHS ferries (*Kennicott* and *Columbia*), have full-service, sit-down dining rooms. The others have cafeteria-style facilities that serve hot meals and beverages. There are also vending machines on all of the boats, which dispense snacks and drinks. Food prices—ranging from $2 for a vending machine snack to $10 for a hot meal in the dining room—are not included in the fares.

ACTIVITIES   No organized activities, but lots of scenic viewing.

ITINERARIES   The ferries operate in two distinct areas—year-round in the Southeast or Inside Passage (from Bellingham to Skagway/Haines), and in the summer months across to the Aleutians (in Alaska's Southwestern region) by way of Prince William Sound and the Kenai Peninsula. The Aleutians service is dependent on the weather: The seas become too rough, the fog too thick, and the cold too intense for the ferries to operate safely or profitably in the winter. See the website (www.dot.state. ak.us/amhs) for details on the many routes that the AMHS offers and the ports that it services.

CHILDREN'S PROGRAM   None.

ENTERTAINMENT   None.

SERVICE   Service is not one of the things that the Alaska Marine Highway System is noted for. The small American staff on each vessel works enthusiastically but without a great deal of distinction.

CRUISETOUR & ADD-ON PROGRAMS   None.

CABINS   The great majority of the cabins are small and spartan to say the least, coming in two- and four-bunk configurations, and either inside (without windows) or outside (with windows). For a premium, you can reserve a more comfortable sitting-room unit on some vessels. Most cabins have tiny private bathrooms with showers. Try to get an outside cabin so that you can watch the world go by. Cabins can be stuffy, and the windowless units can be claustrophobic as well. (If you're used to a veranda cabin when you cruise, forget about traveling on the Alaska Marine Highway System!)

Travelers who do not book their ferry passage in time to snag a cabin must spend their time curled up in chairs in the lounges if it's cold, or out on deck in a tent when the days lengthen and the sun stays high until late into the night. The patio-furniture lounge chairs on the covered outdoor solarium, on the top deck, are the best public sleeping spot on board, in part because the noise of the ship covers other sounds. If you're tenting, the best place is behind the solarium, where it's likely to be less windy. On the *Columbia,* that space is small, so grab it early. Bring duct tape to secure your tent to the deck in case you can't find a sheltered spot, as the wind over the deck of a ship in motion blows like an endless gale. The recliner lounges are comfortable, too, but can be stuffy. If the ship looks crowded, grab your spot fast to get a choice location. Showers are available, although there may be lines. Lock valuables in the coin-operated lockers.

RATES   Booking your passage on the Alaska Marine Highway System can be a complicated affair. First, there's the basic cost for the trip. The journey between, say, Bellingham, Washington, the southernmost port in the system, and Juneau (a trip that takes 39½ hr.), costs $326 one-way. From Ketchikan to Sitka, a much shorter journey (23 hours), the fare is just $83 one-way. (In winter, the ferries drop some lesser-visited ports from their itineraries. As a result, the prices also drop—to as low as $260 one-way in the first routing above and to $64 one-way in the other). Children between the ages of 6 and 11 are charged roughly half the adult fare throughout the system.

Once you've booked your passage, you choose and pay for the cabin that you will sleep in. That's extra. For the Bellingham/Juneau leg, a two-berth outside cabin, with facilities, goes for $393 (a little less for an inside room). Want a three-berth room? Four berth? There are several options for each vessel. Some rooms are inside, some are outside, some have private facilities, and some don't. And, of course, the prices are different for each category. See what we mean about being complicated?

After you've reserved and paid for your passage on the boat and your cabin, you then have to pay still more to bring your automobile onboard, if you're taking one along. The prices vary widely by size of vehicle. You also have to pay if you take along a kayak, inflatable boat, or bike. (Only in Alaska!)

PUBLIC AREAS   All of the ferries have warm, if somewhat sparse, interiors, with room for all when the weather is foul. They have solariums with high windows for viewing the passing scenery.

POOL, FITNESS, SPA & SPORTS FACILITIES   Are you kidding?

The Ports of Embarkation

Most Alaska cruises operate either round-trip from Vancouver or Seattle, or one-way northbound or southbound between Vancouver or Seattle and Seward/Anchorage. Whittier, an unprepossessing little place that has the advantage of being 60 miles closer to Anchorage, has become the northern turnaround port for Regent Seven Seas and most (but not all) of Princess's and its sister company, Carnival's, cruises in the Gulf of Alaska. Seattle and San Francisco are other popular ports of embarkation: This year, Princess will have a ship in Alaska rotation out of San Francisco. Norwegian, Princess, Cruise West, Holland America, and American West Steamboat Company are using Seattle as a base. Most of the small adventure-type vessels sail from popular Alaska ports

of call such as Juneau, Ketchikan, and Sitka. In this chapter, we'll cover the most common of these home ports: Anchorage, Seward, Vancouver, Seattle, Juneau, and Whittier.

Consider traveling to your city of embarkation at least a day or two before your cruise departure date. You can check out local attractions, and if you're traveling from afar, give yourself time to overcome jet lag.

Use the port-city information provided here; in addition, you may want to refer to *Frommer's Alaska 2008*, *Frommer's Vancouver & Victoria 2008*, *Frommer's Seattle 2008*, or *Frommer's San Francisco 2008* for more details, particularly if you're planning to spend a few days in the port.

1 Anchorage

Anchorage, which started as a tent camp for workers building the Alaska Railroad in 1914, stands between the Chugach Mountains and the waters of upper Cook Inlet. It was a remote, sleepy railroad town until World War II, when a couple of military bases were located here and livened things up a bit. Even with that, though, Anchorage did not start becoming a city in earnest until the late 1950s, when oil was discovered on the Kenai Peninsula, to the south.

Fortunes came fast and development was haphazard, but the city seems at this point to have settled into its success. It now boasts good restaurants, fine museums, and a nice little zoo. In addition, the **Alaska Native Heritage Center,** a 26-acre re-creation of the villages of Alaska's five Native groups, welcomes visitors. Anchorage is, without argument, Alaska's only cosmopolitan city, but surrounded as it is by wilderness, moose regularly annoy gardeners in the town, and even bears occasionally show up in the streets. It's unlikely, though, that you'll run into such critters in the height of the cruise season.

Anchorage's downtown area, near Ship Creek, is about 8 by 20 blocks wide, but the rest of the city spreads some 5 miles east and 15 miles south. Most visitors, whether heading off on a cruise ship or not, spend a day or two in town before going somewhere more remote. The city center is pleasant, but we recommend you try to see more than just the streets of tourist-oriented shops. Check out the **coastal trail** and the **museums,** and if you have time, plan a day trip about 50 miles south along **Turnagain Arm** to explore the receding **Portage Glacier** and visit the mountains.

And don't forget the **Alaska Native Heritage Center** we mentioned above. It's well worth a visit, even at $24 a head, providing an introduction to the state's Native groups through storytelling, dance, music, a crafts workshop, a museum, and an outdoor area in which five traditional homes have been constructed. Most lines' shore-excursion books include it this year. If you're doing it on your own, it's an easy 10-minute drive north of downtown.

GETTING TO ANCHORAGE & THE PORT

Cruise ships dock in Seward or Whittier on the east coast of the Kenai Peninsula, to avoid the extra day that cruising around the peninsula to Anchorage adds to Gulf of Alaska itineraries. It's quicker to transport passengers between the towns in motor-coaches or by train than it is to sail all the way around the peninsula. Most visitors will use Anchorage as a hub because, thanks to the international airport, it's where Alaska connects to the rest of the world. We recommend spending a day or two in Anchorage before or after your cruise.

BY PLANE   If you're arriving or leaving by plane, you'll land at the **Ted Stevens Anchorage International Airport** (how come they always name airports after politicians?). The facility is located within the city limits, a 15-minute drive from downtown. Taxis run about $25 for the trip downtown. **Alaska Shuttle** (© **907/338-8888;** www.akshuttle.com) charges $14 for up to three people traveling together.

BY CAR   By car, there is only one road into Anchorage from the rest of the world: the Glenn Highway. The other road out of town, the Seward Highway, leads to the Kenai Peninsula.

EXPLORING ANCHORAGE

INFORMATION   The **Anchorage Convention and Visitor Bureau** (© **907/276-4118;** www.anchorage.net) maintains five information locations. The main one is the Log Cabin Visitor Information Center at 4th Avenue and F Street (© 907/274-3531). It's open daily from 7:30am to 7pm June through August, and from 8am to 6pm in May and September. Visit the bureau's website for everything you need to know before you go.

GETTING AROUND   Most car-rental companies maintain a counter at the airport. A compact car costs about $50 a day, with unlimited mileage. (There aren't many of those $30-a-day specials that you see advertised in some other states!) Advanced bookings are strongly recommended in midsummer. Anchorage's bus system is an effective way of moving to and from the top attractions and activities. The buses operate between 6am and 10pm daily, and passage costs $1.75 for adults and $1 for ages 5 to 18. In the 20-block downtown area, which consists of 5th and 6th avenues between Denali and K streets, the bus operates as a free people mover.

ATTRACTIONS WITHIN WALKING DISTANCE

With its old-fashioned grid of streets, Anchorage's downtown area is pleasant, if a bit touristy. The 1936 **Old City Hall,** at 4th Avenue and E Street, offers an interesting display on city history in its lobby, including dioramas of the early streetscape. For a better sense of what Alaska's all about, though, you'll want to check out the heritage

Anchorage

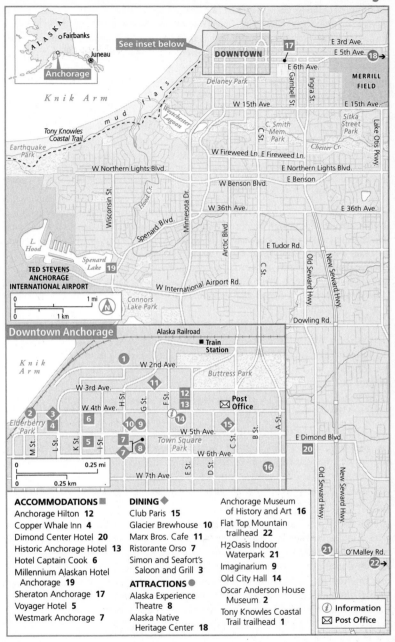

ACCOMMODATIONS ■
Anchorage Hilton **12**
Copper Whale Inn **4**
Dimond Center Hotel **20**
Historic Anchorage Hotel **13**
Hotel Captain Cook **6**
Millennium Alaskan Hotel
Anchorage **19**
Sheraton Anchorage **17**
Voyager Hotel **5**
Westmark Anchorage **7**

DINING ◆
Club Paris **15**
Glacier Brewhouse **10**
Marx Bros. Cafe **11**
Ristorante Orso **7**
Simon and Seafort's
Saloon and Grill **3**

ATTRACTIONS ●
Alaska Experience
Theatre **8**
Alaska Native
Heritage Center **18**

Anchorage Museum
of History and Art **16**
Flat Top Mountain
trailhead **22**
H2Oasis Indoor
Waterpark **21**
Imaginarium **9**
Old City Hall **14**
Oscar Anderson House
Museum **2**
Tony Knowles Coastal
Trail trailhead **1**

ⓘ **Information**
⊠ **Post Office**

museums or take a ride outside the city to the Chugach Mountains. You can also take a walk on the **Tony Knowles Coastal Trail,** which comes through downtown and runs along the water for about 11 miles, from the western end of 2nd Avenue to Kincaid Park. You can hop onto the trail at several points, including Elderberry Park, at the western end of 5th Avenue.

The Alaska Experience Theatre Think Alaska, think big. This 40-minute Omnivision wraparound presentation, *Alaska the Greatland,* is a cool introduction to some of the places you'll be touring, but be aware Omnivision (like IMAX) may cause motion sickness in some people. You can also visit the Alaska Earthquake Exhibit—it really shakes—for a separate admission.

705 W. 6th Ave., on the northwest corner of 6th Ave. and G St., partly in a dome tent. ✆ 877/276-3730 or 907/276-3730. www.alaskaexperiencetheatre.com. Admission $8 adults, $4 children 5–11. Summer daily 9am–9pm; winter noon–6pm. The film is screened on the hour. Alaska Earthquake Exhibit admission $6 adults, $4 children 5–11. Combination discount: $10 adults, $7 children.

Anchorage Museum of History and Art In the Alaska Gallery, you can enjoy an informative walk through the history and anthropology of the state, and in the art galleries you can see what's happening in Alaska art today. Special exhibits are frequent. A branch of the Marx Bros. Cafe (see listing below) serves excellent lunches, and Native dancers perform in the auditorium daily at 12:15, 1:15, and 2:15pm.

121 W. 7th Ave. ✆ 907/343-4326. www.anchoragemuseum.org. Admission $8 adults, free for children 17 and under (though a $2 donation is suggested). A combined Anchorage Museum/Native Heritage Center admission ticket is available for $25. May 15–Sept 15 Fri–Wed 9am–6pm, Thurs 9am–9pm; Sept 16–May 14 Wed–Sat 10am–6pm, Sun 1–5pm.

The Imaginarium This science museum is geared toward kids, with concise explanations and lots of fun learning experiences. There's a strong Alaska theme to many of the displays. The saltwater touch tank, one of the stars of the museum, is like an indoor tide pool.

737 W. 5th Ave., Suite G. ✆ 907/276-3179. www.imaginarium.org. Admission $5.50 adults, $5 ages 2–12. Mon–Sat 10am–6pm; Sun noon–5pm.

The Oscar Anderson House Museum This house museum shows how an early Swedish butcher lived. It's a quaint dwelling surrounded by a lovely little garden, and the house tour provides a good explanation of the city's short history. Furnishings include a working 1909 player piano.

420 M St., in Elderberry Park. ✆ 907/274-2336. Admission $3 adults, $1 children 5–12. Summer Mon–Fri noon–5pm; closed in winter.

ATTRACTIONS OUTSIDE THE DOWNTOWN AREA

The Alaska Native Heritage Center This 26-acre center introduces visitors to the lives and cultures of the state's five major Alaska Native groupings: the Southeast (Inside Passage) region's Tlingits, Eyaks, Haida, and Tsimshians; the Athabascans of the Interior; the Iñupiat and St. Lawrence Island Yup'ik Natives of the far north; the Aleuts and Alutiiqs of the Aleutian Islands; and the Yup'ik and Cup'ik tribes of the extreme west. A central Welcome House holds a small museum, a theater, a workshop where Native craftspeople demonstrate techniques, and a rotunda where storytelling, dance, and music performances are presented throughout the day. Outside, spaced along a walking trail around a small lake, five traditional dwellings represent the five regional Native groupings, each hosted by a member of that group. You can catch a

The Iditarod

Few things fire up Alaska's residents like the **Iditarod Trail Sled Dog Race,** a 1,000-mile run from Anchorage to Nome that takes place in mid-March. Winners cover the distance in 9 or 10 days, which includes mandatory stopovers of up to 24 hours to rest the dogs. (The 2007 winner, Lance Mackey, completed the course in 9 days, 5 hr., 8 min., and, oh yes, 41 sec.) The race is big news—TV anchors speculate on the mushers' strategies at the top of the evening news, and school children plot the progress of their favorite teams on maps. Its start, in downtown Anchorage, has been covered repeatedly by ABC's *Wide World of Sports.* When the event hits Nome, the town overflows with visitors kept busy by the many local events and activities that coincide with the race. Even if the first team crosses the finish line at 3am in –30°F (–34°C) weather, a huge crowd turns out to congratulate the musher.

This is Alaska's Super Bowl, its World Series. The victors are feted and admired throughout the state as much as any sports star ever is in the Lower 48. They're not compensated quite as well, mind you. First prize in the grueling event varies but usually runs about $65,000—with sometimes a truck thrown in for good measure! The cruise lines long ago recognized the significance of the Iditarod, even to non-Alaskans. Princess, for instance, has a contract with Libby Riddles, the first woman to win the race, in 1985. She comes aboard in Juneau with a slideshow to talk about her mushing experience. The *Riverboat Discovery* is a popular day cruise on the Chena River in Fairbanks, an outing cruise lines include in their cruisetour itinerary if they have programs in the Denali Corridor. The boat stops for a while on each of its sailings at the dog yard where the late Susan Butcher—an Alaska legend who won the Iditarod four times (1986, 1987, 1988, and 1990)—kept some of her champion dogs. The Iditarod Trail Sled Dog Race headquarters is located in Wasilla, near Anchorage, and is also a part of the shore-excursion schedule of virtually all Gulf of Alaska cruise operators.

Cruise aficionados may never be in the state to see the race itself, since it takes place off season—*way* off season. But they are likely to see and hear plenty about it during their summer vacations.

complimentary shuttle to the Center from the Anchorage Museum of History and Art and other Anchorage locations; check www.alaskanative.net for details.

From the Glenn Hwy., take the North Muldoon exit. © 800/315-6608 or 907/330-8000. www.alaskanative.net. Admission $24 adults, $21 seniors and military, $16 children 7–16; free for children 6 and under. Family rate (2 adults, 2 children) $69. A combined Anchorage Museum/Native Heritage Center admission ticket is available for $25. Summer daily 9am–5pm.

The Alaska Zoo Don't expect a big city zoo. Instead, come to experience a little Eden complete with Alaska bears, seals, otters, musk oxen, mountain goats, moose, caribou, and waterfowl. There are also decidedly non-Alaska elephants, tigers, and the like here.

4731 O'Malley Rd. © 907/346-3242. www.alaskazoo.org. Admission $10 adults, $8 seniors, $6 children 3–17, free under 2. Tues and Fri 9am–9pm; Mon, Wed–Thurs, Sat–Sun 9am–6pm. New Seward Hwy. to O'Malley Rd., then turn left and go 2 miles; it's 20 min. from downtown, without traffic.

Flat Top Mountain   Rising right behind Anchorage, this mountain is a great and easy climb, and perfect for an afternoon hike. The parking area at Glen Alps, above the tree line, is a good starting point.

In the Chugach Mountains. From the New Seward Hwy., drive east on O'Malley Rd., turn right on Hillside Dr. and left on Upper Huffman Rd., then right on the narrow, twisting Toilsome Hill Dr.

The H₂Oasis Indoor Waterpark   This aquatic attraction features a lazy river perfect for idling away an hour, a wave pool that generates rollers that can reach up to 4 feet, a water coaster more than 40 feet high and 500 feet long, a 150-foot-long enclosed slide, and a children's lagoon with a pirate ship and water cannons.

The Castle on O'Malley, 1520 O'Malley Rd. (about 5 miles from downtown). ℭ **907/522-4420.** www.h2oasis waterpark.com. Day pass $22 adults, $17 children 3–12. Daily 10am–9pm. Take the New Seward Hwy. from downtown past O'Malley Rd. Park is between O'Malley and Huffman rds.

Portage Glacier   In 1985, the National Forest Service spent $8 million building a visitor center at Portage. Imagine its chagrin when the glacier then started receding, moving away from the center so fast that at this point you can't even see one from the other. You must now board a tour boat to get close to the glacier face. Portage is not the best glacier Alaska has to offer—it's relatively small—but if you haven't had enough of them after your cruise (or want a preview beforehand), it's well worth a stop. The visitor center itself is worth a visit; it's a sort of glacier museum and an excellent place to learn about what you'll be seeing (or saw) on your cruise. Many bus tours are offered (your cruise line may offer one, too), including a 7-hour **Gray Line of Alaska** (ℭ **907/277-5581;** www.graylinealaska.com) trip from Anchorage, which includes the boat ride to the glacier and a stop at Alyeska Ski Resort, where you can have lunch on your own at the Alyeska Prince Hotel and take an optional tram ride to the top of the mountain. The cost is $69 adults, $35 children, and the trip is offered twice daily in the summer.

About 50 miles south of the city on the Seward Hwy. (toward Seward). Visitor Center Memorial Day to Labor Day daily 9am–6pm; Labor Day to Memorial Day Sat–Sun 10am–5pm. Free admission.

BEST CRUISE-LINE SHORE EXCURSIONS
See the "Anchorage City Tour," on p. 160.

EXCURSIONS OFFERED BY LOCAL AGENCIES
Anchorage Historic Properties   This 2-hour tour covers 2 miles, and the volunteer guides are both fun and knowledgeable. Meet at the lobby of Old City Hall, next door to the Log Cabin Visitor Information Center (p. 150).

645 W. 3rd Ave. ℭ **907/274-3600.** Guided walking tour of historic downtown Anchorage June–Aug weekdays at 1pm, for a reasonable $5 adults, $1 children. Combination ticket available for $6.50 (kids $2) with the Oscar Anderson House Museum (p. 152).

WHERE TO STAY
Rooms can be hard to come by in Anchorage in the summer, so be sure to arrange lodging as far in advance of your trip as possible, whether through your cruise line or on your own. In addition to the listings below, you can try the luxurious **Anchorage Hilton,** 500 W. 3rd Ave. (ℭ **800/245-2527** or 907/272-7411; www.hilton.com); the **Hotel Captain Cook,** 4th and K streets (ℭ **800/843-1950** or 907/276-6000; www.captaincook.com); the **Westmark Anchorage,** 720 W. 5th Ave. (ℭ **800/544-0970** or 907/276-7676; www.westmarkhotels.com); the **Sheraton Anchorage,** 401 E. 6th Ave. (ℭ **800/325-3535** or 907/276-8700; www.sheraton.com); the small and charming **Historic Anchorage**

Hotel, right next door to the **Hilton** on E Street (© **800/544-0988** or 907/272-4553; www.historicanchoragehotel.com); the **Dimond Center Hotel,** 700 E. Dimond Blvd. (© **866/770-5002** or 907/770-5000; www.dimondcenterhotel.com); or the **Millennium Alaskan Hotel Anchorage,** 480 Spenard Rd. (© **800/544-0553** or 907/245-2300; www.millenniumhotels.com). It's not a cheap city: Room rates in Anchorage, before discounts, range upward of $200. Hotels accept all major credit cards. The hotels mentioned above are among the city's more upscale. The following are some lower-priced alternatives:

Copper Whale Inn   There's a wonderfully casual feeling to this place. A pair of clapboard houses overlooks the water and Elderberry Park right on the coastal trail downtown, with charming rooms of every shape and size. The rooms in the newer building, lower on the hill, are preferable, with cherry-wood furniture and high ceilings. All rooms are wired for TVs, phone, and voice mail—you just have to ask for the actual instrument to be connected. A few bikes are available for loan, and a full breakfast is included in the price.

440 L St., Anchorage, AK 99501. © **907/258-7999.** Fax 888/WHALE-IN or 907/258-6213. www.copperwhale.com. 14 units, 12 with bathroom. $165 double with shared bathroom; $165–$195 double with private bathroom. Extra person in room $10. AE, DC, DISC, MC, V.

The Voyager Hotel   The Voyager is just about right. The size is small, the location central, the rooms large and light (all with kitchens), and the housekeeping exceptional. The desks have modem ports and extra electrical outlets, and the hospitality is warm yet highly professional. There's nothing ostentatious or outwardly remarkable about the hotel, yet the most experienced travelers rave about it the loudest. There's no smoking.

501 K St., Anchorage, AK 99501. © **800/247-9070** or 907/277-9501. Fax 907/274-0333. www.voyagerhotel.com. 38 units. $139–$179 single or double. Extra person in room $10 extra. AE, DC, DISC, MC, V.

WHERE TO DINE

Club Paris STEAK/SEAFOOD   Walking from a bright spring afternoon under a neon Eiffel Tower into midnight darkness, past a smoke-enshrouded bar, and sitting down at a secretive booth for two, we felt as if we should have been plotting a shady 1950s oil deal. And we would probably not have been the first. Smoky Club Paris may be too authentic for some, but it's essence of the old Anchorage boomtown years, when the streets were dusty and an oilman needed a classy joint in which to do business. Beef, of course, is what to order, and it'll be done right. Club Paris has a full liquor license.

417 W. 5th Ave. © **907/277-6332.** www.clubparisrestaurant.com. Reservations recommended. Lunch $7–$27; dinner $18–$47. AE, DC, DISC, MC, V. Mon–Sat 11:30am–2:30pm and 5–11pm; Sun 5–10pm.

Glacier Brewhouse GRILL/SEAFOOD   A tasty, eclectic, and ever-changing menu is served in a large dining room with lodge decor, where the pleasant scent of the wood-fired grill hangs in the air. This place brews five hearty beers behind a glass wall. It's noisy and active, with lots of agreeable if trendy touches, such as the bread—made from spent brewery grain—that's set out on the tables with olive oil. An advantage for travelers is the wide price range—a feta cheese, spinach, and artichoke pizza is under $11.

737 W. 5th Ave. © **907/274-BREW.** www.glacierbrewhouse.com. Reservations recommended for dinner. Lunch $9.50–$17; dinner $9.50–$37. AE, DC, DISC, MC, V. Summer 11am–11pm; winter Mon 11am–9:30pm, Tues–Thurs 11am–10pm, Fri–Sat 11am–11pm, Sun 4–9:30pm.

Shopping Smart for Native Art

If you're interested in Native Alaskan art, know that there is a large market in fakes: More than one shopkeeper's assistant has been spotted removing MADE IN TAIWAN stickers from supposedly Native art objects.

Before you buy a piece of Native art, ask the dealer for a biography of the artist and ask whether the artist actually carved the piece (rather than just lending his or her name to knockoffs). Most dealers will tell you where a work really comes from—you just have to ask.

Price should also be a tip-off to fakes, as real Native art is pricey. An elaborate mask, for instance, should be priced at $3,000, not $300. Be particularly wary of soapstone carvings, as most are not made in Alaska.

There are two marks used for Alaska products: a MADE-IN-ALASKA polar bear sticker, which means the item was at least mostly made in the state, and a silver hand sticker, which indicates authentic Native art. An absence of the label, however, does not mean the item is not authentic; it may just mean the artist doesn't like labels. So just ask if you're curious about a piece of artwork that doesn't have a sticker.

Marx Bros. Cafe ECLECTIC/REGIONAL   A restaurant that began as a hobby among three friends nearly 20 years ago is still a labor of love and has become a standard of excellence in the state. The cuisine is varied and creative, ranging from Asian to Italian, but everyone orders the Caesar salad made tableside. The decor and style are studies in casual elegance. Beer and wine are served.

627 W. 3rd Ave. ✆ **907/278-2133.** www.marxcafe.com. Reservations required. Main courses $30–$45. AE, DC, MC, V. Summer Tues–Sat 5:30–10pm; winter Wed–Sat 5:30–10pm.

Ristorante Orso ITALIAN   Despite its Italian orientation (excellent pastas, great sauces), this restaurant also offers superb wood-grilled steaks and locally caught seafood in an elegant, comfortable setting.

737 W. 5th Ave. ✆ **907/222-3232.** www.orsoalaska.com. Reservations recommended. Lunch $8.50–$15; dinner $14–$37. AE, DC, DISC, MC, V. Summer lunch 11:30am–4pm daily; dinner Sun–Fri 5–10pm, Fri–Sat 5–11pm.

Simon and Seafort's Saloon and Grill STEAK/SEAFOOD   This is one of the city's great dinner houses, with turn-of-the-century decor, a cheerful atmosphere, warm service, and fabulous sunset views of Cook Inlet. Prime rib and seafood are the specialties. Light meals are served in the bar.

420 L St. ✆ **907/274-3502.** www.r-u-i.com/sim. Reservations recommended (days in advance in summer). Lunch $7.95–$18; dinner $19–$55. AE, MC, V. Mon–Fri 11am–2:30pm; daily 4:30–10pm.

SHOPPING

Anchorage is truly an international city, but when all is said and done, it's a part of Alaska, and for that reason, if for no other, visitors should shop for genuine products of the 49th state. **Alaska Unique,** at 3601 Minnesota Dr. (✆ **907/561-9498**), offers a selection of Native-crafted articles—in ivory, soapstone, gold, and other materials. **4th Avenue Market Place,** 411 W. 4th Ave. (✆ **907/222-4853**), in the heart of downtown, has a number of stores, some quite touristy, some more upscale, offering similar kinds of goods, less expensively.

DIY (do-it-yourself) clothes makers may enjoy **The Quilt Tree,** 341 Benson Blvd. (© **907/561-4115;** www.quiltree.com), with its wide selection of Alaska-pattern fabrics. During the height of cruise season, expect these and other stores to be open from 9am to 7pm, but in the early and late weeks of the season (early May or mid-Sept), they tend to close a little earlier.

2 Seward

Since Seward is the northern embarkation and disembarkation port for most Gulf of Alaska cruise operators, passengers can almost be forgiven if they sometimes think the correct name of this Resurrection Bay community is "Seward-the-port-for-Anchorage." Although the majority of 7-day Gulf cruises are advertised as "Vancouver to Anchorage" (or the reverse), the ships don't actually sail to Anchorage proper. Instead, they dock in Seward and guests are carried by motorcoach (or, more recently, by rail) to or from Anchorage. Why? Because Seward—and Whittier—lie on the south side of the Kenai Peninsula, and Anchorage on the north. Sailing around the peninsula would add another day to the cruise.

As such, most people pass through Seward on their way to or from their ship, but never really see much of the town. And that's a pity. Seward, which traces its history back to 1793 when the Russian poobah, Alexander Baranof, first visited, is an attractive little town rimmed by mountains and ocean, with streets lined with old woodframe houses and fishermen's residences. It's also home to the spectacular **Alaska SeaLife Center** (a marine research, rehabilitation, and public education center where visitors can watch scientists uncovering the secrets of nearby **Prince William Sound**). Seward is an ideal spot from which to make wildlife-watching day trips by boat into the sound or to begin one of a variety of road and rail trips through the beautiful **Kenai Peninsula.** Seward was hit hard on Good Friday 1964 when a massive earthquake rattled Anchorage, the peninsula, and everything in between. The villagers (there were only about 2,500 of them) watched the water in the harbor drain away after the shaking stopped and realized immediately what was about to happen: a tidal wave. Because they were smart enough to read the signs and run for high ground, loss of life was miraculously slight when the towering 100-foot wall of water struck. (For more info, read the section "The Trembling Earth," on p. 246.) The town itself, however, was heavily damaged, so many of the buildings that visitors see today are of a more recent vintage than might be expected. However, care has been taken to rebuild them in the style of the town's earlier days.

GETTING TO SEWARD

Most cruise passengers will arrive at Seward either by ship (at the end of their cruise) or by bus.

By Plane   The nearest major airport, Ted Stevens Anchorage International Airport, is 130 miles away.

By Bus   The bus trip from the airport takes about 3 hours, passing through the beautiful Chugach National Forest. If you haven't made transportation arrangements through your cruise line, **Seward Bus Line** (© **907/224-3608**) offers one trip a day (9am check-in) from Anchorage for $45 one-way. **Gray Line of Alaska's Alaskan Express** (© **800/544-2206**) does the same for $50, but only for passengers going to or coming from certain ships, most notably but not exclusively those of Gray Line's owner, Holland America.

By Car For those arriving by car, Seward and the Kenai Peninsula are served by a single major road, the Seward Highway.

By Train The train ride to or from Anchorage with a stop at Seward goes through some truly beautiful scenery; it costs $65 one-way adults ($109 round-trip) and $33 one-way for kids ($55 round-trip) on the **Alaska Railroad** (© 800/544-9552 or 907/265-2494). The route is prettier than going by road; you'll see gorges, rushing rivers, and tunnels cut through mountains.

EXPLORING SEWARD

INFORMATION The **Seward Chamber of Commerce** (© 907/224-8051; www.sewardak.org) operates an information booth right on the cruise-ship dock; it's open from 8am to noon and 3 to 7pm daily. If you have time, stop by **Kenai Fjords National Park Visitor Center,** near the waterfront at 500 Adams St. (© 907/224-7500), to learn about what's in the area, including nearby hiking trails. It's open May through Labor Day daily from 9am to 6pm, off season Monday through Friday from 9am to 5pm.

GETTING AROUND The downtown area is within walking distance of the cruise-ship dock, and you can easily cover downtown Seward on foot. If it's not raining, consider a bike ride through town. **Seward Bike Shop** (© 907/224-2448), 411 Port Ave., in a railcar near the depot at the harbor, rents high-performance mountain bikes that are good for getting around town and into the surrounding hills, plus other equipment. A cruiser is $14 for a half-day, $23 for a full day. For motorized transport, the **Chamber of Commerce Trolley** runs every half-hour from 10am to 7pm daily in summer; it goes south along 3rd Avenue and north on Ballaine Street, stopping at the railroad depot, the cruise-ship dock, the Alaska SeaLife Center, and the harbor visitor center. The fare is $2 per trip, or $5 for an all-day pass. A little bus known as the **Seward Trolley** will carry you between the downtown area and the waterfront. It costs $15 for an all-day pass, $5 for a one-way trip. The trip isn't much more than a mile, though, so it's a pleasant walk if the weather cooperates.

ATTRACTIONS WITHIN WALKING DISTANCE

Downtown Seward can be explored with the help of a **walking-tour map,** available from the Chamber of Commerce visitor center near the cruise-ship docks and at establishments throughout town.

The Alaska SeaLife Center Opened in 1998, this facility allows scientists to study, in their natural habitat, Steller's sea lions, porpoises, sea otters, harbor seals, fish, and other forms of marine life that abound in the area, as well as the umpteen species of local seabirds—colorful rock puffins, cormorants, and more. The important thing, of course, is that you can study them, too—through windows that show you the undersea world. The center itself is something of a phoenix, rising from the metaphorical ashes of the 1989 *Exxon Valdez* disaster that so drastically affected the area's marine ecology and the creatures that inhabit the sound. Much of the $60 million needed to create the center came from an oil-spill reparation fund established by Exxon Corporation. It would be nice to record that the center has been an unqualified financial success, but it hasn't. The planners overestimated the potential visitation, and the facility, strapped for cash, has been given state government grants to cover the shortfall. The

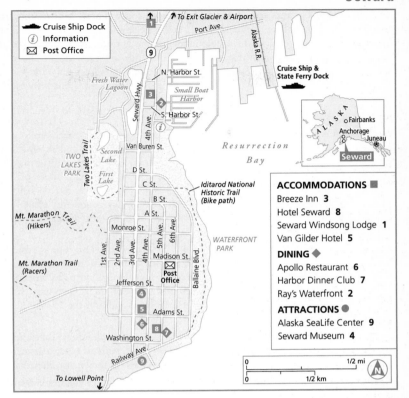

failure of this great facility to turn a consistent profit is a pity—and probably caused by the fact that visitors tend to land in Seward and almost immediately board trains and coaches for Anchorage, leaving very little time for touring and sightseeing. Nevertheless, the SeaLife Center will continue operations and should be on everybody's must-see list.

301 Railway Ave. ✆ 800/224-2525 or 907/224-6300. www.alaskasealife.org. Admission $15 adults, $12 children 7–12, free for children 6 and under. Apr 15–Sept 15, daily 8am–7pm; Sept 16–Apr 14 daily 10am–5pm.

The Seward Museum This is a charming grandma's attic of a place, with clippings, memorabilia, and curiosities recalling town history, painter Rockwell Kent, and the ways of the past. An interesting exhibit revolves around the Russian ships built here in the 18th century.

Corner of 3rd Ave. and Jefferson St. ✆ 907/224-3902. Admission $3 adults, 50¢ children 5–18, free for children under 5. Summer daily 9am–5pm.

ATTRACTIONS BEYOND THE PORT AREA

Caines Head State Recreation Area Parts of this 7-mile coastal trail, south of town, are accessible only at low tide, so it's best done with someone picking you up and/or dropping you off by boat beyond the beach portion; **Miller's Landing water taxi** (✆ **866/541-5739** or 907/224-5739) offers this service for $38 per person one-way,

$45 round-trip. The trail has some gorgeous views, rocky shores, and the concrete remains of Fort McGilvray, a World War II defensive emplacement. Take flashlights and you can poke around in the spooky underground corridors and rooms. For an easy 2-mile hike to Fort McGilvray, start with a boat ride to North Beach. The main trail head is on Lowell Point Road. Stop at the Kenai Fjords National Park Visitor Center at the boat harbor for tide conditions and advice. Check out www.alaska stateparks.org for more about these local trails.

BEST CRUISE-LINE SHORE EXCURSIONS

Anchorage City Tour (3–9 hr.; $99): A restroom-equipped motorcoach takes you on a 3-hour drive from Seward through the Chugach National Forest and along Turnagain Arm between Seward and Anchorage. Once you hit Anchorage, the bus makes a circuit through the downtown area, pointing out sights of interest, good shops, and popular restaurants. You'll then be free for a few hours to shop, eat, or visit the Museum of History and Art. The tour is either an all-day round-trip affair from Seward or a half-day trip that ends in Anchorage (either downtown at Egan Center or at the Anchorage Airport).

Portage Lake and Glacier (8 hr.; $71 adults, $59 children): This tour is typically done en route to Anchorage by motorcoach. *The MV Ptarmigan,* an enclosed cruiser with an open-top deck, sails up Portage Lake for an hour-long sojourn that sometimes brings you within 300 yards of the glacier. The tour continues on to Anchorage, where you will see some of the city's historical points of interest and tour the 25-acre Alaska Native Heritage Center.

Resurrection River Float Trip (2½ hr.; $75 adults, $40–$49 children): Take a relaxing trip on an inflatable raft along the Resurrection River, with an expert oarsman as your pilot. Sights include Exit Glacier and expansive views of the Resurrection Valley.

Kenai Fjords National Park Cruise (9–10hr.; $149 adults, $75 children): Board a dayboat for a wildlife and glacier cruise in the park. Keep an eye out for whales, sea lions, and otters. You'll also view a massive tidewater glacier and enjoy the stunning sight of glacially carved cliffs (typically offered with a transfer to Anchorage).

EXCURSIONS OFFERED BY LOCAL AGENCIES

Alaska Railroad (© 800/544-0552; www.akrr.com) offers a variety of day tours from Seward, including a 4½-hour cruise (offered with Major Marine Tours) that explores Resurrection Bay. The cruise is narrated by a park ranger and costs $191 per person; advance reservations are suggested. Kenai Fjords Tours (© 800/478-8068 or 907/224-8068; www.kenaifjordstours.com) has a variety of land excursions and day cruises in Resurrection Bay and the Kenai Fjords National Park. A 6-hour cruise is priced at $129 for adults and $65 for children, while a 9½-hour, 150-mile cruise, including deli-style lunch, is priced at $159 for adults, $80 for children under 12. The company also offers kayaking day trips in Resurrection Bay for $149. **IditaRide dog-sled tours,** Old Exit Glacier Road, 3¾ miles off the Seward Highway (© 800/478-3139 or 907/224-8607), offers dog-sled demonstrations and rides on a wheeled dog sled.

In addition to these tours, **fishing charters** are available from various operators in the harbor.

WHERE TO STAY

The Breeze Inn   Located right at the boat harbor, this large, three-story motel-style building offers good standard accommodations with the most convenient location for a fishing or Kenai Fjords boat trip. Twenty new rooms, at the upper end of the price range, are especially nice. A restaurant and lounge are across the parking lot.

1306 Seward Hwy. (P.O. Box 2147), Seward, AK 99664-2147. © **907/224-5238.** Fax 907/224-7024. www.breeze inn.com. 100 units. $129–$219 double. Extra person in room $10 extra. AE, DC, DISC, MC, V.

Hotel Seward   The rooms here are large, fresh, and attractively decorated. Many rooms have big bay windows, and all have TV/VCRs, refrigerators, dataports, and coffeemakers. Rooms with a view of Resurrection Bay go for a premium. Avoid the south-facing rooms, with views of the back of another hotel. The cheaper economy rooms are smaller but have the same amenities as the standard rooms.

221 5th Ave., Seward, AK 99664. © **907/224-2378.** Fax 907/224-3112. www.hotelsewardalaska.com. 38 units. $199–$224 double; economy rooms $155. Extra person in room $10. AE, MC, V.

The Seward Windsong Lodge   This hotel is the only one near Kenai Fjords National Park with a national park atmosphere. The location is out of town, among spruce trees in the broad, unspoiled valley of the Resurrection River. The collection of buildings goes on and on, with rooms set in separate lodges with entry from exterior porches. All accommodations have a crisp feel and feature two queen beds, rustic-style furniture, and good amenities.

Mailing address: 2525 C St., Ste. 405, Anchorage, AK 99503. © **888/959-9590** or 907/224-7116. www.sewardwindsong. com. 108 units. $215 double. Extra person (over 11) $15. AE, DC, MC, V. Exit Glacier/Herman Leirer Rd. Continue for ½ mile.

The Van Gilder Hotel   This charming if creaky old place was founded in 1916 and is listed on the National Register of Historic Places. Some rooms have a lot of charm, but authenticity means they tend to be small and unique, so choose carefully. The bathrooms are small and some are shared—one bathroom per two bedrooms. So know what you're signing on for when booking here.

308 Adams St. (P.O. Box 609), Seward, AK 99664. © **800/204-6835** or 907/224-3079. Fax 907/224-3689. www.vangilderhotel.com. 24 units. $149–$179, double with private bath, $109 double with shared bath. Extra person $10. AE, DC, MC, V.

WHERE TO DINE

Apollo Restaurant MEDITERRANEAN/SEAFOOD   Greek atmosphere, with a number of Greek dishes on the menu, along with fresh local seafood, pizza, pastas, and more.

229 4th Ave. © **907/224-3092.** Main courses $11–$18. MC, V. Daily noon–11pm.

The Harbor Dinner Club STEAK/SEAFOOD   This old-fashioned family restaurant has been the same reliable place as long as anyone can remember. With white tablecloths and a menu that ranges from fine seafood to a basic but delicious hamburger, you don't have to spend a lot of money to eat in a quiet, well-appointed dining room.

220 5th Ave. © **907/224-3012.** Main courses $9.50–$19; lunch $7–$15. AE, DC, DISC, MC, V. Daily 11am–2:30pm and 5–11pm.

Ray's Waterfront STEAK/SEAFOOD   The lively, noisy dining room here has big windows that look out across the small-boat harbor. This is where the locals will send you, and for good reason: The food is just right, and the atmosphere is fun. The specialty is salmon served on a cedar plank. To eat well and less expensively, order the delicious fish chowder and a small Caesar salad. Don't count on speedy seating or service.

1316 4th Ave. © **907/224-5606.** Lunch $8–$15; dinner $16–$25. AE, DISC, MC, V. Mid-Mar to Sept daily 11am–11pm; closed Oct to mid-Mar.

SHOPPING

Seward isn't exactly a shopping mecca. But given the arty nature of the place, there are some local products to be found. One of the more interesting facilities is the **Resurrection Coffee House Art Gallery** (℃ **907/224-7161**), located in a converted church at 320 3rd Ave. It's a neat place to buy art or just to schmooze with the residents over a cup of java. **Softly Silk,** at 416 4th Ave. (℃ **907/224-6088**), is another worthy art stop.

3 Vancouver

Located in the extreme southwestern corner of British Columbia, Vancouver has the good fortune to be surrounded by both mountains and ocean. The city has been expanding and growing rapidly, thanks to an influx of foreign money (especially from Hong Kong), and has undergone a major construction boom. But the development has not diminished the quality of life in Vancouver, which has a rich cultural heritage that includes Northwest Coast Native tribes and a flourishing Asian community.

The city also has a thriving **arts** scene, including numerous summertime festivals focusing on various forms of entertainment such as folk music, jazz, comedy, and even the art of fireworks display. Residents and visitors alike relish the proximity to **outdoor activities:** You can sailboard, rock-climb, mountain-bike, wilderness-hike, kayak, and ski on a world-class mountain here. For day-trippers, the city offers easily accessible attractions, including the historic **Gastown district,** with its shops and cafes, and a thriving **Chinatown.**

With the U.S. and Canadian dollar practically even—at press time the exchange rate was US$1 = C$1.06, shopping on Robson Street and Granville Island is not the bargain it once was, but the shops are still enticing. You'll likely visit Vancouver at the beginning or end of your Alaska cruise, as it's the major southern transit point. We recommend that you try to visit for at least a day before or after your cruise so you have time to explore.

Note: Rates below are calculated in U.S. dollars and may change based on the exchange rate at the time of your trip.

GETTING TO VANCOUVER

Most cruise ships dock at **Canada Place** (℃ **604/666-7200**) at the end of Burrard Street. A landmark in the city, the pier terminal is noted for its five-sail structure, which reaches into the harbor. It's located at the edge of the downtown district and is just a quick stroll from the **Gastown** area (see below), filled with cafes, art galleries, and souvenir shops, and Robson Street, a mecca for trendy clothes stores. Right near the pier are hotels, restaurants, and shops, as well as the **Tourism Vancouver Infocentre.** Ships also sometimes dock at the **Ballantyne** cruise terminal, a 5-minute cab ride from Canada Place.

BY PLANE **Vancouver International Airport** is located 13km (8 miles) south of downtown Vancouver. The average taxi fare from the airport to downtown is about $30. **Vancouver Airporter** (℃ **604/946-8866;** www.yvrairporter.com) buses offer service one-way to the city for about $13 per person for adults (less for kids and seniors). **Limo Jet Gold** (℃ **604/273-1331;** www.limojetgold.com) offers flat-rate limousine service at $37 for up to six passengers.

BY CAR Take Granville Street in and hope that the traffic's light.

Downtown Vancouver

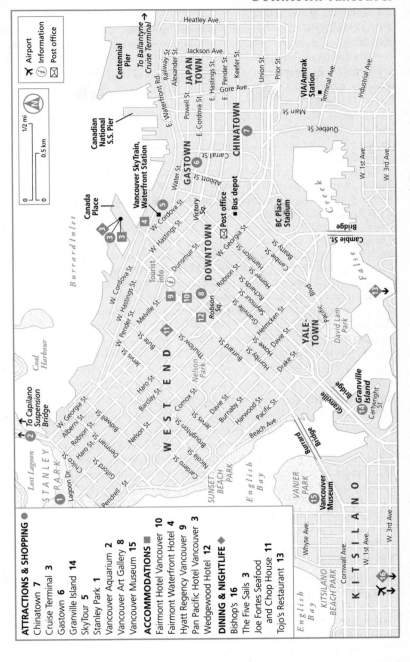

ATTRACTIONS & SHOPPING ●
Chinatown **7**
Cruise Terminal **3**
Gastown **6**
Granville Island **14**
SkyTour **5**
Stanley Park **1**
Vancouver Aquarium **2**
Vancouver Art Gallery **8**
Vancouver Museum **15**

ACCOMMODATIONS ■
Fairmont Hotel Vancouver **10**
Fairmont Waterfront Hotel **4**
Hyatt Regency Vancouver **9**
Pan Pacific Hotel Vancouver **3**
Wedgewood Hotel **12**

DINING & NIGHTLIFE ◆
Bishop's **16**
The Five Sails **3**
Joe Fortes Seafood
and Chop House **11**
Tojo's Restaurant **13**

✈ Airport
ⓘ Information
✉ Post office

EXPLORING VANCOUVER

INFORMATION The Tourism **Vancouver Infocentre,** 200 Burrard St. (© **604/ 683-2000**), is open May to Labor Day daily from 8am to 6pm, daily 8:30am to 5:30pm the rest of the year.

GETTING AROUND Because of its shape and setting, Vancouver has lots of bridges—Burrard Bridge, Granville Bridge, Cambie Street Bridge, and, of course, Lions Gate Bridge. Cruise ships pass under the Lions Gate Bridge on their way to and from Canada Place. The bridges sometimes make driving in Vancouver a slow endeavor. The **Aquabus ferries** shuttle visitors from Granville Island and elsewhere. Fares are $2.50 for adults, $1.25 for seniors and children (© **604/689-5858;** www. theaquabus.com).

Car-rental agencies with local branches include Avis, Budget, Hertz Canada, and Thrifty. You can easily walk the downtown area of Vancouver, but if you want transportation, you've got a few options. The **Translink system** (schedules and trip info © **604/953-3333** [6:30am–11:30pm daily]; www.translink.bc.ca) includes electric buses, ferries, and the magnetic-rail SkyTrain Service (see "Attractions within Walking Distance," below); on the main routes, it runs from 5am to 2am daily. Schedules are available at many hotels and online. **Taxis** are available through **Black Top** (© **604/ 731-1111**), **Yellow Cab** (© **604/681-1111**), and **MacLure's** (© **604/731-9211**), and can be either called or found around the major hotels.

You can rent a bicycle from **Bayshore Bicycle Rentals** (which also rents inline skates), 745 Denman St. (© **604/688-2453;** www.bayshorebikerentals.com), or **Spokes Bicycle Rentals,** 1798 W. Georgia St. (© **604/688-5141;** www.vancouverbikerental.com); rates are about $5.60 per hour, $16 for a half-day, and $22 for a full day. Helmets (required by law) and locks are included in the rate. The city has several great bicycle runs, including Stanley Park, the Seawall Promenade on the park's north end, and Pacific Spirit Park.

ATTRACTIONS WITHIN WALKING DISTANCE

Chinatown Vancouver's Chinatown is one of the largest in North America (though it doesn't hold a candle to those in New York and San Francisco), and, like Gastown, it's also an historic district. Chinese architecture and the **Dr. Sun Yat-sen Garden,** 578 Carrall St. (© **604/689-7133;** www.vancouverchinesegarden.com; admission $8.75 adults, $7 seniors/students, 4 and under free; open daily June–Oct; closed Mon Nov–May; May 1–June 14 and Sept 10am–6pm, Jun 15–Aug 31 9:30am–7pm, Oct–Apr 10am–4:30pm), are among the attractions, along with great food and shops selling Chinese wares. In addition to photogenic Chinese gates, bright-red buildings, and open-air markets, you'll find the amazing 6-foot-wide **Sam Kee Building** at 8 W. Pender St.

In the area bordered by E. Pender and Keefer sts., from Carrall St. to Gore Ave.

Gastown Gastown is named for "Gassy" Jack Deighton, who in 1867 built a saloon in Maple Tree Square (at the intersection of Water, Alexander, and Carrall sts.) to serve the area's loggers and trappers. The Gastown of today offers cobblestone streets, historic buildings, gaslights, a steam-powered clock (near the corner of Water and Cambie sts.), street musicians, and a touch of bohemia. It's so close to the ship pier that it's a must-see. Boutiques, antiques stores, and art galleries stand beside lots of touristgeared shops and restaurants, clubs, and cafes.

Located in the area bordered by Water and Alexander sts., from Richard St. east to Columbia St.

SkyTour   In summer 2006, the Vancouver SkyTrain launched the world's first auto-mated guided tour of a region using headsets on a public transit system. The SkyTour service allows visitors to rent headsets that provide commentary of the SkyTrain jour-ney in six languages (English, French, German, Spanish, Mandarin, and Japanese). Global positioning system (GPS) technology directs the headset users to get off the SkyTrain and take guided walking tours of the historic areas of Gastown or New West-minster. Tickets are available at the Waterfront Station near the cruise terminal.

Waterfront Station. Translink *ⓒ* 604/953-3333 (info 6:30am–11:30pm daily). www.translink.bc.ca. Tickets about $24 for adults, $19 for children.

Stanley Park   Just a few miles from downtown and the green-space pride of the city—it's Canada's largest urban park—Stanley Park was damaged by high winds in December 2006, with some 3,000 trees toppled or otherwise destroyed and parts of the seawall damaged (forcing the seawall promenade to be closed). Millions of dollars were committed to a repair effort. Its 405 hectares (1,000 acres) contain rose gardens, totem poles, a yacht club, a kids' water park, miles of wooded hiking trails, great views of Lions Gate Bridge, and the outstanding **Vancouver Aquarium (*ⓒ* 604/659-FISH [3474];** www.vanaqua.org; admission $20 adults, $15 seniors/students, $12 children 4–12, ages 3 and under free; open summer daily 9:30am–7pm, winter daily 10am–5:30pm). Summer hours for the park are 9:30am to 7pm daily.

Downtown Vancouver, northwest of the cruise-ship terminal.

Vancouver Art Gallery   Located within easy walking distance of the pier, the gallery is housed in a building constructed in 1906 as the provincial courthouse. It contains an impressive collection that includes works by British Columbia artist Emily Carr and the Canadian Group of Seven. Also on display are international and other regional paintings, sculptures, graphics, photography, and video ranging from classic to con-temporary. The Annex Gallery features rotating educational exhibits geared toward younger audiences.

750 Hornby St. *ⓒ* 604/662-4719. www.vanartgallery.bc.ca. Admission $20 adults, $15 seniors, $14 students, $6.50 for children 5–12, free for children under 4. Mon and Fri–Sun 10am–5:30pm; Tues and Thurs 10am–9pm.

Vancouver Museum   This museum offers a history of the city, from the Coast Sal-ish Indian settlement to the arrival of early pioneers, to European settlement, to 20th-century expansion. The exhibit allows visitors to walk through the steerage deck of a 19th-century immigrant ship, peek into a Hudson's Bay Company trading post, and sit in an 1880s Canadian-Pacific passenger car. Re-creations of Victorian and Edwar-dian rooms show how early Vancouverites decorated their homes. A new permanent exhibit focuses on Vancouver as gateway to the Pacific and the impact of World War II on that relationship (including the government's registering of all Canadians of Japanese descent); objects displayed include a 1906 Oldsmobile, Vancouver's first gas station, and ashes from Hiroshima.

1100 Chestnut St. *ⓒ* 604/736-4431. www.vanmuseum.bc.ca Admission $10 adults, $8 seniors, $6.50 youth, chil-dren 4 and under free. Tues–Sun 10am–5pm (Thurs 10am–9pm in summer).

ATTRACTIONS BEYOND THE PORT AREA
Capilano Suspension Bridge   Sure, it's touristy, but it's still a kick to cross this nar-row, historic, 137m (449-ft.) walking bridge, located 70m (230 ft.) above the Capilano River in North Vancouver (about a 10-min. drive, or a $17 cab ride, from downtown). From this vantage point, even the towering evergreens below look tiny (this attraction

is not for those with a fear of heights). The adjacent park offers hiking trails, history and forestry exhibits, a carving center, and Native American dance performances (only in summer), as well as restaurants and a gift shop. A new Treetops Adventure (included in admission price) lets you walk across 197m (646 ft.) of cable bridges high in the forest.

3735 Capilano Rd., North Vancouver. ℂ 604/985-7474. www.capbridge.com. In-season admission (May 1–Oct 31) $27 adults, $25 seniors, $21 students 17-plus w/ID, $16 youth 13–16, $8 children 6–12, free for children 5 and under; off-season admission: $24 adults, $22 seniors, $18.50 students 17-plus w/ID, $14 youth 13–16, $7.40 children 6–12, free for children 5 and under May–Sept daily 9am–7:30pm; Oct–Apr daily 9am–5pm.

BEST CRUISE-LINE SHORE EXCURSIONS

Capilano Canyon Nature Tour (4 hr.; $79 adults, $45 ages 12 and under): Walk alongside the canyon and through a rainforest with 500-year-old trees, as guides describe the ecosystem and wildlife habitats. Then cross the Lions Gate Bridge, with its spectacular views of the skyline, and eat a picnic lunch before returning to the airport or your downtown hotel.

City Tour (2½–3½ hr.; $39–$50 adults, $32 children): This bus tour covers major sights like Gastown, Chinatown, Stanley Park, and high-end residential areas. You'll also visit Queen Elizabeth Park, the city's highest southern vantage point and home of the Bloedell Conservatory, which commands a 360-degree city view and features an enclosed tropical rainforest complete with free-flying birds. May also include Granville Island.

Note: This tour is usually offered after the cruise and is available only to passengers with late-afternoon or evening flights. At the end of the tour, you are dropped off at the airport for your flight home.

EXCURSIONS OFFERED BY LOCAL AGENCIES

Stanley Park Horse-Drawn Tours (ℂ **604/681-5115;** www.stanleyparktours.com) has offered tours of the 405-hectare (1,000-acre) Stanley Park by horse-drawn trolley for more than a century. The narrated 1-hour tours depart from the Coal Harbour parking lot beside the Stanley Park information booth on Park Drive. Tickets are $25 adults, $24 seniors and students, $15 kids 3 to 12. The **Vancouver Trolley Company** (ℂ **888/451-5581** or 604/801-5515; www.vancouvertrolley.com) has old-fashioned (engine-powered) trolleys offering narrated tours on a circuit that includes Gastown, Chinatown, Granville Island, Stanley Park, and other areas of interest. You can get off and on as you like. Stop no. 1 is in Gastown. Tickets are $35 for adults and $19 for kids. **A Wok Around Chinatown** (www.awokaround.com) is a 4-hour walking tour that takes visitors around the colorful and flavorful neighborhood. The tour is offered Friday through Monday at 10am and leaves from Dr. Sun Yat-sen Garden (see listing for "Chinatown" in "Attractions within Walking Distance," above); the tour costs $85 and includes a dim sum lunch.

WHERE TO STAY

Almost all of Vancouver's downtown hotels are within walking distance of shops, restaurants, and attractions, although you might want to avoid places around Hastings and Main after dark. Granville Street downtown is an area that has been "cleaned up" and is now home to some lower-end, boutique-type hotels. The area has clubs and an active nightlife, but also lots of panhandlers.

The Fairmont Hotel Vancouver   After extensive renovations, the grande dame of Vancouver's hotels has been restored beyond its former glory. Designed on a generous scale, with a copper roof, marble interiors, and massive proportions, the hotel conveys unparalleled luxury and spaciousness in its lobby and public areas. High tea is a proud tradition here. Guest rooms have marble bathrooms and mahogany furnishings, and offer city, harbor, and mountain views.

900 W. Georgia St., Vancouver, BC V6C 2W6. ℭ 800/257-7544 or 604/684-3131. Fax 604/662-1929. www.fairmont. com. 544 units. $260–$389 double; from $400 suite Children under 18 stay free in parents' room. AE, DC, DISC, MC, V. Parking $28 per night.

The Fairmont Waterfront Hotel

This ultra-modern hotel comprising 23 stories of blue reflective glass takes advantage of its harborside location, offering spectacular waterfront and mountain views from 70% of the rooms. A concourse links the hotel to the rest of Waterfront Centre, Canada Place, and the Alaska cruise-ship terminal.

900 Canada Place Way, Vancouver, BC V6C 3L5. ℭ 800/257-7544 or 604/691-1991. Fax 604/691-1999. www.fairmont. com. 518 units. $310–$450 double; from $450 suite. AE, DC, MC, V. Parking $26 per night.

Hyatt Regency Vancouver

The Hyatt is a modern white tower built over the Royal Centre Mall, which contains 60 specialty shops. The very large guest rooms are tastefully decorated with understated yet comfortable furnishings. Corner rooms on the north and west sides have balconies with lovely views.

655 Burrard St., Vancouver, BC V6C 2R7. ℭ 800/233-1234 or 604/683-1234. Fax 604/689-3707. www.hyatt.com. 644 units. From $220–$305 double; $442 suite. AE, DC, DISC, MC, V. Parking $23.

Pan Pacific Hotel Vancouver

Vancouver's most distinctive landmark is Canada Place Pier, with five gleaming white Teflon sails that recall a giant sailing vessel. The pier houses the Vancouver Trade and Convention Centre as well as the Alaska cruise-ship terminal. It also offers a splendid **IMAX Theatre** (ℭ 604/682-4629; www.imax. com/vancouver) where, for about $7, cruise passengers can while away an hour or so viewing the wonders of Alaska, Mount Everest, the Galapagos Islands, and other places. Atop the terminal is the spectacular 23-story Pan Pacific Hotel. This and the Fairmont Waterfront Hotel are the closest accommodations to the cruise-ship dock. All of the guest rooms are modern, spacious, and comfortably furnished. All come with such amenities as coffeemakers, irons, and ironing boards. Try to book a harborside room for the best view. The new and luxurious Spa Utopia and Salon offers a Roman-inspired sanctuary with towering pillars and cascading waterfalls—an excellent place to recover from jet lag (or end-of-cruise blues).

300–999 Canada Place, Vancouver, BC V6C 3B5. ℭ 800/937-1515 or 604/662-8111. Fax 604/685-8690. www.pan pac.com. 504 units. $368–$443 double; from $1,000 suite. AE, DC, MC, V. Parking $24.

Wedgewood Hotel

This small boutique property near the Robson Street shops features individually furnished rooms filled with nice amenities. Penthouse suites also offer fireplaces, wet bars, Jacuzzis, and scenic garden terraces. Public rooms have antiques and fresh flowers, and the hotel has one of the best watering holes in town, Bacchus, an upscale piano bar where you can sink into a plush chair or couch, enjoy an excellent martini, and take in the local scene. The Bacchus restaurant has also won awards for its fine cuisine.

845 Hornby St., Vancouver, BC V6Z 1V1. ℭ 800/663-0666 or 604/689-7777. Fax 604/608-5348. www.wedgewood hotel.com. 89 units. $250–$350 double; $450–$675 suite. AE, DC, MC, V. Parking $17.

WHERE TO DINE

Bishop's PACIFIC NORTHWEST   The atmosphere is all candlelight, white linen, and soft jazz; the service is impeccable; and the food is even better. Owner John

Bishop greets you personally, escorts you to your table, and introduces you to an extensive catalog of fine wines and a menu he describes as "contemporary home cooking"—which means dishes such as roast duck breast with sun-dried Okanagan Valley fruits and candied ginger glacé, steamed smoked black cod with new potatoes and horseradish sabayon, and marinated sirloin of lamb. If you have only one evening to dine out in Vancouver, spend it here.

2183 W. 4th Ave. ℭ **604/738-2025.** www.bishopsonline.com. Reservations required. Main courses $32–$38. AE, DC, MC, V. Mon–Sat 5:30–11pm; Sun 5:30–10pm.

The Five Sails PACIFIC NORTHWEST/SEAFOOD   The Five Sails' view of Coal Harbour, Stanley Park, and the Coast Mountains is pure magic, a vision of the rugged nirvana that is Vancouver; the Five Sails' excellent cuisine, inventive without being too clever, is the perfect accompaniment. The restaurant is sparkling after a major renovation last year. The menu features West Coast ingredients including local produce and lake trout. The Five Sails Seafood Tower is a special treat for two or more guests, literally bursting with fresh local shellfish (priced at market price).

999 Canada Place Way, in the Pan Pacific Hotel. ℭ **604/891-2892.** www.fivesails.ca. Reservations recommended. Main courses $25–$40. AE, DC, MC, V. Daily 5:30–10pm.

Joe Fortes Seafood and Chop House SEAFOOD   This place has been winning awards—for its food, its wine list, and its oysters—for years. This two-story dark-wood restaurant with an immensely popular bar is always filled with Vancouver's young and successful. The decor and atmosphere are reminiscent of an oyster bar, and the spacious covered and heated roof garden (where cigar smokers gather) is pure Vancouver. Pan-roasted oysters are a menu staple. A daily selection of up to a dozen types of oysters is offered raw or cooked in a variety of ways, along with fresh fish, Dungeness crab, and live lobsters (at market prices).

777 Thurlow St. ℭ **604/669-1940.** www.joefortes.ca. Reservations recommended. Most main courses $23–$40. AE, DC, DISC, MC, V. Daily 11am–4pm lunch menu (Sat–Sun brunch); 4–10:30pm dinner.

Tojo's Restaurant JAPANESE   Located above an A&W burger joint, this restaurant has an unimpressive decor but nice city views if you can snag a window seat. And Hidekazu Tojo's sushi is Vancouver's best, attracting Japanese businessmen, Hollywood celebrities, and anyone else who's willing to pay for the finest. Tell Tojo how much you want to spend, and he'll prepare an incredible meal to fit your budget.

777 W. Broadway. ℭ **604/872-8050.** www.tojos.com. Reservations required for sushi bar. Complete meals $40–$80 and up. A la carte menu available. AE, DC, MC, V. Mon–Sat 5–10pm.

SHOPPING

Granville Island is a shopper's paradise, with its vibrant daily market and streets lined with fine-art studios (it's a hearty walk from downtown, so depending on where you're staying, you may want to take a cab or a water taxi). Downtown, **Robson Street** is chockablock with boutiques, souvenir shops, coffeehouses, and bistros. The massive **Pacific Centre Mall** fills the city blocks between Robson, Dunsmuir, Howe, and Granville streets and is within easy walking distance of the pier. Fran can attest to the fine offerings at **Hill's Native Art** (ℭ **604/685-4249;** www.hillsnativeart.com), 165 Water St. in Gastown; she has a totem pole from this shop in her dining room. The store also sells moccasins, ceremonial masks, silkscreen prints, and jewelry. Down the road at 164 Water St., **Images for a Canadian Heritage** (ℭ **604/685-7046**) is a government-licensed First Nations gallery featuring both traditional and contemporary works—check out the glass totems.

4 Seattle

Americans now have more opportunities than ever to begin and end their Alaska-bound cruises on U.S. soil. In recent years, Americans' growing interest in the 49th state and their clear preference for American gateways and destinations has had the cruise lines falling over themselves to deploy more of their Alaska ships in Seattle. And because many Americans remain skittish about long-distance air travel to Europe, Alaska's popularity continues to increase. Consequently, so does Seattle's—which is all to the cruise passenger's benefit. Vancouver is bursting at the seams with cruise ships (so many cruise passengers need air transportation into the Canadian city that the airlines are frequently unable to accommodate them all). Seattle has become an attractive alterative home port for large oceangoing passenger liners bound for the Northland. In 2000, only one major ship was based in Seattle for the Alaska cruise season. In 2008, eight large vessels will be based in the city. And they will be joined by Cruise West's small (80–140 passengers) ships and the vessels of other smaller lines that have operated a few cruises out of Seattle every summer for years.

As cruise ports go, Seattle need bow the knee to no other. Known as the Emerald City because of the abundant greenery to be found in every direction, it is every bit as scenically appealing as Vancouver. Its skyline is dominated by the 607-foot-high revolving Space Needle, built in 1962 for the World's Fair (known at the time as the Century 21 Exposition). It's linked to the heart of downtown by a monorail. Seattle has shopping, fine restaurants, attractions galore, good air service, culture, a wide range of accommodations, internal transportation—everything you need, in fact, to enjoy a day or two before or after your cruise.

Seattle is very much a water-oriented city, set between Puget Sound and Lake Washington, with Lake Union in the center. Practically everywhere you look, the views are of sailboats, cargo ships, ferries, windsurfers, and anglers—and trees and parklands, of course. One of our favorite pastimes on nice days in Seattle is to take one of the local ferries—to anywhere—just for the fun of it.

The **Seattle Waterfront,** along Alaskan Way from Yesler Way North to Bay Street and Myrtle Edwards Park, is one of the city's single most popular attractions, and much like San Francisco's Fisherman's Wharf area, that's good and bad. Yes, it's very touristy, with tacky gift shops, saltwater taffy, T-shirts galore, and lots of overpriced restaurants, but it's also home to the Seattle Aquarium and the Pike Place Market. Your ship will dock right along this strip. There are companies located here that offer sailboat and sea-kayak tours.

At Pier 54, you'll find companies offering sea-kayak tours, sportfishing trips, jet-boat tours, and bicycle rentals. At Pier 55, boats leave for 1½-hour harbor cruises, as well as the **Tillicum Village** excursions to Blake Island (see "Attractions Beyond the Port Area," below). At Pier 57 you'll find the **Bay Pavilion,** which has a vintage carousel and a video arcade to keep the kids busy. At Pier 59 you'll find the **Seattle Aquarium** and a waterfront park. Meanwhile, Pier 69 is the dock for the ferries that ply the waters between Seattle and Victoria. Sunset and jazz cruises also leave from this pier.

If you are in the city for a day or two you may want to venture 20 minutes from downtown (by car, cab, or bus) to Ballard, a waterfront area that has recently moved from blue collar to trendy with a variety of boutiques, hip eateries, and nighttime spots.

GETTING TO SEATTLE

BY PLANE   **Seattle-Tacoma International Airport** (© **800/544-1965** or 206/431-4444), also known as **Sea-Tac**, is located about 14 miles south of Seattle. It's connected to the city by Interstate 5. Generally, allow 30 minutes for the trip between the airport and downtown. Since the Bell Street passenger ship pier is superbly located a few minutes' walk from the heart of downtown, airport taxis will drop you at the terminal for about the same price as they would charge to go to any of the major Seattle hotels.

A **taxi** between the airport and downtown will cost you between $35 and $40. **Gray Line Airport Express** (© **800/426-7532** or 206/626-6088; http://graylineseattle.com/airportexpress1.cfm) provides service between all the airport terminals and seven downtown hotels, with the first hotel pickup at 4:50am and continuing every half-hour through the day until the last pickup at 11:20pm. The fares are $10 one-way, $17 round-trip; children ages 2 to 12 pay $7.25 one-way, $12 round-trip. **Shuttle Express** (© **425/981-7000;** www.shuttleexpress.com) also gets you between Sea-Tac and downtown. The company's check-in desk is on the third floor of the parking garage at the airport, and a one-way fare for up to two people is $29 ($4 for the third rider) to most downtown areas. The public **Seattle Metro** (© **800/542-7876** or 206/553-3000) operates service from the airport to downtown for as little as $1.25 in the off-peak hours, clearly the least expensive transportation. But the bus drops passengers only at the Seattle Convention Center, not at the hotel of their choice, so it's not necessarily the most convenient.

BY CAR   The major freeway running through Seattle is Interstate 5. Follow it south from downtown to Sea-Tac. Interstate 5 runs north to the Canadian border, which leads, ultimately, to the road to Vancouver. Alaskan Way, a busy street, runs along the waterfront and past the cruise-ship terminal. It's only a very short car or cab ride from any city hotel to the cruise terminal, which is not more than 10 minutes from even the most distant of the hotels listed here.

EXPLORING SEATTLE

INFORMATION   The **Seattle-King County Convention and Visitors Bureau** operates a visitor information center in the Washington State Convention and Trade Center, 800 Convention Place, Galleria Level, at the corner of 8th Avenue and Pike Street (© **206/461-5840**). It's open 8:30am to 5pm Monday through Friday, 10am to 4pm Saturday and Sunday late May through August, and varying shorter hours during the remainder of the year.

GETTING AROUND   Nearly every major car-rental company has an outlet at Sea-Tac, and many also have offices in downtown hotels. Prices will depend on the season and even on the day of the week (rentals on Fri, for example, when cruise passengers are likely to arrive in large numbers, will probably cost more than they will on, say, Wed). **Seattle Metro** (© **800/542-7876** or 206/553-3000) offers free bus transportation within the downtown area between the hours of 6am and 7pm, and charges a couple of dollars for rides to some areas outside the downtown area. The company also operates a waterfront service using old-fashioned streetcars, some of it in the ride-free area, some of it outside.

ATTRACTIONS WITHIN WALKING DISTANCE

Pike Place Market   City officials have worked overtime to ensure that the Pike Place Market, begun in 1907 and one of Seattle's most enduring institutions, remains

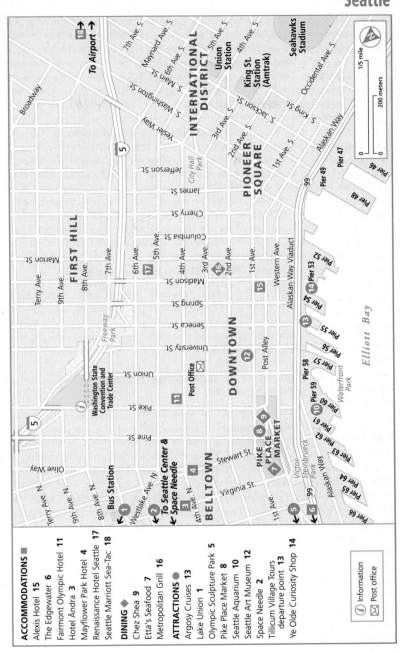

Seattle

To Airport → **18** →

Broadway

7th Ave. S.
Maynard Ave. S.
5th Ave. S.
4th Ave. S.

S. Main St.
S. Washington St.
S. Jackson St.

Union Station

King St. Station (Amtrak)

Seahawks Stadium

INTERNATIONAL DISTRICT

Yesler Way

Occidental Ave. S.

3rd Ave. S.
2nd Ave. S.
1st Ave. S.

PIONEER SQUARE

City Hall Park

Jefferson St.
James St.
Cherry St.
Columbia St.
Madison St.

99

Pier 49
Pier 47
Pier 46

Pier 48

FIRST HILL

Marion St.

Terry Ave.
9th Ave.
8th Ave.
7th Ave.
6th Ave.
5th Ave.
4th Ave.
3rd Ave.
2nd Ave.
1st Ave.

17
16
15

Western Ave.
Alaskan Way Viaduct

Pier 52
Pier 53
Pier 54
Pier 55
Pier 56

14
13

Freeway Park

Spring St.
Seneca St.
University St.

DOWNTOWN

Post Alley

12

Post Office ✉

11

Elliott Bay

Union St.
Pike St.
Pine St.

Washington State Convention and Trade Center

To Seattle Center & Space Needle ↑

Bus Station ←

Olive Way

Terry Ave. N.
9th Ave. N.
8th Ave. N.
Westlake Ave. N.
4th Ave. N.

1 ←
2 ↑
3
4

BELLTOWN

Stewart St.
Virginia St.

8 **9**
7

PIKE PLACE MARKET

1st Ave.

5 ←
6 ←

99

Victor Steinbrueck Park

Waterfront Park

Alaskan Way

Pier 57
Pier 58
Pier 59
Pier 60
Pier 61
Pier 62
Pier 63
Pier 64
Pier 65
Pier 66

10

1/5 mile
200 meters
0
0

ACCOMMODATIONS ■

Alexis Hotel **15**
The Edgewater **6**
Fairmont Olympic Hotel **11**
Hotel Ändra **3**
Mayflower Park Hotel **4**
Renaissance Hotel Seattle **17**
Seattle Marriott Sea-Tac **18**

DINING ◆

Chez Shea **9**
Etta's Seafood **7**
Metropolitan Grill **16**

ATTRACTIONS ●

Argosy Cruises **13**
Lake Union **1**
Olympic Sculpture Park **5**
Pike Place Market **8**
Seattle Aquarium **10**
Seattle Art Museum **12**
Space Needle **2**
Tillicum Village Tours departure point **13**
Ye Olde Curiosity Shop **14**

ⓘ Information
✉ Post office

true to its roots. Just a few blocks from the passenger pier, the city made a big push a few years ago to add more tourist-friendly T-shirt and souvenir shops, but the market vendors fought to keep the emphasis on food and flowers and were at least partly successful. The market remains the single best place in the city to find fresh produce and seasonal specialties like Rainier cherries, Washington asparagus, fresh king salmon, and Northwest hazelnuts. Go hungry: The grazing opportunities here are unsurpassed. We strongly recommend that you don't leave without trying a Dungeness crab cocktail, a fresh-baked cinnamon roll or *piroshki* (Russian meat pie), and, of course, coffee from any number of vendors, including the *original* Starbucks. Go underground to explore wonderful specialty shops, including one of the best stores devoted to magic and old magic posters in the country, a fragrant store dedicated to spices, and an exotic bird store where the parrots squawk in your face. A 90-minute **Market Heritage Tour,** beginning at the Market Heritage Foundation Visitor Center on Western Avenue, is offered Wednesday through Sunday at 11am and 2pm ($8 adults; $6 seniors/children under 18); make reservations at www.pikeplacemarket.org or call ② **206/774-5249.** A free map of the complex is available at the information booth at the 1st Avenue entrance. At night the vendors clear out, but several excellent restaurants, bars, and theaters in the market keep hopping.

Between Pike and Pine sts., at 1st Ave. ② 206/682-7453. Mon–Sat 9am–6pm; Sun 11am–5pm.

The Seattle Aquarium   The Seattle Aquarium presents well-designed exhibits dealing with the watery worlds of the Puget Sound region. One of the aquarium's most popular exhibits is an interactive tide pool and discovery lab that re-creates Washington's wave-swept intertidal zone. From the underwater viewing dome, you get a fish's-eye view of life beneath the waves. Each September you can watch salmon return up a fish ladder to spawn.

1483 Alaskan Way, Pier 59, Waterfront Park. ② 206/386-4320. www.seattleaquarium.org. Admission $15 adults, $10 ages 4–12, 3 and under free. Daily 9:30am–7pm.

Seattle Art Museum and Olympic Sculpture Park   Closed in 2006 for a major expansion, the art museum reopened in spring 2007 with nearly double its original museum space. The new design features two floors of public space, 70% more gallery space, a new restaurant, and a store. The museum is a repository for everything from African masks, old masters, and Andy Warhol to one of the nation's premier collections of Northwest Coastal Native art. In addition, the new, free outdoor Olympic Sculpture Park opened in spring 2007. Transforming an industrial site on downtown Seattle's waterfront, the 9-acre Olympic Sculpture Park has paths that zigzag down to the bay through four ecosystems. Works and special commissions by artists Louise Bourgeois, Richard Serra, Alexander Calder, Teresita Fernandez, Roy McMakin, Mark Dion, and other leading contemporary artists are on display.

100 University St., 2 blocks from Pike Place Market. ② 206/654-3100. www.seattleartmuseum.org. Admission is a suggested donation of $13 adults, $10 seniors, $7 students and youths 13–17, free for children 12 and under, free to all 1st Thurs of the month. Tues–Sun 10am–5pm (to 9pm Thurs). The Olympic Sculpture Park is at 2901 Western Ave.

The Space Needle   From a distance, this structure resembles a flying saucer on top of a tripod. When it was built for the World's Fair, it was meant to suggest future architectural trends; today the soaring structure is the quintessential symbol of Seattle. At 518 feet above ground level, the views from the observation deck are stunning. High-powered telescopes let you zoom in on distant sights, and there's a lounge and two very expensive restaurants inside.

203 6th Ave. N., Seattle Center. ℂ 206/443-2111. www.spaceneedle.com. Admission $16 adults, $14 seniors, $8 children 4–13, 3 and under free. Daily 9am–midnight.

Ye Olde Curiosity Shop   It's weird! It's tacky! It's always packed! A cross between a souvenir store and Ripley's Believe It or Not!, Ye Olde Curiosity Shop features an oddball collection started in 1899 by Joe Standley. It's the place (the only place, probably) to see Siamese-twin calves, a natural mummy, the Lord's Prayer on a grain of rice, a narwhal tusk, shrunken heads, a 67-pound snail, fleas in dresses, and walrus and whale oosiks (the bone of the male reproductive organ).

1001 Alaskan Way, on Pier 54. ℂ 206/682-5844. www.yeoldecuriosityshop.com. Free admission. Mon–Fri 9:30am–6pm; Sat–Sun 9am–6pm.

ATTRACTIONS BEYOND THE PORT AREA

Lake Union   A $10 cab ride from the port, glacially carved Lake Union, in the central part of Seattle, is worth a visit. It's pretty and is home to hundreds of pleasure craft and houseboats and some naval vessels. While the lake is big, it's becoming smaller as city planners, in the name of "progress," fill in parts of it for construction.

Tillicum Village/Tillicum Village Tours   Located at Blake Island State Marine Park across Puget Sound from Seattle, and accessible only by tour boat or private boat, **Tillicum Village** was built in conjunction with the 1962 Seattle World's Fair. The "village" is actually a large restaurant and performance hall fashioned after a traditional Northwest Coast Indian longhouse. With totem poles standing vigil out front, the forest encircling the longhouse, and the waters of Puget Sound stretching out into the distance, it's a beautiful spot. **Tillicum Village Tours** operates tours that include the scenic boat ride to and from the island, a lunch or dinner of alder-smoked salmon, and a performance by traditional masked dancers—members of 11 Northwest tribes. After the meal and the dance performance, you can strike out on forest trails to explore the island.

Pier 56. ℂ 206/443-1244. www.tillicumvillage.com. 4-hr. tour $79 adults, $72 seniors, $30 children 5–12, 4 and under free.

BEST CRUISE-LINE SHORE EXCURSIONS

Seattle City Tour (2–3½ hr.; $49–$54 adults, $39 children): A basic spin around Pike Place Market, the World's Fair site, downtown Seattle, Lake Union, and more, offered by virtually all cruise lines. May include a stop at the Space Needle.

Seattle Boats, Buildings & Billionaires (3½ hr.; $69 adults, $49 children): Take a narrated bus drive to Lake Union and board a sightseeing boat for a 1½ hr. cruise of Lake Union and Lake Washington. See the historic houseboat and floating home communities including the home featured in the movie *Sleepless in Seattle*. You'll also see the world's longest floating bridge and catch a glimpse of the residence of Bill Gates.

Seattle Highlights & Winery (4hr.; $54): Combine a narrated drive through the downtown area with a visit to the renowned Woodinville Wine District. Here you'll visit either the Chateau Ste Michelle or Columbia Winery. Tasting is of course included.

EXCURSIONS OFFERED BY LOCAL AGENCIES

Argosy Cruises (ℂ **206/623-4252**; www.argosycruises.com) offers a variety of short cruises around the Seattle area, including a **Seattle harbor cruise,** a cruise through the **Hiram Chittenden Locks to Lake Union,** and cruises around **Lake Washington** (which, among other things, take you past the fabled Xanadu built by Bill Gates on the shore of Lake Washington). Cruises depart from Pier 55. Tickets for the 1-hour Harbor Cruise are $18 for adults, $7.80 for children 5 to 12, and free for children under 5; the 2-hour Lake Cruise goes for $27 for adults, $9 for children 5 to 12, and free for children under 5. **Gray Line of Seattle** (www.graylineseattle.com) recently introduced a new 4-hour tour that takes visitors 30 miles from downtown to the Future of Flight Aviation Center and Boeing Tour at Paine Field Airport in Everett, a cutting-edge facility offering interactive aviation exhibits (you also visit the Boeing factory) for $47.

WHERE TO STAY

Alexis Hotel Unbelievable as it sounds, this elegant boutique hotel, located in an enviable location halfway between Pike Place Market and Pioneer Square, and only 2 blocks from the waterfront, was once a parking garage. Now listed in the National Register of Historic Places, the 90-year-old building is a sparkling gem, with a pleasant mix of old and new and a friendly staff. Classic styling prevails in the guest rooms, each of which is a little different (the nicest by far are the splurge-worthy fireplace suites).

1007 1st Ave. (at Madison St.), Seattle, WA 98104. © 800/426-7033 or 206/624-4844. Fax 206/621-9009. www.alexishotel.com. 109 units. $299–$315 double; $419–$599 suite. AE, DC, MC, V. Valet parking $30.

The Edgewater Built on a pier, Seattle's only waterfront hotel is incongruously designed to resemble a deluxe mountain lodge. Somehow, it works. A vaulted open-beamed ceiling, a deer-antler chandelier, a river-stone fireplace, and a wall of glass that looks out on busy Elliott Bay and gorgeous sunsets all combine to make the lobby a great place to hang out. Rooms feature rustic lodge-pole-pine furniture. Because the least expensive rooms here overlook the parking lot (and city), you really should opt for a water-view or partial-water-view room. It makes all the difference.

Pier 67, 2411 Alaskan Way, Seattle, WA 98121. © 800/624-0670 or 206/728-7000. Fax 206/441-4119. www.edge-waterhotel.com. 236 units. $149–$419 double; $525–$2,000 suite. AE, DC, DISC, MC, V. Valet parking $26.

Fairmont Olympic Hotel This is one of the biggest and absolutely one of the most elegant hotels in Seattle. Reminiscent of an Italian Renaissance palace, complete with crystal and gilt chandeliers, marble facings, and dark-oak walls and pillars, the hotel offers a health club, shopping area (upscale, of course), concierge, complimentary overnight shoeshine, and much more. It's located on a hill in the city's financial district, affording good views all around. Not cheap, but worth it.

411 University St., Seattle, WA 98101. © 800/332-3442 or 206/621-1700. Fax 206/682-9633. www.fairmont.com. 450 units. $299–$429 double; $369–$3,000 suite. AE, DC, DISC, MC, V. Valet parking $30.

Hotel Andra Part Art Deco, part Buzz Lightyear—that describes this boutique hotel located in the trendy Belltown enclave, an easy walking distance from Pike Place Market, the Seattle Art Museum, and downtown shopping. Originally built in 1926, the classic brick and terra-cotta building was thoroughly reinvented in 2004 with design elements that meld the Northwest (the extensive use of woods and stones) with high-tech toys such as flat-screen TVs, wireless Internet connections, and blue-glass bedside lamps. All rooms score high for creature comforts, too, especially with the Frette towels and plump goose-down pillows and comforters. One of Seattle's hottest restaurants beckons downstairs: Lola, from top chef Tom Douglas, with a menu that ranges from local seafood to Greek cuisine.

2000 4th Ave., Seattle, WA 98121. © 877/448-8600 or 206/448-8600. Fax 206/441-7140. www.hotelandra.com. 119 units. $206–$325 double; $320–$2,100 suite. AE, DC, DISC, MC, V. Valet parking $29.

Mayflower Park Hotel   If shopping and sipping martinis are among your favorite recreational activities, there's no question of where to stay in Seattle. The Mayflower Park Hotel, built in 1927 and completely renovated a few years back, is connected to the upscale shops of Westlake Center and is flanked by Nordstrom and Bon Marché department stores. The hotel also serves up the best martinis in Seattle, at Oliver's Lounge. (It's won the annual martini contest sponsored by a local newspaper umpteen times!) Most rooms are furnished with an eclectic blend of contemporary Italian and traditional European furnishings. If you crave space, ask for one of the large corner rooms or splurge for a suite. The smallest rooms here are very cramped.

405 Olive Way, Seattle, WA 98101. (C) 800/426-5100, 206/382-6990, or 206/623-8700. Fax 206/382-6997. www. mayflowerpark.com. 192 units. $169–$220 double; $245–$400 suite. AE, DC, DISC, MC, V. Valet parking $28.

Renaissance Hotel Seattle   Despite its large size and its location a stone's throw from the freeway, this hotel manages to stay quieter and less hectic than most convention hotels. With its rooftop restaurant and swimming pool with a view, it's a good choice for leisure travelers. All rooms are larger than average and many have views of either Puget Sound or the Cascade Range. For the best views, ask for a room on the west side of the hotel.

515 Madison St., Seattle, WA 98104. (C) 800/468-3571 or 206/583-0300. Fax 206/622-8635. www.renaissance hotels.com. 631 units. $165–$229 double; $250–$2,000 suite. AE, DC, DISC, MC, V. Valet parking $18; self-parking $15.

Seattle Marriott Sea-Tac   If you want to stay near the airport, this is a fantastic bet—a resortlike hotel with a huge central atrium that has a swimming pool, dense tropical greenery, a bar, two whirlpool tubs, and a scattering of totem poles. Rooms are sizable and comfortable, some with a view (on a clear day) of Mount Rainier.

3201 S. 176th St., Seattle, WA 98188. (C) 800/228-9290 or 206/241-2000. Fax 206/248-0789. www.marriotthotels. com/seawa. 464 units. $109–$165 double; $225–$550 suite. Children under 18 stay free in parent's room. Cheaper rates on weekends. AE, DC, DISC, MC, V. Free parking.

WHERE TO DINE

Chez Shea PACIFIC NORTHWEST   Quiet, dark, and intimate, Chez Shea is one of the finest restaurants in Seattle. Its dozen candlelit tables with views across Puget Sound to the Olympic Mountains are the perfect setting for a romantic dinner. The menu changes with the season, and ingredients come primarily from Pike Place Market, conveniently located below the restaurant. There are usually five entree choices, along the lines of rabbit braised in wine with balsamic vinegar, sweet peppers, leeks, and rosemary; or halibut sautéed with blood-orange coulis, gaeta olives, red onion, coriander, white wine, and garlic. While there are equally fine restaurants in the city, few have quite the quintessential Seattle atmosphere of Chez Shea.

Corner Market Building, Suite 34, 94 Pike St., Pike Place Market. (C) 206/467-9990. www.chezshea.com Reservations highly recommended. Main dishes $20–$36; fixed-price 8-course Chef's Special dinner $75; add $32 for wine pairing. AE, MC, V. Tues–Sun 5:30–10:30pm.

Etta's Seafood SEAFOOD   Etta's offers the best seafood in town. Located in the Pike Place Market area, this place serves chef/owner Tom Douglas's signature crab cakes (crunchy on the outside, creamy on the inside) and more. Consider the seared ahi tuna if it's on the menu. This almost-sushi has a wonderful texture. If you're not a lover of seafood, fear not: Even though seafood makes up most of the menu, there are other fine options, too.

2020 Western Ave. (C) 206/443-6000. www.tomdouglas.com Reservations recommended. Main dishes $12–$27. AE, DC, DISC, MC, V. Mon–Thurs 11:30am–10pm; Fri 11:30am–11pm; Sat 9am–11pm; Sun 9am–10pm.

Metropolitan Grill STEAK The Metropolitan is dedicated to carnivores. When you walk in, you'll see various cuts of meat, from filet mignon to triple-cut lamb chops, displayed on ice. Green-velvet booths and floral-design carpets create a sophisticated atmosphere, and mirrored walls and a high ceiling trimmed with elegant plasterwork make the dining room feel larger than it actually is. Perfectly cooked steaks are the prime attraction, and a baked potato and a pile of thick-cut onion rings complete the perfect steak dinner.

818 2nd Ave. (② 206/624-3287. www.themetropolitangrill.com Reservations recommended. Main dishes lunch $11–$44, dinner $21–$60. AE, DC, DISC, MC, V. Mon–Fri 11am–3:30pm and 5–11pm; Sat 4–11pm; Sun 4:30–10pm.

SHOPPING

You can't be in Seattle without visiting the **Nordstrom** department store in the heart of downtown at 500 Pine St. (② **206/628-2111**). Seattle is, after all, where the company originated—in 1901. (It was financed, incidentally, by money earned by founder John W. Nordstrom in the Klondike gold rush.) This Nordstrom store is the second-biggest attraction for tourists in town—after Pike Place Market—and worth a visit for its historical significance, if for nothing else. There's a **Nordstrom Rack**—the discounted version of the department store—nearby at 1601 2nd Ave. (② **206/448-8522**).

Elliott Bay Book Company, First Avenue South and Main Street (② **800/962-5311**), in an area known as Pioneer Square, has a tremendous selection of titles and a bargain books floor of some repute. Another book outlet—**Beyond the Closet,** 518 E. Pike St. (② **206/322-4609**)—is Seattle's largest gay and lesbian bookshop.

5 Juneau

Since Juneau is also a major port of call, please see the Juneau section in chapter 8, "Ports & Wilderness Areas along the Inside Passage," for a map and information on attractions and tours.

GETTING TO JUNEAU

BY PLANE Juneau is served by **Alaska Airlines** (② **800/426-0333** or 907/789-9791) with daily nonstop flights from Seattle and Anchorage. Because weather can wreak havoc with landing conditions, it's especially advisable if you're flying to Juneau to plan on getting there a day or two before your cruise embarkation date.

BY BOAT The vessels of the **Alaska Marine Highway** (www.dot.state.ak.us/amhs; commonly known as the Alaska Ferry) link Juneau with Alaska, British Columbia, and U.S. gateways as far south as Bellingham, Washington, but unless you have 2 or 3 days to spare, you probably won't use that service to get to your ship.

BY CAR You can't drive to Juneau (there are no road links to the outside world) or get there by train. That leaves you with airplanes or long boat trips, period.

EXPLORING JUNEAU

INFORMATION The **Visitor Information Center** is in Centennial Hall at 101 Egan Dr., near the State Museum (② **888/581-2201** or 907/586-2201; fax 907/586-6304; www.traveljuneau.com). It's open May through September daily from 8:30am to 5pm, October through April Monday through Friday from 9am to 4:30pm. The visitor center at the cruise-ship dock is open during the summer when the ships come in.

GETTING AROUND A cab from the airport to downtown will cost about $25. The **Capital Transit city bus** (② **907/789-6901**) comes to the airport at 11 minutes past the hour on weekdays from 7:11am to 5:11pm and costs $1.50; your luggage has to fit under your seat or at your feet. Ask the driver for the stop closest to your hotel; you may need a short cab ride from there. The public bus can also get you to the city's top visitor attraction, Mendenhall Glacier (p. 210). The passenger cruise-ship pier is right in town and an easy walk. However, with baggage it might be necessary to take a taxi, which shouldn't cost more than $8. Major car-rental companies have offices at the airport.

WHERE TO STAY

Breakwater Inn   Located in a residential area close to downtown, and across from the Aurora Boat Harbor, this casual motel property offers decent-size rooms and complimentary van service to downtown. Units with kitchenettes are available and the restaurant serves steak and seafood.

1711 Glacier Ave., Juneau, AK 99801. ℰ **800/544-2250** or 907/586-6303. Fax 907/463-4820. www.breakwaterinn. com. 49 units. $120–$150 (off season $70–$95). Children under 12 stay free with parents or grandparents. AE, DISC, MC, V.

Goldbelt Hotel Juneau   This is a recently renovated hotel with large, nicely appointed rooms favored by business travelers. The rooms in the front (which are more expensive) overlook the Gastineau Channel. The atmosphere is quiet and almost hermetic. Chinook's Restaurant, decorated with museum-quality Native American art and offering Southeast Alaska–inspired cuisine, is just off the lobby.

51 W. Egan Dr., Juneau, AK 99801. ℰ **888/478-6909** or 907/586-6900. Fax 907/463-3567. www.goldbelttours.com. 105 units. $169–$179 double. Extra person in room $15 extra. AE, DC, DISC, MC, V.

Prospector Hotel   The Prospector is a comfortable hotel right on the waterfront, with large standard rooms in attractive pastel colors. More than two dozen rooms have kitchenettes, and some of the more expensive ones are like nice furnished apartments. Those facing the channel have good views. The lower level, called the first floor, is half basement and somewhat dark. The hotel has a full-service restaurant and lounge called T. K. Maguire's.

375 Whittier St., Juneau, AK 99801-1781. ℰ **800/331-2711** or 907/586-3737. Fax 907/586-1204. www.prospector hotel.com. 58 units. $149–$155 double; $129–$135 off season. AE, DC, DISC, MC, V.

Westmark Baranof   In winter, the venerable old Baranof acts like an annex of the state capitol for conferring legislators and lobbyists; in the summer, it's more like a branch of the package-tour companies. The nine-story concrete building, built in 1939, has the feel of a grand hotel, although some rooms are on the small side. The upper-floor rooms are modern and have great water views. There are many room configurations, and some rooms have kitchenettes, so discuss the options with your reservationist to make sure you get what you want. The hotel has two restaurants. The Art Deco **Gold Room** is Juneau's most traditional fine-dining establishment, although the food varies greatly in quality year to year. Most entrees are $20 to $25.

127 N. Franklin St., Juneau, AK 99801. ℰ **800/544-0970** or 907/586-2660. Fax 907/586-8315. www.westmarkhotels. com. 193 units. $149–$199 double. AE, DC, DISC, MC, V.

WHERE TO DINE

Red Dog Saloon SALOON FOOD   This is not by any means an elegant eatery—it's more of an experience. The Red Dog is a Juneau landmark, and its restaurant serves good, wholesome food in a frontier atmosphere. Just don't go looking for speedy or particularly distinguished service. Enjoy the honky-tonk piano and banjo and the emcee's constant stream of one-liners while you're waiting for your grub. It's noisy. It's crowded. And it's fun!

728 S. Franklin St. (C) **907/463-3777**. www.reddogsaloon.cc Main courses $8–$14. AE, MC, V. Summer daily 11am–11pm.

Twisted Fish Company SEAFOOD/PIZZA/BURGERS Right near the cruise-ship pier but still popular with locals, this casual publike eatery serves up fish tacos (salmon or halibut), pizzas topped with salmon, salmon served on a cedar plank, and an excellent Caesar salad. Wash your meal down with some Alaskan Pale Ale. Several tables offer views of Gastineau Channel and there is outdoor dining when the weather is warm. It's our new favorite in Juneau.

550 S. Franklin St. (behind Taku Smokeries). (C) **907/463-5033**. Lunch main courses $7–$15; dinner $12–$30. AE, DISC, MC, V. Daily 11am–10pm.

Wild Spice This restaurant, opened in 2007, offers meals cooked Mongolian style on an open grill (you pick your ingredients and the chefs prepare them in front of you, or chose one of the chef's suggestions). It's the brainchild of the award-winning local coffee roaster Heritage Coffee, which also has several cafe locations around Juneau serving good coffee and sandwiches.

140 Seward St. (C) **907/523-0344**. Lunch main course $8–$14; dinner $13–$26. V, M, AE. Open daily, lunch 11am–2pm, appetizers 4–5pm, dinner 5–9pm.

6 Whittier

Unless you're getting on or off a cruise ship or are going sightseeing in Prince William Sound, there's little reason to go to Whittier. Unless, that is, you're on a quest to find America's oddest towns. Most of the townspeople (181 as of the 2000 census) live in a single 14-story concrete building, Begich Towers, with dark, narrow hallways. The grocery store is on the first floor and the medical clinic is on the third. The rest of the people live in one other building.

Begich Towers was built during the 1940s, when Whittier's strategic location on the Alaska Railroad and at the head of a deep fjord made it a key port in the defense of Alaska. Today, with its barren gravel ground and ramshackle warehouses and boat sheds, the town maintains a stark military-industrial character. The pass above the town is a funnel for frequent whipping winds, it always seems to rain, and the glaciers above the town keep it cool even in summer. The official boosters look on the bright side: Having everyone live in two buildings saves on snow removal in a place that gets an average of 20 feet per winter. The kids don't even have to go outside to get to school—a tunnel leads from the tower to the classroom. It's an unusual setup even for Alaska.

No matter how odd or dreary Whittier may seem, it has assumed huge importance to the Princess and Carnival lines—and vice versa. In 2005, the two companies' five Gulf ships made a combined 50-odd turn-around stops there during the season, exposing more than 120,000 embarking and disembarking visitors to the city. Norwegian Cruise Line also visits Whittier as a port of call. How much money any of those thousands of passengers will spend on goods and services is open to question. But the cruise lines' docking fees alone are worth big bucks to Whittier. An **ATM** is located at the liquor store near the boat harbor, but Whittier lacks a bank and other services, so bring what you need.

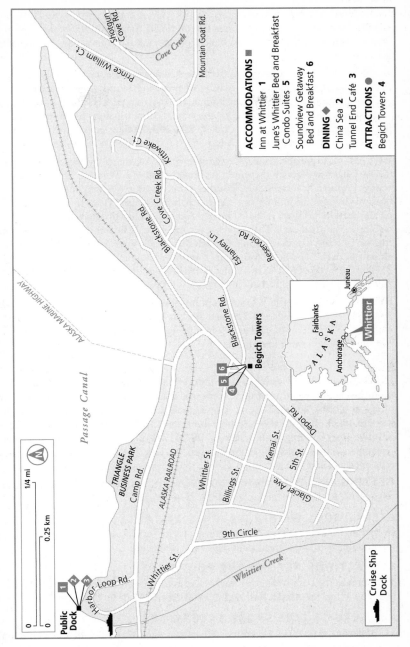

Whittier

ACCOMMODATIONS ■
Inn at Whittier **1**
June's Whittier Bed and Breakfast
Condo Suites **5**
Soundview Getaway
Bed and Breakfast **6**

DINING ◆
China Sea **2**
Tunnel End Café **3**

ATTRACTIONS ●
Begich Towers **4**

GETTING TO WHITTIER

BY PLANE   Fly to the **Ted Stevens International Airport** in Anchorage, and the drive is about 1½ hours. You are best off booking a transfer through the cruise line to get there.

BY BUS   The **Magic Bus** departs from the Anchorage Museum of History and Fine Art (at 7th and A sts.) at 3pm Monday, Wednesday, and Saturday, and arrives in Whittier some 90 minutes later. Luggage is limited to two bags per passenger (extra luggage is taken on a space-available basis, for an extra fee). The trip costs $56 for adults, $28 for kids each way. For reservations, call © **800/208-0200**, or go to www.alaskatravel.com/bus-lines/anchorage-whittier.html.

BY CAR   It is possible to drive to Whittier from Anchorage by way of the Portage Glacier Highway through the Anton Anderson Memorial Tunnel at Whittier. But be warned: Although, theoretically, Whittier is only a couple hours' drive or train ride from Anchorage, the journey can take much, much longer. That's because the tunnel on the outskirts of town is shared by both vehicular and rail vehicles, and while one is using it, the other can't. They switch every half-hour or so, but it can make for some frustrating waits. Get the schedule through the tunnel's website (go to **www.dot.state. ak.us** and click "Traveler Information"), through its phone recording (© **877/611-2586** or 907/566-2244), or by tuning to 1610AM in Portage or 530AM in Whittier. The toll for cars is $12. Parking in Whittier is $5 per day.

BY RAIL   You can get to Whittier from Anchorage on the Alaska Railroad (© **800/ 544-0552** or 907/265-2494). The new dock is near the mouth of Whittier Creek. Nothing in Whittier is more than a 5-minute walk away. Don't look for taxi ranks or free shuttles—you won't need them.

EXPLORING WHITTIER

INFORMATION   Probably because it doesn't have much to promote, Whittier has no tourist board, per se, and there is no visitor center, but you can contact the city offices at © **907/472-2327**, ext. 101 (admin@ci.whittier.ak.us). The people at the harbormaster's office are also helpful and maintain public toilets and showers; it's the only two-story building at the harbor (© **907/472-2327**, ext. 110 or 115). And a new phenomenon here, inside the cruise terminal, is a rack with brochures promoting area tour operators and the like.

GETTING AROUND   You can walk everywhere, but there's also a cab or two in town. Look for them when you get off the boat or train.

ATTRACTIONS WITHIN WALKING DISTANCE

Everything's within walking distance; there just isn't much to see. Visit the yacht harbor and the town's apartment building—that's about it.

ATTRACTIONS BEYOND THE PORT AREA

You can take the train straight to Anchorage, a fun scenic ride, for $58 one-way, $29 ages 2 to 11 on the **Alaska Railroad** (© **800/544-0552** or 907/265-2494).

BEST CRUISE-LINE SHORE EXCURSIONS

The following two cruises are offered only to passengers with a pre- or post-cruise stay in Anchorage or those with departing flights after 5pm.

Blackstone Glacier Adventure Cruise (5½ hr.; $112 adults, $59 children): Cruise a glacier-carved fjord and view two tidewater glaciers. The vistas of the unspoiled wilderness are breathtaking. Marine science activities and a baked Alaska halibut lunch are included.

Kayaking in Prince William Sound (3 hr.; $99): Learn the basics, then follow your guide into the pristine waters of Prince William Sound. He or she will point out the native flora, fauna, and marine life.

EXCURSIONS OFFERED BY LOCAL AGENCIES

Several companies compete for your business for day-trip tours to the sound's western glaciers. Besides having incredible scenery, the water is calm, making seasickness unlikely—for the queasy, this is a much better choice than Kenai Fjords National Park. Each operator times departures to coordinate with the daily Alaska Railroad train from Anchorage, described above, which means they have up to 6 hours for the trip. Some try to see as much as possible, while others take it slower to savor the scenery and wildlife sightings. **Phillips' Cruises and Tours** (© 800/544-0529 or 907/276-8023; www.26glaciers.com) offers a 26-glacier cruise of the sound on a fast three-deck catamaran, counting the glaciers as they go. The boat ride is 4½ hours and costs $129 for adults, $79 for children under 12.

Major Marine Tours (© 800/764-7300 or 907/274-7300; www.majormarine. com) operates a smaller 149-passenger vessel at a slower pace than Phillips'—they hit a mere 10 glaciers but spend more time waiting for them to calve. The route goes up Blackstone Bay. The boat is comfortable, with reserved table seating. They also put more emphasis on their food, which costs extra; the all-you-can-eat salmon and prime rib buffet is $15. Time on the water is 5 hours; the price is $99 adults, $49 children under 12 (food not included).

Sound Eco Adventures (© 888/471-2312 or 907/472-2312; www.soundeco adventure.com) is operated by a retired wildlife biologist who spent years researching the waterfowl and ecology of Prince William Sound. The 30-foot wheelchair-accessible boat carries up to six passengers at a time on wildlife, whale, and glacier tours and does kayak drop-offs as well. Prices range from $180 per person for an 8-hour wildlife-viewing cruise to $210 per person for a whale and wildlife adventure. Lunch and a snack are included.

Honey Charters (© 888/477-2493 or 907/472-2493; www.honeycharters.com) is a family-run small-boat business licensed to carry 6 to 10 passengers. For larger groups, their *Qayaq Chief* can carry 18 kayakers or 22 visitors on a sightseeing cruise. No food is available on board, so bring lunch and snacks with you. For a 3-hour cruise, the price is $99 per person; for a 4 to 6-hour cruise, it's $149 per person; inquire about longer trips.

WHERE TO STAY

Inn at Whittier   Located at the mouth of the harbor, this new luxury property is taking advantage of the town's cruise boom. It has a timber-framed design with a lighthouse structure as its centerpiece. Get a room with views of Prince William Sound or of the mountains, if you prefer. All rooms have TVs and dataports. Junior suites have Jacuzzi tubs, and the two, two-story town house suites include Jacuzzis and fireplaces. The hotel has a 150-seat restaurant (serving three meals a day) and the chef will prepare your day's catch if you go fishing. Otherwise, the dinner menu features seafood including Copper River King Salmon as well as such meat dishes as filet mignon and crab-stuffed pork tenderloin; the lunch menu has crab cakes, Rueben sandwiches, and the like.

P.O. Box 609, Whittier, AK 99693. ℂ **866/472-5757** or 907/472-7000. Fax 902/472 5081. www.innatwhittier.com. 25 units. Rates $229–$299 double; $350–$599 suite. DC, MC, V.

June's Whittier Bed and Breakfast Condo Suites   Nine of these condo units are in the top two floors of the Begich Towers, the concrete building that dominates Whittier. It allows guests to live as Whittier people do, with great views and hummingbirds feeding at the windows. All have full kitchens. The hotel provides a free shuttle service to the harbor.

P.O. Box 715, Whittier, AK 99693. ℂ **888/472-2396** or 907/472-2396. Fax 907/472-2503. www.breadnbutter charters.com. 10 units. $115–$375 double. AE, MC, V.

Soundview Getaway Bed and Breakfast   These ocean- and mountain-view condos are located in the historic Bachelor's Officers Quarters that date back to Whittier's military days in the '40s and '50s. Some of the original fixtures remain. Each unit comes with a full kitchen and sitting area. Continental breakfast is included in the room rate. The units sleep two to four people.

WMCA 8, #9 Blackstone, Whittier, AK 99693. ℂ **800/515-2358** or 907/472-2358. No fax. www.soundviewalaska. com. 6 units. $120–$145. Extra person $25. AE, MC, V.

WHERE TO DINE

Most meals served in Whittier are for people grabbing a sandwich while waiting for a boat or otherwise passing through. Several such restaurants are in the triangle at the east end of the harbor, including a Chinese place, the Korean-owned **China Sea** (ℂ **907/472-2222**). It's okay. Lunch there is $8 or $9, dinner $12 to $19, and in the summer they serve specials such as kung pao halibut. Hours are 11am to 10pm daily. The **Tunnels End Café** (ℂ **907/472-3000;** www.tunnelsendcafe.com), at 12 Harbor Loop Rd., serves espresso, breakfast (including egg burritos), and sandwiches ($6.95–$8.95), as well as seafood and steak. Dinner entrées range from $9 to $27. Hours are 7am to 10pm Wednesday through Monday.

SHOPPING

Don't even think about it. There isn't really a store in town worthy of the name, but if you happen to run out of toothpaste, the grocery store is on the first floor of the Begich Building. Of course, we say this now, but with the cruise crowd growing, entrepreneurs are likely to move in.

8

Ports & Wilderness Areas along the Inside Passage

The Inside Passage runs through the area of Alaska known as the **Southeast.** It's that narrow strip of the state—islands, mainland coastal communities, and mountains—that stretches from the Canadian border in the south to the start of the Gulf in the north, just above Glacier Bay National Park. It's also known as The Panhandle. Since the typical cruise itinerary begins or ends in Vancouver, British Columbia, or, increasingly, in Seattle (both of which are covered in chapter 7, "The Ports of Embarkation"), we've arranged the ports chapters geographically, moving northward.

For ports and wilderness areas in the Gulf of Alaska, see chapter 9.

1 Victoria, British Columbia

Yes, we know it's in Canada, not Alaska, but cruises that start in Seattle or San Francisco typically include Victoria (on Vancouver Island) as a port of call while traveling northward. This lovely city, the capital of British Columbia, offers Victorian architecture and a very proper British atmosphere—some say it's more British than Britain itself—with main attractions that include high tea and a visit to **Butchart Gardens** with its incredible botanical displays.

A former British outpost, Victoria has a history filled with maritime lore. Whalers and trade ships once docked in the city's harbors, transporting the island's rich bounty of coal, lumber, and furs throughout the world. One of the great sights of any visit to Victoria is its Inner Harbor, framed by the venerable (ca. 1908) Empress Hotel and the British Columbia Parliament Building. It is, by any yardstick, a panorama of great beauty. The big ships don't dock there (see "Coming Ashore," below). The Inner Harbour is a great spot to begin a walking/shopping tour of the city, though.

Take a tour around the island and you'll see gorgeous homes and gardens, with views that include the snowcapped mountains of Washington State.

COMING ASHORE   Spectacular as it would be to dock in the Inner Harbor, it's too small for major cruise ships, which park instead at the Ogden Point terminal on Juan De Fuca Strait. It's about a mile into town, so if you don't mind a stretch of the legs, walk west along Dallas Street from the dock and north on Oswego Street or Menzies Street, and you'll find yourself in the heart of the action—right on the Inner Harbor. Every cruise ship, of course, operates a shuttle service to the Empress Hotel, where flowers, milling crowds, and street performers—including, usually, a lone bagpiper—enliven the scene.

Beautifully maintained old wooden water taxis ply the harbor. It's worth taking a jaunt, even if you're going nowhere! Be sure to bring lots of film: Victoria's Inner Harbor is one of the most photogenic sights on the planet.

Note: Rates below have been translated into U.S. dollars based on the conversion rate at press time: US$1 = C$1.06.

INFORMATION   You can pick up a map of the city at the **Visitors Information Center** (✆ 250/953-2033), on the waterfront at 812 Wharf St. It's open daily from 9am to 5:30pm in May and June, 9am to 6:30pm throughout the summer, reverting to the shorter hours in the fall and winter.

BEST CRUISE-LINE SHORE EXCURSIONS

Note that shore excursion prices quoted here are representative of what's available but may differ slightly from cruise line to cruise line.

English Tea at Butchart Gardens (4 hr.; $109 adults, $69 children 12 and under): The bus makes the 13-mile trip from the ship to world-renowned Butchart Gardens along Brentwood Bay, where you'll have time to explore the 131-acre grounds and enjoy an elegant traditional afternoon tea, with finger sandwiches, scones and cream, and all kinds of goodies, washed down with honest-to-goodness brewed English tea.

Victoria Pub Crawl (3½ hr.; $75, adults only): Flowers and greenery may be what most people think of when they think of Victoria, but the city also boasts some fabulous English-style pubs. The tour, mostly on foot, takes visitors to several of these to sample the local brews. *Note:* Minimum age 19.

Victoria by Horse-Drawn Trolley (1½ hr.; $50 adult, $29 children 12 and under): A romantic way to see the sights of the city—the Inner Harbor, Chinatown, the historic James Bay residential area, and much more.

EXCURSIONS OFFERED BY LOCAL AGENCIES

Several local operators greet passengers right at the pier, offering rides into the city and longer tours using various modes of transportation. **Heritage Tours and Daimler Limousine Service** (✆ 250/474-4332; www.islandnet.com/~daimler) does tours using stretch limos, Rolls-Royces, and Daimlers. Fares range from about $70 an hour per vehicle for a small stretch limo to $90 an hour per vehicle for a plush eight-passenger stretch limousine. **Classic Car Tours** (✆ 250/883-8747) has a similar concept, offering tours in classic convertibles (perfect on a sunny day), with commentary that we found colorful and delightful. Fares are $65 an hour per car; the cars seat up to four guests. The bicycle rickshaws operated by **Kabuki Kabs** (✆ 250/385-4243) and competing firms offer an unusual way to get around the city for about $50 an hour (for two people). For those seeking a more traditional bus tour, **Gray Line of Victoria** (✆ 250/388-5248; www.graylinewest.com) offers a wide variety of tours of Victoria and the surrounding area, including one to Butchart Gardens, leaving from near the Empress Hotel, for $46 adults, $15 ages 5 to 12. Among the company's other offerings are a 2½-hour Grand City Tour and Craigdarroch Castle package for $30 for adults and $16 for children age 5 to 11.

ON YOUR OWN: WITHIN WALKING DISTANCE

The Fairmont Empress Hotel   Located right by the Inner Harbour, this ivy-covered 1908 landmark has a commanding view of the harbor and an opulent lobby. This is the place to go for your British-style high tea, and the Empress pulls out all the stops. The tea includes fresh seasonal fruit and cream, sandwiches (with cucumber,

Southeast Alaska

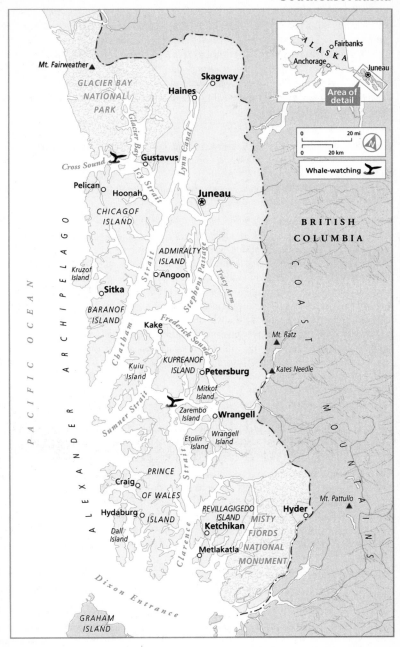

Mt. Fairweather ▲

GLACIER BAY NATIONAL PARK

Skagway

Haines

Cross Sound

Gustavus

Pelican

Hoonah

Juneau ⊛

CHICAGOF ISLAND

Glacier Bay

Icy Strait

Lynn Canal

ADMIRALTY ISLAND

Angoon

Stephens Passage

Tracy Arm

Kruzof Island

Sitka

BARANOF ISLAND

Chatham Strait

Kake

Frederick Sound

Mt. Ratz ▲

KUPREANOF ISLAND

Petersburg

Kuiu Island

Kates Needle ▲

Mitkof Island

Zarembo Island

Wrangell

Sumner Strait

Etolin Island

Wrangell Island

PRINCE OF WALES ISLAND

Craig

Clarence Strait

Hydaburg

Dall Island

REVILLAGIGEDO ISLAND

Ketchikan

MISTY FJORDS NATIONAL MONUMENT

Hyder

Mt. Pattullo ▲

Metlakatla

Dixon Entrance

GRAHAM ISLAND

PACIFIC OCEAN

ALEXANDER ARCHIPELAGO

BRITISH COLUMBIA

COAST MOUNTAINS

ALASKA

Fairbanks

Anchorage

Juneau ⊛

Area of detail

0   20 mi
0   20 km

Whale-watching

B.C. salmon and cream cheese, shrimp mousse, and curry-mango chicken salad), raisin scones with Devonshire cream and strawberry preserves, pastries, truffles, tarts, shortbread cookies, and the rest of the trimmings. Tea at the Empress has become almost a status symbol and is in great demand. Call ahead for reservations. Expect to pay about $52 to $63 per person. It's pricey, but such a treat! And please observe the dress code: no torn jeans, short shorts, jogging pants, or tank tops allowed.

721 Government St. ℂ **250/384-8111;** for tea reservations 250/389-2727. www.fairmont.com. Daily seatings noon–5:15pm.

Miniature World Museum   Around the back of The Fairmont Empress Hotel, you'll find what's billed as "The Greatest Little Show on Earth," with quirky displays that include big dollhouses, the world's smallest working sawmill, and a model of London in 1670.

649 Humboldt St. ℂ **250/385-9731.** www.miniatureworld.com. Admission $8 adults, $6.50 youths 12–18, $5.50 children 5–11. Summer hours 8:30am–9pm daily.

Royal British Columbia Museum and National Geographic IMAX Theatre
Outside the entrance to this modern, three-story concrete-and-glass museum is a glass-enclosed display of towering totem poles and other large sculptural works by Northwest Native artists. Inside, exhibits showcase the natural history of the province, illustrate Victoria's recent past, and demonstrate how archaeologists study ancient cultures using artifacts from numerous local tribes. There's also an IMAX theater showing features on places such as the Amazon, Africa, and Mount Everest. (The schedule changes every few months.) Behind the museum is **Thunderbird Park,** with Native totem poles and a ceremonial house. **Helmecken House,** 10 Elliot St., next to the park, is one of the oldest houses in British Columbia. It was the home of a pioneer doctor, and there are enough torturous-looking medical tools to make you shudder. Admission to these exhibits is free. If you want to learn about British Columbia's past, this complex is the place to go.

675 Belleville St. ℂ **888/447-7977** or 250/356-7226. www.royalbcmuseum.bc.ca. Museum admission $24 adults, $19 seniors, $17 ages 6–18, free for children age 5 and under, family admission (2 adults, 2 kids under 18) $65. Daily 9am–5pm; until 10pm most Fri–Sat evenings in summer. IMAX admission $10 adults, $8 seniors and ages 6–18, $4.75 children 5 and under, family admission $35.50. Daily 10am–8pm. Combined museum/IMAX ticket $32 adults, $26 seniors, $24 youth, $4.75 children, family admission $100.

Spinnakers Gastro Brewpub   It's not exactly Victoria's version of Carlos n' Charlie's (the boisterous drink spot in the Caribbean), but this recently expanded pub/restaurant is Canada's oldest brewpub, and a worthy place for brew fans to visit— the handcrafted ales are brewed using the finest hops and grain. The summer raspberry ale uses locally grown berries. You can also play a game of darts here. There's a waterfront deck, and a new viewer-friendly area lets visitors watch the culinary team in action.

308 Catherine St. ℂ **877/838-2739** or 250/386-2739. www.spinnakers.com. Open daily 11am—11pm.

ON YOUR OWN: BEYOND THE PORT AREA

Butchart Gardens   A ride by cab, public bus, or other transportation (see "Excursions Offered by Local Agencies," above) and several free hours will be required for a visit to this world-renowned attraction. The gardens lie 13 miles north of downtown Victoria on a 131-acre estate and feature English-, Italian-, and Japanese-style plantings, as well as water gardens and rose beds. There are also restaurants and a gift shop

Victoria, British Columbia

Legend (map):

Butchart Gardens **1**
Craigdarroch Castle **5**
Cruise Terminal **6**
Fairmont Empress Hotel **3**
Miniature World Museum **3**
Royal British Columbia Museum and National Geographic IMAX Theatre **4**
Spinnakers **2**

(i) Information

0   1/2 mi
0   0.5 km

on-site. *Note:* You can catch a public bus from downtown Victoria for less than $3 each way. A cab will cost you about $30 each way.

800 Benevenuto Ave., in Brentwood Bay. © 250/652-5256. www.butchartgardens.com. Admission $23 adults/seniors, $12 children 13–17, $2.85 kids 5–12, free for kids 4 and under. Summer hours 9am–10:30pm.

Craigdarroch Castle   You have to take a cab to see Craigdarroch Castle, the elaborate home of millionaire Scottish coal-mining magnate Robert Dunsmuir, who built the place in the 1880s. The four-story, 39-room Highland-style castle is topped with stone turrets and furnished in opulent Victoria splendor.

1050 Joan Crescent. © 250/592-5323. www.craigdarrochcastle.com. Admission $11 adults, $10 seniors, $3.50 children age 6–18, children 5 and under free. Summer hours 9am–7pm.

SHOPPING

It may seem strange, but your summertime cruise stop in Victoria is the perfect time to start thinking about Christmas. Victoria has two of the best Christmas shops, each jam-packed with ornaments, village scenes, Santas of every conceivable style, and nativity scenes—anything you might desire to celebrate the holiday season. As a bonus, in the middle of the year when cruise passengers visit, the prices are a bargain. **The Original Christmas Village** store is at 1323 Government St. (© **250/380-7522**), and the **Christmas House** is at 1209 Wharf St. (© **250/388-9627**); both are a short walk from the Inner Harbor.

Book lovers shouldn't miss **Munro's Books,** at 1108 Government St. (© **250/382-2464**), offering an impressive selection of thousands of titles in every subject, from metaphysics to mystery, biography to biology, and sports to self-help.

2 Canada's Inside Passage

Canada's Inside Passage is simply the part of an Inside Passage cruise that lies in British Columbia, south of the Alaskan border and running to Vancouver. On big ships, the first day out of Vancouver (or the last day going south) is usually a day at sea. Passengers get the chance to enjoy the coastal beauty of the British Columbia mainland to the east and Vancouver Island to the west, including some truly magnificent scenery in Princess Louisa Inlet and Desolation Sound.

In most cases, that's all the ships do, though: Go past the scenery—much of it at night. In their haste to get to Ketchikan, the first stop in Alaska, they invariably sail right past much of the Canadian Inside Passage.

One of the Canadian Inside Passage's loveliest stretches is **Seymour Narrows,** 5 or 6 hours north of Vancouver, just after the mouth of the Campbell River. It's so narrow that it can be passed through only at certain hours of the day, when the tide is right, which is often late in the day or in the wee small hours. On the long days of summer, it is often possible to enjoy Seymour Narrows if you're prepared to stay up late.

The U.S./Canada border lies just off the tip of the Misty Fjords National Monument, 43 sailing miles from Ketchikan (and 403 miles from Glacier Bay, for those who are keeping count).

3 Prince Rupert, British Columbia

Until recently, this sleepy Canadian port just a few miles from the Alaska border registered just a tiny blip on the cruise industry's radar screen. Now, however, with the number and size of ships in the Alaska trade growing, the need for alternative ports of call en route has focused some attention on Prince Rupert's Northland Dock at Cow Bay. In response, the city has spiffed up the facility, mostly used by cargo ships from Asia, and upgraded a small complex of retail stores alongside it.

Despite its best promotional efforts, though, Prince Rupert still gets only a small number of major cruise ship visits—two ships a week in summer 2007. As a B.C. cruise destination, it ranks a distant third to Vancouver and Victoria. The town was named in 1670 for the first governor of the Hudson's Bay Company. He was Rupert, the son of Frederick V, king of Bohemia, and Elizabeth Stuart, daughter of James I of England. Today many of its 13,000 inhabitants work in commercial fishing. There is also a flourishing artists' colony, the results of whose efforts can be seen in the Cow Bay galleries right next to the passenger-ship dock. The town has two shopping malls, a number of good-quality stores, and some good, if hardly gourmet, restaurants.

Prince Rupert's location makes it an ideal jumping-off point for visits to Southeast Alaska, the Queen Charlotte Islands, Vancouver Island, and the interior of British Columbia. The town is served year-round by both the **BC Ferries** system (© **888/ BC-FERRY [223-3779];** www.bcferries.com) and the **Alaska Marine Highway System** (© **800/642-0066;** www.dot.state.ak.us/amhs). Both ferry systems offer up to five departures a week during the summer to a number of Alaskan Inland Passage ports.

By road, Prince Rupert is accessible via the Yellowhead Highway to Vancouver in the south, and to Dawson Creek, B.C. (not to be confused with Dawson City, the Yukon Territory gold-rush capital) and Alberta in the east. **VIA Rail Canada** (© **888/VIA-RAIL [842-7245]**; www.viarail.ca) operates daily between Prince Rupert and Jasper National Park, and **Air Canada** (© **888/247-2262**; www.aircanada.com) has two flights a day to Vancouver.

Note: Rates below have been translated into U.S. dollars based on the conversion rate at press time: US$1 = C$1.06.

COMING ASHORE   The passenger pier is a very short distance from town. However, there's a little uphill walking to be done, especially right by the pier from which 1st Avenue, the main thoroughfare into town, has a steepish climb of 50 yards or so. It's not a mountain, but enough to test the mettle of anybody whose legs aren't as limber as they used to be.

INFORMATION   A walk of a few yards will get you from the ship to the pier's **Prince Rupert Visitor Information Center** at 215 Cow Bay Rd. (© **800/667-1994** or 250/624-5637; www.tourismprincerupert.com), open daily from 9am to 6pm (later if cruise ships are in town for evening stays).

BEST CRUISE-LINE SHORE EXCURSIONS

Bear-Watching Adventure (4 hr.; $380): Visit, via a 27-mile floatplane ride, the Khutzeymateen area, in which resides the largest concentration of grizzlies in B.C. This tour may also be offered by boat for $199 (for a 5-hr. excursion including lunch), though with less viewing time than the floatplane option.

Historic North Pacific Cannery (3½ hr.; $71): Declared a National Historic Site by the B.C. government on its 100th anniversary in 1989, the structure is an example of the kind of residential cannery—where people both worked and lived—that was common in British Columbia a century ago. You also view the historic downtown sights, with time to explore the Museum of Northern B.C.

Whale-Watching (4 hr.; $119): Orcas, humpbacks, grays, and minkes inhabit the waters off Prince Rupert in their season. Whales are the primary object of the search, but participants are likely also to see eagles, seals, sea lions, and an abundance of other kinds of wildlife.

Tsimshian Traditional Canoe Quest & Rainforest Walk (4 hr.; $109): Travel on a 29-foot canoe of Native design, the means of travel that enabled the Tsimshian First Nations people to reach their fishing and hunting destinations. You'll visit McNichol Creek Beach, a salmon spawning stream, and explore the nearby rainforest.

EXCURSIONS OFFERED BY LOCAL AGENCIES

You can book a whale-watching tour with **Seashore Charters** (© **800/667-4393**; www.seashorecharters.com) to see the migrating humpbacks, orcas (May to early July only), minkes, and grays, and probably lots of other marine life, too (porpoises included). Departures are at 1pm and 4pm; the tours are $92 for adults and $73 for children 5 to 12 (under 5 free). The same company also offers kayak and canoe excursions that are led by First Nation guides. Bear lovers can view the outskirts of the Khutzeymateen Grizzly Bear Sanctuary with **Palmerville Adventures** (© **888/580-2234** or 250/524-8243; www.palmerville.bc.ca/tour.html). First you take a plane or helicopter and then a boat to the sanctuary, the only grizzly bear home in Canada where you can get up close and personal (sort of) with the furry creatures. You view

Prince Rupert, British Columbia

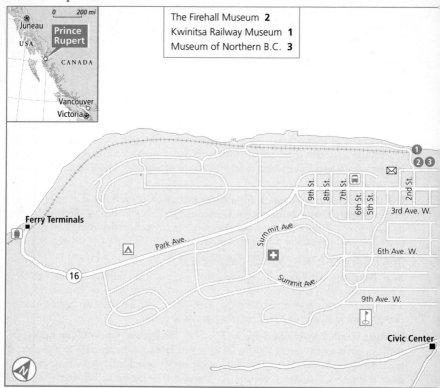

The Firehall Museum **2**
Kwinitsa Railway Museum **1**
Museum of Northern B.C. **3**

the bears from the boat in Khutzeymateen Inlet, and rates are from about $375 per person.

ON YOUR OWN: WITHIN WALKING DISTANCE

The Museum of Northern B.C.   This well-designed facility traces the cultures and development of the Native peoples of B.C. (Tsimshian, Haida, Nisga'a, and others). The museum begins in the impressive longhouse lobby, with its cedar timbers and glass artworks. It continues through the Great Hall, the Hall of Nations, and the Treasures Gallery, which among them contain a striking collection of archaeological artifacts, ceremonial art and dress, weaponry from Indian wars, canoes, and much more. Television monitors in these rooms run oral histories of the area from its Indian origins right up to the modern-day commercial fishing and the creation of the city itself. At frequent intervals during the day, live performances by Indian dancers and musicians take place. The museum—a must-see for visitors to Prince Rupert—is located only a few hundred yards from the passenger terminal. But it should be noted that the first half of the road is steeply uphill.

100 1st Ave. W. (C) 250/624-3207. www.museumofnorthernbc.com. Admission $5 adults, $2 children (6–12). Mon–Sat 9am–8pm; Sun 9am–5pm.

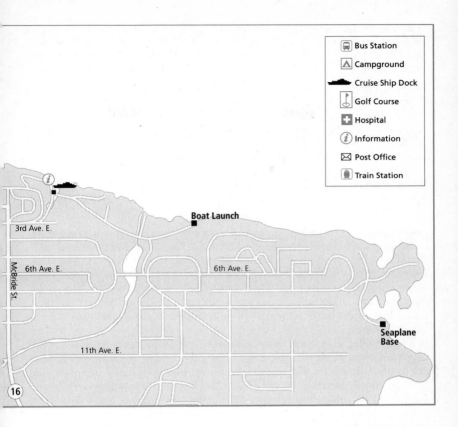

The Kwinitsa Railway Museum   Located in the city's Waterfront Park, very close to the Prince Rupert Museum, the facility explains the evolution of Prince Rupert, from a tent town terminus for the Grand Trunk Railway, through incorporation as a city in the 1920s.

110 Bill Murray Way. © **250/624-3207**. Free admission. Daily 9am–noon and 1–5pm.

The Firehall Museum   This attraction features a display of a rebuilt R.E.O. Speed-wagon (ca. 1925) and illustrates the history of the Prince Rupert Fire Department through pictures and artifacts.

200 1st Ave. West. © **624/627-1248**. Free admission. Mon–Sat 1–5pm.

ON YOUR OWN: BEYOND THE PORT AREA
The North Pacific Historic Fishing Village   This living history museum is about 12 miles from Prince Rupert and is home to the oldest surviving salmon cannery in British Columbia. Here you'll learn through videos and displays what it was like to live in a company town, and discover all you need to know about fishing and canning methods. The 28 buildings date from 1889 to 1964. You can also view one of the largest model railroads on display in Western Canada. The site is operated by the non-profit Port Edward Historical Society.

Prince Edward, B.C. ⓒ 250/628-3538. www.cannery.ca. Admission is $11 adults, $9 seniors/students, $7.50 youths ages 6–18, children under 6 free. Mid-May through June, Tues–Sun, 10am–5pm (closed Mon); July to mid-Aug, daily 10am–5pm; mid-Aug to mid-Sept Tues–Sun 10am–5pm (closed Mon); open late Sept to pre-booked groups only; closed to visitors rest of year.

SHOPPING

Right around Cow Bay, at Atlin Terminal, where the cruise ships dock, there are some excellent, funky little art shops offering some great pieces of jewelry, pottery, and sculpture by local artists, both native and non. The **Blue Heron Gallery,** at 123 Cow Bay Rd. (ⓒ **250/624-5700**), is one of the best. Also recommended is **MacGregor Studios** (ⓒ **250/627-7171**), a little to the east, at 2161 Seal Cove Circle.

In the town proper, try the well-laid-out art stores of historic **Old Town Prince Rupert,** whose walkways are lined with totem poles, fountains, and flowerbeds. The area also provides easy access to a stairway from which one can enjoy spectacular views of the city and its harbor.

4 Ketchikan

Ketchikan is the southernmost port of call in Southeast Alaska, and its 7,410 residents sometimes refer to it as "the first city." That's not because it's the most important city to the region's economy, or that it's the biggest, or even that it was literally the first built. The name comes from the fact that Ketchikan is usually the first city visited by cruise ships on the Inside Passage, when ships are running northbound out of Vancouver or Seattle.

The first thing most cruise visitors encounter upon arrival at the dock is a Liquid Sunshine Gauge, which the city put up to mark the cumulative rainfall for the year, day by day. We once checked and saw that the mark showed over 36 inches—and it was only June. Even at that, the gauge had a long way to go. The average annual rainfall is about 160 inches (more than 13 ft.!) and has topped 200 inches in the rainiest years. Precipitation is so predictable here that the locals joke that if you can't see the top of nearby Deer Mountain, it's raining; if you can see it, it's going to rain!

But here's a strange thing: Through the years, we've been in Ketchikan at least once in every month of the season, and we can recall only two real downpours. On one occasion recently, we were there in May and found sunshine and temps in the low 70s (low 20s Celsius). Go figure.

Maybe it's because the weather gods are kind to us that we have a soft spot for this place. Climate notwithstanding, this is a fun port to visit—a glorified fishing village with quaint architecture, history, salmon fishing, the great scenery that is to be found in just about every Inside Passage community, and **totem poles**—lots and lots of totem poles. However, we have to admit concern that the place is getting too touristy and overcrowded. About 70 jewelry stores and dozens of what locals call "trinket shops" cater to cruise-ship passengers. Much of the character we loved is vanishing in favor of touristy attractions like the Great Alaskan Lumberjack Show and Duck Tours (which take you on land and into the water on amphibious vehicles).

You used to catch great views of historic Creek Street from the ship pier, but now the views are blurred by mini-malls. From up close, though—say, on the sidewalk of Stedman Street—the main thoroughfare, Creek Street, still presents a photogenic side. It's often said (perhaps only by the Ketchikan Chamber of Commerce!) that it's the most photographed street in Alaska.

Last year, just in time for the tourist season, the tour company Alaska Travel Adventures introduced a great new way to see Ketchikan. Its stern-wheeler, the 350-passenger *Alaska Queen,* offers a narrated harbor cruise, complete with a calliope, banjo music, honky-tonk piano and live depictions of historical events and people of note. During the 2½-hour cruise, gold rush-era costumes and the stories of poet Robert W. Service ("The Shooting of Dan McGrew," "The Cremation of Sam McGee" et al.) will be much in evidence.

Ketchikan is still a strong center of the Tlingit, Tsimshian, and Haida cultures. These proud Southeast Alaska Native peoples have preserved their traditions and kept their icons intact over the centuries. They've also re-created **clan houses** and made replicas of totem poles that were irretrievably damaged by decades of exposure to the elements. The tall hand-carved poles are everywhere—in parks, in the lobbies of buildings, in the street. It should be no surprise to anyone that there are more totems in Ketchikan than in any city in the world.

A word of caution about that: Unless you're *very* interested in the origins and the meaning of totem poles, choose your shore excursion very carefully. On one particularly cold day, Jerry did the **Totem Bight State Historical Park** tour, but the guide, oblivious to the group's shivery discomfort, seemed intent on sharing with us every fact he'd ever learned about Alaska Native cultures and relating, in infinite detail, the story behind pole after pole after pole. (They're not merely decorative, and each tells the story of an incident in a tribe's life—a battle, a birth, and so on.) The first half-dozen were fine, but then, frankly, the time began to drag. The numbed visitors climbed back on the coach more than 3 hours later, suffering from cold and information overload.

Creek Street, the centerpiece of downtown, comprises a row of buildings on pilings over a stream that the salmon swim up in their spawning season. Today the narrow wood-sidewalk street is lined mostly with funky restaurants, such as the Creek Street Café, and boutiques and galleries specializing in offbeat pieces by local artists. In the early 1900s, this was Ketchikan's red-light district, with more than 30 brothels lining the waterway; a small sign at the head of the street notes that it was where both the fishermen and the fish went up the stream to spawn. The most famous of the courtesans (or, at least, the most enduring) was Dolly Arthur (born Thelma Dolly Copeland). Neither the most successful—nor, according to pictures we've seen, the prettiest—working girl, she nevertheless outlived the rest. Most people can tell you who Dolly Arthur was, although she was only one of a hundred girls working the area. **Dolly's House,** 24 Creek St. ((C) **907/225-6329**), is now a small museum. Like the house's old clientele, you have to pay to get inside. We don't know what they used to pay, but today it'll cost you $5. It's open daily from 8am to 4pm when cruise ships are in town (sometimes earlier or later, depending on cruise-ship schedules).

One of our favorite things to do in Ketchikan, besides booking a shore excursion and getting into the surrounding natural areas, is to walk the few blocks from the ship, past Creek Street, and take the **funicular railway** (round-trip $1) to the **Westcoast Cape Fox Lodge** for lunch. The lunch is satisfying (if hardly gourmet), and the Alaskan Amber Ale is refreshing, but it's the views of the city and of the Tongass Narrows and Deer Mountain, both from the funicular and from parts of the lodge and its grounds, that make the trip worthwhile.

It's also an easy walk from here to the **Deer Mountain Tribal Hatchery and Eagle Center,** at 1158 Salmon Rd. ((C) **907/228-5530;** admission $9; children under 12 free) a Native-run operation where you can learn where salmon come from and see some rescued and healing eagles. It's open May through September daily 8am to 4:30pm. Also nearby is the Totem Heritage Center (see below).

COMING ASHORE   Ships dock right at the pier in Ketchikan's downtown area or, on particularly busy days, in the bay, bringing passengers ashore by tender.

INFORMATION   Our first two stops in Ketchikan are usually the **Ketchikan Visitors Center,** right on the dock at 131 Front St. (© **907/225-6166**), to pick up literature and information on what's new in town (and discount coupons for attractions), and the **Southeast Alaska Discovery Center,** at nearby 50 Main St. (© **907/228-6220**), one of four Alaska Public Lands Information facilities in the state. The latter is more than a mere dispenser of information: It also houses a museum where a number of exhibits and dioramas depict both Native Alaskan cultures and the modern business development of Ketchikan. Admission to the exhibits is $5. The visitor center is open whenever a cruise ship has docked. The Discovery Center is open May through September daily from 8:30am to 4:30pm, October through April Monday to Friday 8:30am to 4:30pm.

BEST CRUISE-LINE SHORE EXCURSIONS

Alaska Queen (2½ hr; $59 adult, $39 children 12 and under): A fun way to enjoy Ketchikan's colorful past. The 4-deck stern-wheeler departs from a point just north of downtown and heads south past the cruise ship docks and Creek Street to Saxman Village where it turns around. Ketchikan's history takes on a new meaning when seen from the deck of a vessel such as this—the kind of boat that was once the major form of transportation in Alaska.

Alaska Amphibious Tours (1½ hr.; $36 adult, $22 children under 12): See Ketchikan by both land and sea. This fun outing, in a high-riding "duck" vehicle, takes guests through rustic streets (past the salmon ladder, Creek Street, and Totem Heritage Center) and into the harbor where they can eye the aquatic wildlife, check out the leisure and fishing boats, and get an up-close look at the floatplanes taking off. Be forewarned that, as you hit the water, there may be splashes (which typically elicit squeals of delight).

Misty Fjords Flightseeing (2 hr.; $239–$269): Everyone gets a window seat aboard the floatplanes that run these quick flightseeing jaunts over Misty Fjords National Monument. There's no ice fields and glaciers on this trip, but Misty Fjords has another kind of majesty: You'll see sparkling fjords, cascading waterfalls, thick forests, and rugged mountains dotted with wildlife. Then, you'll come in for a landing on the fjord itself or on a nearby wilderness lake. Once you've landed, you can get out and stand—carefully—on the pontoons to take pictures.

Mountain Point Snorkeling Adventure (3 hr.; $95–$99): Believe it or not, you can snorkel around Ketchikan, where the climate is warm for Alaska. Still, it's not the Caribbean, and insulating wetsuits are provided on this excursion, as well as hot beverages for when you get out of the water. Undersea are fish, starfish, sea urchins, sea cucumbers, and more.

Saxman Native Village and Ketchikan City Tour (2½ hr.; $54): This modern-day Native village, situated about 3 miles outside Ketchikan, is a center for the revival of Native arts and culture. The tour includes either the telling of a Native legend or a performance by the Cape Fox dancers in the park theater, plus a guided walk through

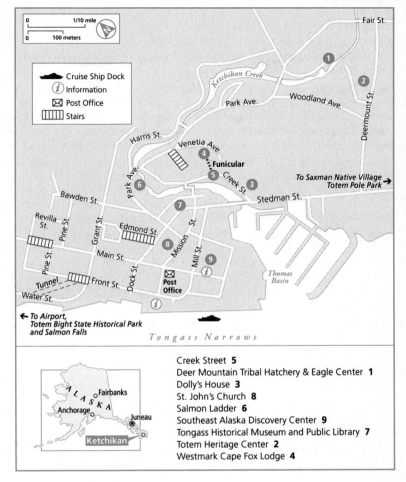

Creek Street **5**
Deer Mountain Tribal Hatchery & Eagle Center **1**
Dolly's House **3**
St. John's Church **8**
Salmon Ladder **6**
Southeast Alaska Discovery Center **9**
Tongass Historical Museum and Public Library **7**
Totem Heritage Center **2**
Westmark Cape Fox Lodge **4**

the grounds to see the totem poles and learn the stories behind them. Craftspeople are sometimes on hand in the working sheds to demonstrate totem-pole carving.

Note: You can visit the Saxman Native Village (© **907/225-4846**) on your own (frankly, we don't advise it) if you take a cab from the ship for about $15 (tour admission, of course, will be extra for independents: $38 adults, $18 children 12 and under).

Tatoosh Island Sea Kayaking (4 hr.; $135 adults, $107 children 8–12): There are typically two kayaking excursions offered in Ketchikan: This one (which requires you to take a van and motorized boat to the island before starting your 90-min. paddle) and a trip that starts from right beside the cruise-ship docks. Of the two, this one is far more enjoyable, getting you out into a wilder area rather than just sticking to the busy port waters. The scenery is incredible, and you have a good chance of spotting bald eagles, seals (whether swimming around your boat or basking on the rocks), and leaping salmon.

Clover Pass Bicycle Ride (2½ hr.; $82): Pedal your way around the beautiful pass along the water's edge, soaking in the peace and quiet of the wilderness within easy reach of bustling Ketchikan proper.

Totem Bight State Historical Park and City Tour (2–2½ hr.; $36–$39 adults, $19–$27 children 12 and under): This tour takes you by bus around Ketchikan and through the Tongass National Forest to see the historic Native fish camp, where a ceremonial clan house and totem poles sit amid the rainforest. There's a fair amount of walking involved, making the tour a poor choice for anyone with mobility problems.

Rain Forest Ropes & Zip Challenge (3¾ hr.; $129): This tour allows guests to traverse a zipline in harnesses between trees before rappelling to the ground. It's a new way to appreciate the Alaskan rainforest. This is real ziplining (unlike the offering in Icy Strait Point which is more of a ride than lining). Instruction will be given, and only minimal skill is required. A similar option is available in Juneau.

Great Alaskan Lumberjack Show (1 hr. 10 min.; $34 adults, $17 children aged 2–10): Chopping, sawing, speed climbing, log rolling and more. And all within a short walk of the cruise ship pier. The performers are in the open air but the spectator seats are covered and the area heated.

Alaska Undersea Tours (1½ hr.; $49 adults, $29 children under 12): Board the Nautilus V for an exploration of the harbor—just 6 feet below the surface, where the state's unique aquatic life looms, followed by a surface cruise around the neighboring islands and shoreline.

Seawind Aviation (1 hr.–3 hr. ranging from $99–$345 per person): Fly over the Ketchikan city/harbor area or as far afield as Misty Fjords National Monument. Transportation is in a six-seat (all window) Dehavilland Beaver, with voice-activated headsets to ensure that all passengers can easily hear the pilot's narration.

EXCURSIONS OFFERED BY LOCAL AGENCIES

A bevy of tour operators sell their offerings at the **Ketchikan Visitors Center,** on 131 Front St. (© **907/225-6166**), right at the dock. Schoolteacher Lois Munch of **Classic Tours** (© **907/225-3091;** www.classictours.com) makes her tours fun: She wears a poodle skirt to drive visitors around in her '55 Chevy, accompanied by '50s mood music. A 2-hour tour to the Saxman totem poles is $84; a 3-hour tour adds a natural-history stop and costs $99. Rates are per person and include the admission to Saxman and tax. The maximum group size is five. Lois is also happy to customize a tour (price based on itinerary) for you, if you call in advance and tell her what you want ($125 per hr. for one or two people, up to $175 an hr. for five people). **Allen Marine Tours** (© **888/747-8101;** www.allenmarinetours.com) offers cruises from Ketchikan to Misty Fjords National Monument on a high-speed catamaran built at the company's own boatyard in Sitka. A 4-hour tour is $149 for adults, $99 for children 3 to 12. Other locals offer tours, too; check at the town visitor center (see above) for many more choices. **South Sea Kayaks,** on Millar Street (© **907/225-1258;** paddle@ketchikan.com), offers excursions such as a 2½-hour paddle ($79 for adults and $59 for children under 12).

Ketchikan City Tours (© **907/617-9772;** http://citytours.alaskamade.com) also offers tours to **Totem Bight State Historical Park** (also listed in "Best Cruise-Line

Shore Excursions," above) for $35 for adults, $17 for kids, in addition to the shore excursion. The tour is by double-decker bus, a fun way to travel. The company also offers Saxman Native Village in a 2-hour package, also for $35 per person. ***Note:*** We do not recommend taking a cab to Totem Bight State Park: It's a long way out, and the fare is hefty.

ON YOUR OWN: WITHIN WALKING DISTANCE

Creek Street   This former red-light district is now arguably Ketchikan's number-one tourist attraction, jewelry stores and tourist shops aside. The view of Creek Street from the bridge over the stream on Stedman Street (the main thoroughfare) is striking, to say the least. It lays claim to the title "Most photographed street in the world" and, even allowing for a little chamber of commerce hyperbole, it just might be!
Off Stedman St., along Ketchikan Creek.

St. John's Church   St. John's Church is the oldest place of worship in town. Both the church (Episcopal, by the way) and its adjacent Seaman's Center—built in 1904 as a hospital and now a commercial building—are interesting examples of local early 1900s architecture.
On Bawden St., at Mission St.

The Salmon Ladder   We could spend hours on the observation deck at the artificial salmon ladder just off Park Avenue, watching these determined fish make their way from the sea up to the spawning grounds at the top of Ketchikan Creek. How these creatures can keep throwing their exhausted bodies up the ladder at the end of their long journey from the ocean, never giving up though they fail in three out of four leaps, is one of those mysteries of nature that we will never understand—and never tire of observing.
Off Park Ave., in Ketchikan Creek.

Tongass Historical Museum and Public Library   This museum offers Native cultural displays and other fine exhibits. It also contains one of the city's grizzlier relics: the bullet-riddled skull of Old Groaner, a brown bear that took to attacking humans and was shot for its troubles. In the same building, the attractive Ketchikan Public Library is a great place to recharge, especially in the children's section downstairs, where big windows look out on Ketchikan Creek's falls.
In the Centennial Building, 629 Dock St. ℂ 907/225-5600. Admission $2 summer. Summer daily 8am–5pm.

Totem Heritage Center   The Totem Heritage Center, built by the city of Ketchikan in 1976, has the virtue of being indoors, so weather isn't a factor. The museum houses a fine collection of 33 original totem poles from the 19th century, retrieved from the Tlingit Indian villages on Tongass and Village islands and the Haida village of Old Kasaan. The Tsimshian people are also represented in some exhibits. There's a nice nature path outdoors. Be aware it's a long walk to the museum unless you take the funicular, which allows you to avoid some of the uphill hike.
601 Deermount St. ℂ 907/225-5900. Admission $5. May–Sept daily 8am–5pm; Oct–Apr, open Mon–Fri, 1–5pm.

ON YOUR OWN: BEYOND THE PORT AREA

In Ketchikan, we strongly recommend that you leave the out-of-port tours to either the cruise lines or tour operators in town.

SHOPPING

Ketchikan, much to our dismay, has become a tourist shopping spot. Most of the shops are owned by folks who come here just for the summer to cater to cruise passengers. But there are still some hidden gems, our favorite being a friendly hole-in-the-wall called **Salmon, Etc.** (✆ 800/354-7256; www.salmonetc.com), a few blocks from the ship pier at 322 Mission St., where you can buy cans of yummy smoked salmon. The shop has been in town since the early 1980s and is locally owned. Its smoked-fish products are so good that on our last visit we bought a 24-can case of smoked salmon (for $139) and hauled it home (you can also have it shipped). That price was about $40 cheaper than at the shops at Salmon Landing, a mini-mall closer to the ship pier. Ketchikan has a decent arts scene, and a good place to check out what's new is the Main Gallery of the **Ketchikan Arts and Humanities Council,** near Creek Street at 716 Totem Way (✆ 907/225-2211; www.ketchikanarts.org). Shows change monthly. Fish-art aficionados should go directly to Ray Troll's **Soho Coho,** at 5 Creek St. (✆ 800/888-4070; www.trollart.com); his SPAWN TILL YOU DIE T-shirts have become classics.

5 Misty Fjords National Monument

The 2.3-million-acre, Connecticut-size area of Misty Fjords starts at the Canadian border in the south and runs along the eastern side of the Behm Canal. Revillagigedo Island, where Ketchikan is located, is on the western side of the canal. It is topography, not wildlife, that makes a visit to Misty Fjords worthwhile. Among the prime features of Misty Fjords are New Eddystone Rock, jutting 237 feet out of the canal, and the Walker Cove/Rudyerd Bay area, a prime viewing spot for marine life, eagles, and other wildlife. Volcanic cliffs (up to 3,150 ft. high), coves (some as deep as 900 ft.), and peace and serenity are the stock in trade of the place.

Only passengers on small ships will see Misty Fjords close up, as its waterway is too narrow in most places for big ships. The bigger ships pass the southern tip of the Misty Fjords National Monument and then veer away northwest to dock at Ketchikan. Unfortunately, this means that large-ship passengers miss one of the least spoiled of all wilderness areas. Unless, that is, you book a flightseeing trip to see the place (see the section on Ketchikan excursions above).

Archaeologists believe local Indian tribes (Haida, Tlingit, and Tsimshian primarily) lived here as far back as 10,000 years ago. The only way you are likely to see any trace of their existence now, though, is from a kayak or small boat that can get close enough to the rock face that you can discern the few remaining pictographs etched into the stone along the shore.

Anglers in Misty Fjords are liable to think they've died and gone to heaven. The pristine waters yield a rich harvest of enormous Dolly Varden, grayling, and lake trout. It is possible to walk in the park, but only the hardy and the experienced are advised to do that. And it is necessary to follow some simple rules. Let somebody know where you are going and when you expect to return. Keep to the trails. (The wildlife—especially bears—doesn't always appreciate intruders.) And carry out everything you carried in; that's the law.

By the way, the name Misty Fjords comes from the climatic conditions. Precipitation tends to leave the place looking as though it was under a steady mist much of the time. It also gives the waterway an almost spooky look. President Jimmy Carter protected it and named it a national treasure in 1978.

6 Admiralty Island National Monument

About 15 miles due west of Juneau, this monument contains almost a million acres and covers about 90% of Admiralty Island. It's another of those Alaska areas that cruise passengers on the bigger ships will never see. The villages here, some of them Native, have recently begun to attract some small-ship operators. The Tlingit village of **Angoon,** for example, welcomes small groups of visitors off ships. Small ships (such as those operated by Cruise West) may also ferry passengers ashore in a more remote area of the island for a hike.

Admiralty Island is said to have the highest concentration of **bears** on earth. Naturalists estimate that there may be as many as four of these creatures per square mile. Bears, though, don't have a monopoly on the island. Also plentiful are **Sitka black-tailed deer** and **bald eagles,** and the waters around teem with sea lions, harbor seals, and whales. One of the largest concentrations of bald eagles in Southeast (second, perhaps, only to that in Haines in the fall) is to be found in the bays and inlets on the east side of the island. An estimated 4,000 of the eagles congregate there because the food supply is more abundant and is easier to get at.

A 25-mile-long canoe trail system links the major lakes on the island, with some overland portions where visitors must carry their canoes. Travelers who are willing to work are rewarded by magnificent scenery and quiet.

Angoon itself is not particularly close to the natural wonders of Admiralty Island. There's not much to do there except walk along the beach to an old cemetery that houses some interesting headstones.

7 Tracy Arm & Endicott Arm

Located about 50 miles due south of Juneau, these long, deep, and almost claustrophobically narrow fjords are a striking feature of a pristine forest and mountain expanse with a sinister name: **Tracy Arm–Ford's Terror Wilderness.** The place came by its name honestly after a 1889 incident in which a crewman from a U.S. naval vessel (name: Ford; rank: unknown) rowed into an inlet off Endicott Arm and found himself trapped for 6 hours in a heaving sea as huge ice floes bumped and ground around and against his flimsy craft. He survived, but the finger of water in which he endured his ordeal was forever after known as Ford's Terror.

The Tracy and Endicott arms, which reach back from Stephens Passage into the Coastal Mountain Range, are steep-sided waterways, each with an active glacier at its head—the **Sawyer Glacier** in Tracy Arm and **Dawes Glacier** in Endicott. These calve constantly, sometimes discarding ice blocks of such size that they clog the narrow fjord passages, making navigation difficult. When the passage is not clogged, ships can get close enough for amazing viewing of and listening to the calving glaciers (the sound of white thunder is amazing!). And on a Regent Seven Seas ship recently, we were thrilled when the captain ordered the tenders out at Sawyer Glacier for a great photo op.

A passage up either fjord offers eye-catching views of high cascading waterfalls, tree- and snow-covered mountain valleys, and wildlife that might include **Sitka black-tailed deer, bald eagles,** and possibly even the odd **black bear.** Around the ship, the animals you're most likely to see are whales, sea lions, and harbor seals.

8 Baranof Island

Named after the Russian trader Alexander Baranof, Russian America's first appointed honcho, the island's main claim to fame is **Sitka,** on the western coast, the center of Russian-era culture and the seat of the Russian Orthodox Church in Alaska. (The island name, by the way, is often spelled Baranov, which some people contend is the way Alexander himself spelled it.) **Peril Straits,** off the northern end of the island, separating Baranof from Chichagof Island, is a scenic passageway too narrow for big cruise ships, but some of the smaller ones can get through.

9 Sitka

Sitka differs from most ports of call on the Inside Passage cruises in that, geographically speaking, it's not on the Inside Passage at all. Rather, it stands on the outside (or western) coast of Baranof Island. Its name, in fact, comes from the Tlingit Indian *Shee Atika,* which means "people on the outside." For the relatively short time it takes ships to get to Sitka, they must leave the protected waters of the passage and sail with nothing between them and Japan but the sometimes turbulent Pacific Ocean. If you're going to run into heavy seas at any point on an Inside Passage cruise, this is where you're most likely to find them. This is also one of the ports in Alaska where you're more likely to have to tender to shore (in small boats) rather than dock at the harbor. Be that as it may, the idea of missing this delightful port of call is unthinkable to many people.

Step off your cruise ship here, and you step into the Russian Alaska of yesteryear. This is where, in 1799, trader Alexander Baranof established a fort in what became known as New Archangel. Today **St. Michael's Cathedral,** with its striking onion-shape dome and its ornate gilt interior, reflects that heritage, as does the all-female troupe the **New Archangel Dancers,** who perform during the cruise season in **Harrigan Centennial Hall.** The colorfully costumed, 30-strong troupe performs a program of energetic Russian folk dances several times a day. Once a week, the New Archangel Dancers get together with a Tlingit dance troupe for a joint performance in the Sheet'ka Kwaan Naa Kahidi Community House on Katlian Street (p. 204).

Most attractions in Sitka are within walking distance of the passenger docks. The **Sitka National Historical Park** (p. 204), a must-do attraction with its impressive (mostly reproduction) totem poles and excellent views, is about a 10-minute walk from the passenger docks. One attraction that is too far to walk to but ought not to be missed is the **Alaska Raptor Rehabilitation Center** (p. 205). A nonprofit venture supported by tour companies, cruise lines, and public donations, the center was opened in 1980 to treat sick or injured birds of prey (primarily eagles) and to provide an educational experience for visitors. We don't mind admitting that the sight of our majestic national bird close up, with its snowy white head and curved beak, gives us goose bumps. Go as part of a shore excursion or take a taxi for about $15.

Every year in June, this town of 880 year-round residents hosts a celebration of chamber music, performed by world-class practitioners of the art in various halls throughout the town. The **Sitka Summer Music Festival** has been held every year since 1972 under the guidance of renowned violinist Paul Rosenthal. Performances are Tuesday and Friday evenings; admission prices vary. We recommend it as a perfect complement to the more frenzied, more modern entertainment found on cruise ships. All this culture is particularly impressive when you consider Sitka has more boats than people.

Sitka

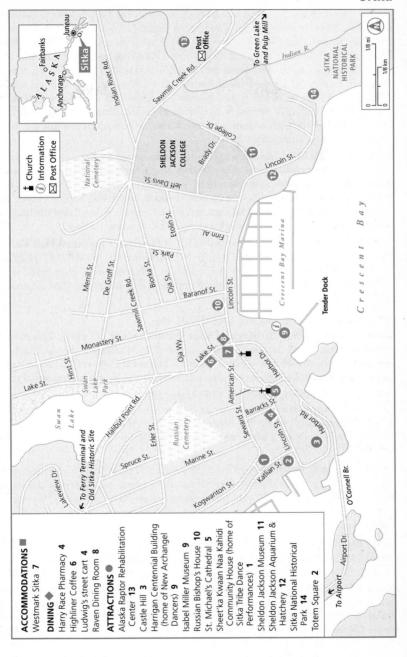

ACCOMMODATIONS ■
Westmark Sitka **7**

DINING ◆
Harry Race Pharmacy **4**
Highliner Coffee **6**
Ludwig's street cart **4**
Raven Dining Room **8**

ATTRACTIONS ●
Alaska Raptor Rehabilitation Center **13**
Castle Hill **3**
Harrigan Centennial Building (home of New Archangel Dancers) **9**
Isabel Miller Museum **9**
Russian Bishop's House **10**
St. Michael's Cathedral **5**
Sheet'ka Kwaan Naa Kahidi Community House (home of Sitka Tribe Dance Performances) **1**
Sheldon Jackson Museum **11**
Sheldon Jackson Aquarium & Hatchery **12**
Sitka National Historical Park **14**
Totem Square **2**

If you get the munchies, stop by **Ludwig's** street cart (on Lincoln) to try their fantastic clam chowder (spicy sausage is their secret ingredient) and other treats. Eat them at the nearby waterfront Totem Square (p. 205). The cart is next door to **Harry Race Pharmacy,** 106 Lincoln St., which has a cool 1950s-style soda fountain (and also serves ice cream). At the **Westmark Sitka,** at 330 Seward St., you can get a fancier restaurant meal at the **Raven Dining Room,** which offers a sea view and fine service (thanks to a bunch of energetic and friendly young people). **Highliner Coffee,** in Seward Square Mall (327 Seward St.), offers lattes, other coffee drinks, and excellent baked goods (try the giant oatmeal cookies); it also has computers you can use (for a fee) to e-mail your friends back home.

COMING ASHORE   Most passengers will arrive by tender because the harbor is too small to accommodate large ships. Tenders drop you right by the downtown area, but shuttle buses are also available to ferry you to local sights for a few dollars. But unless you have a very specific distant destination in mind (the Raptor Center, for instance), we don't recommend taking a taxi or bus. Sitka is so small and the heart of town so close to the passenger pier that it's ideal for exploring on foot.

INFORMATION   A kiosk in the city-operated **Harrigan Centennial Hall Visitor Center,** next to the Crescent Boat Harbor at 330 Harbor Dr. (© 907/747-3225), is the only walk-in information stop. It is staffed by volunteers only when cruise ships are in town. The hall is open Monday through Friday from 8am to 10pm, Saturday 8am to 5pm, and sometimes Sunday.

BEST CRUISE-LINE SHORE EXCURSIONS

Russian Sitka and New Archangels Dance Performance (4 hr.; $140): This motorcoach excursion hits all the historic sights, including St. Michael's Cathedral, the Russian Cemetery, Castle Hill, and Sitka's National Historical Park, with its totem poles and forest trails, and returns for the dance extravaganza at Harrigan Centennial Hall.

Sea Otter & Wildlife Quest (3 hr.; $109 adults, $85 children 12 and under): A naturalist accompanies passengers on this jet-boat tour to point out the various animals you'll encounter and explain the delicate balance of the region's marine ecosystem. They're so sure you'll see a whale, bear, or otter that they offer a partial cash refund if you don't.

Wildlife Quest & Beach Walk (3 hr.; $159 adults, $99 children 12 and under): This offering is more intimate than the above tour, taking guests in a 12-person catamaran for wildlife viewing and onto a remote island to explore its rugged coast. The captain designs the itinerary based on the weather and tides of the day. You may spot whales, puffins, sea otters, and brown bears.

Silver Bay Nature Cruise and Hatchery Tour (2 hr.; $47–$49 adults, $23–$34 children 12 and under): An excursion vessel takes you through beautiful Silver Bay to view wildlife, scenery, the ruins of the Liberty Prospect Gold Mine, and a salmon hatchery.

Salmon Fishing (4 hr.; $189): An experienced captain will guide your fully equipped boat to a good spot for halibut and salmon; the rest is up to you. Your catch can be frozen or smoked and shipped to your home if you wish. *Note:* A $10 fishing license and a $10 king-salmon tag are extra.

EXCURSIONS OFFERED BY LOCAL OPERATORS

Owned by the Sitka Tribe of Alaska, **Tribal Tours** (© 907/747-7290; www.sitka tours.com) offers a cultural-tour program that relates the history of Sitka, with an emphasis on Native history and culture. Tickets can be purchased at the Sheet'ka Kwaan Naa Kahidi Community House at 200 Katlian St. (near the tender docks). A 2½-hour comprehensive tour, priced at $45, includes a 45-minute narrative drive, a half-hour stop at the Sheldon Jackson Museum, a stop at the Sitka National Historical Park, and a performance by the Tlingit Indian Dance Troupe (not to be confused with the New Archangel Dancers).

ON YOUR OWN: WITHIN WALKING DISTANCE

Castle Hill   At first, we found the prospect of a climb up to the top of the hill—by way of a lengthy flight of stairs from the western end of Lincoln Street—a little daunting, but after climbing to the top, we have two words of advice: Do it. The reward is panoramic views of downtown Sitka. This is where the first post–Alaska Purchase U.S. flag was raised, in 1867. The place is steeped in history. It was on this site, in the 1830s, that the marauding Russians drove off the resident Kiksadi clan of Tlingit Indians and built a stronghold from which to conduct their fur-trading business. The last of the buildings within the walls of the stronghold was used by the first Russian America governor and was called Baranof's Castle (hence: Castle Hill). The structure burned some 60 years later, and its remains can still be seen, along with a lot of other reminders of those pre-Purchase days. Castle Hill is a National Historic Landmark, managed by the Alaska State Parks Department.

Climb stairs near intersection of Lincoln and Katlian sts.

Isabel Miller Museum   Sharing a building with the New Archangel Dancers (see below), this museum, operated by the Sitka Historical Society, illustrates the city's history with art and artifacts. There's also a large diorama of Sitka as it was in 1867 when the land was transferred from Russia to the United States.

In the Harrigan Centennial Building, 330 Harbor Dr., near the tender docks. Free admission (donations accepted). May 4–Sept 22 daily 8am–5pm; off season Tues–Sun 10am–4pm.

New Archangel Dancers   Just watching the way these Russian folk dancers throw themselves around the stage makes us tired. Where do they get the energy? The dancers are all women—they even play the men's parts, complete with false beards if the dance requires it. When the troupe was organized in 1969, the men of the town pooh-poohed the idea. It'll never work, they said. Later, when the original handful of women proved that it could work, some of the men expressed the feeling that they might not mind joining in. Too late, guys. The founders decided to keep the show all female. The 30-minute show is presented at least twice a day and sometimes as often as four times most days in the summer, largely determined by the number of cruise ships in town.

Performances (on most days that a cruise ship is in port) are held in the Harrigan Centennial Building, 330 Harbor Dr., near the tender docks. © **907/747-5516**. Admission $8. Call for performances times, which change daily. Tickets must be purchased at least half-hour before the show.

Russian Bishop's House   Bishop Innocent Veniaminov, born in 1797, translated scriptures into Tlingit and trained deacons to carry Russian Orthodoxy back to their Native villages. Unlike most of the later Protestant missionaries led by Sitka's other historic religious figure, Sheldon Jackson, Veniaminov and his followers allowed parishioners to use their own language, a key element to saving Native cultures. The house was built in 1842 for Veniaminov and is now owned and operated by the National

Parks Service. Ranger-led tours include the bishop's furnished quarters and an impressive chapel. Exhibits downstairs trace the development of New Archangel into Sitka.

Lincoln and Monastery sts. No phone; call Sitka National Historical Park Visitor Center ((C) **907/747-0110**). Admission $4 per person or $15 per family. Summer daily 9am–5pm.

St. Michael's Cathedral   Even if you're not a fan of religious shrines, you'll probably be impressed by the architecture and the finery of this rather small place of worship. One of the 49th state's most striking and photogenic structures, the current church is actually a replica; the original burned to the ground in 1966. So revered was the cathedral that Sitkans, whether Russian Orthodox or not, formed a human chain and carried many of the cathedral's precious icons, paintings, vestments, and jeweled crowns from the flames. Later, with contributions of cash and labor from throughout the land, St. Michael's was lovingly re-created on the same site and rededicated in 1976. A knowledgeable guide is on hand to answer questions or give talks when large groups congregate. Sunday services are sung in English, Slavonic, Tlingit, Aleut, and Yupik.

At Lincoln and Cathedral sts. (C) **907/747-8120**. Suggested donation $2. Summer Mon–Fri 9am–4pm, Sat–Sun varies (call in advance).

The Sheldon Jackson Museum   Located on the grounds of a college founded by Presbyterian missionary Sheldon Jackson as a vocational school for young Tlingits (founded in 1878, it was the first educational institution in Alaska), the museum contains a fine collection of Native artifacts—not just those of the Tlingits, but also those of the Aleut, Athabascan, Haida, and Tsimshian peoples, as well as the Native peoples of the Arctic. The museum has a decent gift shop. In a rustic building across the street, the Sheldon Jackson Aquarium & Hatchery allows visitors to pick up and touch creatures (in five tanks) taken from local waters, including bright anemones and starfish in shades ranging from red/orange to purple. Outside is a hatchery for king salmon.

104 College Dr. (at Lincoln St.). (C) **907/747-8981**. Admission $4 to museum, free for ages 18 and under. Aquarium admission free. Mid-May to mid-Sept daily 9am–5pm; mid-Sept to mid-May Tues–Sat 10am–4pm.

Sitka National Historical Park   At just 107 acres, this is the smallest national park in Alaska, but don't let that discourage you—the place breathes history. This is where the Russians and the Tlingits fought a fierce battle in 1804. Within the park are a beautiful totem-pole trail (which you can visit on a ranger-led tour or on your own) and a visitor center where exhibits explain the art of totem carving, and Native artisans from the Southeast Alaska Indian Cultural Center create totems, jewelry, and Native drums. The admission price below applies to the visitor center only; you can tour the park grounds for free.

106 Metlakatla St. (about a 10-min. walk from the tender pier). (C) **907/747-6281**. Admission $4. Visitor center summer daily 8am–5pm. Park summer daily 6am–10pm.

Sitka Tribe Dance Performances   The Sheet'ka Kwaan Naa Kahidi, Sitka's Community House, stands on the north side of the downtown parade ground. It is a modern version of a Tlingit clan house, with an air-handling system that pulls smoke from the central fire pit straight up to the chimney. The magnificent house screen at the front of the hall, installed in 2000, is the largest in the Pacific Northwest. Performances last 30 minutes and include three dances and a story. It's entirely traditional and put on by members of the tribe. You can also sign up for tours and activities in the lobby.

200 Katlian St. (C) **888/270-8687** or 907/747-7290. www.sitkatribal.com. $8 adults, $5 children. Call for times.

Totem Square   This area was originally underwater. It served as the Russian ship-yard, which was reclaimed from the sea from 1940 to 1941. It now contains Russian cannons, huge anchors believed to have come from ships lost in Sitka Harbor in the 1700s, and other historical memorabilia.

Katlian St., at the west end of Lincoln St. Free admission. Open 24 hr.

ON YOUR OWN: BEYOND THE PORT AREA

Alaska Raptor Rehabilitation Center   Local informational literature claims that the center is 20 minutes on foot from town, but these must be some kind of special chamber of commerce minutes because it seems to take at least that long by bus. How-ever you get there, though (and every cruise line offers it as a shore excursion), the cen-ter is well worth seeing. It's not a performing-animal show with stunts and flying action, but a place where injured raptors (birds of prey) are brought and, with luck, healed to the point that they can be returned to the wild. Some eventually can; those that cannot are housed permanently at the center or sent to zoos. Very few are eutha-nized. A flight-training center, completed in 2003, comprises a little rainforest in an aviary where recuperating birds learn to fly again. Visitors walk through in a tube with one-way glass so they can watch the birds without disturbing them. The tour through the center and on a wheelchair-accessible nature trail in the surrounding rainforest takes about an hour.

1101 Sawmill Creek Rd. (milepost .9), just across Indian River. © 907/747-8662. Admission $12 adults, $6 ages 3–12. Summer Sun–Fri 8am-4pm.

SHOPPING

Unlike some of the other towns including Skagway and Ketchikan, in Sitka all the shops are locally owned. One of Fran's favorite shops on the whole Southeast route is **Sitka Rose Gallery** (© 888/236-1536; www.sitkarosegallery.com), in a pretty Victo-rian house at 419 Lincoln St. The gallery features the works of more than 100 Alaskan artists (no MADE IN TAIWAN merchandise here) at prices that are more reasonable than at the bigger ports like Ketchikan. Fran's daughter, Erin, snagged a lovely pair of antique walrus tusk earrings for only $29. On another visit, Fran bought a fossilized whale bone sculpture. On her most recent trip, however, Fran was most obsessed with the **Winter Song Soap Company** shop, now in the back of the gallery. Their home-made soaps come in fragrances like Alaskan Herb & Flowers, and they also sell nice wooden soap dishes. Another little find is **Tea-Licious Tea House,** at 315 Lincoln St. (© 907/747-4535), where you can get a tea or latte, as well as scones and other pas-tries, but which also has a nice selection of amber jewelry at really reasonable prices (Fran snagged a nice blingy ring for only $59).

10 Juneau

Quick quiz: Can you name a state capital that cannot be reached by road from any-where else in the state? Juneau it is! Fronted by the bustling Gastineau Channel and backed by Mount Juneau (elevation 3,819 ft.) and Mount Roberts (elevation 3,576 ft.), the city is on the mainland of Alaska but is cut off by the Juneau Icefield to the east and wilderness to the north and south. To be sure, there are roads—150 miles of them, in fact—but they all dead-end against an impenetrable forest or ice wall.

In 1900, Congress moved the territorial capital to Juneau from Sitka, which had fallen behind in the flurry of gold-rush development. Not all Alaskans believe Juneau is the right and logical place for a legislative center. Its inaccessibility, some argue, disenfranchises many voters, and every few years somebody puts a "move the capital" initiative on the ballot. So far all of the proposals have been defeated, which is good news for Juneau's 12,500 civil servants. In Juneau, government is the city's biggest industry. However, tourism is not far behind: Besides the thousands of independent visitors who arrive by air and ferry, many thousands more come ashore during the 500 or so passenger-ship port calls made here each summer.

On any given day, four or five cruise ships might be in port, ranging from the biggest in the fleets of Princess, Celebrity, Holland America, and the rest, to the small ships of Cruise West and others. The small ships and most of the large ships usually find a dock, but depending on how many large ships are in port that day, some might have to anchor in the channel and tender their guests ashore.

While the city is tourism dependent, not everyone loves the crowds and it's easier to grasp the residents' unhappiness when you think of the number of cruise passengers who pour into the city. We were in Juneau once on a day when there were so many ships in port—four of the biggest, plus two smaller vessels, as we recall—that there might have been as many as 10,000 cruise visitors in town. That's more than a quarter of the permanent population of Juneau!

Juneau is a product of Alaska's golden past. It was no more than a fishing outpost for local Tlingit Indians until 1880, when gold was discovered in a creek off the Gastineau Channel by two prospectors, Joe Juneau and Richard (Dick) Harris. To be accurate, the gold was discovered first by Chief Kowee of the Auk Tlingit clan, who, in return for 100 warm blankets (more important to him than gold), passed the information on to a German engineer named George Pilz. Pilz, then surveying sites around the Inside Passage for mineral deposits, gave the hitherto unsuccessful Juneau and Harris directions to the spot described by Chief Kowee—and they couldn't find it! Only when Kowee accompanied them on a second expedition did they succeed in pinpointing the source of the precious metal. And the rush was on. Mines sprang up on both sides of the channel. So rich was the area's gold yield that mines continued to open for the next 3 decades, including the most successful of them all, the **Alaska-Juneau Mine** (aka the A-J), which produced a whopping 3.5 million ounces of gold before it closed in 1944.

The town, incidentally, was originally called Harrisburg, until Harris fell out with his neighbors and the citizens opted to name it instead for his better-liked partner.

Today Juneau is arguably the most handsome of the 50 state capitals, despite a glut of souvenir shops near the pier (where you can buy anything from "I Love Alaska" backscratchers to fur coats). The city runs with a mix of quiet business efficiency and easygoing informality. It has a good deal more sophistication to it than any city in Alaska outside of Anchorage, and yet it also has a frontier-style saloon.

Red Dog Saloon, 278 S. Franklin St., is a sawdust-floored, swing-door, memorabilia-filled pub (offering food and drink) whose old-time raucousness may be tempered by its pursuit of the tourist buck (and by its location adjacent to the Juneau Police headquarters) but whose appeal is undeniable. Another place to enjoy a not-so-quiet drink is the bar of the **Alaskan Hotel,** nearby at 167 S. Franklin St., built in 1913. On the National Register of Historic Sites, the Alaskan is Juneau's oldest operating hotel.

For those who can tear themselves away from that cool drink, Juneau offers another major attraction: the **Mendenhall Glacier,** at the head of a valley a dozen miles away. The glacier is one of Alaska's most accessible and most photographed ice faces. If your tummy is growling after a glacier hike, check out **Twisted Fish Company,** right near

Downtown Juneau

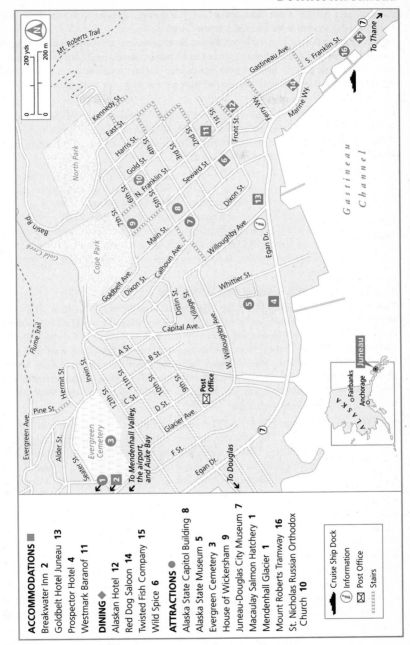

ACCOMMODATIONS ■
Breakwater Inn **2**
Goldbelt Hotel Juneau **13**
Prospector Hotel **4**
Westmark Baranof **11**

DINING ◆
Alaskan Hotel **12**
Red Dog Saloon **14**
Twisted Fish Company **15**
Wild Spice **6**

ATTRACTIONS ●
Alaska State Capitol Building **8**
Alaska State Museum **5**
Evergreen Cemetery **3**
House of Wickersham **9**
Juneau-Douglas City Museum **7**
Macaulay Salmon Hatchery **1**
Mendenhall Glacier **1**
Mount Roberts Tramway **16**
St. Nicholas Russian Orthodox
Church **10**

▲ Cruise Ship Dock
ⓘ Information
⊠ Post Office
▨▨▨▨▨ Stairs

the ship pier behind **Taku Smokeries** (see "Shopping," below) and have some fish tacos or pizza topped with smoked salmon. Yummy.

A note to smokers: Cigarette smoking has been banned in certain bars and lounges, though the law has not yet been extended to all public places. Speaking of addictions, Web addicts will want to know there's free public Internet access at the Juneau Public Library, the big concrete building on the left past the ship pier but before you get to the Red Dog.

COMING ASHORE   Unless you arrive on one of the busiest days of the year, your ship will dock right in the downtown area, along Marine Way. The pier is directly adjacent to the downtown area, but there is also shuttle bus service available that travels back and forth along the waterfront road.

INFORMATION   Midway down the cruise-ship wharf, a blue building houses the visitor information facility; stop in to pick up a walking-tour map and visitor's guide before striking out to see the sights. Another **Visitor Information Center** is in Centennial Hall at 101 Egan Dr., near the State Museum (© **888/581-2201** or 907/586-2201; fax 907/586-6304; www.traveljuneau.com). It's open May through September daily from 8:30am to 5pm, and October through April Monday through Friday from 9am to 4:30pm. The visitor center at the cruise-ship dock is open during the summer when the ships come in.

BEST CRUISE-LINE SHORE EXCURSIONS

Deluxe Mendenhall Glacier & City Highlights Tour (4 hr.; $96 adults, $62 children 12 and under): Twelve miles long and 1½ miles wide, Mendenhall is the most visited glacier in the world and the most popular sight in Juneau. This trip will take you by bus to the U.S. Forest Service Observatory, from which you can walk up a trail to within half a mile of the glacier (which feels a lot closer), or take one of the nature trails, if time allows. After this, you will visit Juneau's historic highlights and you might, on some tours, also visit the Macaulay Salmon Hatchery, the Alaska State Museum, and other local attractions.

Four Glacier Helicopter (3½ hr.; $325): This is definitely not a trip for the faint of heart or the out-of-shape. The excursion involves a flight on to the Juneau Icefield and to four glaciers found there. There is some walking involved (always in the company of a trained mountain guide) so unless you're fit, we suggest that you choose something else for your Juneau adventure. A version of the tour that includes a dog-sled ride on the Icefield costs $499.

Glacier Helicopter Trek (4 hr.; $399): Here's another chance to walk on the face of a glacier. After transferring to the airport by bus, guests board helicopters bound for Mendenhall, Norris Glacier, or other glacier areas. The tour may include one or two stops on a glacier, and you will soar over the jagged peaks carved by the massive Juneau Icefield. If special equipment (boots, rain slickers, and so on) is required, it will be provided.

Gold Mine History Tour (4 hr.; $59 adults, $30 children 12 and under): Juneau's gold-rush history comes to life (especially for kids) as you visit the ruins of the Alaska Gastineau mine and don a hard hat for a walk along a 360-foot tunnel for a demonstration of early-20th-century mining equipment and methods.

Mendenhall River Float Trip (3½ hr.; $117 adults, $75 children under 12): Board a 10-person raft on the shore of Mendenhall Lake, and an experienced oarsman will guide you out past icebergs and into the Mendenhall River. You'll encounter moderate rapids and stunning views, and be treated to a snack of smoked salmon and reindeer sausage somewhere along the way.

Taku Wilderness Lodge Adventure (3–3½ hr.; $262 for adults, $232 for kids): Fly on a floatplane over breathtaking glaciers and land at a wilderness lodge for an all-you-can-eat salmon bake. Your hosts will tell stories of Alaska's past, and after your meal you can take a guided hike (black bears are occasionally sighted).

EXCURSIONS OFFERED BY LOCAL OPERATORS

The **Juneau Trolley Car Company** (⟨ **907/789-4342**) provides narrated tours around the downtown area. Pickup is at the Tram Center at the pier. You can get off and on as you like at sites including the Alaska State Capitol and the Alaska State Museum. Fares are $19 for adults, $9 for kids under age 12. The trolley operates every day except Friday. Also at the pier you'll find booths operated by various independent tour operators selling city and glacier tours starting at about $25 a head. Ziplining is the new adventure offering in Juneau and locally owned Alaska Zipline Adventure can get you all harnessed up to fly above the treetops (www.alaskazip.com) for $115 for adults, $95 for kids 10 and 11 (not offered for under age 10) for a 3½-hour ride. The company also offers combo zipline and mountain-bike tours and ziplining combined with an Alaskan feast.

ON YOUR OWN: WITHIN WALKING DISTANCE

Alaska State Capitol Building   We've often wondered how so lovely a capital city could come up with such an unprepossessing legislative home. The interior is worth a visit, though, to see the old-fashioned woodwork and interesting decorative details.

4th St., between Main and Seward sts. ⟨ **907/465-3800.** Free admission. Tours during the summer start every half-hour Mon–Fri 9am–4:30pm.

Alaska State Museum   This place opened as a territorial museum in 1900 and has a wildlife exhibit, a first-class collection of artifacts reflecting the state's Russian history and Native cultures, and exhibits illustrating the history of the city's mining and fishery industries.

395 Whittier St. ⟨ **907/465-2901.** Admission $5 adults, free for ages 18 and under. Summer daily 8:30am–5:30pm.

Evergreen Cemetery   At this beautiful cemetery, which slopes toward the ocean, you can view the gravesites of Joe Juneau, Richard Harris, and other pioneers. The old Alaska Native graves are located in the wooded area on the far side of the cemetery.

12th St., just west of the downtown area.

House of Wickersham   This house was built in 1899 and bought in 1928 by Judge James Wickersham, who did much to shape the face of Alaska. Wickersham was the first territorial delegate to the U.S. Congress, was in the vanguard of the fight for statehood, and founded the University of Alaska. The house was in the family from 1928 until the state bought it in 1984, so it still contains Wickersham's belongings. Highlights include an Edison cylinder gramophone he took to Fairbanks, and his assignment to go to Alaska, signed by Theodore Roosevelt. *Note:* The house is at the top of a very steep hill.

7th St. ⟨ **907/586-9001.** A live-in guide requests a $2 donation. Daily mid-May to late Sept 10am–noon and 1–5pm.

Juneau-Douglas City Museum   This museum highlights the development of the city from its golden beginnings to statehood and also has exhibits on Tlingit culture. The facility specializes in programs and displays geared toward youngsters.

Corner of 4th and Main sts. ℂ **907/586-3572.** Admission $4 adults, free for ages 18 and under. Summer Mon–Fri 9am–5pm; Sat–Sun 10am–5pm.

Mount Roberts Tramway   The best place to take in Juneau's lovely position on the Gastineau Channel is from high up on Mount Roberts. The ascent of the mountain used to entail a strenuous hike but is now an easy 6-minute ride in the comfortable 60-passenger cars of the Mount Roberts Tramway. Operated by Goldbelt, a Tlingit corporation, the tramway rises from a base alongside the cruise-ship docks and whisks sightseers 2,000 feet up to a center with a restaurant/bar, a gift shop, a museum, cultural film shows, a series of nature trails (bring mosquito repellent!), and a fabulous panorama. Don't miss it, but on the other hand, don't bother if the day is overcast: Many visitors have paid the fees for an all-day pass, reached the top, and been faced with a solid wall of white mist.

At the cruise-ship docks. ℂ **888/461-TRAM** or 907/463-3412. All-day pass $25 adults, $14 children 7–12, 6 and under free. Mar–Nov daily 9am–9pm.

Red Dog Saloon   This is the place to go for a taste of frontier Alaska—and of the scrumptious locally brewed Alaskan Amber Ale. Look up on the wall behind the bar, where, among other things (many other things), they've got one of Wyatt Earp's pistols. Also look at the rest of the walls, where you'll see scrawled messages from legions of cruise-ship passengers who came before you.

278 S. Franklin St., right by the cruise-ship docks. ℂ **907/468-3535.** Main courses $8–$14. AE, DISC, MC, V. Summer daily 11am–11pm.

St. Nicholas Russian Orthodox Church   This tiny, ornate, octagonal structure is altogether captivating. It was built in 1893 by local Tlingits, who, under pressure from the government to convert to Christianity, chose the only faith that allowed them to keep their language. Father Ivan Veniaminov had translated the Bible into Tlingit 50 years earlier, when the Russians were still in Sitka.

5th and Gold sts. $2 donation requested. Lengthy services are sung in English, Tlingit, and Slavic for Sat vespers at 6pm and Sun at 9am; the congregation stands throughout the service. Otherwise, the church is open for visitors during the summer Mon–Sat 9am–5pm; Sun noon–5pm.

ON YOUR OWN: BEYOND THE PORT AREA

Mendenhall Glacier   Mendenhall is the easiest glacier to get to in Alaska and the most visited glacier in the world. Its U.S. Forest Service visitor center has glacier exhibits, a video, and rangers who can answer questions. Check out the trail descriptions and choose from several that'll take you close to the glacier. The easiest are a .3-mile photo trail (which takes about 20 min. and provides an excellent glacial photo op) and a .5-mile Trail of Time self-guided nature trail (which takes about 1 hr. to complete). The 3.5-mile Eastern Glacier Loop follows the glacial trim line, with a lot of time in the forest. It takes about 2 hours and includes some moderate uphill climbing. If you hike, bring water, sunscreen, and bug spray. Bears occasionally are spotted in the forest. If you do encounter one, stand still but make a lot of noise.

Mendenhall is about 13 miles from downtown, and taxis and local bus services are readily available in town (the bus costs $1.50 each way, taxis about $22) for those who want to visit independent of a tour. If you take a taxi out, make arrangements with the driver to also pick you up—and negotiate a round-trip price before you leave. Or take the Mendenhall Glacier Express, a bus that will carry you from the pier to the door of the glacier visitor center and back for $12. No reservation is needed; just walk off the ship and get on one of the buses parked 50 yards away (just past the Mount Roberts Tramway). It's an old-school bus—not necessarily the most comfortable way to go—but the advantage over the city transportation is that this one really takes you to Mendenhall Glacier, as opposed to dropping you off at the bus stop more than a mile away. Since it doesn't stop to embark and disembark riders en route, the Menden-hall Glacier Express gets you there in 20 minutes; although the city bus is cheaper, the ride takes closer to an hour. The MGE bus also comes with commentary. Fran recently had a Native American driver who shared such wisdom as: "Why does the bald eagle have a white head? Because the raven flies above."

Off Mendenhall Loop Rd. Visitor center ℭ 907/789-0097. Admission to the visitor center $3 adults, free for children under 12. Summer daily 8am–6pm.

Glacier Gardens Rainforest Adventure   Opened in 1998, this botanical garden was created in an area that had been decimated in a landslide. Privately owned, the garden has since expanded to 50 acres of landscaped gardens featuring alpine and other flowers and lush rainforest, including an eagle-viewing area. A golf cart shuttle takes visitors past the blooming flowers as you travel up Thunder Mountain, high above Gastineau Channel, and past trees, waterfalls, and ponds. You can get to the gardens by city bus (for $1.50 per ride) or cab (about $18 each way from downtown). There is also a greenhouse area with beautiful plants hanging, a gift shop and a small cafe serving beverages and sandwiches (locals winter their plants here). Ships also sell pre-booked tours here for those who would rather not travel on their own.

7600 Glacier Highway. ℭ 907/790-3377. www.glaciergardens.com. Admission includes a guided 1½-hr. golf cart tour, $22 adults, $16 children age 6–12, 5 and under free. Open daily 9am–6pm.

SHOPPING

Taku Smokeries (ℭ 800/582-5122; www.takustore.com), right off the ship pier at 550 S. Franklin St., has all kinds of smoked fish for sale and offers delicious free samples. They will ship your purchase home for you. **The Raven's Journey,** 435 S. Franklin St. (ℭ 907/463-4686), specializes in Tlingit and other Northwest Indian carvings and masks, whalebone, ivory, basketry, fossil ivory carvings, and jewelry from the Yup'ik and Iñupiat of western and northern Alaska. **Juneau Artists Gallery,** in the Senate Building at 175 S. Franklin St. (ℭ 907/586-9891; www.juneauartistsgallery. com), is staffed by a co-op of local artists and shows only the members' work: paintings, etchings, photography, jewelry, fabrics, ceramics, and other media. For gifts, try **Annie Kaill's** fine arts-and-crafts gallery at 244 Front St. (ℭ 907/586-2880). It's a little out of the cruise-ship shopping area and gets business from locals. **Ad Lib,** at 231 S. Franklin St. (ℭ 907/463-3031), also is reliable and oriented to authentic items made in Alaska. Many shops in downtown Juneau are very touristy; it's a good place to stock up on Alaska T-shirts and trinkets.

11 Icy Strait Point, Icy Strait & Hoonah

Icy Strait Point wasn't on the map a few years ago. The name was coined to describe a new purpose-built private dock to handle cruise-ship traffic near the Tlingit city of Hoonah, the largest Tlingit settlement in Alaska, with a population of nearly 1,000.

The concept is similar to what the cruise lines did in the Caribbean—with traditional ports (including Juneau) getting full, they created a new venue to get passengers off the ship and onto shore excursions.

Hoonah happens to be strategically located about 22 miles southeast of Glacier Bay National Park. And nature is the calling card here. We're talking prime whale-watching waters. And passengers aboard large ships may well be fortunate enough to see them on their journey. Those in small ships or whale-watching excursions will have an even better chance, since the small ships have the luxury of going places the bigger vessels can't, and their size and maneuverability make it possible for them to get closer to the whales.

Onshore around Hoonah is old-growth rainforest, and brown (grizzly) bear sightings are common. Bald eagles are frequently spotted overhead. Fishermen here go after halibut and five species of salmon.

Hoonah is an old blue-collar village, just now being "discovered," although the Huna Tlingit have resided here for thousands of years.

Development-wise, the Northwest Trading Company came to town opening a store in 1880. A mission and school were created shortly thereafter. The city got its first post office in 1901. Fire destroyed much of the city, including Tlingit artifacts, in 1944. The federal government led a rebuilding effort, and the city was incorporated in 1946.

The cruise dock, built by a Tlingit Indian corporation, opened in 2004 and is now being visited on a regular basis (albeit one shipload at a time) by lines including Royal Caribbean, Celebrity, Holland America, and Princess.

The dock was built to incorporate a historic cannery that dates to 1930—Hoonah was once one of the most productive salmon cannery towns in the state. Fishing and fish processing are still the mainstays of the economy in these parts, along with logging, and tourism is catching on. The other new and big attraction in Icy Strait Point is the world's longest ZipRide, an amusement park–like chance to zip down a mountain.

ICY STRAIT POINT

COMING ASHORE   Cruise passengers are tendered into the dock at the Icy Strait Point Cannery.

INFORMATION   There is an information booth (no phone) at the dock. If you're a hiker, here's the place to ask for directions to local beach and forest trails.

BEST CRUISE-LINE SHORE EXCURSIONS

ATV Expedition (2½ hr.; $137): Traverse the mountains of Chichagof Island in rugged fashion on a 4×4 expedition. You start high in the majestic mountains of Chichagof Island (after a drive by motorcoach through Hoonah). Your guide will provide a little area history, and following a brief orientation, you board your 4×4 Kawasaki Mule off-road vehicle. Ride along a trail, taking in the Alaska wilderness, rainforest, and tremendous views of Icy Strait.

Glacier Bay Flightseeing (2 hr.; $299): Depart Hoonah Airport on a fixed-wing plane and fly over Point Adolphus and Icy Strait, an important feeding ground for many marine mammals; Glacier Bay (note how land that once held glaciers is now deeply forested); and the awesome delights of Glacier Bay National Park, including the massive Brady Glacier.

Hoonah Sightseeing (2 hr.; $39 adults, $29 children): Tour the quaint Alaska village, the largest Tlingit settlement in the 49th state. Your guide will explain the village's history, including how the Huna Tlingits had to flee advancing glaciers. Your motorcoach will stop at an old cemetery and see a Tlingit Shaman gravesite. Modern Tlingit life will be detailed as well.

Tribal Dance Performance (1 hr.; $39 adults, $24 children): Dancers perform in full regalia at the Native Theater, telling the story of the Tlingit. Learn about the ancient significance of the Raven and the Eagle.

Remote Bush Exploration and Grizzly Bear Search (2½ hr.; $105): Explore the wilds of Chichagof Island in search of grizzlies. Your motorcoach will travel through Hoonah en route to the bush country of the Spasski River Valley. Learn about the local flora and fauna on a short hike along gravel and boardwalk-lined paths through a rainforest to viewing platforms overlooking the Spasski River. Keep your eyes out for bears, salmon, bald eagles, and more, though sightings, of course, are not guaranteed.

ZipRider (1 hr., $99): Ride on the world's longest zipline, 5,330 feet long with a 1,300-foot vertical drop. You travel at speeds of up to 60 miles per hour. The highest point is 300 feet above the ground. If you dare to look down you'll enjoy views of Port Fredrick, Icy Strait, and your cruise ship. This ride has you harnessed in a seat; no skill is required.

EXCURSIONS OFFERED BY LOCAL AGENCIES

The setup in Icy Strait Point is tightly controlled by the Hoonah Totem Native Corporation. Tours are offered only in advance, through the cruise line.

ON YOUR OWN: WITHIN WALKING DISTANCE

Icy Strait Point Cannery Beautifully restored and reopened in 2004, the historic cannery, located right where you get off the tender, was once one of the most productive salmon canneries in the state. Its halls are filled with family-owned shops (27 at last count) and a museum with a 1930s cannery display, as well as a cultural center. The original cookhouse is now open for family-style dining.

ON YOUR OWN: BEYOND THE PORT AREA

Hoonah, meaning "village by the cliff," is the largest Tlingit Indian village in Alaska, and it's located just about a mile from the pier. It's an unspoiled little town that sustains itself mostly on fishing and logging. The wilderness is so close that walking along the bay you are likely to see eagles flying overhead; you may even spot whales from the pier. The town has grocery and hardware stores catering to locals. The atmosphere is much different than in ports that are used to the tourist trade. Some visitors may like that; others may not. But this is a chance to catch a glimpse of real Alaska life.

SHOPPING

All the shops at the **Icy Strait Point Cannery** are owned by Alaskans, and you can find local crafts and clever tourist items on sale including the opportunity to have a message canned and shipped to friends back home. In town, **Creations,** 541 Garteeni Hwy. (© **907/945-3478**), carries all the materials and beading supplies a quilter could want.

12 Glacier Bay National Park Preserve

There are about 5,000 glaciers in Alaska, so what's all the fuss about Glacier Bay? Theories on its popularity abound. Some think it's the wildlife, which includes humpback

Glacier Bay National Park

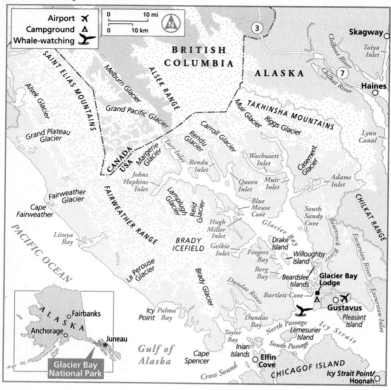

whales, bears, Dall sheep, seals, and more. Some think it's the history of the place, which was frozen behind a mile-wide wall of ice until about 1870. A mere 55 years later, it was designated as a national park, along with its 3.3 million surrounding acres. Those with an interest in geology and glaciology might argue that it's the receding ice faces at the ends of Glacier Bay's various inlets. Thought to be the fastest-moving glaciers in the world, they retreat at some 1½ inches a year. Whatever the reason, Glacier Bay has taken on an allure not achieved by other glacier areas.

The first white man to enter the vast (60-plus-mile) Glacier Bay inlet was naturalist **John Muir** in 1879. Just 100 years earlier, when Capt. James Cook and, later, George Vancouver sailed there, the mouth was still a wall of ice. Today all that ice has ebbed back, leaving behind a series of inlets and glaciers (**Margerie, Johns Hopkins, Muir,** and others) whose calving activity provides entertainment for hundreds of cruisers lining the rails as their ships sit, becalmed, for several hours. Watching massive slabs of ice break away and crash with a roar into the ice-strewn waters is one of our favorite experiences. It can take 200 years for ice that falls off the face of a glacier to reach that point.

Each ship that enters the bay takes aboard a park ranger. The ranger provides commentary over the ship's PA throughout the day about glaciers, wildlife, and the bay's history. On large ships, the ranger may also give a presentation in the show lounge about conservation; on small ships, he or she will often be on deck throughout the day, available for questions.

Glacier Bay is the world's largest protected marine sanctuary. The bay is so vast that the water contained within its boundaries would cover the state of Connecticut. The bay is a source of concern for environmentalists, who would like to see cruise ships banned from entering, or at least have their access severely curtailed. The ship operators, on the other hand, argue that no evidence shows that their vessels have any negative impact on the wildlife of the bay. They feel that they provide an excellent opportunity for the maximum number of people to enjoy the natural wonders of the park at one time, with the minimum of damage to the water's denizens.

There are numerous glaciers in the park. There are 16 major tidewater glaciers (those that go all the way to the water) and 30 valley or alpine glaciers (those that compress between two hills but don't extend all the way to the water). In Tarr Inlet, at the Alaska/Canada border, two notable glaciers meet—Margerie and Grand Pacific. Margerie, on the Alaskan side, is pristine white and very active, calving frequently; Grand Pacific, on the Canadian side of the line, is black, gritty, and not particularly active. The widely differing coloration of the two is caused by the terrain through which each glacier pushes its way to the sea. Margerie cuts through a relatively clean path, while Grand Pacific picks up rocks and dirt along the way. It makes for an interesting contrast for cruise-ship passengers in the inlet.

Visible from much of the bay (on a clear day) is the massive Mount Fairweather (elevation 15,320 ft.). Although Fairweather is taller than any mountain in the Lower 48, it ranks no higher than 19th among Alaska's peaks.

13 Haines

This pretty, laid-back port is an example of Alaska the way you probably thought it would be. It's a small, scenic town with wilderness at its doorstep and only two stop signs. If you are not on one of the few ships that regularly visit Haines (pop., 2,500), you can easily reach the port on a day excursion from **Skagway.** The two communities lie at the northern end of the Lynn Canal, just 17 miles apart by water (350 miles by driving). The ferry trip takes only about 35 minutes by fast ferry and is priced round-trip at $54 adults, $28 kids. It's well worth taking especially for those who have "done" Skagway before.

The thing that's immediately striking about Haines is its setting, one of the prettiest in Alaska. The village lies in the shadow of the Fairweather Mountain Range, about 80 or so miles north of Juneau and on the same line of latitude as the lower reaches of Norway. Framed by high hills, it is more protected from the elements than many other Inside Passage ports. Ketchikan, for instance, gets up to 200 inches of rain in a wet year, Haines a mere 60 inches. That's positively arid by some Southeast Alaska standards!

Haines was established in 1879 by Presbyterian missionary S. Hall Young and naturalist John Muir as a base for converting the Chilkoot and Chilkat Tlingit tribes to Christianity. They named the town for Mrs. F. E. Haines, secretary of the Presbyterian National Committee, who raised the funds for the exploration. The natives called it Da-Shu, the Tlingit word for "end of the trail." Traders knew the place as Chilkoot. The military, which came later and built a fort here in 1903, knew it as Fort Seward or Chilkoot Barracks. In 1897 and 1898, the town became one of the lesser-known access points (it was less popular than Skagway and Dyea) to a route to the Klondike; it was located at the head of what became known as the Jack Dalton Trail into Canada.

At about the same time, gold was discovered much closer to home—in Porcupine, just 36 miles away—and that strike drew even more prospectors to Haines. The gold quickly petered out, though, and Porcupine is no more.

The **old fort** still stands, although its survival was questionable at one point. After World War II, and after 42 years of service, it was decommissioned and the future of the place—and of Haines itself, to some extent—was in doubt. So much of the local economy had depended on the spending of the military personnel stationed there. A group of veterans once stationed at Chilkoot Barracks, however, would not let the fort die. In 1947, they bought the 85 buildings standing on 400 acres. They built a salmon smokehouse, a furniture-making plant, and other cooperative business ventures that they hoped would revive the place that held such a special place in their hearts. They agitated to have Haines included on the Alaska Marine Highway System. They built the Hotel Hälsingland, established art galleries, and funded Indian arts training programs for local youngsters.

The **Officers' Club Lounge** in the Hälsingland Hotel is a dandy place to stop for a libation. It features Alaskan and Yukon beers and a house special known as the Fort Seward Howitzer. The descendants of some of these modern-day pioneers still live in homes their fathers and grandfathers built on the fort grounds. One house on the grounds was recently sold to a Colorado couple who visited Haines on a cruise ship and decided they wanted to live here. Designated a National Historic Site by the U.S. government in 1972, **Fort William Seward** should be a must-see on your list. All lines invariably include a fort shore excursion in their brochure.

Haines is so small that it can be absorbed on foot. You can see almost everything in 1 to 2 hours of reasonably flat walking. Start at **Steve Sheldon's museum** about a quarter mile from the pier; turn west up Main Street (the only uphill part of the journey), with its beautiful views of the Chilkat Mountains. Next is the free **Hammer Museum**—dedicated to hammers. Haines' tallest building—all of four stories high—is a little farther on. Turn right onto Second Avenue and have a drink or a meal at the **Pioneer Bar & Bamboo Room Restaurant,** or visit the nearby **Old City Hall and Fire Station.** Turn left onto Union Street, past the **Lindholm House** (built in 1912), left onto Third Avenue, and right onto Dalton Street, named for Jack Dalton, a turn-of-the-century entrepreneur who helped put Haines on the map. A few blocks later, turn left onto Fifth Avenue and then left again onto Main Street toward the Lynn Canal. In no time at all, you're back at the ship.

The town's gold history, its military background, and its Native heritage draw travelers to Haines. So do the **eagles:** The area is a magnet for these magnificent creatures—a couple hundred are year-round residents. Unfortunately, cruise passengers are unable to experience the annual **Gathering of the Eagles,** which occurs in winter (usually Oct until mid-Feb) and which brings as many as 4,000 birds from all over the Pacific Northwest to the area in search of salmon, which can't be found anywhere else during these months. During this time, trees along a 5-mile stretch of the river (in an area known as the **Alaska Chilkat Bald Eagle Preserve**) are thick with these raptors—often a dozen or more sharing a limb. But even during the cruise season, you're likely to spot at least an eagle or two. We spotted eight in various swooping and tree-sitting poses on a bike ride out to Chilkoot Lake (about 10 miles from the cruise-ship pier) last May.

COMING ASHORE   Thanks to a newly expanded dock, you no longer have to tender from big ships into Haines. Small ships dock at the nearby Native American-owned

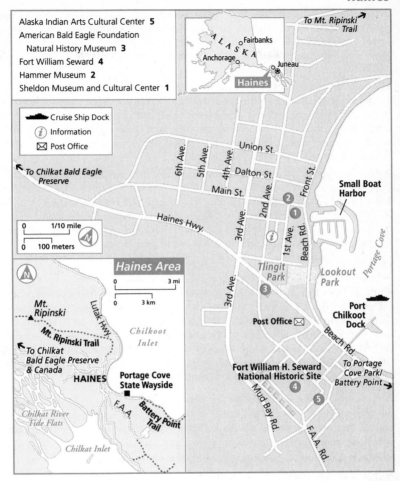

Alaska Indian Arts Cultural Center **5**
American Bald Eagle Foundation
    Natural History Museum **3**
Fort William Seward **4**
Hammer Museum **2**
Sheldon Museum and Cultural Center **1**

A L A S K A
Fairbanks
Anchorage
Juneau
Haines

To Mt. Ripinski Trail

🚢 Cruise Ship Dock
ⓘ Information
✉ Post Office

← To Chilkat Bald Eagle Preserve

6th Ave. 5th Ave. 4th Ave. 3rd Ave. 2nd Ave. 1st Ave. Beach Rd. Front St.

Union St.
Dalton St.
Main St.
Haines Hwy.

Small Boat Harbor

Portage Cove

ⓘ

Tlingit Park

Lookout Park

Port Chilkoot Dock

Post Office ✉

Beach Rd.

0 — 1/10 mile
0 — 100 meters

Haines Area

0 — 3 mi
0 — 3 km

Mt. Ripinski ▲
Mt. Ripinski Trail
← To Chilkat Bald Eagle Preserve & Canada
HAINES

Lutak Hwy.

Chilkoot Inlet

Portage Cove State Wayside

Fort William H. Seward National Historic Site

Mud Bay Rd.

To Portage Cove Park/ Battery Point →

Chilkat River Tide Flats

F.A.A.

Battery Point Trail

Chilkat Inlet

F.A.A. Rd.

ferry terminal, which also has a small shop selling souvenirs. Both docks are within walking distance of many of the town's main attractions.

INFORMATION   Pick up some walking-tour information on Haines at the **visitor center,** on Second Avenue (📞 **800/458-3579** or 907/766-2234). It's open in summer Monday through Friday from 8am to 7pm, Saturday from 9am to 5pm, and Sunday from 11am to 5pm. It's easy to explore the town on foot, or you can rent a bike at **Sockeye Cycle,** on Portage Street right up the street from the cruise-ship dock (📞 **907/ 766-2869;** www.cyclealaska.com); it's $12 for 2-hour rental, $25 for 4 hours, and $35 for the whole day.

BEST CRUISE-LINE SHORE EXCURSIONS

Best of Haines by Classic Motor Car (1 hr.; $64): Explore Haines in style in a 1930s or 1940s six-passenger automobile. The entertaining guides share the history of the area, and you'll get an insight into how Hainesians live.

Eagle Preserve Wildlife Adventure by Jet Boat (3½ hr.; $131 for adults, $69 for children 12 and under): A bus takes you to the world-famous Chilkat Bald Eagle Preserve, where you board small boats specially designed to traverse the narrows of the Chilkat River. Eagle spotting is the thing on this excursion, and you may also see bears, moose, and beavers.

Haines Wilderness Kayak Experience (4 hr.; $109 for adults, $79 for children 7–12): Located as it is at the top of the Inside Passage, Haines is an ideal place for kayaking. A short bus trip will take you to the launch site, and the goal as you glide in your kayak is to see wildlife—depending on your luck, this might include humpback whales, porpoises, seals, sea lions, sea otters, moose, brown bears, and, of course, Haines's famous bald eagles.

A Taste of Haines (2 hr.; $59): Sample some of the fresh products Haines has to offer on this intimate tour, headed by a local guide. You'll visit Dalton City, a gold-rush town created for the 1989 Disney film *White Fang,* tour Haines Brewing Company (with an annual production of only 300 barrels), and sample ales and stouts with the brewmeister. The tour also includes a visit to Dejon Delights to learn how the experts smoke halibut and salmon. Samples are provided, and there's time for shopping (see more in shopping below).

EXCURSIONS OFFERED BY LOCAL OPERATORS

Chilkat Guides, on Portage Street (© **907/766-2491;** www.raftalaska.com), offers a rafting trip twice a day during the summer down the Chilkat River to watch eagles. The rapids are pretty easy—there's a chance you may be asked to get out and push— and you'll see lots of eagles. The 4-hour trip includes a snack and costs $79 for adults, $62 for children. **Alaska Nature Tours** (© **907/766-2876;** www.kcd.com/aknature) offers a variety of escorted tours, including a 4-hour walking tour of the Chilkat Bald Eagle Preserve ($75 with lunch, $60 for kids 12 and under).

ON YOUR OWN: WITHIN WALKING DISTANCE

Alaska Indian Arts Cultural Center Located in the old fort hospital on the south side of the parade grounds, the center has a small gallery and a carvers' workshop where you may be able to see totem carving in progress.

On the south side of the parade grounds. Mon–Fri 9am–5pm and evenings when cruise ships are in town.

American Bald Eagle Foundation Natural History Museum This foundation celebrates Haines's location in the "Valley of the Eagles" with a huge diorama depicting more than a hundred eagles.

At Second Ave. and Haines Hwy. © **907/766-3094.** Admission $3 adults, $1 kids 8–12, free for kids under 8. Mon–Fri 9am–5pm and evenings when cruise ships are in town.

Fort William Seward The central feature of the town, rising right above the docks, Fort Seward was retired after World War II and redone by a group of returning veterans. It's not the kind of place one thinks of when envisioning a fort. It has no parapets, no walls, no nothing—just an open parade ground surrounded by large wood-frame former barracks and officers' quarters that have today been converted into private homes, the Hälsingland Hotel, a gallery and studio, and the Alaska Indian Arts Cultural Center (see above). In the center of the sloping parade ground, you'll find a replica of a Tlingit tribal house. And recently added thanks to a local collector was a harpoon gun on the parade grounds which is now fired on special town occasions (it looks like a cannon).

The area is just inland from the cruise-ship dock. Open all day.

Hammer Museum   You want quirky? Check out this new museum, devoted entirely to the hammer. The collection is that of longshoreman Dave Pahl, who amassed his collection while building his homestead over a span of some 20 years. The prize in the collection is an 800-year-old Tlingit war hammer, but hammer lovers will find some 1,400 instruments from all over the world.

108 Main St. ✆ 907/766-2374. Admission $3, free for children 12 and under. Mon–Fri 10am–5pm.

The Sheldon Museum and Cultural Center   Not to be confused with the Sheldon Jackson Museum in Sitka, this place was established by a local man, Steve Sheldon. Small by some museum standards, it nevertheless has a wonderful collection of Hainesiana: Tlingit artifacts, gold-rush-era weaponry, military memorabilia, and so on.

Corner of Main and Front sts. ✆ 907/766-2366. Admission $3, free for children under 12. Summer Mon–Fri 11am–6pm, Sat–Sun 2–6pm.

ON YOUR OWN: BEYOND THE PORT AREA

Chilkat Bald Eagle Preserve   Haines may be the best place in the world to see bald eagles. And this 48,000-acre park along the Chilkat River is Ground Zero for the species. From around mid-October to December, some 3,000 eagles reside here. But even during cruise season, you are likely to glimpse a few—at least a couple hundred actually live here year-round. The best viewing sights are on the Haines Highway, between miles 18 and 21. The preserve is managed by the Alaska State Parks.

Contact the local ranger's office at ✆ 907/766-2292, or find updated reports at www.alaskastateparks.org.

Shopping

Haines is not a big shopping destination, and we like it that way. But shoppers will find a few enticements. The **Dejon Delights Smokery** (✆ 907/766-2505), on Portage Street near Fort Seward, sells freshly smoked wild Alaska salmon and halibut, and offers free samples so you know what you're buying. They'll ship your purchases if you don't want to carry them. Stop by the nearby outdoor stand **The Local Catch** on Portage Street for a cup of coffee or espresso and sweets (✆ 907/766-3557). On Portage Street just up from the cruise-ship pier, **The Wild Iris** (✆ 907/766-2300) is an art shop selling fine jewelry, including local gold, Eskimo art, watercolors, and silkscreen prints.

14 Skagway

No port in Alaska is more historically significant than this small town at the northern end of the picturesque Lynn Canal. In the late 19th century, a steady stream of prospectors began the long trek into Canada's Yukon Territory, seeking the vast quantities of Klondike gold that had been reported in Rabbit Creek (later renamed Bonanza Creek). Not many of them realized the unspeakable hardships they'd have to endure before they could get close to the stuff. They first had to negotiate either the **White Pass** or the **Chilkoot Pass** through the coastal mountain range to the Canadian border. To do so, they had to hike 20 miles, climbing nearly 3,000 feet in the process, and, by order of Canada's North West Mounted Police, they had to have at least a year's supply of provisions with them before they could enter the country.

Numbed by temperatures that fell at times into the –50s (–40s Celsius), and often blinded by driving snow or stinging hail (they were, after all, hiking through the mountain passes that gave Skagway its name—in Tlingit, *Skagua* means "home of the North Wind"), they plodded upward. They ferried part of their supplies up part of the way, stashing them, and would return to Skagway to repeat the process with another load, always inching their way closer to the summit. The process took as many as 20 trips for some, and often enough, their stashes were stolen by unscrupulous rivals or opportunistic locals. Prospectors who thought themselves lucky enough to be able to afford horses or mules found their pack animals to be less than sound of limb. One stretch of the trail through the White Pass (the more popular of the two routes through the mountains) is called **Dead Horse Gulch.**

Arduous as it was, that first leg was just the beginning. From the Canadian border, their golden goal lay a long and dangerous water journey away, part of the way by lake (and, thus, relatively easy), but most of it down the mighty Yukon River and decidedly perilous.

The gold rush brought to Skagway a way of life as violent and as lawless as any to be found in the frontier West. The Mounties (the law in Canada) had no jurisdiction in Skagway. In fact, there was no law whatsoever in Skagway. Peace depended entirely on the consciences of the inhabitants—saloonkeepers, gamblers, prostitutes, and desperadoes of every stripe.

The most notorious of the Skagway bad men was Jefferson Randolph "Soapy" Smith, an accomplished con man. He earned his nickname in Denver, Colorado, by persuading large numbers of gullible people to buy bars of cheap soap for $1 in the belief that some of the bars were wrapped in larger-denomination bills. They weren't, of course, but the scam made Smith a lot of money. In Skagway he and his gang engaged in all kinds of nastiness, charging local businesses large fees for "protection," exacting exorbitant sums to "store" prospectors' gear (and then selling the equipment to others), and setting up a telegraph station and charging prospectors to send messages home (though the telegraph wire went no farther than the next room).

The gold-rush days of Skagway had their heroes as well. One of them, city surveyor Frank Reid, put an end to Soapy's reign; he shot Smith dead and was himself mortally wounded in the gunfight. In his honor, the local citizenry erected an impressive granite monument over his grave in the Gold Rush Cemetery; Smith's marker, on the other hand, is very simple, and his remains aren't even underneath it (they're 3 ft. to the left, outside consecrated ground). Perversely, though, it is the villain Smith whose life is commemorated each July 8, with songs and entertainment.

Unlike many other Alaska frontier towns, Skagway has been spared the ravages of major fires and earthquakes. Some of the original buildings still stand, protected by the National Park Service. The Klondike Gold Rush National Historic District contains some striking examples of these buildings. Other little touches of history are preserved around town, such as the huge watch painted on the mountainside above town—it was an early billboard for the long-gone Herman Kirmse's watch-repair shop. Also remaining from the old days is the White Pass and Yukon Route narrow-gauge railroad, opened in 1900 to carry late stampeders in and gold out. A ride on the train is a must for visitors. The round-trip to the summit of the pass, following a route carved out of the side of the mountain by an American/Canadian engineering team backed by British money, takes 3 hours from a departure site conveniently located a short walk (or an even shorter shuttle bus ride) from the cruise-ship piers.

ATTRACTIONS ●
The Arctic Brotherhood
  Hall **8**
Case-Mulvihill House
  & Nye House **3**
Eagles Hall and
  Days of '98 Show **5**
Gault House **4**
Gold Rush Cemetery **2**
Historic Moore
  Homestead **7**
Jefferson Smith's Parlor **11**
Klondike Gold Dredge **1**
Mollie Walsh Park **6**
The Red Onion Saloon **10**

Skagway City Hall **8**
Skagway Museum
  & Archives **8**
White Pass and Yukon
  Route Railway **12**

← To Dyea &
  Chilkoot Trail

DINING ◆
Red Onion Saloon **10**
Skagway Brewing
  Company **9**

Cruise Ship Dock
ⓘ Information
⊠ Post Office

Having a sweet little historic town is nice for Skagway's 860 or so year-round residents, of course, but by itself, history doesn't pay the bills. So, though Skagway is trying to hang on to its gold-rush heritage, it's also trying to make money off it. New businesses, including restaurants (a Starbucks!) and jewelry stores, are sprouting up as well, many of which have gold-rush connotations only in the sense that they've opened to cash in on visitor's gold.

On a recent visit, we were actually given a verbal invite (come-on) by a clerk outside one of those fancy jewelry stores that have followed cruise passengers here from the Caribbean. We know he was only doing his job, but really, you used to be able to window-shop in Skagway in peace without having to worry about being lured in. Little Switzerland has left town, closing its two Skagway venues. No net loss, though: Two other jewelry outlets are earmarked to move in.

For a respite from shopping, check out the $3 beer specials at the **1898 Red Onion Saloon** (at Broadway and 2nd Ave.), or, down Broadway, test the product at the **Skagway Brewing Company,** where you can also check your e-mail.

COMING ASHORE   Most ships dock at the cruise pier, at the foot of Broadway, but if many ships are in town, two other docks are available; the walk from those is no longer than 10 minutes, and shuttles are available. From the closest point, it's about a 5-minute walk from the pier across the train tracks to downtown, but shuttle buses are also offered. The only street you really need to know about is Broadway, which runs through the center of town and off which everything branches.

After you've docked, take a few minutes to study the painting of ships' and captains' names and dates that blankets the 400-foot-high cliffs alongside the pier. It's not graffiti; it is a genuine history of the development of the cruise industry in Skagway over the last 4 decades or more. Each of the paintings, mostly of shipline logos, were done by members of the crews of visiting ships. Some of the pictures are placed hundreds of feet up the cliffs. Local authorities have put a stop to it. For several years, it's been a case of "paint a rock, go to jail" and the rock face, which used to be so colorful, is beginning to fade without new creations. Occasionally, some enterprising crew members will attempt to revive the tradition, but they are quickly shepherded away from the cliff and warned against it.

INFORMATION   Walking maps are available at the **Skagway Visitor Information Center** (📞 **907/983-2854**), at the Arctic Brotherhood Hall, 245 Broadway, between 2nd and 3rd avenues. Located in the restored railroad depot, the **National Park Service Visitor Center,** 2nd Avenue and Broadway (P.O. Box 517, Skagway, AK 99840; 📞 **907/983-2921;** www.nps.gov/klgo), is the focal point for activities in Skagway. Rangers answer questions, give lectures, and show films; five times a day, they lead an excellent walking tour. The building houses a small museum that lays the groundwork for the rest of what you'll see. The park service's programs are free. The visitor center is open May through September daily from 8am to 6pm, the rest of the year Monday through Friday from 8am to 5pm.

BEST CRUISE-LINE SHORE EXCURSIONS

Eagle Preserve Float Adventure (6½ hr.; $179 for adults, $153 for children 7–12): Combines a fjord cruise (35 min. to Haines) with a leisurely raft float (no white-water rapids here) through the Chilkat Bald Eagle Preserve. Essential equipment (boots and life jackets, rain poncho if needed) is provided.

Horseback Riding (3½ hr; $145): Giddy-up on horseback to see the remnants of Dyea, once a booming gold-rush town, and explore the scenic Dyea Valley. Participants must, of course, be able to mount a horse and maintain balance in a saddle.

Skagway by Streetcar (2 hr.; $44 adults, $22 children under 12): This is as much performance art as historical tour. Guides in period costume relate tales of the boomtown days as you tour the sights both in and outside of town aboard vintage 1930s Kenworth, Dodge, and White sightseeing limousines. Though theatrical, it's all done in a homey style, as if you're getting a tour from your cousin Martha.

White Pass & Yukon Route Railway (3 hr.; $98 for adults, $49 for children 3-12): The train makes two round-trips a day, three on Thursday. The sturdy engines and vintage parlor cars of this famous narrow-gauge railway take you from the dock past waterfalls and parts of the famous Trail of '98, including Dead Horse Gulch to the White Pass Summit, the boundary between Canada and the United States. Don't take this trip on an overcast day—you won't see anything. If you have a clear day, though, you'll be able to see all the way to the harbor; you might spot a marmot fleeing the train's racket. Or take the train to Fraser, B.C. (in Canada) and get on mountain bikes for the ride back (4 hr.; $150 for adults, $75 for children 3–12). All of the trains are wheelchair accessible.

Yukon Jeep Adventure (6 hr.; $129 adults, $86 children 12 and under): Retrace the steps of the gold miners along the Trail of '98 from the comfort of a four-wheel-drive Jeep Wrangler. Interactive headphones permit drivers in the convoy to keep in touch with guides as they describe the events of '98. Dead Horse Gulch, Tormented Valley, Pitchfork Falls—the convoy passes all of the historic gold rush sights.

EXCURSIONS OFFERED BY LOCAL AGENCIES

Independent tours, representing a number of operators, are sold at a tour center at 7th Avenue and Broadway. Tours are priced in the $40 to $50 range for a 2½-hour city and White Pass Summit tour by van. **Chilkat Cruises** (© **888/766-2103;** www.chilkatcruises.com) offers a fast ferry that takes you to Haines in about 35 minutes. They run several trips a day, costing $30 one-way for adults, half-price for kids 3 to 12. Gold mining never actually happened in Skagway—it was only a transit point—but the town now gets more gold-rush tourists than anywhere else. So **Klondike Gold Dredge Tours,** Mile 1.7, Klondike Highway (© **907/983-3175;** www.klondikegold dredge.com), created an opportunity for visitors to pan for gold. Costumed guides spice up the tour with humor. The tours are $39 for adults, $20 for kids 11 and under (add $5 for 1½ miles of transportation from the cruise-ship pier in Skagway).

ON YOUR OWN: WITHIN WALKING DISTANCE

The Case-Mulvihill House, the Gault House, and the Nye House   All within a block of one another, these three buildings are striking examples of gold-rush-era Skagway architecture. You can view these three, from the street only, as part of a guided walking tour conducted by officers of the National Park Service.

The Case-Mulvihill House and the Nye House are on Alaska St., between 7th and 8th aves. The Gault House is on Alaska St., between 5th and 6th aves.

Eagles Hall and Days of '98 Show   This is the venue for Skagway's long-running (since 1927) *Days of '98* show, a live melodrama of the Gay '90s featuring dancing girls and ragtime music. Follow the events leading up to the historic shootout that led to the end of Smith's crime reign. Daytime performances are offered at 10:30am and 2:30pm, timed so cruise passengers can attend. (Mon there is only a 2:30pm show, and Sat there is only a nighttime show.)

Southeast corner of 6th Ave. and Broadway. © 907/983-2545. Daytime performances $16, kids age 15 and under $8.

Historic Moore Homestead   The Moore Cabin was built in 1887 as the home of Capt. William Moore, the founder of Skagway. The cabin was restored recently by the National Park Service.

5th Ave. and Spring St. Free tours offered 10am–5pm during the summer.

Jefferson Smith's Parlor   Also known as Soapy's Parlor, Jefferson Smith's Parlor was a saloon and gambling joint operated by the notorious bandit in the late 1890s. The building, which tourists can inspect only from the outside, has been relocated twice over the decades but looks pretty much as it did at the time of Smith's death.

2nd Ave., just off Broadway.

Red Onion Saloon   Located near the Arctic Brotherhood Hall, whose eye-catching facade is constructed of thousands of pieces of driftwood, the Red Onion was originally a dance hall and honky-tonk bar (ca. 1898) with the obligatory bordello upstairs.

The bartenders still serve drinks over the same mahogany counter as their turn-of-the-century predecessors did. The waitresses wear dance-hall outfits, and there's often live entertainment. The establishment bears a striking resemblance to Juneau's more famous Red Dog Saloon; it's just as noisy and just as much fun.

205 Broadway, at the corner of 2nd Ave. ℂ 907/983-2222. Summer daily 11am–11pm.

Skagway City Hall　This is not, strictly speaking, a tourist site, but as the town's only stone building, it's worth a peek.

Spring St. and 7th Ave.

Skagway Museum & Archives　In the historic McCabe College building (built 1899–1900), this museum offers a look at Skagway's history through artifacts, photographs, and historical records. Items on display include a Tlingit canoe and Bering Sea kayaks, as well as a collection of gold-rush supplies and tools, and Native Alaskan items including baskets and beadwork.

7th and Spring sts. ℂ 907/983-2420. Admission $2 adults, $1 students, free for children 12 and under. Summer Mon–Fri 9am–5pm; Sat 10am-5pm; Sun 10am–4pm.

ON YOUR OWN: BEYOND THE PORT AREA

The Gold Rush Cemetery　This is the permanent resting place of Messrs. Smith and Reid. The cemetery is small and lies a short walk from the scenic Reid Falls, named after the heroic one-time surveyor. Aside from Reid's impressive monument, most of the headstones at the cemetery are whitewashed wood and are replaced by the park service when they get too worn. You can get a good look at it from the White Pass & Yukon Rail carriages.

About 1½ miles away from the center of downtown, up State St. (walkable if you have the time and inclination).

SHOPPING

The shops in Skagway are pretty touristy, with a lot of the items made outside of Alaska (and most outside the country). But you can find high-end crafts, including hand-carved Tlingit masks and nice silver jewelry, at **Inside Passage Arts,** at 340 7th Ave. (ℂ **907/983-2585**). **Skagway Artworks,** 555 Broadway (ℂ **907/983-3443**), also features regionally made art, jewelry, and crafts. The **Train Shoppe** (ℂ **800/343-7373**), in the White Pass and Yukon Route Depot (on 2nd Ave.), offers memorabilia for train buffs.

9

Ports & Wilderness Areas along the Gulf Route

Remember what we said back in chapter 2: Going on a Gulf cruise does not mean that you miss out on the ports and natural areas of the Inside Passage. It just means that, whereas Inside Passage cruise itineraries typically begin and end in Vancouver or, more recently, Seattle, the Gulf routing is one-way—from Vancouver to Whittier/Seward (ports for Anchorage) or the reverse—and may sail an itinerary that includes Inside Passage stops and attractions like Ketchikan, Juneau, Skagway, and Glacier Bay, plus Gulf ports and attractions like Hubbard Glacier, College Fjord, and Seward.

See chapter 4 for information on shore excursions and a few tips on debarkation, what to bring along with you while ashore, and little matters such as not missing the boat.

1 Petersburg

Visiting this perfect little fishing town on Mitkof Island in the Frederick Sound is like visiting a slice of Norway. In fact, it was founded in 1890 by Norwegian immigrant Peter Buschmann, who came here to found a cannery and killed himself after living here for only 4 years. But that inauspicious history should not hinder your impression. This is "Alaska's Little Norway," and it's lovely.

Petersburg, population 3,300, is the perfect little small town, with an appealing quirkiness—there are so many docks, boardwalks, and wooden walkways that the town almost feels like it's floating on the water. Big cruise ships can't enter the narrow harbor, so cruise passengers who do visit come on small, laid-back ships rather than in big crowds, and that's fine with everyone concerned.

Nordic Drive has businesses catering to its residents, including family-owned grocery and hardware stores. Given the number of blond locals and the neat white clapboard houses decorated with flower boxes, you really might think you're in a fishing village in Scandinavia.

The town is surrounded by water and rainforest. There are wonderful trails for hiking and biking. And on the water, humpback whales frolic—sightings are frequent. Nearby LeConte Glacier is a prime place to visit, and the fishing here is terrific.

In fact, the town's economy is based on fishing for salmon and halibut (note the big commercial fishing fleet) and government work—the Stikine Ranger District of the Tongass National Forest is headquartered here.

Cruise lines usually include a complimentary performance for their passengers of traditional Norwegian folk dances by a costumed local troupe, the Leikarring Dancers, either shipboard or at the Sons of Norway Hall.

COMING ASHORE   The small cruise ships that visit here use the small, welcoming ferry terminal (℗ **907/772-3855**), with a pier from which to watch the boats and marine animals. It's about a mile to the town center.

INFORMATION   The Petersburg Chamber of Commerce **Visitor Information Center,** at the corner of 1st and Fram streets (℗ **907/772-4636;** www.petersburg. org), offers guidance on outdoor activities and distributes trail guides and natural history publications. The center is open in summer Monday through Saturday from 9am to 5pm, Sunday from noon to 4pm; winter Monday through Friday from 10am to 2pm.

BEST CRUISE-LINE SHORE EXCURSIONS

Mitkof Island Tour & Rainforest Experience (2½ hr.; $37): Meet a local guide and learn about life on the edge of North America's largest rainforest. After driving until the road ends, you stroll through old-growth trees, taking in the local flora and fauna. It's an easy walk on a boardwalk past forest, bogs, and a saltwater estuary.

LeConte Glacier Jet Boat (4 hr.; $190): Enjoy an exhilarating trip aboard an 18-passenger, twin-engine vessel that will take you at 30 miles per hour past icebergs to the glacier base. LeConte is the southernmost saltwater terminating glacier in North America.

EXCURSIONS OFFERED BY LOCAL AGENCIES

The full-service **Viking Travel** agency, corner of Nordic Drive and Sing Lee Alley (℗ **800/327-2571** or 907/772-3818; www.alaskaferry.com), specializes in booking local guides for tours, kayaks, whale-watching, flights, fishing charters, and other activities. **Alaska Sea Adventures** (℗ **888/772-8588** or 907/772-4700; www.yacht alaska.com) offers a 4½-hour LeConte Glacier tour leaving mornings and afternoons, for $140 per person (two-person min).

ON YOUR OWN: WITHIN WALKING DISTANCE

Birch Street   This charming little one-lane, one-dock stretch follows the Hammer Slough, the tidal mouth of the creek that runs through town. On the pilings are old, weathered houses that hang over the placid channel. Many have one door opening to the road and another for the water.

Clausen Memorial Museum   Here's the place to learn about Petersburg and its history, although it's mostly geared toward locals. Exhibits include obsolete fishing gear, rugged old nautical equipment, and a model fish trap, outlawed in 1959 when Alaska became a state.

2nd and Fram sts. ℗ 907/772-3598. www.clausenmuseum.alaska.net. Admission $3, free for children 12 and under. Summer Mon–Sat 10am–5pm; call for winter hours.

Eagle's Roost Park   Past the commercial fishing activity of the harborfront, Eagle's Roost Park has a grassy area where you can sit and relax, and a stairway that leads down to the water. At low tide, an interesting but rugged beach walk starts here. Look up in the treetops and you're almost guaranteed to see eagles, which congregate for the fish waste from the nearby cannery.

Nordic Drive.

Sons of Norway Hall   A giant model of a Viking ship used in the Little Norway Festival in May is often parked outside this national historic site, which dates to 1912.

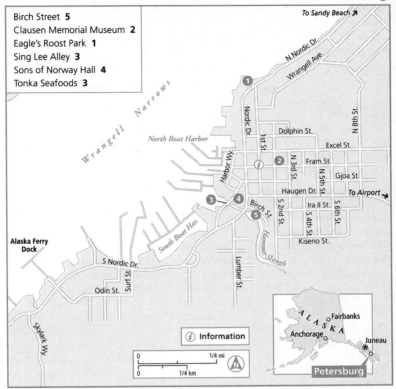

Birch Street **5**
Clausen Memorial Museum **2**
Eagle's Roost Park **1**
Sing Lee Alley **3**
Sons of Norway Hall **4**
Tonka Seafoods **3**

To Sandy Beach

Wrangell Narrows

North Boat Harbor

N Nordic Dr.
Wrangell Ave.
Nordic Dr.
1st St.
N 8th St.
Dolphin St.
Excel St.
N 3rd St.
Fram St.
N 5th St.
Gjoa St.
Haugen Dr.
To Airport
Harbor Wy.
Birch St.
S 2nd St.
Ira II St.
S 6th St.
S 4th St.
Kiseno St.
Hammer Slough
Lumber St.

Alaska Ferry Dock
S Nordic Dr.
Surf St.
Odin St.
South Boat Har.
Skylark Wy.

(i) **Information**

0 — 1/4 mi
0 — 1/4 km

ALASKA
Fairbanks
Anchorage
Juneau
Petersburg

Though you can't go inside, the model ship still makes for a nice photo op. On the pilings next door, the **Fishermen's Memorial Park** is a memorial to Petersburg mariners lost at sea and includes a bronze statue of Bojer Wikan, a fisherman and life-long resident.

23 Indian St., near Sing Lee Alley, on the wooden dock.

Tonka Seafoods   This fish-processing plant has a shop and mail-order operation; they will process your sport-caught fish, too. If you're interested in learning more about the smoking and canning processes, you can take a 1-hour tour in the summer for $15. You can visit the retail shop for free, but you'll probably end up spending some cash for some tins or smoked slabs of salmon.

22 Sing Lee Alley. (C) **888/560-3662** or 907/772-3662. www.tonkaseafoods.com. Tour: $15. Tours offered in summer Mon–Sat at 1:30pm (if there's a crowd the tour is repeated at 3:30pm).

ON YOUR OWN: BEYOND THE PORT AREA
Sandy Beach   Three miles southeast of town on Sandy Beach Road, this beach does not offer fine sand (it's more like fine gravel), nor can you swim in the frigid water. But it's still a pretty spot facing Frederick Sound, and at low tide you can see the outlines of ancient fish traps, dating back some 2,000 years. There are also some petroglyphs

on nearby rocks. Finding the traps and petroglyphs isn't easy—it's best if you can get someone to lead you, perhaps by joining the occasional Forest Service walks (information at the Visitor Information Center; see above). If you go at high tide, you can still beachcomb and may spot a Great Blue Heron or two.

SHOPPING

Sing Lee Alley boasts some nice little shops—none of them of the chain variety. You can find a good collection of books on natural history and local culture at **Sing Lee Alley Books,** 11 Sing Lee Alley (© **907/772-4440**); handmade Norwegian knit souvenirs and arts and crafts supplies at **Cubby Hole,** 14 Sing Lee Alley (© **907/772-2717**); quilt table runners and wall hangings at **WildCat Quilts,** 14 Sing Lee Alley (© 907/772-4848); and canned smoked salmon and smoked halibut, and more fishy products at **Tonka Seafoods,** 22 Sing Lee Alley (© **888/560-3662** or 907/772-3662).

2 Valdez

Until one miserable, overcast day in 1989, probably not many people could have located Valdez (pronounced Val-*deez*) on a map. The town, where tankers come to fill with oil from the Trans-Alaska Pipeline, seldom appeared on tourist agendas, even though its interesting history includes both gold-rush action and a devastating earthquake in 1964 (registering 9.2. on the Richter scale). Then, with a grinding and gurgling, the supertanker *Exxon Valdez* grounded on Bligh Rock just off the harbor and disgorged 11 million gallons of crude oil into the hitherto pristine waters of Prince William Sound. Suddenly, the eyes of the world were on little Valdez. Newspapers carried stories and TV news showed footage, invariably illustrated with a map insert, and suddenly everybody knew where Valdez was.

Nowadays, you can take a boat tour into the Sound without seeing much evidence of the oil spill. A town's tourism image could of course be seriously damaged by a catastrophic event like the *Exxon Valdez* grounding. But since Valdez didn't have much of a tourism image before, it didn't have much to lose.

Today, Valdez is a small town driven by industry. Visitors can tour two small museums and take a hike or a river float. The town has made major strides in improving its appearance, especially on the waterfront, but is still not exactly a charming place. Nevertheless, it does have the benefit of easy access to the Sound and the recreation, wildlife, and views the waterway affords.

COMING ASHORE Cruise ships generally dock at a commercial facility a couple of miles from the town center. Shuttle buses transport visitors to the information center in town.

INFORMATION The Valdez Convention and Visitors Bureau maintains a **Visitor Information Center** at 200 Fairbanks Dr., a block off Egan Drive (P.O. Box 1603), Valdez, AK 99686 (© **907/835-4636;** www.valdezalaska.org). Pick up the free town map and useful *Vacation Planner*. They're open in summer daily 8am to 7pm and winter Monday through Friday 8am to 5pm.

BEST CRUISE-LINE SHORE EXCURSIONS

Canyon Rafting (2 hr; $70): Take an exhilarating rafting trip in Keystone Canyon. There are thrills on the 4½-mile, Class III ride (although for the most part it's mild). Views include sheer canyon walls and waterfalls.

Valdez Sportfishing (4 hrs, $230): It might sound odd given the famous oil spill, but Valdez is a wonderful fishing destination, especially for coho salmon in midsummer. This excursion is designed for beginners and experienced fishermen alike—equipment, tackle, and bait is provided. You need to buy a $10 fishing license on the boat (cash only).

EXCURSIONS OFFERED BY LOCAL AGENCIES

For most visitors, a daylong ride on a tour boat into the Sound is likely to be the most memorable part of a visit to Valdez. The main tour boat company in town is **Stan Stephens Glacier and Wildlife Cruises** (© 866/867-1297 or 907/835-4731; www.stan stephenscruises.com). After passing through the long fjord of Port Valdez, boats enter an ice-choked bay in front of **Columbia Glacier** on a 6-hour tour that often encounters birds, seals, sea otters, and sea lions, and sometimes whales, for $95 adults. **Pangaea Adventures** (© 800/660-9637 or 907/835-8442; www.alaskasummer.com) offers guided sea kayaking from Valdez. **Keystone Raft and Kayak Adventures** (© 907/ 835-2606; www.alaskawhitewater.com) takes five trips a day 4½ miles down the amazing Keystone Canyon, a virtual corridor of rock with a floor of frothing water, past the crashing tumult of the 900-foot Bridal Veil Falls. The white water is rated Class III, meaning it is not too wild for most people. They charge $40 per person.

ON YOUR OWN: WITHIN WALKING DISTANCE

The Valdez Museum and Historical Archive   The museum's primary exhibit is a chronological walk through the area's history from explorers' visits through the oil spill. Objects and photographs show a pride in Valdez as a home town. An annex near the ferry dock (about 4 blocks away) is less polished, but shouldn't be missed—it contains the "Remembering Old Valdez" exhibit, a ½₀-scale model of how Valdez looked at its old site, before the 1964 earthquake forced the town to move. A film puts it in context. The annex is at 436 S. Hazelet Ave. Admission covers both buildings.

217 Egan Dr. © 907/835-2764. www.valdezmuseum.org. $5 adults, $4.50 over age 65, $4 ages 14–17, free for children under 14. Memorial Day to Labor Day both buildings daily 9am–6pm.

ON YOUR OWN: BEYOND THE PORT AREA

Dock Point Hike   This easy hike is a pleasant forest and shore walk, starting at the east side of the small boat harbor (within walking distance of downtown) at the end of North Harbor Drive. You'll find berries along the way in season.

The Solomon Gulch Hatchery   When the pink salmon return from late June to early August, they swarm on the hatchery in a blizzard of fish. The hatchery releases more than 200 million pinks and 2 million silvers (or coho) each year. Seals and birds come in to feed, and you can stand on shore and watch (and smell) the spectacle. Popular tours at the hatchery were suspended by construction through 2007, but managers expected to open to the public again in 2008. Call or ask at the visitor center to learn the current status.

On Dayville Rd. on the way to the tanker terminal. © 907/835-1329.

Maxine & Jesse Whitney Museum   Located at the airport, this museum, operated by Prince William Sound Community College, contains a large collection of Alaska Native arts and crafts and animal mounts accumulated by a couple over 50 years.

303 Airport Rd. © 907/834-1614. www.pwscc.edu. $5. Open May to mid-September daily from 9am–6pm.

SHOPPING

Downtown are a few shops selling T-shirts, jewelry and other souvenirs. **Harbor Landing Gifts,** 100 Harbor Court, near the Small Boat Harbor (© **907/835-2331**) claims to be the town's biggest.

3 Hubbard Glacier

Said to be Alaska's longest cruise-ship-accessible ice face—it's about 6 miles across—Hubbard lies at the northern end of **Yakutat Bay.** The glacier has a rather odd claim to fame: It is one of the fastest moving in Alaska. So fast and far did it move about a dozen years ago that it quickly created a wall across the mouth of **Russell Fjord,** one of the inlets lining Yakutat Bay. That turned the fjord into a lake and trapped hundreds of migratory marine creatures inside. Scientists still can't tell us why Hubbard chose to act the way it did or why it receded to its original position several months later, reopening Russell Fjord.

Cruise ships in Yakutat Bay get spectacular views of the glacier, which, because of the riptides and currents, is always in motion, calving into the ocean and producing lots of white thunder. It should be noted, however, that only one ship can get close to the glacier at a time, and if another ship is hogging the space, your ship may have to wait or may not get close at all.

There is one footnote to the Yakutat Bay cruise experience: Some Alaska residents a few years ago tried to make visitors pay for the privilege of viewing the glacier. Some of the **villagers of Yakutat,** at the mouth of the bay, tried to impose a $1.50 head tax on all ship passengers cruising past to see Hubbard Glacier—even though ships never call at Yakutat. Ultimately, the ship operators and the villagers reached a compromise. Instead of paying a tax on passengers carried into the bay, the lines now buy fish and other area products for use in the dining room, thereby enriching the locals without having to add to the cost of a cruise berth.

4 Prince William Sound

Located at the northern end of the underside of the Kenai Peninsula, this is truly one of Alaska's most appealing wilderness areas, though it suffered mightily following the *Exxon Valdez* oil spill in 1989. The area has recovered nicely from the ravages of that infamous spill, and today visitors are absolutely guaranteed wildlife—whales, harbor seals, eagles, sea lions, sea otters, puffins, and more.

If your cruise doesn't spend time on the sound, day cruises are available out of Whittier and Seward. One company, **Phillips' Cruises and Tours,** 519 W. 4th Ave., Suite 100, Anchorage, AK 99501 (© **800/544-0529** or 907/276-8023; www.26 glaciers.com), markets what it calls a "26 Glaciers Cruise." All in 1 day! That tells you just about as much as you need to know about the scenic beauty of the sound. The cruise—$129 per adult and $79 per child—is well worth taking.

Another operator, **Major Marine,** 411 W. 4th Ave., Anchorage (© **800/764-7300** or 907/274-7300; www.majormarine.com), offers a slightly more modest cruise on the Sound. It features a *mere* 10 glaciers. The 5-hour cruise costs $99 for adults and $49 for kids 11 and under. Food is extra—$15 for a salmon and prime rib buffet.

Perhaps the most spectacular of the sound's ice faces is **Columbia Glacier,** whose surface spreads over more than 400 square miles and whose tidewater frontage is more than 5 miles across. Columbia is receding faster than most of its Alaska counterparts.

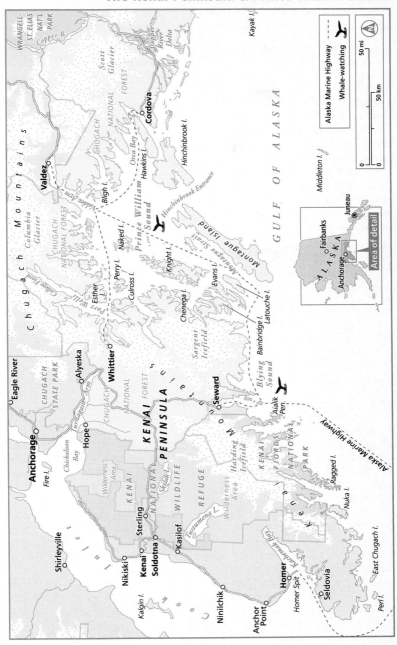

Scientists reckon it will retreat more than 20 miles in the next 20 to 50 years, leaving behind nothing but another deep fjord—just what Prince William Sound needs.

5 College Fjord

College Fjord is in the northern sector of Prince William Sound, roughly midway between Whittier and Valdez. It's not one of the more spectacular Alaska glacier areas, being very much overshadowed by Glacier Bay, Yakutat Bay (for Hubbard Glacier), and others, but it's scenic enough to merit a place on a lot of cruise itineraries, mostly for **Harvard Glacier,** which sits at its head. On a visit in 2005, Fran got within 1,000 feet of the glacier on the *Carnival Spirit,* and it was calving every few minutes. Without thinking what this may mean in terms of global warming, it was an unforgettable sight to behold.

The fjord was named in 1898 by an expedition team that opted to give the glaciers lining College Fjord and their neighbor, Harriman Glacier, the names of Ivy League and other prominent Eastern universities—hence, Harvard, Vassar, Williams, Yale, and so on.

6 Seward

Seward is the main northern embarkation/debarkation port for north- and southbound Alaska cruises. For information on attractions, shore excursions, tours, accommodations, and dining, see chapter 7, "The Ports of Embarkation."

10

Cruisetour Destinations

No matter how powerful your binoculars, you can't see all of Alaska from a cruise ship, and that's why the cruise lines invented the cruisetour. In this chapter, we'll give you info on the most popular cruisetour destinations. (See "Cruisetours: The Best of Land & Sea," in chapter 2, for a discussion of the various cruisetour packages offered; for much more in-depth information on these destinations, pick up a copy of *Frommer's Alaska 2008*.)

1 Denali National Park & Preserve

This is Alaska's most visited—environmentalists say overvisited—wilderness area, with almost one million people a year coming by bus and train to soak up the park's scenic splendor. It used to be difficult to overnight anywhere in or near the park, but it's gotten easier in recent years with the opening of the Talkeetna Alaskan Lodge and the Princess McKinley Lodge—both with spectacular views of the Alaska Range and Mount McKinley. These added valuable new accommodations to what was previously a rather "thin" selection. An addition to the McKinley Chalet Resort 3 years ago brought the room count in the area around the mountain to 345. That's not by any means a lot, but it has made stopping over by the park much easier. There are, however, times when demand outstrips supply, so book early.

Wildlife is the thing in Denali—somewhere in the realm of 161 bird species, 37 mammal species, and no fewer than 450 plant species are to be found there.

The **Alaska Railroad** operates daily between Anchorage and Fairbanks alongside the park, towing the private railcars of Holland America Line and Princess, as well as those of Royal Celebrity Tours (Royal Caribbean and Celebrity Cruises' joint tour product). You can do the tour in either direction. In 2006 Alaska Railroad added its own domed viewing cars in addition to its more basic (but less expensive and perfectly adequate) carriages. (The trains do not actually enter the park; they run along its perimeter and deposit passengers at stations just outside the boundary.)

Besides the wildlife, the focal point of the park is North America's highest peak, **Mount McKinley** (also known by its original Native name, Denali, which means "the great one"). You could argue that McKinley comprises the two highest peaks in North America: Its north face towers over the Alaska Range at 20,320 feet, while its south face rises to 19,470 feet. Permanently snow-covered mountains dominate the expanse. There's Mount Foraker, which stands a mere 17,400 feet; Mount Silverthrone, at 13,320 feet; Mount Crosson, at 12,800 feet; and many, many more giant heaps. It's an awesome sight, even from on the ground at one of the nearby lodges. You just have to hope you can see it.

As with all enormous mountains, The Great One creates its own weather system, and foggy seems to be its favorite flavor. Sadly, it's possible to be in the area for days

A Mountain by Any Other Name . . .

We've long been taught that the Athabascans of Interior Alaska named the mountain Denali, meaning "the high one" or "the great one." But at least one historian contends that the word *Denal'iy* actually referred to a mountain near Anchorage, now known as Pioneer Peak, and means "one that watches," and that the Native word for McKinley, "the high one," is actually *Doleika*. In any event, Alaska Natives seldom made use of the area, as it produced little fish or game, and white men came only in search of gold. In 1896, a prospector named the mountain after William McKinley of Ohio, who was elected president of the United States that year.

All well and good, except that most Alaskans prefer the name Denali and since 1975 have petitioned to officially change it back. Ohio won't allow it. Although congressmen from Alaska and Ohio compromised on the issue in 1980, changing the name of the national park to Denali and leaving the mountain named McKinley, Alaskans have kept pushing for Denali. However, the U.S. Board on Geographical Names has refused to take up the issue. The board has a rule against considering an issue that is also before Congress, and the Ohio Congressional delegation repeatedly introduces a one-paragraph bill stating that the name should stay the same. This bill never goes anywhere, but just introducing it has been enough to thwart any name change.

and never catch a glimpse of the Alaska Range. Trust us, though: When you do get to see it in all its splendor, you'll find that the wait was well worth it. It is Jerry's favorite Alaska view. (He once sat on a bench on the viewing platform at the Talkeetna Lodge for so long late one summer's evening that a young lady from the reception desk came out to see if he was okay. She was concerned that he might have taken ill—or worse. She seemed a little bemused when he assured her that it was only the grandeur of the view that kept him glued to the bench.)

Most people cannot drive far into the park. Private vehicles are tightly restricted, for environmental reasons, and are allowed only to about Mile 15 on the park road. That cuts down on your wildlife-viewing chances. However, you can sign up for the park concessionaire's coaches (some are school buses; others are nonpolluting), which are allowed to penetrate much more deeply into the park. The buses leave from the few local hotels. The drivers of these buses are all expert in the flora and fauna of the area. They always seem to be able to spot Dall sheep on the hillside, or caribou in the tall grass—even bears. When that wildlife is close enough, the driver/guide will ask for quiet so as not to startle the animals. And you'd better be quiet! The tour demands a long day—about 8 hours in not particularly luxurious vehicles—but if the weather holds and the viewing is good, it'll be the best $30 you ever spent.

2 Fairbanks

Alaska's second-largest city (after Anchorage) is friendly, unpretentious, and easygoing in the Alaska tradition, although its downtown area is drab and a little depressing.

Fairbanks' major attraction is the *Riverboat Discovery*, 1975 Discovery Dr. (© **866/479-6673** or 907/479-6673), a three-deck stern-wheeler that operates 4-hour cruises twice a day throughout the summer on the Chena (*Chee*-nah) and Tanana (*Ta*-na-naw) rivers. The boat visits a re-created Indian village, a sled-dog training school, and an Athabascan Indian fish camp tour (with narration), as well as a flyby performed by a bush pilot. The cruise costs $50 for adults, $35 for kids ages 3 to 12, and is free for kids under 3. Sailings are mid-May to mid-September. The vessel used for the cruise is the third in the *Riverboat Discovery* series.

The Binkleys, the family that owns the stern-wheeler, also own **El Dorado Gold Mine,** off the Elliott Highway, 9 miles north of town (© **866/479-6673** or 907/479-6673). Here visitors can pan for gold and, while riding on the open-sided Tanana Valley Railroad, study the workings of the mine just as it was a century ago. It's hokey, of course, but it's good fun, especially for youngsters. Tours, which run daily (call for times), are $35 for adults, $23 for ages 3 to 12, and free for kids under 3. If you buy the Gold Mine tickets at the same time as you do the riverboat cruise, you can save $2 a head off the combined price.

Pioneer Park (formerly **Alaskaland**), at the intersection of Airport Way and Peger Road (© **907/459-1087**), is a low-key Native culture–themed park with a couple of small museums, a playground, and a little tour train. It will never be confused with Disneyland. The park is open year-round, but the attractions operate only Memorial Day weekend to Labor Day daily from 11am to 9pm. And the best part of all? Admission is free.

Your cruisetour may include a tour of the gold mine or a visit to **Gold Dredge No. 8,** a huge monster of a machine that dug gold out of the hills until 1959 and is now on display for visitors. Shore excursions and cruisetours almost always include the *Riverboat Discovery* and the El Dorado Gold Mine.

3 Prudhoe Bay

Prudhoe Bay is located at the very end of the Dalton Highway, also known locally as the Haul Road, a 414-mile stretch built to service the Trans-Alaska Pipeline. The road connects the Arctic coast with Interior Alaska and passes through wilderness areas that include all sorts of scenic terrain—forested rounded hills, the rugged peaks of the Brooks Range, and the treeless plains of the North Slope. The route offers lots of wildlife-spotting opportunities, with strong chances of seeing caribou, Dall sheep, moose, and bear.

But the real reason to come way up here is the **Prudhoe Bay Oilfield.** Although touring an oil field may not be high on your vacation must-do list, the bay complex is no ordinary oil field. It's an historic and strategic site of great importance and a great technological achievement. (And chances are, you'll be the only one on your block who's actually been there!) The industry coexists here with migrating caribou and waterfowl on wet, fragile tundra that permanently shows any mark made by vehicles. (Visits to the oil field were curtailed following the Sept 11, 2001, terrorist attacks, but a modified version has since resumed under stricter security rules.) Tours (2 hr.; $36 adults $18 for children 12 and under) are operated by the **Arctic Caribou Inn,** P.O. Box 340111, Prudhoe Bay, AK 99734 (© **907/659-2368**). They will need your name and an identification number that British Petroleum can use to run a background check before allowing you on the oil field: A driver's license, passport, or Social Security

First to the Top

It's the biggest. That's why climbers risk their lives on Mount McKinley. You can see the mountain from Anchorage, more than 100 miles away. On a flight across Alaska, McKinley stands out grandly over waves of other mountains. It's more than a mile taller than the tallest peak in the other 49 states. It's a great white triangle, always covered in snow, tall but also massive and strong.

The first group to try to climb Mount McKinley came in 1903, led by Judge James Wickersham, who also helped explore Washington's Olympic Peninsula before it became a national park. His group made it less than halfway up, but on the trip they found gold in the Kantishna Hills, setting off a small gold rush that led to the first permanent human settlement in the park area. Wickersham later became the Alaska Territory's nonvoting delegate to Congress and introduced the bill that created the national park, but the government was never able to get back land in the Kantishna area from the gold miners. Today, that land is the site of wilderness lodges, right in the middle of the park.

On September 27, 1906, renowned world-explorer Dr. Frederick Cook announced to the world by telegraph that he had reached the summit of Mount McKinley after a lightning-fast climb, covering more than 85 miles and 19,000 vertical feet in 13 days with one other man, a blacksmith, at his side. On his return to New York, Cook was lionized as a conquering explorer and published a popular book of his summit diary and photographs.

In 1909, Cook again made history, announcing that he had beaten Robert Peary to the North Pole. Both returned to civilization from their competing treks at about the same time. Again, Cook was the toast of the town. His story began to fall apart, however, when his Eskimo companions mentioned that he'd never been out of sight of land. After being paid by Peary to come forward, Cook's McKinley companion also recanted. A year later, Cook's famous summit photograph was re-created—on a peak 19 miles away and 15,000 feet lower than the real summit.

In 1910, disgusted with Cook, four prospectors from Fairbanks took a more Alaskan approach to the task. Without fanfare or special supplies—they carried doughnuts and hot chocolate on their incredible final ascent—they marched up the mountain carrying a large wooden flagpole they could

number will work. Entry is by advance booking only. There are no walk-ins. Included in the tour is a short stop on the shores of the Arctic Ocean. Brrrrr!

To get here, you usually drive the Dalton Highway in buses one-way and fly the other, with either **Fairbanks** or **Anchorage** being the other connecting point. The trip includes an overnight in **Coldfoot.**

Be aware: The bus trip is a long one over not particularly good roads and not always terribly comfortable.

plant on top to prove they'd made it. But on arriving at the summit, they realized that they'd climbed the slightly shorter north peak. Weather closed in, so they set up the pole there and descended without attempting the south peak. Then, when they got back to Fairbanks, no one could see the pole, and they were accused of trying to pull off another hoax.

In 1913, Episcopal archdeacon Hudson Stuck organized the first successful climb to reach the real summit—and reported he saw the pole on the other peak. Harry Karstens led the climb (he would become the park's first superintendent in 1917), and the first person to stand at the summit was an Alaska Native, Walter Harper.

Although McKinley remains one of the world's most difficult climbs, about 10,000 people have made it to the top since Hudson Stuck's party. Since 1980 the number of climbers has boomed. Garbage and human waste disposal are a major problem. One recent June day, 115 climbers made it to the summit. In 1970, only 124 made the attempt all year; now more than 1,200 try to climb the peak each year, with about half making it to the summit. The cold, fast-changing weather is what usually stops people. From late April into early July, climbers fly from the town of Talkeetna to a base camp at 7,200 feet elevation on the Kahiltna Glacier. From there, it takes an average of about 18 days to get to the top, through temperatures as cold as −40°F (−4°C).

Climbers lose fingers, toes, and other parts to frostbite, or suffer other, more severe injuries. More than 90 climbers have died on the mountain, not counting plane crashes. During the season, the park service stations rescue rangers and have an emergency medical clinic at the 14,200-foot level of the mountain, and they keep a high-altitude helicopter ready to go after climbers in trouble. In 2002, under pressure from Congress, the park service started charging climbers a $150-a-head fee, defraying a portion of the rescue costs. The park and the military spend about half a million dollars a year rescuing climbers and sometimes much more. The cost in lives is high as well. Volunteer rangers and rescuers die as well as climbers. Plane crashes, falls, cold, and altitude all take a toll. Monuments to those who never returned are in the cemetery near the airstrip in Talkeetna.

—*Charles Wohlforth*

4 Nome & Kotzebue

There's no place like Nome. Well, we had to say it. But, really, this Arctic frontier town is a special place, combining a sense of history, a hospitable and silly attitude (we're talking about a place that holds an annual Labor Day bathtub race), and an exceptional location on the water before a tundra wilderness.

What it does not have is anything that remotely resembles a tourist destination. Anthropological, yes. Touristy, no! It's little more than a collection of beat-up residences and low-rise commercial buildings. It looks like the popular conception of a

Denali Changes

Massive changes to the main Denali National Park visitor area underway for several years have been pretty well completed. Other changes farther inside the park are just getting started. Here are the major upheavals either finished or pending as we went to press:

- The Eielson Visitor Center, 66 miles inside the park, has been rebuilt much larger than the original. The project started in 2005 and was opened to great acclaim in May 2007. The shuttle bus from the village of Denali costs from $21 to $36 per person, depending on the length of the ride chosen.
- The 3-year-old Murie Science and Learning Center is a fine educational resource in the easily accessible front-country area.
- The Visitor Center Campus was completed last year. The campus has programs, exhibits, a theater, food courts, a bookstore, parking, and so on.
- What was formerly the Visitor Access Center is now a transit center, just for boarding buses and getting tickets and permits for the buses, campgrounds, and backcountry.

century-old gold-rush town—which isn't really surprising, since that's what it is. But if it seems to be in need of a face-lift—and how!—the inhabitants make up for all that by the warmth of their welcome. Probably they're glad to see a strange face in the summer because they know they'll see precious few in the winter when the weather turns ugly and the sun disappears for 3 or 4 months. There are local roads but no highway link with the rest of the state.

The name Nome is believed to have been an error by a British naval officer in 1850, who wrote "? Name" on a diagram. The scrawl was misinterpreted by a mapmaker as "Nome." The population boom here in 1899 also happened by chance, when a prospector from the 1898 gold rush was left behind on the beach due to an injury. He panned the sand outside his tent and found that it was full of gold dust.

Undoubtedly, on your visit, you'll find time to try gold panning. The city also has a still sloppy, gold-rush-era-style saloon scene, and bargains on **Iñupiat Eskimo** arts and crafts.

Your tour will also visit **Kotzebue** (pronounced *Kot*-say-bue) to the north, one of Alaska's largest and oldest Iñupiat Eskimo villages. Here you'll tour the **NANA Museum of the Arctic,** run by a regional Native corporation representing the 7,000 Iñupiat people who live in the northwest Arctic region.

To get here, you fly from Anchorage, fly between Nome and Kotzebue, and fly back to Anchorage, as part of itineraries that typically include an overnight in Anchorage and a visit to Denali and Fairbanks. Cruise West has a couple of sailings each year between Anchorage and Nome, by way of the Aleutians and the Russian Far East.

5 The Kenai Peninsula

The Kenai (*Kee*-nye) Peninsula, which divides Prince William Sound and Cook Inlet, offers glaciers, whales, legendary sportfishing, spectacular hiking trails, bears, moose, and high mountains. And it's easy to get to, to boot. At least, it's not a long ways away and there's a good road to help you get there. The trouble is, there's an awful lot of traffic on it. The traffic jams on Friday evenings and Saturday morning especially can make the most jaded Los Angelenos forget the crush on the I-405 at rush hour, or New Yorkers the Lincoln Tunnel. But try to get to Anchorage a day or two before your cruise begins (or stay a day or two afterward) and make the trip in midweek. The scenery alone is well worth the effort. There are two main towns on the peninsula, Kenai and Soldotna, the former slightly bigger than the latter, but neither by any stretch of the imagination a major metropolis.

People from Anchorage come here for the weekend to hike, dig clams, paddle kayaks, and, particularly, fish. There's a special phrase for what happens when the red salmon are running in July on the Kenai and Russian rivers: **combat fishing.** Anglers stand elbow to elbow on a bank, each casting into his or her yard-wide slice of river, and still catch plenty of fish.

Cruisetours to the Kenai Peninsula include options for fishing, **river rafting,** and other soft-adventure activities.

You typically travel here by bus or rail from Seward. Princess includes an overnight at its own Kenai Princess Lodge, a wilderness resort with a gorgeous setting on a bluff overlooking the river, and other cruise lines offer overnights at other properties. Some tours combine a visit to Kenai Peninsula with an overnight in Anchorage.

6 The Yukon Territory

You'll pass plenty of beautiful scenery along the way, but today the real reason to cross the Canadian border into this region is the same as it was 100 years ago: **gold** (or, rather, gold-rush history).

Gold was discovered in the Canadian Klondike's Rabbit Creek (later renamed Bonanza Creek—for fairly obvious reasons) in 1896. In a matter of months, tens of thousands of people descended into the Yukon for the greatest gold rush in history, giving birth to Dawson City, Whitehorse, and a dozen other tent communities. By the turn of the century, the gold rush was on in earnest, and in 1900, the White Pass Yukon rail route opened from Skagway to the Canadian border to carry prospectors and their goods.

Once part of the Northwest Territories, the Yukon is now a separate Canadian territory bordered by British Columbia and Alaska. The entire territory has a population of just over 33,000, two-thirds of them living in **Whitehorse,** the capital of the region since 1953. Located on the banks of the Yukon River, Whitehorse was established in 1900, 2 full years after the stampeders began swarming into Dawson City. Today the city serves as a frontier outpost, its tourism influx also giving it a cosmopolitan tinge complete with nightlife, good shopping opportunities (with some smart boutiques and great outdoor shops), fine restaurants, and comfortable hotels. The up-to-the-minute nature of the town, with the Canada Games Center, a sports/convention center, its modern Visitor Information Center, its Waterfront Trolley rail service ($2 one-way) that runs from the Games Center all the way to the other end of town, allowing passengers to disembark at any of several stations along the way, puts it at some contrast with most of the Yukon—with the next-largest community in the territory, for instance . . .

Dawson City was once the biggest Canadian city west of Winnipeg, with a population of 30,000, but it withered to practically a ghost town after the gold-rush stampeders stopped stampeding. Dawson today is the nearest thing to an authentic gold-rush town the world has to offer, with old buildings, vintage watering holes, dirt streets flanked with raised boardwalks, shops (naturally), and some particularly good restaurants. On a visit to Dawson last year, Jerry was much impressed by the excellent La Table, in the Aurora Inn at the corner of 5th Avenue and Harper Street, an eatery that would do credit to the dining opportunities in the nation's largest cities. There is always, of course, the Dawson staple—Diamond Tooth Gertie's Gambling Hall (full-service bar, poker, blackjack, roulette, and slots) where one can eat a casual meal in truly fun surroundings. There is a $5 admission charge for adults—and don't bring the kids! The place is operated by the Klondike Visitors Association and it's all in fun. The proceeds go to maintain the gold-rush-style architecture and ambience of the town. Another establishment worth a visit is Bombay Peggy's Inn & Pub on 2nd Street. The pub features—along with a selection of locally brewed libations—artworks by Dawson area artists. (And no, there is no plan to change the name to Mumbai Betty's!) Take a look also at the city museum, in The Old Territorial Building on 5th Avenue, one of the most comprehensive recountings of the tumultuous years of the gold rush to be found anywhere.

If you're on a Holland America cruisetour—highly likely, since that company operates more Yukon cruisetours than any other—you'll travel between Dawson City and the tiny Alaskan town of Eagle via the *MV Yukon Queen II,* a high-speed, 115-passenger catamaran. It makes the trip along the Yukon River in 5 hours, passing through incredibly beautiful wilderness scenery, where the only sign of civilization is the occasional fisherman.

Holland America also has two more Yukon strings to its bow—exclusive rights to enter the UNESCO World Heritage Site known as **Kluane National Park,** a protected Canadian wilderness area that was hitherto all but inaccessible (a few backpackers, campers, and cyclists made up just about the only traffic into the park), and **Tombstone Territorial Park,** about a 90-minute drive from Dawson City.

7 The Canadian Rockies

Canadian Rockies cruisetours typically include travel by bus and/or train between Vancouver and either Seattle or Calgary.

Highlights of the tour include a visit to the parks at **Jasper** and **Banff,** which together comprise 17,518 sq. km (6,832 sq. miles). The parks are teeming with wildlife, with some animals—like bighorn sheep, mountain goats, deer, and moose—meandering along and across highways and hiking trails. There are also coyotes, lynx, and occasional wolves (though they tend to give humans a wide berth), as well as grizzlies and black bears, both of which are unpredictable and best photographed with a telephoto lens.

The two "capitals," Banff and Jasper, are 287km (178 miles) apart and connected by scenic Highway 93. Banff is in a stunningly beautiful setting, with the mighty Bow River, murky with glacial till, coursing through town.

The **Banff Springs Hotel** (© **403/762-2211**) was built in 1888 as a destination resort by the Canadian Pacific Railroad. Ever since then, tourists have been visiting this area for its scenery and hot springs, plus nearby fishing, hiking, and other outdoor activities. Today the streets of Banff are also an attraction, lined with trendy cafes and exclusive boutiques offering international fashion.

Lake Louise is located 56km (35 miles) north of Banff and is a famed spot, deep green from the minerals it contains (ground by the glaciers above the lake) and surrounded by forest-clad snowcapped mountains. The village near the lake is a resort destination in its own right. Nearly as spectacular as the lake is **Chateau Lake Louise,** 111 Lake Louise Dr., Lake Louise (© **800/441-1414** or 403/522-3511), built by the Canadian Pacific Railroad and one of the most celebrated hotels in Canada.

Between Lake Louise and Jasper is the **Icefields Parkway,** a spectacular mountain road that climbs through three deep-river valleys, beneath soaring, glacier-notched mountains, and past dozens of hornlike peaks. Capping the route is the **Columbia Icefields,** a massive dome of glacial ice and snow that is the largest nonpolar ice cap in the world.

Jasper isn't Banff. It was born as a railroad division point, and the town does not offer the glitz of its southern neighbor. **Jasper National Park** is Canada's largest mountain park and offers an outdoor-oriented experience with opportunities to hike, ride horses, fish, or even climb mountains.

Appendix A:
Alaska in Depth

by Charles Wohlforth

To discover Alaska is something apart from statistics, although the numbers do give you a general idea of scale. Once you've driven across the continental United States and know how big that is, seeing a map of Alaska placed on top of the area you crossed, just about spanning it, provides some notion of size. Alaskans always like to threaten that they'll split in half and make Texas the third-largest state. Alaska has a population of just 670,053, according to Alaska's state government in 2006—the third-least-populous state in the Union. If you placed them an equal distance apart, each resident would be almost a mile from any other. Of course, that couldn't happen. No human has ever set foot in some of the most remote parts of Alaska.

But none of that expresses what really matters. It's not just a matter of how big Alaska is or how few people it contains. It's not an intellectual concept at all. None of that crosses your mind when you see a chunk of ice the size of a building fall from a glacier and send a huge splash and wave surging outward, or when you feel your sea kayak lift on a wave caused by the fall of a breaching humpback whale. A realization of what Alaska means can also come in a simple little moment. It can come standing on an Arctic Ocean beach, when you look around at the sea of empty tundra behind you, the sea of green water before you, and your own place on what seems to be the edge of the world. Or you might simply be sitting on the sun-warmed rocks of a beach in Southeast or Southcentral Alaska when you discover that you're occupying only one of many worlds—a world of intermediate size, lying in magnitude between the tiny tide-pool universes of life all around you and the larger world as seen by an eagle gliding through the air high above.

1 Natural History: Rough Drafts & Erasures

THE SURGING ICE

In 1986, Hubbard Glacier, north of Yakutat, suddenly decided to surge forward, cutting off Russell Fjord from the rest of the Pacific Ocean. A group of well-intentioned but ill-advised wildlife lovers set out to save the marine mammals that had been trapped behind the glacier. Catching a dolphin from an inflatable boat isn't that easy—they didn't accomplish much, but they provided a lot of entertainment for the locals. Then the water burst through the dam of ice, and the lake became a fjord again, releasing the animals anyway. In 2002, it happened again (no rescue this time). Ships were warned away as the 70-square-mile lake, having risen 61 feet above sea level, quickly drained through a 300-foot-wide channel with a whoosh.

Bering Glacier, the largest in North America (about 30×145 miles in area), can't decide which way to go. Surging and retreating on a 20-year cycle, it reversed course in 1995 after bulldozing a wetland migratory bird stopover, and speedily contracted back up toward the mountains. Yanert Glacier surged 100 yards a day in 2000 after moving only 100 yards a year since 1942. The next year,

Tokositna Glacier started galloping after 50 years of quiet. In 1937, surging Black Rapids Glacier almost ate the Richardson Highway. In Prince William Sound, Meares Glacier has plowed through old-growth forest. On the other hand, some glaciers are so stable that they gather a layer of dirt where trees and brush grow to maturity. When Malaspina Glacier retreated, the trees on its back toppled. On a larger scale, all the land of Glacier Bay—mountains, forests, sea floor—is rising a little each year as it rebounds from the weight of melted glaciers that 100 years ago were a mile thick and 65 miles longer.

Yet these new and erased lands are just small corrections around the margins compared to all the earth has done in setting down, wiping out, and rewriting the natural history of Alaska. In the last ice age, 15,000 years ago, much of what Alaska is today was one huge glacier. Looking up at the tops of granite mountains in Southeast Alaska, especially in the Lynn Canal, a passageway created by nature and enjoyed by cruise-ship passengers traveling between Juneau and Skagway, you can see a sort of high-water mark—the highest point to which the glaciers came in the ice age. Even looking from the deck of a boat, thousands of feet below the upper reaches of the mountains, you can see that many mountain shoulders were rounded by the passage of ice and thus are much smoother than the sharp, craggy peaks just above that stuck out of that incredible sheet of ice.

It's possible that a glacier could get Juneau—the city fronts on the huge Juneau Icefield—but there would be at least a few centuries' warning before it hit. Glaciers are essentially just snow that doesn't get a chance to melt. It accumulates at higher altitudes until it gets deep enough to compress into ice and starts oozing down the sides of the mountain. When the ice reaches the ocean, or before, the melting and calving of icebergs at the leading edge reaches a point of equilibrium with the snow that's still being added at the top. The glacier stops advancing, becoming a true river of ice, moving a snowflake from the top of the mountain to the bottom in a few hundred years. When conditions change—more snow or colder long-term weather, for example—the glacier gets bigger, which is called "advancing"; when there is less snow and warmer weather, the glacier gets smaller, which is known as "retreating." Sometimes something strange will happen under the glacier and it will surge. Bering Glacier started to float on a cushion of water, and Yanert Glacier slid on a cushion of mud. But most of the time, the advance or retreat is measured in no more than inches or feet per year.

Dateline

- **Approximately 15,000 years ago** First human explorers arrive in Alaska from Asia.
- **1741** Vitus Bering, on a mission originally chartered by Peter the Great, finds Alaska; ship's surgeon and naturalist Georg Steller goes ashore for a few hours on Kayak Island, the first white to set foot in Alaska.
- **1743** Russian fur traders enter the Aleutian Islands; Aleuts are either enslaved to hunt sea otter or massacred; when they try to revolt, Aleut cultural traditions are eliminated. Over the coming decades, Aleuts relocate as far south as California.
- **1772** Unalaska, in the Aleutian Islands, becomes a permanent Russian settlement.
- **1776–79** British Capt. James Cook makes voyages of exploration to Alaska, seeking the Northwest Passage from the Pacific to the Atlantic, and draws charts of the coast.
- **1784** Russians build a settlement at Kodiak.
- **1799** Russians establish a fort near present-day Sitka, which will later become their capital; Tlingits attack and destroy the fort but are later driven off in a counterattack. The Russian-America Company

continues

An Iceberg by Any Other Name

When a glacier calves, the icebergs formed are classified differently depending on their size, a system that allows one ship's captain to warn another of the degree of danger represented by the ice hazard. Very large chunks are officially called **icebergs;** pieces of moderate size (usually 7–15 ft. across) are known as **bergy bits; growlers** are slightly smaller still, at less than 7 feet across, with less than 3 feet showing above water; and **brash ice** is any random smaller chunks. And remember the old adage: What you're seeing is only the tip—most of the ice is below the water.

It took some time to figure out how glaciers work. The living glaciers of Alaska, like living fossils from the last ice age, helped show the way. In the 1830s, scientists in Switzerland found huge rocks (now called glacial erratics) that appeared to have moved miles from where they had once been a part of similar bedrock. Scientists theorized that ancient glaciers shaping the Alps must have moved the rocks. John Muir, the famous writer and naturalist, maintained in the 1870s that the granite mountains of Yosemite National Park had been rounded and polished by the passing of glaciers that melted long ago (he was only part right). He traveled to Alaska to prove it. Here glaciers were still carving the land—they had never finished melting at the end of the last glacial period—and Muir could see shapes like those at Yosemite in the act of being created. Glacier Bay, which Muir

"discovered" when guided there by his Alaska Native friends, was a glacial work in progress, as it still is today.

When you visit, you can see for yourself how the heavy blue ice and white snow are streaked with black rock and dust that were obviously gouged from mountains and left in hills at the faces and along the flanks of the glaciers, in debris piles called **moraines.** At Exit Glacier, in Kenai Fjords National Park, you can stand on a moraine that wraps the leading edge of the glacier like a scarf and feel the cold streaming off spires of clicking ice—like standing in front of a freezer with the door open. Find another hill like that, no matter where it is, and you can be pretty sure a glacier once came that way. Likewise, you can see today's glaciers scooping out valleys in the mountains.

Today Alaska's 100,000 glaciers cover about 5% of its landmass, mostly on the

receives a 20-year exclusive franchise to govern and exploit Alaska.

■ **1824** Boundaries roughly matching Alaska's current borders are set by treaty between Russia, Britain, and the United States.

■ **1839** The British Hudson's Bay Company, surpassing Russia in trade, begins leasing parts of Southeast Alaska and subsequently extends trading outposts into the Interior.

■ **1867** In need of money and fearful that Russia couldn't hold on to Alaska anyway, Czar Alexander II sells Alaska to the United States; Sec. of State William Seward negotiates the deal for a price of $7.2 million, roughly 2¢ an acre; the American flag is raised in Sitka, and the U.S. military assumes government of Alaska.

■ **1870** The Alaska Commercial Company receives a monopoly

on harvesting seals in the Pribilof Islands and soon expands across the territory. (The company remains a presence in the Alaska Bush today.)

■ **1879** Naturalist and writer John Muir explores Southeast Alaska by canoe, discovering Glacier Bay with Native guides.

■ **1880** Joe Juneau and Richard Harris, guided by local Natives, find gold on Gastineau Channel and founded the city of southern coast. There are no glaciers in the Arctic—the climate is too dry to produce enough snow. The northernmost large glaciers are in the Alaska Range, such as those carving great chasms in the side of Mount McKinley. At that height, the mountain creates its own weather, wringing moisture out of the atmosphere and feeding its glaciers. The Kahiltna Glacier flows 45 miles from the mountain, going 15,000 feet downhill over its course. The Ruth Glacier has dug a canyon twice as deep as the Grand Canyon, half filled with mile-deep ice. The glaciers of the 50 ice ages that have covered North America in the last 2.5 million years are the most likely explanation for the fjords and valleys that appear all over Alaska.

Glaciers come in several different varieties. **Tidewater glaciers** are the kind most often seen on postcards; they spill down out of the mountains and run all the way to the sea. **Piedmont glaciers** are two glaciers that have run together into one. When seen from above, piedmonts resemble a highway interchange, edged by road slush, with the median moraine looking like lane dividers. **Hanging glaciers** are glaciers that are draped over hillsides but don't come all the way down to the bottom of the hill. They "hang" up there, resting against the hillside, a few

hundred feet or more above the foot of the hill. There are also **mountain glaciers** (also known as alpine glaciers), which are confined by surrounding mountain terrain; **valley glaciers,** which are mountain glaciers confined by valley walls; and **cirque glaciers,** which sit in basins near ridge crests and are usually circular (as opposed to the typical river shape).

It's still not known exactly why glacial periods come and go. The best theory to date holds that the wobbles and imperfections in the earth's spin and orbit around the sun alter energy flow into the global ecosystem, which in turn changes the balance of carbon dioxide in the atmosphere. Carbon dioxide traps heat on the earth. The earth is warming today in time with its normal cycles of cold and warm, but the warmth may also be accelerated by human release of carbon dioxide into the atmosphere from the burning of fossil fuels. Those effects are felt more strongly in the Arctic than anywhere else on Earth. Forests are moving north, wetlands are drying, sea ice is thinning and withdrawing, and permanently frozen ground is warming. Glaciers are shrinking.

Some of the most visited glaciers on the various cruise itineraries include **Glacier Bay National Park and Preserve** and its 16 tidewater glaciers (p. 213), **Hubbard Glacier** in Yakutat Bay (p. 230),

Juneau; gold strikes begin to come every few years across the state.

- 1884 Military rule ends in Alaska, but residents still have no right to elect a legislature, governor, or congressional representative, or to make laws.
- 1885 Protestant missionaries meet to divide up the territory, parceling out each region to a different religion; they begin to fan out across

Alaska to convert Native peoples, largely suppressing their traditional ways.

- 1898 After prospectors arrive in Seattle with a ton of gold, the Klondike gold rush begins; gold rushes in Nome and Fairbanks follow within a few years; Americans begin to populate Alaska.
- 1906 Alaska's first (nonvoting) delegate in Congress takes office; the capital moves from Sitka to Juneau.

- 1908 The Iditarod Trail, a sled-dog mail route, is completed, linking trails continuously from Seward to Nome.
- 1913 The first territorial legislature convenes, although it has few powers; the first automobile drives the Richardson Highway route, from Valdez to Fairbanks.
- 1914 Federal construction of the Alaska Railroad begins;

continues

Mendenhall Glacier outside Juneau (p. 210), **North and South Sawyer Glaciers** in Tracy Arm (p. 199), and the many glaciers of **College Fjord** (p. 232).

THE TREMBLING EARTH

Alaska has an average of 13 earthquakes a day, or 11% of all the earthquakes in the world, including three of the six largest ever recorded.

Any part of Alaska could have an earthquake, but the Pacific Rim from South-central Alaska to the Aleutians is the shakiest. This is where Alaska is still under construction. The very rocks that make up the state are something of an ad hoc conglomeration, still in the process of being assembled. The floor of the Pacific Ocean is moving north, and as it moves, it carries islands and mountains with it. When they hit the Alaska plate, these pieces of land, called **terranes,** dock like ships arriving, but slowly—an island moving an inch a year takes a long time to travel thousands of miles. Geologists studying rocks near Mount McKinley have found a terrane that used to be tropical islands. In Kenai Fjords National Park, fossils have turned up that are otherwise found only in Afghanistan and China. The slowly moving crust of the earth brought them here on a terrane that makes up a large part of the south coast of Alaska.

The earth's crust is paper thin compared to the globe's forces, and, like paper, it folds where the two edges meet. Alaska's coast is bending down, and farther inshore, where McKinley stands, it is bowing up. At Kenai Fjords National Park, you can see steep little rock islands filled with birds: They are old mountaintops, shrinking down into the earth. The monolith of McKinley is a brand-new one growing higher.

Living in such an unsettled land is a matter of more than abstract interest. More than 80 volcanoes have been active in Alaska in the last 200 years. Earthquakes between 7 and 8 on the Richter scale occur once a year on average, and huge quakes over 8 averaged every 13 years over the last century. The worst of the quakes, on March 27, 1964, was the strongest ever to hit North America. It ranked 9.2 on the Richter scale, lowering an entire region of the state some 10 feet and moving it even farther laterally. No other earthquake anywhere ever moved so much land (until December 26, 2004, when a massive earthquake in the Pacific Ocean off Sumatra generated tsunami waves that killed hundreds of thousands of people).

The 1964 Alaska earthquake destroyed much of Anchorage and several smaller towns, and killed about 131 people, mostly

the first tents go up in the river bottom that will be Anchorage, along the rail line.
- **1917** Mount McKinley National Park is established.
- **1920** The first flights connect Alaska to the rest of the United States; aviation quickly becomes the most important means of transportation in the territory.
- **1923** President Warren Harding drives the final spike on the Alaskan Railroad at

Nenana, then dies on the way home, purportedly from eating bad Alaskan seafood.
- **1925** Leonhard Seppala and other dog mushers relay diphtheria serum on the Iditarod Trail to fight an epidemic in Nome; Seppala and his lead dog, Balto, become national heroes.
- **1934** Federal policy of forced assimilation of Native cultures is officially discarded

and New Deal efforts to preserve Native cultures begin.
- **1935** New Deal "colonists," broke farmers from all over the United States, settle in the Matanuska Valley north of Anchorage.
- **1940** A military buildup begins in Alaska; bases built in Anchorage accelerate city's growth into a major population center.
- **1942** Japanese invade Aleutian territory, taking Attu and

in sea waves created by underwater landslides. In Valdez, the waterfront was swept clean of people. In the Prince William Sound village of Chenega, built on a hill along the water, people started running for higher ground when the wave came. About half made it. But the earthquake could have been much worse. It occurred in the early evening, on Good Friday, when most public buildings were empty. An elementary school in Anchorage that broke in half and fell into a hole had no one inside at the time.

But even that huge earthquake wasn't an unusual occurrence, at least in the earth's terms. Geologists believe the same Alaska coast sank 6 feet in an earthquake in the year 1090.

THE FROZEN TUNDRA

The northern Interior and Arctic parts of the state are less susceptible to earthquakes and, since they receive little precipitation, they don't have glaciers, either. But there's still a sense of living on a land that's not permanent, since most of northern Alaska is solid only by virtue of being frozen practically all of the time. When it does occasionally thaw, it turns to mush. The phenomenon is caused by **permafrost,** a layer of earth a little below the surface that hardly ever thaws—or at least, you'd better hope it doesn't. Buildings erected on permafrost without some

mechanism for dispersing their own heat—pilings, a gravel pad, or even refrigerator coils—thaw the ground below and sink into a self-made quicksand. You occasionally run across such structures.

The Arctic and much of the Interior are a swampy desert. Annual precipitation measured in Barrow is the same as in Las Vegas. Most of the time, the tundra is frozen in white; snow blows around, but not much falls. It melts in the summer, but it can't sink into the subsoil, which remains frozen. Water on top of the permafrost layer creates huge shallow ponds. Alaska is a land of 10 million lakes, with 3 million larger than 20 acres. Birds arrive to feed and paddle around those circles and polygons of deep green and sky blue. Flying over the Arctic in a small plane is disorienting, for little pattern emerges from the flat green tundra and the irregularly shaped patches of water that stretch as far as the eye can see. Pilots can find their way by following landmarks like tractor tracks etched into the tundra. Although few and far between, the tracks remain clearly delineated for decades after they're made, appearing as narrow parallel ponds reaching from one horizon to the other.

Sea ice is the frozen ocean that extends from northern Alaska to the other side of the world. For a few months of summer,

Higher, Higher

The Eskimo blanket toss—the game of placing a person in the center of a walrus-skin blanket and bouncing him or her high in the air—was traditionally used to get hunters high enough to see over the pressure ridges so they could spot game.

it pulls away from the shore. Then, in September or October, icebergs float in toward land, cemented by new ice forming along the beach. But even when the ice covers the whole ocean, it still moves under the immense pressure of wind and current. The clash creates towering pressure ridges—piles of broken ice that look like small mountain ranges and are about as difficult to cross. At its extreme, in March, the ice normally extends all the way south to the Pribilof Islands. Then it is possible to drive a dog team across the Bering Sea to Siberia. The National Weather Service keeps track of the ice pack and issues maps and predictions; you can find them online at www.arh.noaa.gov. In Barrow, the sun doesn't rise for more than 65 days in the winter. In February, the average daily high temperature is –12°F (–24°C), and the average low is –24°F (–31°C). The Iñupiat people learned to survive in this climate for millennia, but life was short and terribly hard. Today they've made some sensible allowances—well-lighted hallways in

many rooms in their homes, for instance, and indoor playgrounds in schools.

THE RAINFOREST

By comparison, southern coastal Alaska is warm and biologically rich. Temperate rainforest ranges up the coast from Southeast Alaska into Prince William Sound, with bears, deer, moose, wolves, and even big cats living among the massive western hemlock, Sitka spruce, and cedar. This old-growth forest, too wet to burn in forest fires, is the last vestige of the virgin, primeval woods that seemed so limitless to the first white settlers who arrived on the east coast of the continent in the 17th century. The trees grow on and on, sometimes rising more than 200 feet high, with diameters of 10 feet, and falling only after hundreds or even thousands of years. When they fall, the trees rot on the damp moss of the forest floor and return to soil to feed more trees, which grow in rows upon their nursery trunks.

Here at least, Alaska does seem permanent. That sense helps explain why logging the rainforest is so controversial. Just one of these trees contains thousands of dollars' worth of wood, a prize that drives the logging industry. Some Southeast lands owned by Alaska Native corporations, alas, have been stripped of their old trees. Nowadays, the federal government is putting the brakes on tree felling in some of the more environmentally sensitive areas.

The rivers of the great coastal forests bring home runs of big **salmon** that clog the waters in spawning season like a busy sidewalk at rush hour. The fish spawn only once, returning by a precisely tuned sense of smell to the streams where they were hatched as many as 7 years before. When the fertilized eggs have been left in the stream gravel, the fish conveniently die on the beach, making a smorgasbord for bears and other forest animals. The huge **Kodiak brown bear,** topping 1,000 pounds, owes everything to the millions of salmon that return to Kodiak Island each summer. By comparison, the **grizzly bears** of the Interior—the same species as browns, but living on grass, berries, and an occasional ground squirrel—are mere midgets, their weight counted in the hundreds of pounds. Forest-dwelling black **bears** grow to only a few hundred pounds.

TAIGA

Rainforest covers only a small fraction of Alaska. In fact, only a third of Alaska is forested at all, and most of the forests are the boreal forests that cover the central part of the state, behind the rain shadow of coastal mountains that intercept moist clouds off the oceans. Ranging from the Kenai Peninsula, south of Anchorage, to the Brooks Range, where the Arctic begins, you'll find **taiga**—a moist, subarctic forest of smaller, slower-growing, hardier trees that leave plenty of open sky between their branches.

THE LIGHT & THE DARKNESS

In summer it never really gets dark at night. In Fairbanks in June, the sun sets in the north around midnight, but it doesn't go down far enough for real darkness to settle, instead rising again 2 hours later. It's always light enough to keep hiking or fishing and, in clear weather, always light enough to read by. You may not see the stars from early May until sometime in August (in the climate chart in chapter 4, "The Cruise Experience," gives seasonal daylight for Anchorage and Juneau). Visitors have trouble getting used to it: Falling asleep in broad daylight is hard. Alaskans deal with it by staying up late and being active outdoors. In the winter, on the other hand, Alaskans forget what the sun looks like. Kids go to school in the dark and come home in the dark. The sun rises in the middle of the morning and sets after lunch. At high

Bay cruise-ship summer entry permits it will issue from 107 to 139. The increase is immediately challenged in federal court by a coalition of environmental groups.

- **1999** Alaskans vote 87% against a plan to use Permanent Fund earnings to cover a state budget shortfall.

- **2000** Alaska initiates new regulations to control cruise-line waste discharge after a number of "dumping" incidents in local waters. Ship operators voluntarily respond by instituting new practices, installing new equipment on board some ships, and offering environment-sensitivity training programs to key employees.

- **2001** Bush Administration proposes tapping the oil reserves in the vast (almost 20 million acres) Arctic National Wildlife Refuge, home to an estimated 160,000 caribou, moose, wolves, and other animals. The area in question consists of the coastal plain in the northeast corner of Alaska, on the Canada border. Environmentalists protest the proposed project's negative impact on wildlife migration patterns.

continues

noon in December, the sun hangs just above the southern horizon with a weak orange light—a constant sunset. Animals and people go into hibernation.

As you go north, the changes in the length of the days throughout the year get larger. In Ketchikan, on the summer solstice (the longest day of the year), direct sunlight lasts 17 hours, 28 minutes; in Fairbanks, 21 hours, 48 minutes; and in Barrow, the longest day lasts more than 2 months. In contrast, in Seattle the longest day is 16 hours, and in Los Angeles, 14 hours, 26 minutes. On the equator, days are always the same length: 12 hours. At the North and South poles, the sun is up half the year and down the other half.

In the north, on a long, summer evening, you can almost feel the planet leaning toward the sun. Come feel it for yourself.

2 A Short Gold-Rush History

The biggest event in Alaska history happened 108 years ago: the 1898 Klondike gold rush. If you're coming to Alaska, you'll hear a lot about it. Here's some context for the barrage of anecdotes you can expect.

A small number of prospectors sought gold even before Russia sold Alaska to the United States in 1867. After the American flag went up over Sitka, prospectors slowly worked their way into Alaska's vastness, often led by or in partnership with Natives, who knew the country. Called **sourdoughs** for the yeast and flour mixture they carried to make their bread, these were tough wilderness men, living way beyond the law or communications with the outside world.

A few of them struck it rich. In 1880, a major find on the Gastineau Channel started the city called Juneau and decades of industrial, hard-rock mining there.

Finds followed on the Fortymile River in 1886 (on the Taylor Hwy.), near Circle in 1893 (on the Steese Hwy.), and near Hope on the Kenai Peninsula in 1895 (on the Seward Hwy.). Gold slowly brought more people to Alaska, but not enough to catch the nation's attention.

In 1896, white prospector George Carmack and his Native partners, Tagish Charlie and Skookum Jim, found gold on the Klondike River, a tributary of the Yukon in Canada. Word traveled downriver to the goldfields in Fortymile country, and within 48 hours, that area was empty and claims on the Klondike were being staked. The miners dug gravel from the creek that winter and when they washed it, it yielded big chunks of solid gold, a massive discovery. Some were instant millionaires at a time when a million dollars really meant something.

■ 2001 A federal judge orders the National Park Service to roll back the number of Glacier Bay cruise authorizations to 107.

■ 2004 Gov. Frank Murkowski proposes a $15-a-head "wildlife conservation pass" for visitors to the state. The proposal died in the state legislature.

■ 2004 A group of Anchorage residents, calling themselves the Campaign to Safeguard America's Waters, announces a plan to put on the ballot in 2006 a proposal to levy a $50-per-head tax on cruise passengers, plus a 33% tax on ships' casino operations, and begins collecting the 23,000 signatures required to qualify the initiative for the ballot.

■ 2005 North West Cruise Ship Association, an association of ship operators, hires an ex–Secret Service forgery/handwriting specialist to verify that the signatures collected by the ballot seekers are valid.

■ 2006 Voters approve the ballot initiative to levy a $50 head tax on arriving cruise passengers as well as imposing taxes on casino profits. (See 2004 entry above.) At the same time, they vote to put pollution inspectors, to

It's hard to imagine today the impact of the news on the outside world. The U.S. economy was in a deep depression. The dollar was on the gold standard and the scarcity of that precious metal had caused a deflationary vise that in 1893 brought a banking collapse and unemployment of 18%. Suddenly, in 1897, a steamer arrived in Seattle bearing men from a place called the Klondike with trunks and gunnysacks full of gold. The supply of money suddenly grew and economic confidence returned. The national economy turned around on the news and, in 1898, some 100,000 people set off for Alaska (the easiest jumping-off point for the Canadian interior) in hopes of getting rich, too, plunging off into a trackless wilderness for which they were completely unprepared.

The **Klondike gold rush** marks the start of contemporary Alaska. Before the gold rush, Alaska largely remained as it had been for thousands of years, ruled and inhabited by indigenous people. As late as the 1880 census, the territory had fewer than 500 white residents and not more than 4,000 by 1890. In 1898, the gold stampede began, bringing an instant population. Even the mayor of Seattle left for Alaska. Within a few years, Alaska had cities, telegraph lines, riverboats, and sled-dog mail routes. About 30,000 made

it all the way to Dawson City in the Yukon Territory. Few of the miners struck it rich, but those entrepreneurs who built the towns and businesses to serve them did. Suddenly there were saloons and brothels, dress shops and photo studios. Promoters sold credulous public plans for newly laid-out towns on supposed routes to the gold mines, including many that were virtually impassable.

The White Pass above Skagway and the Chilkoot Pass above Dyea carried the most stampeders. Gold seekers arrived in the crazily lawless settlements by steamer from Seattle, got robbed and cheated, and then hauled their goods on their backs over one or other of the passes to Lake Bennett. The Canadian authorities wisely required each stampeder to bring a ton of supplies, a rule that undoubtedly prevented famine but which made the single-file journey over the passes a miserable ordeal. Prospectors sometimes had to make dozens of trips up the trail to get their supplies over the pass. At **Lake Bennett,** the stampeders built boats and rafts, crossed the lake, and then floated down the Yukon River, through the dangerous Five Finger Rapids to **Dawson City**—a 500-mile journey from the sea. Many of them didn't make it.

Imagine the disappointment of those who did when they found, upon arrival, that the gold claims had all been staked

---

be known as Ocean Rangers, on every big-ship cruise in Alaska waters during the season and to require cruise lines to disclose how much they are paid by tour operators for inclusion in shore excursion programs.

■ 2006 Republican Sarah Palin, the mayor of Wasilla, a community 40 miles from Anchorage, is elected Governor of Alaska (replacing one-term Governor Frank Murkowski).

■ 2007 Ocean Rangers program runs into implementation problems. Legislature notes that the cost of putting an inspector on every ship would be prohibitive, requiring about 80 new hires. It orders a compromise: inspectors will now board ships only after they dock.

■ 2007 After threats of a lawsuit by tour operators included in shorex programs, the Legislature demands only that disclosure of the fact that they pay shiplines something to be included in shore tour brochures—*not* how much.

and big companies were taking over. Prospectors looking to strike it rich had humbling choices. The smart ones started businesses to make money off the others, and some of them did quite well. Others worked for wages or went home. But many continued their quest for the next big find. Their wild chase for gold drew the modern map of Alaska, founding dozens of towns. Many of these gold-inspired communities disappeared as soon as the frenzy cooled and now are entirely forgotten, or live on only as place names in memory. But some became real cities. **Nome** was born in 1899; **Fairbanks** in 1902; **Kantishna,** now within Denali National Park, in 1905; **Iditarod** in 1908; and many others until the rush finally ended with the start of World War I in 1914.

Upon completion of the railroad through the **White Pass** in 1901, Dyea and the **Chilkoot Pass** were abandoned, but Skagway lived on (see chapter 8).

Even without a rush, there's still gold to be dug. Small-time prospectors are still looking all over Alaska and working their claims, and sometimes someone makes a significant strike. In 1987, a find north of Fairbanks produced as much as 1,000 ounces of the precious metal every day for years.

But there's a bigger, safer business: mining the tourist trade. The rush of visitors each summer dwarfs the number who came in 1898. In the true spirit of the event whose history they celebrate, the gold-rush towns of Skagway, Dawson City, Fairbanks, and Nome know there's more money to be made from people than from gold.

3 An Introduction to Southeast Alaska's Native Cultures

This essay was written for us by Jan Halliday, a former editor of Alaska Airlines Magazine *and author of* Native Peoples of the Northwest *(Sasquatch Books) and* Native People of Alaska: A Traveler's Guide to Land, Art, and Culture *(Sasquatch Books), both of which describe Native tours interpretive centers, museums, art galleries, artists' studios, lodges, B&Bs, and restaurants in their area of coverage, and provide detailed contact information.*

Welcome to the islands of the Inside Passage, the traditional and contemporary home of the Tlingit (pronounced *klink-get*) Indians. Although the Tlingit's language is related to the language of the Athabascan of Interior Alaska and Canada, and to the language of the Navajo of the American Southwest, no one knows for sure when the group settled on this strip of Alaska coastline and islands. The Tlingit may be descendants of the first wave of ice-age travelers who crossed the Bering Sea from Asia into North America, or they may trace their ancestry from a later wave of immigrants who returned to this fish-rich area from the interior of the North American continent more than 10,000 years ago, after ice-age glaciers retreated.

Until the last century, Tlingits used channels between islands and river passageways through barrier mountains as their highways. In the 1700s, Tlingit paddlers, steering huge cargo canoes carved from cedar logs, were sighted as far south as the Channel Islands off the coast of Los Angeles, reportedly to take slaves. In the 18th and 19th centuries, before epidemics decimated their communities, the Tlingit people were trade partners with the Russians, British, Americans, and interior tribes of Canada, controlling the waterways of Southeast Alaska and demanding tolls for their use. In the 1800s, the Tlingits allowed gold miners to travel over the rugged Chilkoot Pass between Skagway and the Klondike gold fields, but only after they paid a substantial fee.

Newcomers to Southeast Alaska include the Haida and Tsimshian Indians, who came into Tlingit territory from British Columbia in the last 2 centuries. The Haida, from the Queen Charlotte Islands, settled on Prince of Wales Island in the late 1700s; the Tsimshian Indians, from the Prince Rupert area, settled Annette Island as a utopian Christian community in the late 1800s.

Today many Natives live in small villages on remote islands (such as Angoon on Admiralty Island, Hoonah on Chichagof Island, and Kake on Kupreanof Island) and in centers of commerce such as Juneau, Ketchikan, and Sitka. In smaller villages, away from the bustle of larger towns, you may see Natives drying seaweed in front of their houses on a sheet of plywood or filleting and drying salmon—both of these are traditional foods. But visitors should not expect people, villages, or towns to look as they did when photographers froze their images 100 years ago, any more than you'd expect to see people in Oregon dressed in pioneer garb, making soap over a wood fire. Although many Natives do live traditional subsistence lifestyles, gathering and preserving fish and shellfish, beach greens, and berries, nowadays they also order bulk groceries from Costco in Juneau. The primary source of income for villagers is logging and commercial fishing. All small communities use fuel-burning generators for electrical power and have well-stocked stores, with larger items arriving by barge and cargo jet, and fresh goods arriving daily by smaller planes.

It's important for visitors to remember that Native history and culture was and is influenced by the cultural and economic impact of the Russian, British, and American traders of the early 1800s; the gold miners of the late 1800s; and the timber, fishing, canning, and mining industries of the 20th century. Southeast Alaska clans led (and won) the fight for Native civil rights years before Martin Luther King, Jr., led the civil rights movement for blacks in the 1960s. Many clan members have served in the U.S. military, many own businesses, and several are Alaska state legislators.

In 1971, Natives gained economic clout when the Alaska Native Claims Settlement Act settled the 100-year-old question of aboriginal land rights. Under dispute were 375 million acres of land in Alaska. Under provisions of the act, Congress deeded title to 44 million acres, spread throughout the state, to Alaska Natives, and a payment of close to $1 billion was made to compensate for the loss of the remaining 331 million acres. The act created 13 regional corporations and more than 230 village corporations to receive federal money and manage land on behalf of Native shareholders. In Southeast Alaska, Native corporations such as Goldbelt, CIRI, Cape Fox, and Huna Totem have taken the lead in tourism development, investing in first-class hotels, cruise ships, air taxis, and passenger-ferry sightseeing boats. Huna Totem Corporation owns the *Alaskan Southeaster,* a magazine about the region. In Juneau, Goldbelt owns and operates the tram to the top of Mount Roberts and a modern hotel. CIRI owns hotels and sightseeing and tour operations. Sealaska Heritage Foundation, the nonprofit arm of Sealaska, another Juneau-based Native corporation, supports scholarly work, publishing videos, language-learning materials, and such books as *Haa Shuka, Our Ancestors: Tlingit Oral Narratives,* by poet Nora Marks Dauenhauer, written in both Tlingit and English. Even small corporations, such as the Organized Village of Kake, have built lovely little hotels for visitors, overlooking beautiful vistas of seacoast and snow-covered mountains.

Alaska Natives don ceremonial regalia (robes decorated with clan insignia and magnificent carved headdresses inlaid with abalone shell) only during celebrations.

(The largest of these traditional events, simply called Celebration, is held in Juneau every 2 years for 4 days in June, with clans gathering from throughout Southeast Alaska to celebrate their cultural heritage and perform traditional dances.) As in most of corporate America, Native Alaskans wear business suits when running their corporations, which are located in some of Juneau's finest office buildings.

Having said this, there are many facets of Native culture for you to enjoy in Southeast Alaska. Distinctive Tlingit, Haida, and Tsimshian totemic art is prevalent. In Ketchikan, for example, there are more than 70 standing totem poles, plus a museum dedicated entirely to the oldest poles collected from abandoned Tlingit villages. There are also two traditional clan houses, reminiscent of dozens of large houses that lined the waterfront in the last century, constructed from hand-hewn cedar and adorned with carved house posts and decorated house screens. Both houses are open to the public. You can observe Native carvers working on commissioned masks, canoes, and totem poles at places such as Saxman Village, 3 miles south of Ketchikan, and in private studios. Many Native artists, such as carvers Amos Wallace and Nathan Jackson, and Chilkat blanket weaver Delores Churchill, have their work in private and museum collections throughout the world.

Most towns in Southeast Alaska have fascinating museums filled with artifacts and traditional art. Those with the largest collections are the Alaska State Museum in Juneau and the Sheldon Jackson Museum in Sitka, but smaller museums shouldn't be missed.

Raven and Eagle clan symbols, representing the two major clan divisions to which every Haida, Tsimshian, and Tlingit Native belongs, adorn everything from bags of fresh-roasted coffee to beach blankets and T-shirts. These clan symbols, plus other totem figures such as salmon, killer whales, frogs, and bears, represent the strong family ties that reach back far into the past and bind contemporary Native people in this region. Rather than describe complicated clan lineage systems in this guide, I suggest you learn firsthand about the clans from Native tour guides and at Native-based shore excursions designed especially for the time frame that cruise ship passengers have in port—Saxman Village in Ketchikan, Metlakatla's tour and salmon bake, or one of Sitka Tribal Tours' bus or walking tours of the old Russian/Tlingit capital of Alaska.

When I researched my guidebook to the Native peoples of Alaska, I stayed at Native-owned hotels, visited with artists (one of the best places to meet carvers, weavers, painters, silversmiths, and bead workers while they work is at the Southeast Alaska Indian Cultural Center in Sitka), gazed in wonder at museum collections, saw the old Chilkat and Ravenstail woven robes come out from behind the glass windows to be worn, and danced to the resonant beat of box drums at Celebration. I watched the Sheet'ka Kwaan Naa Kahidi Community House, a gorgeous hall modeled after the old clan houses, being constructed in Sitka. I listened as Native guides explained how each totem pole tells a unique family story or honors a fallen clan member. I went fishing with Natives on their charter boats and toured canneries, fish-processing plants, and salmon hatcheries owned by Natives (one had a standing totem pole right in the center of the creek, with an opportunistic eagle perched on top, eyeing the spawning salmon below). In Metlakatla, I scaled Yellow Hill on the boardwalk and stairs that Terry Booth, a Tsimshian, built for his wife years ago, and watched the sun bathe the village in first morning light. They were all unforgettable experiences. I hope your trip will be an unforgettable experience as well.

Appendix B:
Alaska on the Wild Side

by Charles Wohlforth

The variety of wildlife found in our 49th state is mind-boggling, whether it rules on land or in the ocean or in the air. The one thing that an Alaska cruise can guarantee is that passengers will see some of these creatures—from the decks of their ship, during organized shore excursions specifically planned to search for them, or even when just walking the streets of the communities their ships visit. Majestic bald eagles, the symbol of this nation, are all over the place and, thankfully, are now well and truly back, having been placed on the protected species list several years ago. Bears roam the woods, Dall sheep dot the hillsides, and caribou and moose inhabit parts of the Interior of the state. The waters of the Inside Passage, Glacier Bay, and Prince William Sound teem with harbor seals, sea otters, sea lions, and—most spectacularly of all—whales. It is highly unlikely that you will ever take a cruise to Alaska without seeing the telltale flukes and condensation spouts in the vicinity of your vessel.

So that you can recognize what you're seeing, here's a short rundown on the creatures you may encounter along the way.

1 Whale-Watching 101

Imagine standing on the deck of a ship, looking out onto the calm silver waters of an Alaskan bay. Suddenly, the surface of the water pulls back and an immense yet graceful creature appears, moving silently, the curve of its back visible for a moment before the water closes over it again. You wait for it to reappear. And wait. And wait. Then, just as you're beginning to think it's gone forever, the creature leaps straight out of the water, twisting around in midair before falling back with a gigantic kersploosh! That's followed a half-second later by an equally distinctive sound: that of 1,000 cruise-ship passengers saying "Oooh!," "Aaah!," and "Marty! Marty! Did you see that?!"

On most large cruise ships, the captain or officer on watch will make an announcement when he or she spots a whale, but due to its strict schedule, the ship probably won't be able to stop and linger. A few lines, though (mostly the small-ship lines), feature whale-watching as a major component of their cruises. Their ships visit areas favored by whales—for instance, waters near Petersburg or Sitka, near Gustavus and Glacier Bay National Park, and near Seward and Kenai Fjords National Park. Once in position, they will spend time waiting for an encounter, or will monitor marine-traffic radio broadcasts and deviate from course to go where whale sightings have been reported. Most ships, both large and small, will offer lectures about whales at some point during each cruise.

To get you ready for your whale encounters, we've prepared the following little whale primer. Study up so you'll know what you're looking at.

THE HUMPBACK WHALE These migratory whales spend their summer in Alaska feeding, then swim to Mexican or Hawaiian waters for the winter, where they give birth to their young and then fast until going north again in spring. The cold northern waters produce the small fish and other tiny creatures that humpbacks filter through their baleen—the strips of stiff, fibrous material that humpbacks have instead of teeth. A humpback is easy to recognize by its huge, mottled tail; by the hump on its back, just forward of its dorsal fin; and by its armlike flippers, which can grow to be 14 feet long. Most humpback sightings are of the whales' humped backs as they cruise along the surface, resting, and of the flukes of their tails as they dive.

The Humpback Whale. Maximum length: 53 ft.

Humpbacks weave nets of bubbles around their prey, then swim upward through the schooled fish, mouths wide open, to eat them in a single swoop, sometimes finishing with a frothy lunge through the surface. Feeding dives can last a long time and often mean you won't see that particular whale again, but if you're lucky, the whale may just be dipping down for a few minutes to get ready to leap completely out of the water, a behavior called **breaching.** No one knows for sure why whales do this; it may simply be play. Breaching is thrilling for viewers and, if you happen to be in a small boat or kayak, a little scary (paddlers should group their boats and tap the decks to let the whales know where they are). Humpbacks are highly sensitive to noise, so keep quiet to see longer displays.

Humpbacks tend to congregate to feed, making certain spots with rich supplies of food reliable places to watch them. In Southeast Alaska, the best humpback-watching spots include the waters of **Icy Strait,** just outside Glacier Bay; **Frederick Sound,** outside Petersburg; and **Sitka Sound.** In Southcentral Alaska, **Resurrection Bay,** outside Seward near Kenai Fjords National Park, has the most reliable sightings.

THE ORCA (KILLER WHALE)   The starkly defined black-and-white patches of the orca, the ocean's top predator, recall the sharp, vivid look of the Native American art of the Pacific Northwest and Southeast Alaska. Moving like wolves in highly structured family groups called pods, and swimming at up to 25 knots (about 29 mph), orcas hunt salmon, porpoises, seals, sea lions, and even juvenile whales. There's never been a report of one attacking a human being. Like dolphins, orcas often pop above the surface in a flashing, graceful arc, giving viewers a glance at their sleek shape and tall dorsal fin.

Unlike humpbacks and other whales that rely on a predictable food supply, orcas' hunting patterns mean it's not easy to say exactly where you might find them. **Resurrection Bay** and **Prince William Sound** both have pods that are often sighted in the summer, and we saw a pod of orcas from the beach in Gustavus, but they could show up anywhere in Southeast Alaska waters. For cruisers coming to Alaska from Vancouver, a top spot to see orcas is **Robson Bight,** an area in Johnstone Strait (between Vancouver Island and mainland British Columbia).

The Orca, or Killer Whale. Maximum length: 30 ft.

THE BELUGA WHALE   This small white whale with a cute rounded beak is one of only three types that spend all their lives in cold water rather than heading south for the winter. Belugas are more likely to be mistaken for dolphin than any other whales. However, the beluga is larger and fatter than a dolphin and lacks the dolphin's dorsal fin. Adults are all white, while juveniles are gray. Belugas swim in large packs that can number in the dozens. It is the only whale that can turn its head, and is one of a few species with good eyesight.

The Beluga Whale. Maximum length: 16 ft.

Belugas feed on salmon, making the mouths of rivers with salmon runs the best places to see them. Occasionally, a group will strand itself chasing salmon on a falling tide, swimming away when the water returns. The Cook Inlet group of belugas is the most often seen: If you're in Anchorage after your cruise, take the Seward Highway south of town, and keep your eyes on the **Turnagain Arm,** or watch from the beach near the mouth of the **Kenai River** in Kenai.

THE MINKE WHALE   The smallest of the baleen whales, the minke is generally under 26 feet long and has a blackish-gray body with a white stomach, a narrow triangular head, and white bands on its flippers. Along with the humpback and (occasionally) the gray whale, it is the only baleen whale commonly seen in Alaskan waters.

When breaching, minkes leap something like dolphins, gracefully reentering the water headfirst—unlike humpbacks, for instance, which smash down on their sides. Also unlike the humpbacks, they don't raise their flukes (the tips of their tails) clear of the water when they dive. Minkes are easy to confuse with dolphins: Watch for the dark skin color to tell the difference.

The Minke Whale. Maximum length: 26 ft.

THE GRAY WHALE   Here's one whale you'll probably see only if you take a shoulder-season cruise (in May or very late Sept), and then only if you're lucky. The grays spend their winter months off the coast of California and in the Sea of Cortez (between Baja and mainland Mexico), and their summer months off northern Alaska, meaning that cruise passengers sailing in the Inside Passage and Gulf of Alaska can spot one only while it's on its migration.

The Gray Whale. Maximum length: 45 ft.

Like the humpback, grays are baleen whales. They're also about the same size as the humpback, though they lack the humpback's huge flippers. Their heads are pointed, and they have no dorsal fin. Grays will often smack the water with their flukes and are very friendly—it's not uncommon for them to swim right up to a small boat and allow their heads to be patted.

2 Alaskan Wildlife

Large mammals other than humankind still rule most of Alaska—even in the urban areas, there sometimes remains a question of who's in charge. In this section, we'll describe some of the more common forms of wildlife. For visitors, the chances of seeing the animals described below are excellent.

BALD EAGLE   Now making a comeback all over the United States, the bald eagle has always been extremely common in Alaska. Every fishing town is swarming with eagles, and they even soar over the high-rise buildings of downtown Anchorage. Only adult eagles have the familiar white head and tail; juveniles of a few years or less have mottled brown plumage and can be hard to tell from a hawk. Eagles are most often seen soaring on rising air currents over ocean or river waters, where they are likely looking for fish to swoop down and snatch, but you also can often see them perched on beach driftwood or in large trees. **Haines** is a prime eagle-spotting area, where thousands of birds congregate in the fall; **Sitka** and **Ketchikan** both have raptor centers where you can see eagles in enclosures.

The eagle represents one of the two main kinship groupings in the matrilineal Tlingit culture (the other group is represented by the raven), so eagles frequently appear on totem poles and in other Southeast Alaska Native art.

Bald Eagle

Raven

RAVEN   A member of the Corvidae family, which includes jays, crows, and magpies, the raven is found throughout the Northern Hemisphere and is extremely common in Southeast Alaska. You can tell a raven from a crow by its larger size, heavy bill, shaggy throat feathers, and unmistakable call, a deep and mysteriously evocative "kaw" that provides a constant soundtrack to the misty forests of Southeast. The raven figures importantly in Southeast Alaska Native stories and in the creation myths of many other Native American peoples. It is portrayed as a wily and resourceful protagonist with great magical powers, an understandable personality for this highly impressive and intelligent scavenger.

BLACK BEAR   Black bears live in forests all over Alaska, feeding on fish, berries, insects, and vegetation. In Southeast Alaska they can be so common that they are sometimes considered pests, and many communities have adjusted their handling of garbage to keep bears out of town. Although not typically dangerous, blackies still deserve caution and respect: They stand about a yard tall at the shoulders and measure 5 or 6 feet from nose to tail. Black bears are usually black but can also be brown, blond, or even bluish—color is not the best way to tell a black bear from a brown bear. Instead, look for smaller size, a blunt face, and the shape of the back, which is straight and lacks the brown bear's large shoulder hump. You're liable to find black bears pretty much anywhere in Southeast Alaska where the popular Inside Passage ports are located. Mostly, you will spot them along riverbanks and near salmon streams. On a cruise on the Island Princess, I saw one swimming across the mouth of Johns Hopkins Inlet in Glacier Bay. Quite a sight!

Black Bear

Brown Bear

BROWN BEAR   Also known as grizzly bears, brown bears are among the largest and most ferocious of all land mammals. Size depends on the bear's food source. In coastal areas where salmon are plentiful, such as Southeast Alaska and Katmai National Park (near King Salmon, Alaska), brown bears can grow well over 1,000 pounds and even approach the 1-ton mark. The largest bears are found on salmon-rich Kodiak Island. Inland, at Denali National Park and on similar tundra landscape (where they feed on rodents, berries, and insects), brown bears top out closer to 500 pounds. Bears can also take larger prey, but that's less common. You can recognize brown bears by their prominent shoulder humps, long faces, and large sizes; color can range from almost black to blond. Among the best places to see them are **Pack Creek** (on Admiralty Island near Juneau), at **Denali and Katmai national parks,** and on bear-viewing floatplane excursions from **Homer.** Of these, Denali is the only inexpensive option.

MOOSE   In winter, when they move to the lowlands, moose can be an absolute pest, blocking roadways and eating expensive shrubbery. In the summer, they're a little more elusive, most often seen standing in forest ponds, eating the weeds from the bottom or pruning streamside willows. The largest member of the deer family, with males reaching 1,200 to 1,600 pounds, moose are found primarily in the boreal forest that covers Interior and Southcentral Alaska. You'll be likely to see one if you're on a pre- or post-cruise land package such as the Anchorage-Denali-Fairbanks route. They are unmistakable. As big as a large horse, with bristly, ragged brown hair; a long, bulbous nose; and huge, mournful eyes, moose seem to crave pity—though they get little from the wolves and people who hunt them or from the trains and cars that run them down, and they give little to anyone in their way when they're on the move. Males grow large antlers, which they shed after battling for a mate every fall. Females lack antlers, are smaller, and give birth to one to three calves each year.

Moose

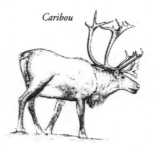

Caribou

CARIBOU   Alaska's barren-ground caribou are genetically identical to reindeer but were never domesticated as reindeer were in Europe. For Iñupiat and Athabascan people, they continue to be an essential source of food and hides, and caribou hunting remains a necessity. By law, nobody is allowed kill caribou for sport or recreation in Alaska. Both males and females have antlers that they shed annually. Caribou travel the arctic tundra and Interior foothills, often in herds of thousands of animals, a stunning sight witnessed by only a lucky few, as the migration routes lie in remote regions. You can, however, often see caribou in smaller groups of a few dozen at Denali National Park, along the Dalton and Denali highways, and on other northern rural roads above the tree line.

SITKA BLACK-TAILED DEER   The Sitka black-tailed deer is a relatively small deer found in the coastal rainforests of Alaska. Males typically weigh in at around 120 pounds and have small antlers. Both males and females sport a reddish-brown coat in summer. They can be found throughout the Southeast, in Prince William Sound, and on Kodiak Island.

Sitka Black-Tailed Deer

Dall Sheep

DALL SHEEP   Dall sheep resemble the more familiar bighorn sheep but are smaller, with males weighing up to 300 pounds and females topping out at 150 pounds. Like the bighorn, males have curling horns, which they butt against each other to establish dominance for mating. Their habitat is high, rocky places, where their incredible agility makes them safe from predators. Except in a few exceptional spots (such as on the **cliffs above the Seward Highway** just south of Anchorage on Turnagain Arm), you almost always need strong binoculars to see Dall sheep. **Denali National Park** is a good place to see them in the usual way: from a great distance. Scanning the mountains, look for white spots, then focus in on them. The sheep often move in herds of a dozen or more.

MOUNTAIN GOAT   Another animal that you won't see unless you bring your binoculars, mountain goats inhabit the same craggy mountain habitat as Dall sheep, including the prime viewing area around **Turnagain Arm.** From a distance, it's easy to confuse mountain goats with female Dall sheep, but mountain goats are shaggier; have short, straight black horns (which appear in both male and female); have the typical goat beard; and have a much more pronounced hump at the shoulders.

*Mountain
Goat*

Sea Otter

SEA OTTER   Possibly number one in Alaska's "cute critter" category, the sea otter is a member of the weasel family (as are minks and river otters) and spends almost all of its life in the water. Extensively hunted for its rich coat from the mid–18th century (when Russian explorer Vitus Bering brought back pelts from his voyage of discovery and initiated extensive Russian settlement of Alaska) until the early 20th century, the sea otter was almost driven to extinction—in 1911, there were probably fewer than 2,000 of them left in Alaska. But by the mid-1970s, that number had risen above 150,000. Adult males weigh between 70 and 100 pounds, while females average 40 to 60 pounds. Adults average 4½ feet in length. Their fur is generally brown to black, often with a silvery or gray tinge, particularly in older animals. You typically see sea otters floating on their backs, sometimes cradling a rock on their stomachs (which they use to crack open shellfish), or sometimes just watching the cruise ships float by.

SEA LION   You'll hear 'em—and smell 'em—before you see 'em. An argumentative honking, like cars stalled in traffic, mixes with a low undertone that sounds like elephants with sinus problems. Then the smell hits you: fishy beyond belief. Still, when you get close enough to know what you're smelling, you won't mind because it's quite a sight: Sea lions typically haul out in the hundreds onto small islands, where they loll in the sun, argue, occasionally fight, go fishing, and breed—just like people on vacation. Their bodies are huge, blubbery, tubular affairs that are perfect for the cold northern waters but appear impossibly ungainly on land, over which they bounce and bound on perfectly inadequate-looking front flippers. Still, even on land you wouldn't want to mess with one: The average adult male weighs approximately 1,250 pounds and measures 10½ feet long, while adult females average 580 pounds and are 8½ feet long. Most adult females are brownish yellow, while males typically are a bit darker, some with a reddish coat.

Sea Lion

Index

See also Accommodations and Restaurant indexes, below.

The new way to
get AROUND town.

Make the most of your stay. Go Day by Day!

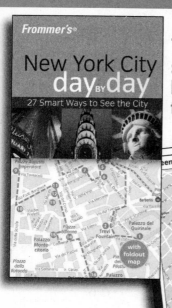

The all-new Day by Day
series shows you the
best places to visit and
the best way to see them.

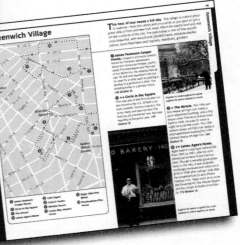

- Full-color throughout, with hundreds of photos and maps
- Packed with 1–to–3–day itineraries, neighborhood walks, and thematic tours
- Museums, literary haunts, offbeat places, and more
- Star-rated hotel and restaurant listings
- Sturdy foldout map in reclosable plastic wallet
- Foldout front covers with at-a-glance maps and info

The best trips start here. **Frommer's®**

A Branded Imprint of ⊕**WILEY**
Now you know.

A Guide for Every Type of Traveler

Frommer's Complete Guides

For those who value complete coverage, candid advice, and lots of choices in all price ranges.

Pauline Frommer's Guides

For those who want to experience a culture, meet locals, and save money along the way.

MTV Guides

For hip, youthful travelers who want a fresh perspective on today's hottest cities and destinations.

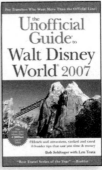

Day by Day Guides

For leisure or business travelers who want to organize their time to get the most out of a trip.

Frommer's With Kids Guides

For families traveling with children ages 2 to 14 seeking kid-friendly hotels, restaurants, and activities.

Unofficial Guides

For honeymooners, families, business travelers, and others who value no-nonsense, *Consumer Reports*–style advice.

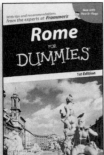

For Dummies Travel Guides

For curious, independent travelers looking for a fun and easy way to plan a trip.

Visit Frommers.com

Now you know.

Explore over 3,500 destinations.

Frommers.com makes it easy.

Find a destination. ✓ Book a trip. ✓ Get hot travel deals.
Buy a guidebook. ✓ Enter to win vacations. ✓ Listen to podcasts. ✓ Check o
the latest travel news. ✓ Share trip photos and memories. ✓ And much more

Frommers.com

FROMMER'S® CRUISE GUIDES

Alaska Cruises & Ports of Call
Cruises & Ports of Call
European Cruises & Ports of Call

FROMMER'S® NATIONAL PARK GUIDES

Algonquin Provincial Park
Banff & Jasper
Grand Canyon

National Parks of the American West
Rocky Mountain
Yellowstone & Grand Teton

Yosemite and Sequoia & Kings
 Canyon
Zion & Bryce Canyon

FROMMER'S® MEMORABLE WALKS

London
New York

Paris
Rome

San Francisco

FROMMER'S® WITH KIDS GUIDES

Chicago
Hawaii
Las Vegas
London

National Parks
New York City
San Francisco

Toronto
Walt Disney World® & Orlando
Washington, D.C.

SUZY GERSHMAN'S BORN TO SHOP GUIDES

France
Hong Kong, Shanghai & Beijing
Italy

London
New York

Paris
San Francisco

FROMMER'S® IRREVERENT GUIDES

Amsterdam
Boston
Chicago
Las Vegas

London
Los Angeles
Manhattan
Paris

Rome
San Francisco
Walt Disney World®
Washington, D.C.

FROMMER'S® BEST-LOVED DRIVING TOURS

Austria
Britain
California
France

Germany
Ireland
Italy
New England

Northern Italy
Scotland
Spain
Tuscany & Umbria

THE UNOFFICIAL GUIDES®

Adventure Travel in Alaska
Beyond Disney
California with Kids
Central Italy
Chicago
Cruises
Disneyland®
England
Florida
Florida with Kids

Hawaii
Ireland
Las Vegas
London
Maui
Mexico's Best Beach Resorts
Mini Mickey
New Orleans
New York City

Paris
San Francisco
South Florida including Miami &
 the Keys
Walt Disney World®
Walt Disney World® for
 Grown-ups
Walt Disney World® with Kids
Washington, D.C.

SPECIAL-INTEREST TITLES

Athens Past & Present
Best Places to Raise Your Family
Cities Ranked & Rated
500 Places to Take Your Kids Before They Grow Up
Frommer's Best Day Trips from London
Frommer's Best RV & Tent Campgrounds
 in the U.S.A.

Frommer's Exploring America by RV
Frommer's NYC Free & Dirt Cheap
Frommer's Road Atlas Europe
Frommer's Road Atlas Ireland
Great Escapes From NYC Without Wheels
Retirement Places Rated

FROMMER'S® PHRASEFINDER DICTIONARY GUIDES

French
Italian
Spanish

CLOSED
due to
accidental demolition

WEGEN BISSIGEN
EICHHÖRNCHEN GESCHLOSSEN

CERRADO
CABRAS

Κλειστό
Μετεωρίτες

POOL CLOSED
プ ー ル も

ELECTRIC EELS

閉
鎖
中

Hotel
closed for
facelifting

FERMÉ POUR
RAISON
DE GRÈVE
DES BONNES

FECHADO!
POR CAUSA DE
ATAQUES DOS CROCODILOS

— I don't speak
sign language.

A hotel can close for all kinds of reasons.
Our Guarantee ensures that if your hotel's undergoing construction, we'll
let you know in advance. In fact, we cover your entire travel experience.
See www.travelocity.com/guarantee for details.

travelocity®
You'll never roam alone.